The Bloomsbury Reader in the Study of Religion and Popular Culture

Also Available from Bloomsbury

The Bloomsbury Reader in Cultural Approaches to the Study of Religion, edited by Sarah J. Bloesch and Meredith Minister

The Bloomsbury Reader in Religion, Sexuality, and Gender, edited by Donald L. Boisvert and Carly Daniel-Hughes

The Bloomsbury Reader on Islam in the West, edited by Edward E. Curtis

The Bloomsbury Reader in the Study of Religion and Popular Culture

Edited by
Lisle W. Dalton, Eric Michael Mazur,
and Richard J. Callahan, Jr.

BLOOMSBURY ACADEMIC
LONDON • NEW YORK • OXFORD • NEW DELHI • SYDNEY

BLOOMSBURY ACADEMIC
Bloomsbury Publishing Plc
50 Bedford Square, London, WC1B 3DP, UK
1385 Broadway, New York, NY 10018, USA
29 Earlsfort Terrace, Dublin 2, Ireland

BLOOMSBURY, BLOOMSBURY ACADEMIC and the Diana logo are trademarks of Bloomsbury Publishing Plc

First published in Great Britain 2022

Cover design: Dani Leigh
Cover image © Soasig Chamaillard

A catalogue record for this book is available from the British Library.

Library of Congress Cataloging-in-Publication Data
Names: Dalton, Lisle W., editor. | Mazur, Eric Michael, editor. | Callahan, Richard J., 1967- editor.
Title: The Bloomsbury reader in the study of religion and popular culture / edited by Lisle W. Dalton,
Eric Michael Mazur, and Richard J. Callahan, Jr.
Description: London ; New York : Bloomsbury Academic, 2022. | Includes bibliographical references and index. | Summary: "This is the first anthology to trace broader themes of religion and popular culture across time and theoretical methods. It provides key readings as well as new approaches and cutting-edge work, encouraging a broader methodological and historical understanding. With a combined teaching experience of over 30 years dedicated to teaching undergraduates, Richard J. Callahan, Jr., Lisle W. Dalton, and Eric Michael Mazur have ensured that the pedagogical features and structure of the volume are valuable to both students and their professors. The book: - is divided into a number of units based on common semester syllabi - provides a blend of materials focused on method with materials focused on subject - begins with an introduction to the texts for each unit - follows each unit with questions designed to encourage and enhance post-reading reflection and classroom discussion - has a glossary of terms from the unit's readings, as well as suggestions for further reading and investigation. The Reader is suitable as the foundational textbook for any undergraduate course on religion and popular culture, as well as theory in the study of religion"– Provided by publisher.
Identifiers: LCCN 2021033873 (print) | LCCN 2021033874 (ebook) | ISBN 9781472509604 (pb) | ISBN 9781472514660 (hb) | ISBN 9781472586254 (ebook) | ISBN 9781472586247 (epdf)
Subjects: LCSH: Popular culture–Religious aspects–Miscellanea.
Classification: LCC BL65.C8 .B57 2022 (print) | LCC BL65.C8 (ebook) | DDC 306.6–dc23
LC record available at https://lccn.loc.gov/2021033873
LC ebook record available at https://lccn.loc.gov/2021033874

ISBN: HB: 978-1-4725-1466-0
PB: 978-1-4725-0960-4
ePDF: 978-1-4725-8624-7
eBook: 978-1-4725-8625-4

Typeset by Deanta Global Publishing Services, Chennai, India
Printed and bound in India

To find out more about our authors and books visit www.bloomsbury.com and sign up for our newsletters

This volume is dedicated to our teacher Cathy Albanese, and to the memory of our teacher Phil Hammond, and to our partners Rebekah Ambrose-Dalton, Claudia Mazur, and Melissa Click, for all of their help and patience.
- The Editors

Contents

Permissions

Acknowledgments

The editors would like to thank Lalle Pursglove for her extraordinary patience as we developed this project, and the long process behind it; it has been a trying few years for all three of us, but we were committed to the idea of this *Reader*, and Lalle enabled us to see it through. We would also like to thank our students at Hartwick College, the University of Missouri, Gonzaga University, and Virginia Wesleyan University who "test drove" some of the readings and helped us think through this material. Supplemental funding for copyright permissions was received from Virginia Wesleyan University, for which we are extremely grateful.

Volume Introduction

While it may seem commonplace today, the intersection of religion and popular culture—apart from theological apologetics—is in many ways a comparatively new area of study. At the risk of sounding old beyond our years, each of the editors of this volume can recall when this particular field of study blossomed in the later years of the twentieth century and has been (in some way or another) involved in it since. And while it seems that one can find works titled "The Gospel According to . . ." well, almost anything, it hasn't always been this way. In just a few decades, the field has moved in from the periphery. The convergence of a variety of fields of study—cultural studies, feminist studies, media studies, social history, and of course popular culture—in the late 1960s and early 1970s brought attention to the "stuff" in people's lives. At roughly the same time that the cover of *Time* magazine was asking "Is God Dead?" and John Lennon was declaring the Beatles "more popular than Jesus," Protestant theologian Harvey Cox was finding religion hidden in "the secular city," and Methodist minister Robert Short was identifying Christian lessons in Charles Schulz's *Peanuts* comics. Particularly in American society, the coming of age of the "baby boomers"—combined with changes in US immigration law—brought a worldwide market of religious (and religion-like) ideologies to a growing population freed (for a variety of reasons) from any obligation of loyalty to their parents' religious institutions and affiliations. As luck would have it, some of these "boomers"—as well as some of us who are not really "boomers," but are not really "Generation X-ers" either—took up the study of religion in the period after the meanings and behaviors associated with both religion and culture had undergone such dramatic shifts. Like Cox and Short, many of us found religion in the seemingly mundane aspects of lived experience, and some of us have pursued that into the realm often identified as "popular culture." While some have lamented that American society is no longer as seemingly religious as it once was, others disagree and have celebrated it as religious in an entirely different way. For them, it is not that Christianity is gone, but that it—and institution-based religious affiliation generally—no longer monopolizes the ways in which some people create and maintain meaning in their individual and communal lives. It is from this transformation that many scholars of the intersection of religion and popular culture have emerged, and it is from this transformation that many of them start their own investigations.

In the last twenty years or so, work in the field has flowed with increasing volume. Some of these works are theological in nature, either condemnations or explorations of popular culture's impact on religion. Others are working in the "comparative religions" genre, using religious categories (myth, ritual, sacred time and space, etc.) to examine a particular popular cultural phenomenon. And still others are engaging critical cultural studies to interrogate the ways that religion and popular culture shape and are shaped by structures of power. Most of this work is insightful, though much of it tends to focus on the present (or recent past). Some of these limitations have arisen because of the object of study; one might find it odd to begin a study of the impact of Catholic leadership on film censorship before the invention of film. Although one could be inventive and make connections farther back in time—to American anti-Catholicism, for example, or even the American tradition of Puritanism—there is always the need for a historical starting point, a point before which one must say, "This is no longer directly relevant to my topic of study." But because of its tendency to privilege mass media, the field of popular culture studies—from which much of the energy has come for the study of its intersections with religion—as well as film studies and television studies have been conditioned by this limitation. The first chapter of Raymond Betts's *A History of Popular Culture* (2004), for example, is titled "Popular Culture in an Early Twentieth-Century Environment." Given these patterns, it is often a challenge to gain a broader perspective.

Additionally, many of those working in this field are themselves products of the same forces that created the field. The transformations in Western society that have led to the elevation of noninstitutional, non-tradition-based forms of religiosity and spirituality have also had a profound impact on the scholars working in the field. Many of the early scholars of religion and popular culture were trained in more traditional disciplines (history, sociology, theology, etc.) and entered the field as an adjunct to produce work that was in addition to their original area of expertise. (One need only locate work on religion and popular culture from the 1990s, and then identify the dissertation topics of the authors, to see what we mean; the editors of this volume, for instance, produced dissertations on Kentucky coal miners, phrenologists, and 1st Amendment litigation.) Many in this generation felt not only the exhilaration of exploring a new subject and the freedom to do so but also the introspection of examining a topic that was so much a part of their own cultural and intellectual development. To many of them, everything felt new, and fresh, and meaning-filled. Moreover, studying the intersections of religion and popular culture provided a way to transgress the boundaries of the established categories of the academic study of religion. When the American Academy of Religion created a program unit on the topic, it became a meeting ground for scholars who would ordinarily not find themselves in the same room at the organization's annual meeting. For this reason, the field prompted conversations that stirred up new perspectives, comparisons, and critical questions.

Now, the study of religion and popular culture is an established field. Publishers maintain academic series on the subject, colleges and universities regularly offer a variety of courses in the area, and in turn there is a growing number of textbooks. The maturation of the field, we contend, requires now that we revisit foundations for the next generation of students of these various topics. In some cases, foundational texts and scholars will be found wanting. Almost as if coming from another world, the concerns that shaped some of the earlier scholarship of religion and culture do always map well onto the issues that urgently press upon the present. Still, we believe that it is important to become familiar with our ancestors before we slay them. Even among the scholars we have included in this volume (particularly the later ones), readers will find a sense of conversation with these older theorists, as if those of more recent vintage are responding to—or building on, or refuting—the work of their predecessors. This is why we have organized the readings in Unit II chronologically; good or bad, every generation of scholars takes the work of those that came before and refines, corrects, embellishes, or refutes it. We strongly support arguments for expanded inclusion into whatever it might be that one considers a "canon" in the study of religion, or culture, or the intersection of religion and popular culture. We have committed here to present the following theorists in the belief that these theories remain foundational to a lot of what gets done in contemporary work by scholars of religion and popular culture, even as a good deal of more recent scholarship proceeds in tension with, or outright criticism of, these foundations. As Stuart Hall discusses his 1981 essay "Notes on Deconstructing 'The Popular'" (excerpted in this volume), both popular culture and scholarly canons are sites of conflict and contestation. Scholarship, like culture itself, is dynamic and ever-changing. The best scholarship challenges that which precedes it, critically exposing its interests and stakes while building on its insights. Our intention in this volume is to provide students and scholars with the background to confidently enter into the ongoing history of work on religion and popular culture that is so vibrantly active in the present. By looking back across a century or more, we can see the ripples created by earlier generations that have deep significance even still. The energies that led to the creation of those ripples will continue to create them; we have tried here to capture some of the earliest sources and gesture toward the work that has built on, and moved beyond, them.

We have designed this reader to be of use to you no matter how you wish to use it. If you have come across this volume and its contents have interested you, we hope that you will sample broadly from the materials that we have provided and take seriously the additional readings we have suggested along the way. If you are using this in a class, we hope that you will find it to be a foundation for your work, a companion of sorts to provide a map through the field of religion and popular culture. We believe that it will be best if used in conjunction with other materials—texts (written or spoken), visuals (static, digital, or moving), or experiences (yours or others'). Recognizing that far too many materials labeled "for classroom use" often overlook the actual mechanics of the classroom, we have made every attempt to make this volume flexible for a variety of uses, and we encourage you to supplement it in any way you think best achieves your learning goals.

The volume's contents have been designed to provide you with a pyramid-like approach to the academic study of religion and popular culture. Rather than merely putting together an assortment of readings and suggesting that, in some way, they are all important and should be read, we have provided this structure to give you the opportunity to connect the excerpts, providing you with an increasingly focused view of the field that holds together in a way that is organic and yet still provides opportunities for improvisation and spontaneity.

The first unit provides readings for a general approach to the topic, a foundation on which you can build an understanding of some of the issues involved in this area of study, by offering excerpts of writings by two well-respected scholars of the "history of religions" approach to the academic study of religion, Charles Long and David Chidester. The body of Long's scholarly work in the study of religious symbols—particularly in the dynamic of cross-cultural interaction, primarily in the Americas—never focuses specifically on popular culture, but it does raise questions about how religious symbols communicate across increasingly modern platforms. Chidester—often cited as one of the earliest thinkers in the academic study of religion and popular culture—expands on themes first raised in his seminal work "The Church of Baseball, the Fetish of Coca-Cola, and the Potlatch of Rock 'n' Roll: Theoretical Models for the Study of Religion in American Popular Culture" (*Journal of the American Academy of Religion* 64, 4) published in 1996, where he invites his readers to think about mundane objects and experiences in terms of the academic study of religion. These readings are accompanied by a brief digression—what we are calling "Connections"— into the ways some who have worked at the intersection of religion and popular culture have sought to organize and categorize their own thinking. We have also provided a brief glossary, some questions that we hope will lead to deeper conversations about the reading, and suggestions for additional reading to supplement the excerpts.

The second unit is in many ways the heart of this volume, providing a sampling from some of the theorists whose work has been central to many of those who study at the intersections of religion and popular culture. One of the central debates in the academic study of religion is whether or not "religious studies" (or "comparative religions") even constitutes a "discipline" as that term is understood in the academic world. We make no claims to a solution here; as scholars who have worked at the intersection of religion (whatever that might be) and popular culture (whatever that might be) for decades, we merely acknowledge the enormous contribution of scholars of other, more traditionally recognized "disciplines" in the humanities and social sciences. We have here provided excerpts from some of the "great works" of some of those scholars, works that are part of—but by no means all of— the material used by students and scholars of religion and popular culture. These materials are provided here to introduce some of the tools scholars have used to get at the issues raised in this field of study. As with the first set of readings, the readings in this section are accompanied by "Connections" that highlight the ways some who have used a particular theory have made connections between religion and popular culture. And as with the first set of readings, with each theorist we have provided a brief glossary, some questions that we hope will lead to deeper conversations about the reading and suggestions for additional reading to supplement the excerpt.

And lastly, the third unit provides a sampling of investigations into what we call "durable forms"—images and activities that have been around for ages but which have taken on new (and, at times, almost unrecognizable) manifestations in the modern, mediated world. We provide here a few "case studies" of these forms, entryways into the investigation of the specific phenomena often found at the intersections of religion and popular culture. In an attempt to historicize the study of religion and popular culture and get away from an all-to-common "presentist" approach used by many writers in the field, we have organized this unit into five sections: "Who We Are," "Where We are," "What We Know," "Where We Go," and "What We Do." In them, we cover such issues as heroes and monsters, sacred space and time, sacred texts and myth, pilgrimages and epics, and rituals, drawing from the past to illuminate the present. We decided that it would be best if we didn't simply write five chapters on each of these categories; there is plenty of work now being done in religion and popular culture—some of it is really good, some of it is really awful, but in either case the world doesn't need five more from us. Instead, we felt that it would be of more use—particularly in a volume that is intended to serve as a resource for students (young and old)—if we explored how each of the categories *could* be approached. In other words, we felt that it would be of greater use if we constructed five different "how-to" chapters, each one thinking less about a specific data set and more about the process of successfully investigating any topic located at the intersection of religion and popular culture.

One final remark: This collection, focused on "foundational" texts in the study of religion and popular culture, is, largely, a collection of scholarship by white men. We endorse wholeheartedly the works of other editors and authors—not least our colleagues Meredith Minister and Sarah J. Bloesch, who have edited the *Bloomsbury Reader in Cultural Approaches to the Study of Religion* and *Cultural Approaches to Studying Religion: An Introduction to Theories and Methods*, and Chris Klassen, the author of *Religion and Popular Culture: A Cultural Studies Approach*—who have sought to provide readers with authors and their theories that might be considered more diverse, more current, or better suited to particular issues in contemporary culture. And we encourage readers of this volume to continue their reading, be it in volumes like these, or elsewhere. We have provided suggestions for additional reading in the excerpts and Connections in Units I and II. The study of religion and popular culture is as new as the latest cultural product; but we should be mindful that, often (in the words of the author of Ecclesiastes), "there is nothing new under the sun."

NOTE: Many of the following readings were originally published in languages other than English or were first published in the UK; for ease of reading, we have taken the liberty of transforming the style into one more familiar to readers in the United States. For reading ease, we also have omitted most of the original internal citations provided by the author (or translator).

Unit I   The Study of Religion and Popular Culture

Introduction to Unit I

A significant number of authors writing about the intersection of religion and popular culture argue that the study is beset by various distinct—if not always acknowledged—definitional dilemmas. One of these definitional dilemmas has its roots in the older study of religion generally: What is meant by the word "religion"? Scholars of religion (and other disciplines) have debated long and hard over the word's definition, and many have come to agree with the position offered by Jonathan Z. Smith that

> while there is a staggering amount of data, of phenomena, of human experiences and expressions that might be characterized in one culture or another, by one criterion or another, as religious—*there is no data for religion*. Religion is solely the creation of the scholar's study. (1982: xi; emphasis in the original)

This is not (the argument goes) to suggest that there is no evidence of people doing things that they (or others) might identify as "Catholic," or agreeing with ideas that they (or others) might identify as "Hindu." Rather, it is an assertion that there is no such thing specifically identifiable as "religion" that inheres in Catholicism or Hinduism—or that connects them to each other—that one can point to and say, "That is 'religion.'" It is an assertion that the concept of "religion" has been constructed entirely for purposes separate from those central to Catholicism or Hinduism and has been done so after-the-fact. In other words (according to this line of argumentation), Catholics may or may not do Catholic things, but only those of us interested in, say, thinking about them as elements that are part of a broader category of human expression, or comparing them with Hindu things, would call them "religious" things, ostensibly so that we can establish a baseline for comparison. Catholics have, over centuries, determined what is and what is not properly considered Catholicism; however, only scholars of religion (and related disciplines) have debated what is and what is not "religious," possibly involving Catholicism or Hinduism but also involving things seemingly unimportant (or unrecognizable) to Catholics or Hindus.

While cognizant of this line of argumentation and its importance both in the study of religion and in the study of things "religious" (whatever they might be), other scholars have found that it may be more of a "mental exercise"—useful to debate in the classroom or at conferences, but not entirely useful in the "real-time" study of religion "on the ground," where actual people live their actual lives. Part of the reason is that, regardless of who may have created the concept of religion, it is not, as Smith argues, "created for the scholar's analytic purposes by his imaginative acts of comparison and generalization," and it does have an "independent existence apart from the academy" (1982: xi). It is a popular (which is to say, fairly common) term. One would be hard pressed to find a resident of the Western world—including scholars of religion—who did not use it with some degree of frequency, and usually without giving it too much thought. It is, regardless of the academic debates over its meaning, origin, or status in the academic world, a term perfectly acceptable to most people in the "real" world. It means something to the people who use it as well as the people who hear it. Indeed, most of those who use the word frequently would likely find Smith's assertion amusing, confusing, or annoying. It is, like so much in any society, a term of greater use and frequency than it is a term of investigation. "Religion" is—in this regard only—very much like many terms we use in common conversation. In a case involving whether or not the State of Ohio could prohibit the sale of things it considered pornographic, US Supreme Court Justice Potter Stewart wrote in 1964 that he would not "attempt further to define the kinds of materials" he understood "to be embraced within that shorthand description" and admitted that he might "never succeed in intelligibly doing so. But," he asserted with some confidence, "I know it when I see it" (*Jacobellis v. Ohio*, 378 U.S. 184, 1964, at 197). In that sense, while scholars may debate over the definition of the word "religion," and even assert that it is a concept that they themselves created, most people live their lives happy to have a sense that, while they might "never succeed in intelligibly" defining religion, they are confident that they will know it when they see it.

In reality, it is a term accorded significant power, regardless of who created it or for what purpose. For example, the terms "religion" and "religious" both appear in the US Constitution—the former in the First Amendment, the latter in Article VI—but the word "Christian" is entirely absent from the founding document. Most historians would argue that this imbalance was the result of the authors—unanimously Christian (and nearly unanimously Protestant)—presuming that the terms "religion" and "Christian" were synonymous. But among most legal and historical scholars, they cannot be so understood today; the past century is a testament to the expansion of how that term (as it is used in the First Amendment protection against laws either "prohibiting the free exercise of religion" or "respecting an establishment of religion") has broadened beyond simply "Christian," so that adherents of the more familiar forms (Catholics, Jews, Muslims, and others) have been afforded protections, as have adherents of less familiar forms, and no forms at all. The Internal Revenue Service has granted "tax exempt" status to the Temple of the Jedi Order, some states recognize weddings performed by ministers of the Church of Latter-Day Dude, and some states permit members of the Church of the Flying Spaghetti Monster to wear colanders as "religious" head coverings in drivers' licensing photos.

Clearly, governmental officials—judges, administrators, and others—are making determinations for themselves about what is and what is not "religion" as it may (or may not) be protected in the US Constitution. So, in their own way, are the people who seek to write off donations to Jediism, perform Dudeist weddings, or represent the Pastafarian community in official government identification photographs. Some may be consulting with religion scholars, but it is reasonable to presume that many are not. If the study of *religion* and *popular culture* is at the intersection of these terms, the study of the "religion" side of that, it would appear in the early years of the twenty-first century, must begin with the presumption that the "popular" use of the term is just as important—if not more so—as the scholarly use of the term.

The two readings in Unit I open the study of religion and popular culture by providing a glimpse into the origins of the field—an overview of the topics and social processes that are studied, definitions of crucial terms (religion, popular, culture), and perhaps most importantly, a sense of what is at stake in exploring the religious dimensions of popular culture. Written by two prominent scholars of religion, Charles Long and David Chidester, these excerpts put strong emphasis on the social dynamics of "the popular" in relation to other forms of culture, the political implications of the study of religion and popular culture, and the diversity of perspectives that have emerged in this field from the late eighteenth century to the present. We have offered these two readings as a starting point because they raise important questions:

- How are the terms "religion," "religious," and "sacred" to be used? What is the relationship of "the sacred" and "the profane"? What is "religious work," or the "political economy of the sacred"?

- What might be some of the meanings that have emerged for "popular" over time, and how did "popular" culture come to be seen as something in tension with (or opposition to) "high," "elite," "folk," or other forms of culture?

- What might have prompted a moment of "discovery of the people" among European intellectuals? And what was it about folk peasants and non-European small-scale ("tribal") societies that might have been appealing?

- Is the "mode of transmission" important to the meaning of the "popular"? Is there a particular mode, genre, or form of popular culture that might be most attractive to those who study religion, or conducive to its study? And is there something about small-scale societies that distinguish these modes of transmission from more complex industrialized societies?

- As you will see when you read Unit II, some of the later scholars are fairly direct when they situate themselves and their work in terms of other social, psychological, political, and economic forces—the state, the market, redemptive sacrifice, the body, and globalization—and some of them might argue that the earlier ones do it too. Should they make these connections to other elements of the human experience? And should scholars of religion and popular culture do this as well?

In practice, it may be best to remember that, while we noted just a few pages ago that "A significant number of authors writing about the intersection of religion and popular culture argue that the study is beset by various distinct—if not always acknowledged—definitional dilemmas," most of those authors either work out their own definitions, or leave the task of defining to the practitioner, or the reader. We believe that these first two readings will provide a strong foundation for anyone's initial journey into the intersection of religion and popular culture.

Suggested Reading on Religion and/or Popular Culture

Ashby, LeRoy. *With Amusement for All: A History of American Popular Culture since 1830.* Lexington: University Press of Kentucky, 2006.

Beaudoin, Tom. *Virtual Faith: The Irreverent Spiritual Quest of Generation X*. San Francisco, CA: Jossey-Bass, 1998.

Betts, Raymond F., and Lyz Bly. *A History of Popular Culture: More of Everything, Faster and Brighter*, 2nd ed. London: Routledge, 2012.

Bloesch, Sarah J., and Meredith Minister. *Cultural Approaches to Studying Religion: An Introduction to Theories and Methods*. London: Bloomsbury, 2018.

Cullen, Jim, ed. *Popular Culture in American History*, 2nd ed. Malden, MA: Wiley-Blackwell, 2013.

Forbes, Bruce David, and Jeffrey H. Mahan. *Religion and Popular Culture in America*, 1st ed. Berkeley: University of California Press, 2000.

Klassen, Chris. *Religion and Popular Culture: A Cultural Studies Approach*. Oxford: Oxford University Press, 2014.

Martin, Joel, and Conrad E. Ostwalt. *Screening the Sacred: Religion, Myth, and Ideology in Popular American Film*. Boulder, CO: Westview Press, 1995.

McDannell, Colleen. *Material Christianity: Religion and Popular Culture in America*. New Haven, CT: Yale University Press, 1995.

Miles, Margaret R. *Seeing and Believing: Religion and Values in the Movies*. Boston, MA: Beacon Press, 1996.

Moore, R. Laurence. *Selling God: American Religion in the Marketplace of Culture*. New York: Oxford University Press, 1994.

Smith, Jonathan Z. *Imagining Religion: From Babylon to Jonestown*. Chicago: The University of Chicago Press, 1982.

1   Charles H. Long and David Chidester

Born in Little Rock, Arkansas, Charles H. Long (1926–2020) attended the University of Chicago and studied under one of the founders of the "history of religions" field in the academic study of religion, Joachim Wach, writing his dissertation on myth and culture in West Africa. A member of the faculty at the University of Chicago, the University of North Carolina, Syracuse University, and the University of California, Santa Barbara, Long was one of the cofounders (with Mircea Eliade and Joseph Kitigawa) of the influential journal *History of Religions*. He is the co-editor—with Joseph Kitigawa (as well as Jerald Brauer and Marshall Hodgson)—of *Myths and Symbols, Studies in Honor of Mircea Eliade* (1969) and the author of *Alpha: The Myths of Creation* (1963) and *Significations: Signs, Symbols, and Images in the Interpretation of Religion* (1986), as well as numerous articles and book chapters on African and African American religion, religion in the Atlantic World, interpretation, and discourses of power.

Working within the University of Chicago-based "history of religions" tradition, Long emphasized the role of words, signs, and symbols in the communication and transmission of power and the possibility (or often, the likelihood) of the subjugation of one community to the authority of another. Long's work was primarily (but not exclusively) intended for the interactions of Euro- and African American communities in the Atlantic and North American contexts, and he was not often considered a scholar of religion and popular culture as such. But in the late twentieth and early twenty-first centuries, what Long calls the "mode of expression" of religion and religiosity (sometimes labeled "spirituality") has become less institution-based, and the "mode of understanding" has more often been transmitted through film, television, the Internet, and a wide variety of formats, both electronic and static. The boundaries which might once have been more easily distinguishable between "popular religion" and religion in popular culture have become blurred. Much of the expression of power (or the exertion or subjugation of it) has relocated away from religious institutions and is now increasingly communicated through culture. It is no surprise that, as the signs, symbols, and images are now transmitted via popular culture, they convey the Western world's power in the construction of a modern global culture. Long's work provides an important bridge between the academic study of religion and the decades-long avoidance of the popular and contributes to conversations about the expression (or concealment) of power, even in the "popular" cultural productions bought and sold with ease in American society. His notions of "the popular," like much of his work, have proven quite prescient.

"Popular Religion" (2005)[1]

The idea that the positive meaning of a society is represented by the "common people," "the folk," or the peasants may be seen as an expression of "cultural primitivism," the dissatisfaction of the civilized with the quality and style of civilization and the expression of a desire to return for orientation to the archaic roots of the culture. This "discovery of the people," to use Peter **Burke**'s apt phrase, began in the late eighteenth and early nineteenth centuries in Europe. The philosophical justification for this orientation can be seen in the writings of Giovanni Battista **Vico** (1668–1744) and Johann Gottfried **Herder** (1744–1803). Probably more than any others, these two thinkers represented new theoretical approaches to the nature of history, religion, and society. They distinguished the notions of the "*populari*" and "the *volk*" as the basis for an alternate and new meaning of humanism apart from the rationalizing and civilizing processes set in motion by the European **Enlightenment**.

The discovery of two new and different forms of societal orders—one outside Europe (the so-called "primitives"), the other internal to European cultures (the peasants and the folk)—was prompted, in fact, by a search for origins. The search was in some sense antithetical, and in other senses supplementary, to the meaning of the origins of the West in the biblical and Greek cultures. The discovery that the archaic levels of human culture and society had an empirical locus in existing Western cultures became the philosophical, theological, and ideological basis for the legitimation of these new structures of order in modern and contemporary societies.

The notion of popular religion has to do with the discovery of archaic forms, whether within or outside Western cultures. It is at this level that the meaning of popular religion forms a continuum with both primitive religions and peasant and folk cultures in all parts of the world. This continuum is based upon structural similarities defined by the organic nature of all of these types of societies rather than upon historical or genetic causation.

Primitive and peasant-folk societies are, relatively speaking, demographically small. The relationships among people in these societies were thought to be personal in nature. Underlying all modes of communication is an intuitive or empathetic understanding of the ultimate nature and purpose of life.

This is what Herder meant by "the organic mode of life," an idea given methodological precision by the social philosopher Ferdinand **Tonnies**, who made a typological distinction between communities ordered in terms of **Gemeinschaft** and those expressing a **Gesellschaft** orientation to life and the world. Gemeinschaft represents community as organic form; Gesellschaft is society as a mechanical aggregate and artifact. A similar distinction is made by the anthropologist Robert **Redfield** when he describes pre-urban cultures as those in which the moral order predominates over the technical order. The moral order, in this interpretation, is the common understanding of the ultimate nature and purpose of life within the community. The notions of the organic nature of community (Gemeinschaft) and the primacy of the moral order lead to different meanings of the religious life in primitive and folk or peasant cultures as compared to societies in urban Gesellschaft orientations.

---

[1]Charles Long, excerpt from "Popular Religion," in *Encyclopedia of Religion*, ed. Lindsay Jones, vol. 11 (New York: Macmillan Publishing, 2005), 7324–33.

Furthermore, the relationship or the distinction between the religious and the cognitive within the two kinds of societies differs.

While it can be said that religion is present when a distinction is made between the **sacred and the profane**, the locus of this distinction in primitive and folk-peasant cultures is a commonly shared one. There is a unified sense of those objects, actions, and sentiments that are sacred, and those that are profane. The religious and the moral orders tend to be synonymous; thus, the expression of religious faith on the **ordinary and extraordinary** levels of these cultures forms a continuum. The extraordinary expressions are those that commemorate important punctuations of the temporal and social cycles (e.g., a new year, the harvest and first fruits, birth, marriage, and death). The ordinary modes are expressed in the customs, traditions, and mundane activities that maintain and sustain the culture on a daily basis.

One of the goals of the early studies of folk, peasant, and popular cultures was to come to an understanding of the qualitative meaning of religion in human cultures of this kind. Attention was focused on the meaning of custom and tradition, on the one hand, and upon the qualitative meaning and mode of transmission of the traditional values in cultures that were not predominantly literate.

The two early innovators, Herder and, especially, Vico, had already emphasized the modes and genres of language of the nonliterate. Vico based his entire philosophical corpus on the origin and development of language, or, to be more exact, of rhetoric. By the term rhetoric Vico made reference to the manner in which language is produced as a mode of constituting bonds between human beings, the world, and other beings outside the community. Closely related to Herder's philosophy of culture and history is the work of the **Grimm** brothers in their philological studies of the Germanic languages. Their collection of fairy tales, **Märchen**, and folk tales represents the beginning of serious scholarly study of oral traditions. In the work of the Grimms, the first articulation of the relationship between genres of oral literature and modes of transmission is raised. This relationship is important, for, given the presupposed organic form of nonliterate societies, the genres of transmission of ultimate meaning, whether ordinary or extraordinary, defined a locus of the religious. The **romantic** notion (present in Herder and in the theologians Friedrich **Schleiermacher** and Paul **Tillich**), namely, that religion is the ultimate ground and substance of culture, underlies the importance given to transmission, manifestation, and expression of this form of culture as religion. Religion is thus understood to be pervasive in society and culture, finding its expression not only in religious institutions, but in all the dimensions of cultural life.

The genres of the folk tale, folk song, art, and myth became the expressive forms of popular religion. The investigation of poetic meaning and wisdom, and of metaphorical, symbolic expressions, emerged as sources of the religious·sentiment in the traditions of popular religion. The initial "discovery of the people" as an approach to the interpretation of culture and society and as a new form of human value was made under the aegis of intuitive methods within literary studies and from the perspective of a speculative philosophy of history. Once serious scholarly attention was given to the data of the popular, certain ambiguities were noted. The original discovery of the people was based, by and large, on a contrast between the popular and the urban, or the artificiality of the urban mode as a form of civilization. In this sense, the popular represented the archaic and original forms of culture; it was its roots. However, the meaning of the popular could not be limited to the conservative, value-retaining, residual, self-contained unit of a society or culture. One of the basic elements in the meaning of a popular cultural tradition was the mode of its transmission, and it was precisely this element that allowed the meaning of such a tradition to be extended beyond that of the nonliterate strata of society—the rural peasants and the folk.

Varieties and Dimensions. Critical investigations of the meaning of popular culture and religion from the disciplinary orientations of the anthropology and history of religion, and from the sociology of knowledge, revealed a wide variety of the forms of popular religion.

[…]

Of these, the following seven are the most significant.

1. *Popular religion is identical with the organic (usually rural and peasant) form of a society. The religious and moral orders are also identical; in this sense, popular religion is closely related to the meanings of primitive and folk religion.* This is the original meaning of popular religion as the religion of folk and peasant culture. Though the distinction between the folk and peasant religion and the religion of the urban areas is clear-cut in the industrial periods of all cultures, such a distinction does not rest simply on this basis. In the feudal periods of various cultures, this distinction is more pronounced in relationship to certain practices and in the hierarchical structures of the society. Within feudal structures, the upper classes participated in and controlled a form of literacy that was confined within this group. In various cultures, this meant access to an orientation of religious meaning revolving around sacred texts. […]

The limitation of the modes of literacy suggests that though there are authoritative sacred texts, they are situated in a context that is often dominated by illiteracy and oral traditions. The line of demarcation between the culture of literacy and that of the oral traditions is seldom clear-cut. In many cases, the traditions of literacy embody a great deal of the content, form, and style of the oral traditions of the peasants and the folk. Prior to the universalization of the modes of literacy in many cultures, the prestige of literacy was to be found in the belief in, and regard for, the sacred text, which itself was believed to have a magical, authoritative meaning in addition to the content of its particular writings. The written words of the god or gods (the authoritative text) resided with, and were under the control of, elites within the culture.

Another characteristic of folk-peasant societies is that they define the lives of their members within the context of a certain ecological niche (agricultural, pastoral, etc.), and the modes and genres of their existence are attached to this context by ties of tradition and sentiment. The group and the ecological structure thus define a continuity of relationships. The sentiment and the moral order of communities of this kind are synonymous with the meaning of their religion. In agricultural peasant and folk cultures, the rhythms of the agricultural seasons are woven into the patterns of human relationships and sociability. […] Robert Redfield has suggested that the folk-peasant mode of life is an enduring structure of human community found in every part of the world. As such it is not only an empirical datum of a type of human community, but may also represent an enduring source of religious and moral values.

2. *Popular religion as the religion of the laity in a religious community in contrast to that of the clergy. The clergy is the bearer of a learned tradition usually based upon the*

prestige of literacy. Another type of popular religion is notable in religious communities where literacy is by and large limited to the clergy. The clergy carries out the authority of the tradition through the use of religious texts. The laity may memorize and repeat certain of these texts in worship and rituals, but they are not in possession of the instruments and institutional authority of sacred literacy. Both clergy and laity may participate in and honor other traditions that arise from the life of the laity. Such traditions are those related to the sacralization of agricultural seasons and worship centered around the cults of relics and saints, holy persons, pilgrimages, and so on.

Another meaning of this kind of popular religion stems from a society in which literacy is not confined to the clergy or elite. The laity may have access to certain authoritative or quasi-authoritative texts without being in possession of the power of normative interpretation and sanction of these texts. They therefore interpret these texts in their own manner, according to their own needs and sensibilities. [...]

3. *Popular religion as the pervasive beliefs, rituals, and values of a society. Popular religion of this type is a kind of **civil religion** or religion of the public. It forms the general and wide context for the discussion of anything of a religious nature within the society.* [...]

[These] forms of popular religion are found in all cultures where the religious substratum of the culture radiates into, and finds explicit expression — or vague nuances and derivations — in the formation and processes of public institutions other than those dedicated to specific religious ceremonials. As such, this form of popular religion provides a generalized rhetoric and norm for the meaning and discussion of religion within the context of the culture in which it is found. In most cases the meaning of this kind of popular religion is expressed in terms of a dominant religious tradition that has had a profound and pervasive influence upon the culture. [...]

4. *Popular religion as an amalgam of **esoteric** beliefs and practices differing from the common or civil religion, but usually located in the lower strata of a society.* Popular religion in this form more often than not exists alongside other forms of religion in a society. Reference is made here to the religious valuation of esoteric forms of healing, predictions of events not based on logical reasoning, and therapeutic practices that have an esoteric origin and may imply a different **cosmology** than the one prevalent within the society as a whole. In most cases the practitioners and clients have not eschewed the ordinary modes of healing and therapy; the esoteric beliefs and practices are supplementary, representing a mild critique of the normative forms of this kind of knowledge and practice in the society at large. This form of popular religion is present in industrial societies in practices such as **phrenology**, palm reading, astrology, and in the accompanying esoteric, "metaphysical" beliefs. [...]

5. *Popular religion as the religion of a subclass or minority group in a culture.* Particular classes defined by their ethnicity or by an ideology or mythology associated with their work (e.g., miners, blacksmiths, butchers, soldiers, etc.), form another mode of popular religion. In most cases such groups do not represent foreign communities residing in another culture, but pose the problem of "otherness" or strangeness for people outside their communities due to their racial type or occupation. These groups are, nevertheless, integrated into the social structure as a necessary ingredient of a common cultural ideology and its functioning; they constitute "a part of the society by not being a part of it." In most traditional cultures of the world, certain occupations, such as mining or blacksmithing, represent this meaning. They are restricted to certain places of residence within the villages and they in turn have

their own rituals and alternate understandings of the nature of the cosmos. While the role and function of such occupations is understood by the rest of society, and is felt to have a place in its general cosmology, they nevertheless form the basis for an alternate understanding of the nature of society. [...]

6. *Popular religion as the religion of the masses in opposition to the religion of the sophisticated, discriminating, and learned within a society.* This is a variation on the difference between the laity and the clergy in hierarchical and traditional societies. Reference is made in this form of popular religion to a meaning of the masses that is the product of democratic politics and industrialism. Whereas in the older, traditional, hierarchical societies, the clergy and the laity both possessed traditions, the modern definition of "the masses" implies the loss of tradition and **canons** of value and taste, which are now defined in terms of a privileged class order of the elite who have had the benefit of special education. Alexis **de Tocqueville**'s comments on the meaning of democracy in America imply that democracy and mass culture are synonymous. The form of popular religion will tend to express the **existential** and **ephemeral** concerns of the mass population at any moment of its history.

7. *Popular religion as the creation of an ideology of religion by the elite levels of a society.* From the very beginning of the study of popular culture and religion, the discovery, meaning, and valuation of "the popular" were undertaken by elites within the society. Especially with the coming of industrialization and the rise of the nation-state, the provincial traditions of the peasant and rural folk within a culture had to fall under the political and ideological meanings of larger, generalizing and centralizing orders of the state and its bureaucracy. To the extent that the ideological meaning of the rural and peasant cultures served the aims of the state, it was promoted as the older, traditional meaning of the state deriving from its archaic forms. Popular culture and religion in this mode were invented and promoted by the state through **folklore** societies, museums, and by the promotion of historical research into the past of the society. On the basis of a genuine and authentic folk and peasant tradition of culture and religion, a new meaning of the popular forms is now embraced and supported by the state.

Given this variety of forms and meanings of popular religion, it is appropriate to ask what is the common element in all of them. There are two common elements. First of all, "the popular" in any of its varieties is concerned with a mode of transmission of culture. Whether the group be large or small, or whether the content of the religion be sustaining or ephemeral, "the popular" designates the universalization of its mode of transmission. In peasant and folk situations, this mode of transmission is traditionally embodied in symbols and **archetypes** that tend to be long-lasting and integrative. In modern industrial societies, the modes of transmission are several, including literacy, electronic media, newspapers, chapbooks, and so on. Such modes of communication bring into being a popular culture that is different from, but may overlap with, other social strata within the culture. Due to the intensity of these forms of communication, the content of the forms of popular culture is able to change quickly. It is not, however, the content that is at the fore here, but the type of cognition afforded by the modes of transmission. Given the intensification of transmission and the ephemerality of content, this form of popular religion and culture is **semiotic**—it is embedded in a system of signs rather than in symbols and archetypes.

David Chidester

David Chidester (1952–) earned a PhD in religious studies from the University of California, Santa Barbara, where he studied with intellectual historian of religious studies Walter Capps and religion and literature pioneer Richard Comstock. He is currently Emeritus Professor of Comparative Religion at the University of Cape Town in South Africa, and his scholarship covers a wide variety of topics in Christian history, religion in South Africa, and comparative religions. He has also been involved in a number of projects examining aspects of South African religion and culture.

Drawing from what some have identified as a "Santa Barbara school" of focusing on "religion on the ground," Chidester's work blends the University of Chicago-based "history of religions" approach with a focus on the materiality drawn from the lives of those he studies. One of his earlier works, *Salvation and Suicide* (1988), was an award-winning analysis of the teachings of Jim Jones drawn from his writings as well as the many hours of recorded sermons taped by Jones during his ministry (right up to the moment of mass suicide in the South American jungle in 1978) and takes seriously the religious rhetoric and imagery of the man who led hundreds of believers away from their homes in the United States and to their death (mostly, if not all) by suicide. Rather than seeing these people as deluded, and Jones as psychotic, Chidester puts himself into the world of the Peoples Temple, its history, its theology, and its eschatology, and works to make sense of them for the people who experienced it in the jungles of South America.

Chidester's enterprise of taking people seriously when they use terms common to religion to describe their own (often seemingly nonreligious) objects, activities, and ideas reveals the fluidity of those concepts rather than their misuse. It is, for Chidester, less important to measure people's usage of a term against some supposed universal definition than to triangulate a sense of what people—including, it turns out, scholars—think they are saying or doing when they use the lexicon of religion. For Chidester, from the beginnings of the European period of colonialism—when a very Christian notion of religion travelled with Empires around the globe—both the practitioner and the scholar have felt the impact of the introduction, imposition, adoption, and transformation of the concept of "religion" to describe that which people have found important, and that which observers have seen people finding important.

More than anything, it is likely Chidester's 1996 article on religion and American popular culture ("The Church of Baseball, the Fetish of Coca-Cola, and the Potlatch of Rock 'n' Roll") that sparked the most recent interest in the academic study of the intersections of religion and popular culture. It is often cited as one of the generative pieces of scholarship in the field, and has been included in edited volumes on the study of religion and popular culture. As the title of the article suggests, Chidester explores how seemingly everyday items—baseball, Coca-Cola, and "rock 'n' roll"—serve for their users as "church," "fetish," and "potlatch," respectively. Chidester suggests there, and develops more deeply in his 2005 work *Authentic Fakes* (from which the following excerpt is taken), the argument that the term "religion" is less meaningful than the concept of "religious work"—the "performative" aspects, as he puts it below—in understanding human experience.

"Planet Hollywood" (2005)[2]

Religion is a difficult term to define because everyone already "knows" what it means. What passes for common knowledge about religion tends to be organized according to binary oppositions: people know their own religion (as opposed to other religions), true religion (as opposed to false religion), or real religion (as opposed to fake religion). In exploring religion and American popular culture, we need to develop a more complex sense of what we mean by the term religion. Without belaboring the issue of definition, we are confronted with the ambiguity of a word that can be used in a conventional sense as a generic term for distinct religious traditions, communities, institutions, or movements, or in an analytical sense as a generic term for any kind of activity engaged with the transcendent, the sacred, or the ultimate concerns of human life. Both of these senses are important for exploring religion and popular culture. The first focuses our attention on specific religious groups in relation to popular culture; the second directs our attention to potent religious symbols, myths, and rituals that might animate cultural formations.

Fitting the conventional sense of the term, the Muslim organizations in Cape Town, as voluntary religious associations, form part of the rich, complex fabric of Islam in South Africa. Like any religion, Islam embraces a diversity of political positions—progressive, reactionary, and everything in between—in relation to the local social environment. In a **globalizing** world, it also reflects political positions that its adherents adopt in relation to the pervasive presence and power of the United States. Mobilizing in the mosques, some Muslim organizations have taken their religious interests to the streets in opposition to U.S. foreign policy. One of these organizations allegedly bombed [the Cape Town, South Africa] Planet Hollywood, as symbol not only of American popular culture but also of a kind of global religion that has generated like a religious mission. The franchise of Planet Hollywood, which has been described in tourist literature as "the Mecca of movie memorabilia," has restaurants in London and Paris, Jakarta and Tokyo, Dubai and Riyadh, Acapulco and Cancun, and, until 1998, in Cape Town, South Africa, occupying all the major zones of the clashing civilizations identified by political scientist Samuel Huntington as the fractures of conflict in a globalizing world. The bombing in Cape Town appeared to be another violent clash between Muslims and the West, or at least between Muslims and the West that could be imagined as centered in America, a religiously motivated attack on American sacred symbols.

In the aftermath, however, Muslim leaders in Cape Town denounced the bombing. On behalf of the Muslim Judicial Council, Sheikh Achmed Seddik, while acknowledging that Muslims in Cape Town held "heavy anti-American sentiments," strongly condemned the bombing as terrorism. Likewise, a spokesman for Muslims against Global Oppression distanced his organization from the bombing, saying, "This is an act of terror." Although the event was presented in the local and global media as an anti-American act, these Muslim leaders in Cape Town insisted that such an act of terror should also be understood as an anti-Muslim act, since terrorism is inconsistent with the basic religious values of Islam. Nevertheless, while the crime remained unsolved in South Africa, the U.S. State Department placed Muslims against Global Oppression on its list of terrorist organizations.

---

[2]David Chidester, excerpt from "Planet Hollywood," in *Authentic Fakes: Religion and American Popular Culture* (Berkeley: University of California Press, 2005), 11–30.

Back in the United States, meanwhile, religious controversy was generated by the representation of Muslims in Hollywood films. Anticipating the opening of *The Siege* (1998), which depicts a Muslim terrorist group planning bombings in New York, American Muslim groups protested the negative stereotypes about Islam, Muslims, and Arabs that are consistently perpetuated by Hollywood. A prominent Arab American, the disk jockey Casey Kasem, who for decades kept Americans tuned in to the latest hits in popular music on his radio show *American Top 40*, condemned Hollywood's tradition of vilifying Muslims. A film like *The Siege*, Kasem argued, "will leave the audience with the idea that Arabs and Muslims are terrorists and the enemies of the United States."

Coincidentally, *The Siege* stars Bruce Willis, one of the owners of Planet Hollywood. In a thoughtful essay entitled "Bruce Willis versus Bin Laden," published in the Cairo weekly *Al-Ahram* in November 1998, Tarek Atia argued as a Muslim against the extremes represented by both men. In a world saturated by global media, he wrote, "Bruce Willis and Bin Laden have come, more than any other two people alive, to represent the extremes of human existence, pitted against each other. They are, in many ways, the most accessible archetypes of religious and secular extremism." Rejecting both of these extremes, Atia situated his struggles as an effort to lead a moral, spiritual life that is defined by neither fundamentalism nor secularism.

According to Atia, Hollywood is not religiously neutral in this struggle. On the one hand, he argued, specific religious interests, including anti-Muslim interests, are being advanced by the "Jews who invented and remain in charge of Hollywood." Featuring in many conspiracy theories about the secret rulers of the world, Jewish control of Hollywood seems, at first glance, confirmed by history, since four out of five heads of the major film studios founded in the 1920s were from Jewish backgrounds. However, they tended to identify themselves less with Judaism than with Christianity and American nationalism. Louis B. Mayer, head of MGM, changed his birthday to the Fourth of July and attended a Catholic church that was also attended by Henry Cohn, head of Columbia Pictures. Asked to donate money to a Jewish relief fund, Cohn reportedly exclaimed: "Relief for the Jews? How about relief from the Jews? All the trouble in this world has been caused by Jews and Irishmen." Although they exerted a powerful influence on the imagery of religion, race, and America, these Hollywood moguls were not advancing Jewish interests.

On the other hand, Atia maintained, secularist extremism, as embodied in an action hero such as Bruce Willis, can be regarded as a kind of secular religion promoted by Hollywood. Although he identified Willis as an archetype of secularism, Atia recalled sufficient evidence from Willis's popular films to suggest that the actor plays a quasi-religious role in American popular cultures as the country's "savior" from criminals, gangsters, terrorists, and even asteroids. In *The Siege*, he seems to be saving America from Muslims.

Although entertainment is certainly an industry, it has produced superstars such as Bruce Willis and Michael Jackson, who display transcendent or sacred qualities in American popular culture. Following the sociologist Max **Weber**'s definition of charisma, we might recognize these superstars as embodying that "certain quality of an individual personality by virtue of which he is set apart from ordinary men and treated as endowed with supernatural, superhuman and at least specifically exceptional powers and qualities." Although we might want to draw other conclusions about them, we can at least recognize traces of religion—superhuman transcendence, the sacred as set apart from the ordinary—that seem to cling to the charismatic superstars of American popular culture.

[...] Still, we need to ask: Does it make sense to call any of this religion? Most important, does it make any difference to call any of this religion?

Religious Work

How does religion work? Classic definitions of religion have focused on its importance as a way of thinking, as a way of feeling, and as a way of being human in relation to other human beings in a community. As a way of thinking, according to E.B. **Taylor**'s minimal definition, religion depends upon "belief in supernatural beings." More recently, Melford **Spiro** qualified this definition by stipulating that religion involves "culturally patterned interaction with culturally postulated superhuman beings." By this account, religion deals with the supernatural, which by definition cannot be confirmed or disconfirmed by ordinary sensory perception or scientific experimentation. According to this classic definition, religion works to identify certain persons as supernatural, superhuman, or at least as greater in power than ordinary humans. By this account, religion generates beliefs and practices for engaging transcendence.

As a way of feeling, religion cultivates a range of intense emotions, from holy fear to sacred intimacy, which have also received attention in its classic definitions. Following Friedrich Schleiermacher's contention that religion is not a way of thinking but a way of feeling, specifically a feeling of absolute dependence upon a Supreme Being, F. Max **Muller**, the putative founder of the study of religion, defined it as an essentially emotional, even romantic "faculty of apprehending the Infinite." Similarly, focusing on personal feeling, Rudolf **Otto** defined religion as a feeling of holy awe, combining avoidance and attraction, before a mystery; William **James** defined religion as a personal response, in solitude, to whatever might be regarded as divine, and Paul Tillich defined it as a person's "ultimate concern" in the face of death.

As a way of being in society, religion is more than merely a matter of personal thoughts and feelings. Religion involves beliefs and practices, but always in the context of social relations. In fact, as Emile **Durkheim** argued, religion might very well be central to the formation of society. Accordingly, Durkheim defined religion as beliefs and practices in relation to the sacred, with the "sacred" defined simply as that which is set apart of the ordinary, but in such a way that it serves to unify people who adhere to those beliefs and practices into a single moral community. Religious thinking and feeling, action and experience, in Durkheim's formulation, realize their function in the construction of any human society around the sacred.

Social cohesion, according to Durkheim, depends on shared beliefs, practices, experiences, and interactions that can usefully be defined as religious. Generally, most scholars of religion have followed Durkheim in seeing religion as multi-dimensional, as a complex system of mythic and doctrinal belief, of ritual and ethical action, of personal and social experience. Religion has been defined by Clifford **Geertz** as a "symbolic system" that generates powerful moods and motivations and clothes these dispositions in an aura of factuality so that they seem uniquely real in forming personal subjectivity and social solidarity.

[...]

At the same time, the meaning of the term religion is determined by usage. As the great linguist Emile **Benveniste** taught us, religion has been used as a highly charged marker of difference, defined precisely by its opposition to "superstition." Whatever the word might have meant in ancient Greco-Roman discourse, the term religio was consistently used to refer to an authentic human activity in opposition to superstitio, an inauthentic, alien, or even less fully human activity that was allegedly based on ignorance, fear, or fraud.

[...]

Here I am interested not in the denial of religion but in the performative extensions of the term to the production, consumption, and artifacts of popular culture. In an essay I wrote in the mid-1990s on the church of baseball, the fetish of Coca-Cola, and the potlatch of rock 'n' roll . . . I was willing to consider these activities as religious not because I said they were, but because participants, real people, characterized their own involvement in these enterprises as religious. Baseball players, Coca-Cola executives, and rock 'n' rollers testified that what they were doing was a kind of religion. In counterpoint to the classic definitions of religion, I am interested in how the term has actually been used by people to make sense out of their lives. What did they mean when they used the term religion to describe their attachment to a sport, a consumer product, or an entertainment industry?

Connections 1a: Typologies

Much of the earliest work in the study of religion and popular culture analyzed phenomena by genre—for example, in film—or by faith tradition. While valuable work is still done this way, one of the signs of an emerging field has been the publication of "typological" volumes that seek to organize data across genres and faith traditions rather than within one or the other.

Because of the many ways in which these phenomena may be examined, these volumes have taken a variety of approaches to the material. One of the earlier edited volumes to be published in this field (*Religion and Popular Culture in America*) employs an organizational structure reminiscent of that developed by Protestant theologian H. Richard Niebuhr in his 1951 work *Christ and Culture*; the editors, Bruce David Forbes and Jeffrey Mahan, vaguely mirror Niebuhr's categories ("Christ against culture," "the Christ of culture," "Christ above culture," "Christ and culture in paradox," and "Christ the Transformer of Culture") with their own ("religion in popular culture," "popular culture in religion," "popular culture as religion," and "religion and popular culture in dialogue"). The fact that all three men are ordained Protestant ministers may be a factor, but it is just as likely that the categories suggest themselves as natural relationships of two categories. The organizational structure of another early work in the field (*God in the Details*) seems more informed by a comparative ("history of . . .") religions approach than by theology, breaking topics down according to their relative proximity to popular manifestations of religious categories: "popular symbol and myth," "popular ritual," "popular spirituality and morality," and "popular churches." A more recent venture (*Routledge Companion to Religion and Popular Culture*) returns to the "genre and traditions" method but collects materials that, in one section, provides analyses of the presentation of religion in different forms of popular culture "delivery"— "mediated," by which they mean via electronic media; "material," by which they mean via physical formation; and "locative," by which they mean via encounter in a specific location—while in another provides analyses of the place of popular culture in various religious traditions.

As the editors of one of the volumes note in their introduction, the categories "are hardly exhaustive" but are "especially useful because of their inherent elasticity." Their goal in creating such a structure, they note, is to show that "what is going on in these activities . . . may be comparable to religion as it is traditionally understood" while at the same time stretching the categories "and therefore our understanding of religion itself to accommodate the strange new world of religion." It seems that regardless of the method used to organize the various phenomena at the intersection of religion and popular culture, most scholars would likely agree.

Designating popular culture as religion does not always mean accepting its religious legitimacy. Conventional religious institutions, especially conservative coalitions, have sometimes identified a competing cultural formation as religion to raise the stakes in the cultural context. In recent years, conservative Christian groups have argued that humanism, secularism, and the scientific theory of evolution should all count as religions and therefore should be excluded from public schools. If the Christian religion cannot be established in public institutions, they have argued, then these other "religions" should also be removed in accordance with the First Amendment prohibition of any government-established religion.

Even Walt Disney productions have been subjected to such a strategic definition of religion. On June 18, 1997, the Southern Baptist Convention passed a resolution to boycott the Walt Disney Company. Arguing that the company had abandoned "its previous philosophy of producing enriching family entertainment," the convention accused Disney of promoting "immoral ideologies such as homosexuality, infidelity, and adultery." In launching a crusade against Disney, the Southern Baptist Convention argued that Disney was not merely a cultural force working against conservative Christian beliefs, values, and sexual ethics; it was also actually promoting an alternative religion, an earth-based, pagan, and pantheistic religiosity as celebrated in animated features such as *The Lion King* and *Pocahontas*, which represented a religious threat to Christianity. The Southern Baptist Convention boycotted Disney, not only because it presented a secular alternative to religion, but also because the corporation was allegedly advancing a religion of its own, in competition with Christianity.

As this religious crusade against Disney suggests, popular culture can appear from different perspectives as religion. As I maneuver between classic academic definitions and actual popular uses of the term religion, I must admit that I do have a working definition of my own. In my view, something is doing religious work if it is engaged in negotiating what it is to be human. Classification, orientation, and negotiation—these are the processes that I look for when I study religion and religions: the processes of classifying persons into superhuman, human, and subhuman; the processes of orienting persons in time and space; and the contested negotiations over the ownership of those classifications and orientations.

In the world of Walt Disney, these patterns and processes of religious work are certainly evident. Although Disney's animated films evoke supernatural persons, such as fairies and genies, ancestral spirits and celestial kings, their religious work concentrates on playing with conventional distinctions among humans, animals, and machines. Religious classifications of persons put these distinctions at stake: What is it to be a human being, not only in relation to superhuman powers, but also in relation to beings classified as less than human? Consistently, Disney engages in a kind of religious work by trying to clarify these classifications.

At the same time, religious orientations in time and space serve to situate persons in place. In films, television, theme parks, and consumer products, the Walt Disney Company has advanced a temporal orientation based on a poignant nostalgia for a bygone era and an unbounded optimism in scientific progress. Anchoring this temporal orientation, Disney theme parks have provided multiple sacred sites for ritual pilgrimage to the heart of a symbolic, cultural, and arguably religious sense of orientation in the world.

Classifications and orientation, person and place, are inevitably negotiated in religion and popular culture. By negotiation, I refer to the relational, situational, and contested character of the production of religious meaning and power in popular culture. Negotiating the sacred does not occur in a vacuum. These struggles over the production, significance, and ownership of sacred symbols take place within a political economy of the sacred.

By using the phrase "political economy of the sacred," I want to focus attention on the ways in which the sacred is produced, circulated, engaged, and consumed in popular culture. Not merely a given, the sacred is produced through the religious labor of interpretation and ritualization. As I explore the political economy of the sacred, I want to highlight three things: First, I want to focus on the means, modes, and forces involved in the production of sacred values through religious labor. By definition, the sacred might be "set apart," but it is set apart, as Karen **Fields** has observed, "by doing." In the political economy of the sacred, this sacred doing, or doing of the sacred, is not merely religious practice, symbolic performance, or social drama. It is a kind of religious work.

Second, I want to focus on the transformations of scarcity into surplus, the processes by which scarce resources, including symbolic capital, are transformed through religious work into sacred surpluses, especially the surplus of meaning generated through the religious work of interpretation.

Third, I want to focus on the struggles over legitimate ownership of sacred symbols, symbols made meaningful through the ongoing work of interpretation but also made powerful through appropriation, through the inevitably contested claims that are made on their ownership.

So this is what I mean by the "political economy of the sacred"—the terrain and resources, the strategies and tactics, in and through which the sacred is negotiated.

The Popular

According to a quantitative definition, popular culture is popular because it is mass-produced, widely distributed, and regularly consumed by a large number of people. Demographically, the popular might be simply understood as a measure of popularity. A cultural form is popular, in this sense, because many people like it. Implicit in this quantitative definition of the popular is a distinction between "high" culture, maintained by a numerically small social elite, and "low" culture, supported by the majority of people in a society. As a result, the popular, whether in popular culture or popular religion, has tended to be located among the laity rather than the clergy and among rural folk rather than city dwellers or among urban lower classes rather than urban elites. In cultural studies, however, the popular has come to refer to a much more complex range of social positions within the production and consumption of culture.

The mass production of popular culture calls attention to what critical theorist Theodor **Adorno** called the "**culture industry**," the machinery of mass cultural production in a capitalist economy. Instead of assuming that popular culture is mass-produced because many people like it, Adorno argued that people like it because they essentially have no choice. Effectively, the culture industry beats them into submission. Readily available and immediately accessible, mass-produced popular culture emerges as the only option within capitalist relations of production. As cultural production becomes an industry, artwork is transformed into a commodity that is created and exchanged for profit. In the process, the distinction between high culture and popular cultures dissolves, since both "bear the stigmata of capitalism."

The culture industry produces two basic effects in popular culture: uniformity and utility. Rather than meeting the diversity of popular desires for leisure or entertainment, the culture industry creates a new uniformity of desire. "Culture now impresses the same stamp on everything," Adorno and his colleague Max **Horkheimer** complained. "Films, radio and magazines make up a system which is uniform as a whole and in every part." Within the capitalist system of cultural production, leisure is integrated into the cycle of productive labor. Leisure, entertainment, and amusement are extensions of work, employments of "free" time that are organized by the same principle of utility that govern the capitalist system of production. As an integral part of the capitalist economy, the culture industry provides popular cultural diversions that the masses seek "as an escape from the mechanized work process, and to recruit strength in order to be able to cope with it again." In this production-oriented model, therefore, popular culture serves the interests of capital—profitability, uniformity, and utility—by entangling people in a culture industry in which a character such as "Donald Duck in the cartoons . . . gets his beating so that the viewers can get used to the same treatment."

The popular reception, or consumption, of cultural forms, styles, and content calls attention to the many different ways people actually find to make mass-produced culture their own. Following the critical theorist Walter **Benjamin**, many cultural analysts argue that the reception of popular culture involves not passive submission but creative activity. Although recognizing the capitalist control of mass-produced culture, Benjamin nevertheless found that people develop new perceptual and interactive capacities that enable them to transform private hopes and fears into "figures of the collective dreams such as the globe-orbiting Mickey Mouse."

Where Adorno insisted that the productions of the culture industry are oppressive, Benjamin looked for the therapeutic effects, such as the healing potential of collective laughter and even the redemptive possibilities in the reception of popular culture. In the case of Mickey Mouse, for example, Benjamin suggested that audiences are able to think through basic cultural categories—machines, animals, and humans—by participating in a popular form of entertainment that scrambles them. As Benjamin observed, Mickey Mouse cartoons are "full of miracles that not only surpass those of technology but make fun of them." Against the laws of nature and technology, these "miracles" of transformation—changing shape, defying gravity—occur spontaneously "from the body of Mickey Mouse, his partisans and pursuers." For an audience "grown tired of the endless complications of the everyday," Benjamin concluded, these miracles promise a kind of "redemption" in an extraordinary world.

Without necessarily subscribing to the proposition of a therapeutic capacity or redemptive potential of popular culture, cultural analysts adopting the reception-oriented model have concentrated on the creative activity of interpretation as itself a means of cultural production that takes place in the process of cultural consumption. As people actively decode cultural content through interpretation, they also participate in rituals of consumption, rituals of exchange, ownership, and care through which the arts and artifacts of popular culture are personalized.

In between cultural production and consumption, the space of popular culture is a contested terrain in which people occupy vastly different and often multiple subject positions grounded in race, ethnicity, social class, occupation, region, gender, sexual orientation, and so on. As the cultural theorist Stuart **Hall** has established, popular culture is the site of struggle in which various alternative cultural objects contend with the hegemony of the dominant culture. Subcultures develop oppositional positions, perhaps even methods of "cultural resistance," thereby creating alternative cultural formations, which social elites work to appropriate and assimilate into the larger society. Not a stable system of production and consumption, popular culture is a battlefield of contending strategies, tactics, and maneuvers in struggles over the legitimate ownership of highly charged cultural symbols of meaning and power.

Glossary

ADORNO, Theodor (1903–69): German philosopher, sociologist, cultural theorist, writer (see separate entry in this volume).

ARCHETYPES: models for, or patterns of, symbolic systems (such as the biblical Adam used to represent all of humanity).

BENJAMIN, Walter (1892–1940): German literary critic, theorist.

BENVENISTE, Emile (1902–76): French linguist, scholar of semiotics.

BURKE, Peter: author of *Popular Culture in Early Modern Europe* (1978).

CANONS: laws, rules, guidelines, often religious, defining proper behavior and belief.

CIVIL RELIGION: a system of symbols and practices—including the observance of national holidays, singing of national anthems, devotion to the flag, national memorials, cemeteries, and statuary, and other patriotic imagery—that sacralize the state and its core values.

COSMOLOGY: a system—either scientific or religious—for understanding the origin of the cosmos.

CULTURE INDUSTRY: a concept, developed by the Frankfurt School (a collection of social theory and philosophy scholars working at the Goethe University in Frankfurt, Germany, between the First and Second World Wars), of social criticism proposing that the major elements of popular culture, including the major media of film, television, radio, and print, have been industrialized and thus produce uniform content whose message is fundamentally manipulative and serves the interests of those in power.

DURKHEIM, Emile (1858–1917): French sociologist (see separate entry in this volume).

ENLIGHTENMENT: an intellectual, social, and political movement started in seventeenth-century Europe that emphasized the study of nature via science, democratic reforms, and the improvement of society via the dissemination of a more rational worldview.

EPHEMERAL: short-lived, temporary, dream-like.

ESOTERIC: known by a limited group of people possessing special knowledge.

EXISTENTIAL: related to existence or to the reality of the existence of something.

FIELDS, Karen: American sociologist, scholar of race and religion.

FOLKLORE: the academic study of oral traditions, music, artifacts, and other everyday elements of a culture, including stories, jokes, songs, gestures, toys, games, etc. Often includes the study of how these materials are created, circulated, and interpreted.

GEERTZ, Clifford (1926–2006): American anthropologist (see separate entry in this volume).

GEMEINSCHAFT: a sociological term for small-scale societies that provide close social ties, unified moral beliefs, and face-to-face communications; compare to **GESELLSCHAFT**.

GESELLSCHAFT: a sociological term for large-scale societies that provide greater anonymity, formal and legalistic value systems, and impersonal communications; compare to **GEMEINSCHAFT**.

GLOBALIZING: in the process of globalization, a term used to describe the integration of human processes and systems—including communication, commerce, and patterns of human interaction (fashion, culture, etc.)—across national boundaries.

GRIMM, Jacob Carl (1785–1863) and **Wilhelm Carl GRIMM** (1786–1859): German linguists, founders of the modern study of folklore.

HALL, Stuart (1932–2014): Jamaican cultural theorist, sociologist (see separate entry in this volume).

HERDER, Johann Gottfried (1744–1803): German theologian, philosopher of history and culture.

HORKHEIMER, Max (1895–1973): German philosopher, cultural theorist (see separate entry in this volume).

JAMES, William (1842–1910): American philosopher, psychologist, theorist of religious experience.

MÄRCHEN: "fairytales" (German).

MÜLLER, F. Max (1823–1900): German linguist, scholar of religion, mythology.

ORDINARY and EXTRAORDINARY: terms used by scholars of religion to differentiate the levels of human existence. "Ordinary" expressions of life are the everyday customs and patterns of living found in a society; "Extraordinary" expressions are those customs and patterns—such as life cycle events (weddings, funerals), annual observances (seasonal observances)—that occur regularly but infrequently.

OTTO, Rudolf (1869–1937): German philosopher, theologian, author of *Das Heilige* (1917; *The Idea of the Holy*, 1923).

PHRENOLOGY: the study of the shape of the skull as an indicator of mentality and character.

REDFIELD, Robert (1897–1958): American anthropologist, theorist of acculturation and cultural change.

ROMANTIC: of or related to Romanticism, a broad intellectual movement of the late eighteenth and early nineteenth centuries, influential in the arts, philosophy, religion, music, and other fields, that emphasized individualism, emotion, spontaneity, intuition, and the inspirational character of "Nature" (as opposed to "nature").

SEMIOTIC: referring to the study of signs and symbols used in systems of communication, as well as the social networks and conceptual systems that sustain them.

SACRED and the PROFANE: terms used by scholars of religion to characterize the most basic activities of religious groups: to separate the sacred from the profane, especially in connection to ritual. The "profane" is often that which has general use but is not meaning-filled; the "sacred" is often that which has limited (and set-apart) use but is meaning-filled.

SCHLEIERMACHER, Friedrich (1768–1834): German theologian, profoundly influential for modern Protestant theology.

SPIRO, Melford (1920–2014): American anthropologist.

TAYLOR, Edward Burnett "E.B." (1832–1917): British anthropologist, heavily influenced by Charles Darwin's theory of evolution.

TILLICH, Paul (1886–1965): German Protestant theologian (see separate entry in this volume).

de TOCQUEVILLE, Alexis (1805–59): French historian, writer, author of *Democracy in America* (1835–40).

TONNIES, Ferdinand (1855–1936): German sociologist, theorist.

VICO, Giovanni Battista "Giambattista" (1668–1744): Italian philosopher of history and law.

WEBER, Max (1864–1920): German sociologist, author of *The Protestant Ethic and the Spirit of Capitalism* (1904).

Questions for Conversation

Which of Long's seven definitions of "popular religion" serve best to understand its connection to popular culture? How might they inform our notions of religion and popular culture?

For Long, what might be the more significant differences between "popular" and "folk"?

How does Long's notion of "popular culture" (as "the culture of the people") differ from Chidester's notion?

How are Chidester's "conventional sense" of the term "religion" ("distinct religious traditions, communities, institutions, or movements") and his "analytic sense" ("any kind of activity engaged with the transcendent") related?

In what ways does Chidester's notion of "religious work" expand the scope of study of religion and popular culture? In what ways might it diminish traditional notions of "religion"?

What might Chidester mean by "political economy of the sacred," or "legitimate ownership of sacred symbols"?

How does Long's emphasis on "modes of transmission" inform Chidester's notion of "religious work"?

How do Long and Chidester's notions of "popular" differ? What effect does that have on their notions of religion and popular culture?

Suggestions for Additional Reading

Albanese, Catherine L. "Religion and American Popular Culture: An Introductory Essay," *Journal of the American Academy of Religion* 64, no. 4 (1996): 733–42.

Chidester, David. "The Church of Baseball, the Fetish of Coca-Cola, and the Potlatch of Rock 'n' Roll: Theoretical Models for the Study of Religion in American Popular Culture," *Journal of the American Academy of Religion* 64, no. 4 (1996): 743–65.

Clark, Lynn Schofield. "Why Study Popular Culture? Or, How to Build a Case for Your Thesis in a Religious Studies or Theology Department," in *Between Sacred and Profane: Researching Religion and Popular Culture*, ed. Gordon Lynch, 5–20. New York: I.B. Tauris, 2005.

Clark, Lynn Schofield. "When the University Went 'Pop': Exploring Cultural Studies, Sociology of Culture, and the Rising Interest in the Study of Popular Culture," *Sociology Compass* 2, no. 1 (2008): 16–33.

Forbes, Bruce David, and Jeffrey Mahan, eds. *Religion and Popular Culture in America*. Berkeley: University of California Press, 2000.

Lyden, John C., and Eric Michael Mazur, eds. *Routledge Companion to Religion and Popular Culture*. New York: Routledge, 2015.

Mazur, Eric Michael, and Kate McCarthy, eds. *God in the Details: American Religion in Popular Culture*. New York: Routledge, 2000.

Unit II Foundational Texts in the Study of Religion and Popular Culture

Introduction to Unit II

As we suggested in this volume's introduction, the theories we present here are the tools developed by their authors and used by readers who sought to answer the various questions that occurred to them as they engaged their subject matter. Some of those who developed the theories were trained in disciplines like anthropology, or psychology, or sociology; others in literature, or comparative religion, or theology. Their training undoubtedly had a profound impact on how they saw their subject matter, and thus how they formulated their questions. But while their theories were developed in light of particular concerns, they were not limited by discipline; they do not come with warning labels stating, "For Sociologists Only." They are available to all who feel that one particular theory might be of greater use than another in helping to solve a riddle, or provide an insight or an understanding of what stands before them. To continue the "tool" analogy, one needs the right tool to fix any problem and may have to visit the neighborhood hardware store to find it. And while it may be a little intimidating to the person who has never attempted to tackle a "do-it-yourself" project, the store providing the tools is open to all.

This fits the study of religion and popular culture particularly well. Both the academic study of religion and the academic study of popular culture have their roots in disciplinary traditions, but both emerged from those roots and have developed into areas of study whose practitioners use a wide variety of disciplinary methods. While those working in these fields develop a mastery of the detail and data of their particular area of interest, they also become fluent (or, at the very least, conversant) in the theories of various disciplines related to that area of interest, as the needs (and questions) arise. Because both the academic study of religion and the academic study of popular culture are driven by the objects of study rather than specific methodological orthodoxies, so, too, the study of religion and popular culture.

Of course, anyone who has gone into a neighborhood hardware store knows that there is much to be learned not only by browsing among the various tools on offer but also in talking to the store clerks and customers, many of whom seem to have intimate knowledge of the use of the tools. One may possess a box filled with tools but may not understand how each one works, or for the variety of purposes each one may have been designed. Unit II has been designed with that conversational aspect in mind. Like Unit I, we have included glossaries to help with more difficult terms, questions to assist in starting conversations about the theories, and suggestions for deeper reading related to the theory. The excerpts in Unit II are presented chronologically according to when each was published, in part because some of the later theorists' works respond to that of the earlier theorists directly. The selection is meant to be introductory rather than comprehensive, to give you a taste rather than a feast; we encourage you to supplement as you see fit and to draw your own conclusions as they occur to you.

As you will see, a number of the theories were developed by theorists who had little (or no) expressed interest in religion and an even greater number by those who had no expressed interest in popular culture. Many of them are known as foundational thinkers in other disciplines: Sigmund Freud ("the father of modern psychology"), Emile Durkheim ("the founder of modern sociology"), and so on. To address this seeming disconnect, in a way more deliberate than in Unit I, we have designed the "Connections" to be a bit more explicit in the ways in which the theory presented—or those derived from it—have been used by others at the intersection of religion and popular culture, and to help you connect the dots between the excerpt presented and its possible applications in the study of religion and popular culture.

Our goal here is to begin conversations—about some of the more commonly turned-to theorists, about how generally developed theories from various academic disciplines migrate into other disciplines or fields of study, and about how specific questions raised in the study of religion and popular culture can benefit from insights derived from different theorists' works. If you finish Unit II with more to think than you had at its beginning, we will have fulfilled our goal of showing you many of the great variety of tools available in the religion and popular culture "hardware" store.

Suggestions for Additional Reading

Capps, Walter. *Religious Studies: The Making of a Discipline*. Minneapolis, MN: Fortress Press, 1995.

Elliott, Scott S. *Reinventing Religious Studies: Key Writings in the History of a Discipline*. New York: Routledge, 2014.

Pals, Daniel. *Nine Theories of Religion*, 3rd ed. New York: Oxford University Press, 2015.

Sharpe, Eric J. *Comparative Religion: A History*. La Salle, IL: Open Court, 1986.

Smart, Ninian. *Dimensions of the Sacred: An Anatomy of the World's Beliefs*. Berkeley: University of California Press, 1996.

Stone, Jon R. *The Craft of Religious Studies*. New York: St. Martin's Press, 1998.

2   Sigmund Freud

The son of a Jewish wool merchant, Sigmund Freud (1856–1939) lived most of his life in Vienna, Austria, where he trained as a medical doctor, developed a therapeutic practice for clients with neurological and nervous disorders, and collaborated with colleagues on the distinctive theory and practice of mental therapy that came to be known as "psychoanalysis." In 1902 Freud secured a professorship at the University of Vienna and formed a small discussion group, the Vienna Psychoanalytic Society, which included other notable theorists Alfred Adler and Carl Jung. He wrote extensively, including various works on psychological disorders and case histories of the use of "talking cures" wherein patients will delve into the personal details of their lives with a trained therapist. Early psychoanalysis centered on Freud's theoretical works on dreams, the psychological dimensions of everyday life, human personality, and human sexuality. Eventually, he would cast his ideas more broadly in later works on the discontents of modern society and religion. Although framed in biological and medical terminology, especially neurology, Freud's works draw upon a wide range of influences, including clinical use of hypnosis, dream analysis, classical literature, philosophy, sacred texts, and anthropological studies of various forms of religion. Freud's core concepts of the unconscious, infant sexuality, Oedipal conflict, and repression fueled the psychoanalytic tradition, which aimed to be both a novel form of therapy and a potent form of cultural critique. Synthetic, provocative, and willing to challenge norms, Freud's views enjoyed wide influence in the middle decades of the twentieth century and stimulated a wide range of academic disciplines, including those that studied religion and popular culture.

Freud's varied writings on religion address a range of core issues, including the psychological wellsprings of religion in "primitive" societies (*Totem and Taboo*, 1913), the future prospects of religion in modern societies (*The Future of an Illusion*, 1927), and the origins of monotheistic beliefs (*Moses and Monotheism*, 1939). Although Freud occasionally expressed some appreciation for the practical and social role of religion, his essential views were critical. Religion was best understood as a form of mental illness, an "object neurosis" rooted in repressed impulses and childhood complexes that could be traced to the unconscious dimensions of the human mind. As a clinician and therapist, he felt neuroses could be managed, or perhaps even cured, by replacing them with more rational views.

Although the works cited above represent Freud's most famous statements on religion, the relationship between psychoanalytic theory, religion, and popular culture is perhaps best approached from his important early work on everyday life and dream interpretation. In the first of these passages, Freud outlined his general view of religion as projection, and in the second sketched his theory of "dream work" that proceeds according to basic mental processes (repression, condensation, transference, symbolization, dramatization, etc.).

Although deployed by Freud to plumb the unconscious mind, dream work finds application in the analysis of popular culture, particularly those forms with highly symbolic content, like mythology, fairy tales, and fantasy. As he observes, "Dream-symbolism extends far beyond dreams." In Freud's era, the emerging media of film, with its emphasis on dynamic action and vivid imagery, was another rich arena for exploring the close relationship between dream work and popular narratives.

Critique of the psychoanalytical tradition focused on a number of problems with its major assumptions about gender, sexuality, and the scientific character of its theoretical claims. Many critics have faulted Freud's assumptions about the primacy of male sexuality, his speculative readings of his case histories, and the lack of corroborating evidence for his theories of infant sexuality and personality (id-ego-superego) in clinical studies. Such has been the range and thoroughness of this critique that mainstream psychology has all but consigned Freud to history, although other fields, notably many humanities disciplines, find his insights are still valuable. In comparative religion, more nuanced anthropology and historical accounts of world mythological traditions cast suspicion on the possibility of "universal" models of myth and symbol based on general psychological theory. A related critique attends to the way that various forms of culture, including both religion and popular media, serve the interests of power. Thus, various critical theories (covered elsewhere in this volume) address imperial visions, class interests, racial dominance, gender disparities, market economies, and other forms of social dominance. Although these critiques tend to focus on social and political forces, they have a strong psychological element in that individuals must internalize, and thus give conscious or unconscious legitimacy to, forms of dominance. Another form of critique, often arising from within the psychoanalytic movement itself, tempered the assumptions of pathology at the heart of Freud's psychoanalytical theories of religion. Led by Carl Jung and others, these theorists found at least some forms of religion and popular culture holding positive benefits as vehicles for achieving a more mature personality, or as a kind of collective therapeutic force.

"Determinism, Chance, and Superstitious Beliefs" (1904)[1]

I do not believe that an occurrence in which my mental life takes no part can teach me anything hidden concerning the future shaping of reality; but I do believe that an unintentional manifestation of my own mental activity surely contains something concealed which belongs only to my mental life—that is, I believe in outer (real) chance, but not in inner (psychic) accidents. With the superstitious person the case is reversed: he knows nothing of the motive of his chance and faulty actions, he believes in the existence of psychic contingencies; he is therefore inclined to attribute meaning to external chance, which manifests itself in actual occurrence, and to see in the accident a means of expression for something hidden outside of him. There are two differences between me and the superstitious person: first, he projects the motive to the outside, while I look for it in myself; second, he explains the accident by an

---

[1]Sigmund Freud, excerpt from "Determinism, Chance, and Superstitious Beliefs," in *Psychopathology of Everyday Life* (London: T. Fisher Unwin Ltd., 1914), 308–10. [Originally published as *Zur Psychopathologie des Alltagslebens* (1904).]

event which I trace to a thought. What he considers hidden corresponds to the unconscious with me, and the compulsion not to let chance pass as chance, but to explain it as common to both of us.

Thus I admit that this conscious ignorance and unconscious knowledge of the motivation of psychic accidentalness is one of the psychic roots of superstition. *Because the superstitious person knows nothing of the motivation of his own accidental actions, and because the fact of this motivation strives for a place in his recognition, he is compelled to dispose of them by displacing them into the outer world.* If such a connection exists it can hardly be limited to this single case. As a matter of fact, I believe that a large portion of the mythological conception of the world which reaches far into the most modern religions *is nothing but psychology projected into the outer world*. The dim perception (the endopsychic perception, as it were) of psychic factors and relations of the unconscious was taken as a model in the construction of a *transcendental reality*, which is destined to be changed again by science into *psychology of the unconscious*.

It is difficult to express it in other terms; the analogy to paranoia must here come to our aid. We venture to explain in this way the myths of paradise and the fall of man, of God, of good and evil, of immortality, and the like—that is, to transform *metaphysics* into *meta-psychology*. The gap between the paranoiac's displacement and that of superstition is narrower than appears at first sight. When human beings began to think, they were obviously compelled to explain the outer world in an **anthropomorphic** sense by a multitude of personalities in their own image; the accidents which they explained superstitiously were thus actions and expressions of persons. In that regard they behaved just like **paranoiacs**, who draw conclusions from insignificant signs which others give them, and like all normal persons who justly take the unintentional actions of their fellow-beings as a basis for the estimation of their characters. Only in our modern philosophical, but by no means finished, views of life does superstition seem so much out of place: in the view of life of prescientific times and nations it was justified and consistent.

"On Dreams" (1911)[2]

One day I discovered to my amazement that the popular view grounded in superstition, and not the medical one, comes nearer to the truth about dreams. I arrived at new conclusions about dreams by the use of a new method of psychological investigation, one which had rendered me good service in the investigation of **phobias**, obsessions, illusions, and the like, and which, under the name "psycho-analysis," had found acceptance by a whole school of investigators. The manifold analogies of dream life with the most diverse conditions of psychical disease in the waking state have been rightly insisted upon by a number of medical observers. It seemed, therefore, *a priori*, hopeful to apply to the interpretation of dreams methods of investigation which had been tested in psycho-pathological processes. Obsessions and those peculiar sensations of haunting dread remain as strange to normal consciousness as do dreams to our waking consciousness; their origin is as unknown to

---

[2]Sigmund Freud, excerpt from *On Dreams*, trans. M. D. Eder (New York: Rebman Company, 1914), 1–20. [Originally published as *Über den Traum* (1911).]

consciousness as is that of dreams. It was practical ends that impelled us, in these diseases, to fathom their origin and formation. Experience had shown us that a cure and a consequent mastery of the obsessing ideas did result when once those thoughts, the connecting links between the morbid ideas and the rest of the psychical content, were revealed which were heretofore veiled from consciousness. The procedure I employed for the interpretation of dreams thus arose from psychotherapy. [...]

I must further remark that the dream is far shorter than the thoughts which I hold it replaces; whilst analysis discovered that the dream was provoked by an unimportant occurrence the evening before the dream.

Naturally, I would not draw such far-reaching conclusions if only one analysis were known to me. Experience has shown me that when the associations of any dream are honestly followed such a chain of thought is revealed, the constituent parts of the dream reappear correctly and sensibly linked together; the slight suspicion that this **concatenation** was merely an accident of a single first observation must, therefore, be absolutely relinquished. I regard it, therefore, as my right to establish this new view by a proper **nomenclature**. I contrast the dream which my memory evokes with the dream and other added matter revealed by analysis: the former I call the dream's *manifest content*; the latter, without at first further subdivision, its *latent content*. I arrive at two new problems hitherto unformulated: (1) What is the psychical process which has transformed the latent content of the dream into its manifest content? (2) What is the motive or the motives which have made such transformation exigent. The process by which the change from latent to manifest content is executed I name the *dream-work*. In contrast with this is the *work of analysis*, which produces the reverse transformation. The other problems of the dream—the inquiry as to its stimuli, as to the source of its materials, as to its possible purpose, the function of dreaming, the forgetting of dreams—these I will discuss in connection with the latent dream-content. I shall take every care to avoid a confusion between the *manifest* and the *latent content*, for I ascribe all the contradictory as well as the incorrect accounts of dream-life to the ignorance of this latent content, now first laid bare through analysis.

VI.

Although the work of displacement must be held mainly responsible if the dream thoughts are not refound or recognised in the dream content (unless the motive of the changes be guessed), it is another and milder kind of transformation which will be considered with the dream thoughts which leads to the discovery of a new but readily understood act of the dream work. The first dream thoughts which are unravelled by analysis frequently strike one by their unusual wording. They do not appear to be expressed in the sober form which our thinking prefers; rather are they expressed symbolically by **allegories** and metaphors like the figurative language of the poets. It is not difficult to find the motives for this degree of constraint in the expression of dream ideas. The dream content consists chiefly of visual scenes; hence the dream ideas must, in the first place, be prepared to make use of these forms of presentation. Conceive that a political leader's or a barrister's address had to be transposed into **pantomime**, and it will be easy to understand the transformations to which the dream work is constrained by regard for this *dramatisation of the dream content*.

Around the psychical stuff of dream thoughts there are ever found reminiscences of impressions, not infrequently of early childhood—scenes which, as a rule, have been visually grasped. Whenever possible, this portion of the dream ideas exercises a definite influence upon the modelling of the dream content; it works like a centre of crystallisation, by attracting and rearranging the stuff of the dream thoughts. The scene of the dream is not infrequently nothing but a modified repetition, complicated by **interpolations** of events that have left such an impression; the dream but very seldom reproduces accurate and unmixed reproductions of real scenes. The dream content does not, however, consist exclusively of scenes, but it also includes scattered fragments of visual images, conversations, and even bits of unchanged thoughts. It will be perhaps to the point if we instance in the briefest way the means of dramatisation which are at the disposal of the dream work for the repetition of the dream thoughts in the peculiar language of the dream.

Connections 2a: Freud, Psychoanalysis, and the Fairy Tale

Folklorists, literary scholars, and therapists made much of psychoanalytic theory and over the course of the twentieth century wrote extensively on the meaning of fairy tales as a guide to human psychology. Among the most famous of these works was Bruno Bettelheim's *The Uses of Enchantment* (1976) which argued, in largely Freudian terms, for the value of magic and enchantment to the maturation of children.

> In order to master the psychological problems of growing up—overcoming narcissistic disappointments, oedipal dilemmas, sibling rivalries; becoming able to relinquish childhood dependencies; gaining a feeling of selfhood and self-worth, and a sense of moral obligation—a child needs to understand what is going on within his conscious self so that he can also cope with that which goes on within his unconscious. . . . It is here that fairy tales have unequal value, because they offer new dimensions to the child's imagination which would be impossible for him to discover as truly his own. (6–7)

Bettleheim's close readings of famous fairy tales like "Snow White," "Jack and Beanstalk," "Sleeping Beauty," and "Cinderella" looked to their symbolism, character dynamics, and other plot elements as a guide to the inner psychic struggles of children. For example, the famous Grimm version of "Snow White" becomes an extended lesson on the dangers of excessive self-love:

> Narcissism is very much part of the young child's make-up. The child must gradually learn to transcend this dangerous form of self-involvement. The story of Snow White warns of the evil consequences of narcissism for both parent and child. Snow White's narcissism nearly undoes her as she gives in twice to the disguised queen's enticements to make her look more beautiful, while the queen is destroyed by her own narcissism. (203)

Now revealed in their full psychological depth, fairy tales achieved an inner "realism" not matched by the ostensibly more sophisticated literature of adults. Likewise, for many other forms of popular culture, the psychoanalytic school pioneered by Freud opens up new insights and meanings largely invisible to the untrained eye.

The dream thoughts which we learn from the analysis exhibit themselves as a psychical complex of the most complicated superstructure. Their parts stand in the most diverse relationship to each other; they form backgrounds and foregrounds, stipulations, digressions, illustrations, demonstrations, and protestations. It may be said to be almost the rule that one train of thought is followed by its contradictory. No feature known to our reason whilst awake is absent. If a dream is to grow out of all this, the psychical matter is submitted to a pressure which condenses it extremely, to an inner shrinking and displacement, creating at the same time fresh surfaces, to a selective interweaving among the constituents best adapted for the construction of these scenes. Having regard to the origin of this stuff, the term **regression** can be fairly applied to this process. The logical chains which hitherto held the psychical stuff together become lost in this transformation to the dream content. The dream work takes on, as it were, only the essential content of the dream thoughts for elaboration. It is left to analysis to restore the connection which the dream work has destroyed.

The dream's means of expression must therefore be regarded as meagre in comparison with those of our imagination, though the dream does not renounce all claims to the restitution of logical relation to the dream thoughts. It rather succeeds with tolerable frequency in replacing these by formal characters of its own.

By reason of the undoubted connection existing between all the parts of dream thoughts, the dream is able to embody this matter into a single scene. It upholds a *logical connection* as *approximation in time and space*, just as the painter, who groups all the poets for his picture of **Parnassus** who, though they have never been all together on a mountain peak, yet form ideally a community. The dream continues this method of presentation in individual dreams, and often when it displays two elements close together in the dream content it warrants some special inner connection between what they represent in the dream thoughts. It should be, moreover, observed that all the dreams of one night prove on analysis to originate from the same sphere of thought. […]

VII.

We have not exhausted our valuation of the dream work. In addition to condensation, displacement, and definite arrangement of the psychical matter, we must ascribe to it yet another activity—one which is, indeed, not shared by every dream. I shall not treat this position of the dream work exhaustively; I will only point out that the readiest way to arrive at a conception of it is to take for granted, probably unfairly, that it *only subsequently influences the dream content which has already been built up*. Its mode of action thus consists in so co-ordinating the parts of the dream that these coalesce to a coherent whole, to a dream composition. The dream gets a kind of façade which, it is true, does not conceal the whole of its content. There is a sort of preliminary explanation to be strengthened by interpolations and slight alterations. Such elaboration of the dream content must not be too pronounced; the misconception of the dream thoughts to which it gives rise is merely superficial, and our first piece of work in analysing a dream is to get rid of these early attempts at interpretation.

The motives for this part of the dream work are easily gauged. This final elaboration of the dream is due to a *regard for intelligibility*—a fact at once betraying the origin of an action which behaves towards the actual dream content just as our normal psychical action behaves towards some proffered perception that is to our liking. The dream content is thus secured under the pretence of certain expectations, is perceptually classified by the supposition of its intelligibility, thereby risking its falsification, whilst, in fact, the most extraordinary misconceptions arise if the dream can be correlated with nothing familiar. Everyone is aware that we are unable to look at any series of unfamiliar signs, or to listen to a discussion of unknown words, without at once making perpetual changes through *our regard for intelligibility*, through our falling back upon what is familiar.

We can call those dreams *properly made up* which are the result of an elaboration in every way analogous to the psychical action of our waking life. In other dreams there is no such action; not even an attempt is made to bring about order and meaning. We regard the dream as "quite mad," because on awaking it is with this last-named part of the dream work, the dream elaboration, that we identify ourselves. So far, however, as our analysis is concerned, the dream, which resembles a medley of disconnected fragments, is of as much value as the one with a smooth and beautifully polished surface. In the former case we are spared, to some extent, the trouble of breaking down the super-elaboration of the dream content.

All the same, it would be an error to see in the dream façade nothing but the misunderstood and somewhat arbitrary elaboration of the dream carried out at the instance of our psychical life. Wishes and phantasies are not infrequently employed in the erection of this façade, which were already fashioned in the dream thoughts; they are akin to those of our waking life—"day-dreams," as they are very properly called. These wishes and phantasies, which analysis discloses in our dreams at night, often present themselves as repetitions and refashionings of the scenes of infancy. Thus the dream façade may show us directly the true core of the dream, distorted through admixture with other matter. Beyond these four activities there is nothing else to be discovered in the dream work. If we keep closely to the definition that dream work denotes the transference of dream thoughts to dream content, we are compelled to say that the dream work is not creative; it develops no fancies of its own, it judges nothing, decides nothing. It does nothing but prepare the matter for condensation and displacement, and refashions it for dramatisation, to which must be added the inconstant last-named mechanism—that of explanatory elaboration. It is true that a good deal is found in the dream content which might be understood as the result of another and more intellectual performance; but analysis shows conclusively every time that these *intellectual operations were already present in the dream thoughts, and have only been taken over by the dream content*. A **syllogism** in the dream is nothing other than the repetition of a syllogism in the dream thoughts; it seems inoffensive if it has been transferred to the dream without alteration; it becomes absurd if in the dream work it has been transferred to other matter. A calculation in the dream content simply means that there was a calculation in the dream thoughts; whilst this is always correct, the calculation in the dream can furnish the silliest results by the condensation of its factors and the displacement of the same operations to other things. Even speeches which are found in the dream content are not new compositions; they prove to be pieced together out of speeches which have been made or heard or read; the words are faithfully copied, but the occasion of their utterance is quite overlooked, and their meaning is most violently changed.

VIII.

In the foregoing exposition we have now learnt something of the dream work; we must regard it as a quite special psychical process, which, so far as we are aware, resembles nothing else. To the dream work has been transferred that bewilderment which its product, the dream, has aroused in us. In truth, the dream work is only the first recognition of a group of psychical processes to which must be referred the origin of hysterical symptoms, the ideas of morbid dread, obsession, and illusion. Condensation, and especially displacement, are never failing features in these other processes. The regard for appearance remains, on the other hand, peculiar to the dream work. If this explanation brings the dream into line with the formation of psychical disease, it becomes the more important to fathom the essential conditions of processes like dream building. It will be probably a surprise to hear that neither the state of sleep nor illness is among the indispensable conditions. A whole number of phenomena of the everyday life of healthy persons, forgetfulness, slips in speaking and in holding things, together with a certain class of mistakes, are due to a psychical mechanism analogous to that of the dream and the other members of this group.

Displacement is the core of the problem, and the most striking of all the dream performances. A thorough investigation of the subject shows that the essential condition of displacement is purely psychological; it is in the nature of a motive. We get on the track by thrashing out experiences which one cannot avoid in the analysis of dreams.... If, however, I continue the analysis for myself, without regard to those others, for whom, indeed, so personal an event as my dream cannot matter, I arrive finally at ideas which surprise me, which I have not known to be mine, which not only appear *foreign* to me, but which are *unpleasant*, and which I would like to oppose vehemently, whilst the chain of ideas running through the analysis intrudes upon me inexorably. I can only take these circumstances into account by admitting that these thoughts are actually part of my psychical life, possessing a certain psychical intensity or energy. However, by virtue of a particular psychological condition, the *thoughts could not become conscious to me*. I call this particular condition "*Repression*." It is therefore impossible for me not to recognise some causal relationship between the obscurity of the dream content and this state of repression—this *incapacity of consciousness*. Whence I conclude that the cause of the obscurity is *the desire to conceal these thoughts*. Thus I arrive at the conception of the *dream distortion* as the deed of the dream work, and of *displacement* serving to disguise this object. [...]

Connections 2b: Freud, Cultural Critique, Self-help, and Religionized Therapy

Over the course of the twentieth century psychological theory spilled out of the clinic, and advocates used it to critique, reinterpret, refine, and otherwise re-imagine cultural traditions. Often this application was sharply critical, as conventional pieties and sensational entertainments were disparaged as forms of obsessive compulsion, wishful thinking, mental illness, escapism, unhealthy stimulations, or otherwise irrational or immature pursuits. Christopher Lasch has argued that by the late twentieth century, "[t]herapy has established itself as the successor both to rugged individualism and religion" (1979: 13). In the process, however, it had made modern society self-obsessed and narcissistic, leading to a broad cultural malaise.

Other theories, however, were more "religion-friendly," aiming simply to describe different personalities and mental activities of religious persons. Of these, perhaps the most enduring has been the work of American philosopher William James, who was also an important early advocate of the academic study of psychology. In *Varieties of Religious Experience* (originally published in 1902), James explored the psychology of religious feelings by comparing the testimonies of those who claimed mystical illumination, religious rebirth, and other intense and transformative life-events. In doing so, he sketched out various religious personality types, like the "healthy-minded" and the "sick soul," along with psychological profiles of saints, mystics, and converts who often overcome profound despair and melancholy via religious experiences.

A "metaphysical" strain of self-help emerged from to the New Thought movement of the nineteenth century, which connected spiritual ideas and mental transformations to healing, improved relationships, and material success. Many books and movements were built around these assumptions, including two of the towering best sellers of American self-help, Ralph Wald Trine's *In Tune with the Infinite* (1897) and Norman Vincent Peale's *The Power of Positive Thinking* (1952). Both posited that ordinary persons could tap into a vast and abundant spiritual force that governed the cosmos—variously named as "God" or "Higher Power" or "the Infinite"—largely by reorienting their thoughts and ideas toward more positive ideas and images. This was to be accomplished by meditation, prayer, positive affirmations, reading spiritual literature, and habits cultivated in social relationships. More recently, figures like Oprah Winfrey have reshaped this kind of spirituality, adapting it with sensitivity to race and gender (as well as media savvy) by employing formats like the talk show, book clubs, and internet-based marketing.

Other forms of "religionized" psychology have pursued more actively interventionist strategies that see theology and religious practice as curative, or at least complementary, alongside conventional therapies. The Emmanuel Movement, begun by Episcopalians in the early twentieth century, put psychoanalytic practices to work in pastoral settings, often convening individualized and group therapy sessions on church properties. In time, this melding of church and clinic found wide expression in various efforts to combat addiction, especially alcoholism, and eventually a wide range of other alleged vices, including narcotics, gambling, crime, excessive sex, and hoarding. The much-imitated "12 Step Program" of Alcoholics Anonymous, for example, was partially inspired by a small Christian sect, the Oxford Group, which had emphasized collective confessions, belief in a Higher Power, seeking absolution from those the addict wronged, rigorous honesty about one's own failings, and prayer (many twelve-step groups adopted the famous "Serenity Prayer" attributed to Reinhold Niebuhr). Although controversial and often challenged as to their effectiveness, Lance and Zachary Dodes argue that such has been the cultural penetration of 12-Step programs that perhaps 60,000 groups exist in the United States and millions regularly attend meetings (2015). Many other religious groups freely adapt modern psychology, often carefully and selectively, and weave them into their messaging across popular media. For example, many Christian conservatives seek counseling advice for perennial topics like childcare, marriage, and family relationships. James Dobson, an evangelical trained in psychology and pediatrics, built a large following in recent decades through best-selling advice books, television, Internet, and most especially, a popular radio program, *Focus on the Family*. Dobson's views were resolutely conservative on issues like corporal punishment for children, abortion, and homosexual rights and reached perhaps over 200 million listeners across a global net-work of thousands of radio stations. Such was Dobson's influence that he became a key figure in conservative politics, advising and supporting various Republican candidates (see Apostolidis 2000).

X.

There has hitherto been no occasion for philosophers to bestir themselves with a psychology of repression. We must be allowed to construct some clear conception as to the origin of dreams as the first steps in this unknown territory. The scheme which we have formulated not only from a study of dreams is, it is true, already somewhat complicated, but we cannot find any simpler one that will suffice. We hold that our psychical apparatus contains two procedures for the construction of thoughts. The second one has the advantage that its products find an open path to consciousness, whilst the activity of the first procedure is unknown to itself, and can only arrive at consciousness through the second one. At the borderland of these two procedures, where the first passes over into the second, a censorship is established which only passes what pleases it, keeping back everything else. That which is rejected by the censorship is, according to our definition, in a state of repression. Under certain conditions, one of which is the sleeping state, the balance of power between the two procedures is so changed that what is repressed can no longer be kept back. In the sleeping state this may possibly occur through the negligence of the censor; what has been hitherto repressed will now succeed in finding its way to consciousness. But as the censorship is never absent, but merely off guard, certain alterations must be conceded so as to placate it. It is a compromise which becomes conscious in this case—a compromise between what one procedure has in view and the demands of the other. *Repression, laxity of the censor, compromise*—this is the foundation for the origin of many another psychological process, just as it is for the dream. In such compromises we can observe the processes of condensation, of displacement, the acceptance of superficial associations, which we have found in the dream work.

It is not for us to deny the demonic element which has played a part in constructing our explanation of dream work. The impression left is that the formation of obscure dreams proceeds as if a person had something to say which must be disagreeable for another person upon whom he is dependent to hear. It is by the use of this image that we figure to ourselves the conception of the *dream distortion* and of the censorship, and ventured to crystallise our impression in a rather crude, but at least definite, psychological theory. Whatever explanation the future may offer of these first and second procedures, we shall expect a confirmation of our correlate that the second procedure commands the entrance to consciousness, and can exclude the first from consciousness.

Once the sleeping state overcome, the censorship resumes complete sway, and is now able to revoke that which was granted in a moment of weakness. That the *forgetting* of dreams explains this in part, at least, we are convinced by our experience, confirmed again and again. During the relation of a dream, or during analysis of one, it not infrequently happens that some fragment of the dream is suddenly forgotten. This fragment so forgotten invariably contains the best and readiest approach to an understanding of the dream. Probably that is why it sinks into oblivion—i.e., into a renewed suppression.

XII.

Whosoever has firmly accepted this censorship as the chief motive for the distortion of dreams will not be surprised to learn as the result of dream interpretation that most of the dreams of adults are traced by analysis to erotic desires. This assertion is not drawn from dreams obviously of a sexual nature, which are known to all dreamers from their own experience, and are the only ones usually described as "sexual dreams." These dreams are ever sufficiently mysterious by reason of the choice of persons who are made the objects of sex, the removal of all the barriers which cry halt to the dreamer's sexual needs in his waking state, the many strange reminders as to details of what are called perversions. But analysis discovers that, in many other dreams in whose manifest content nothing erotic can be found, the work of interpretation shows them up as, in reality, realisation of sexual desires; whilst, on the other hand, that much of the thought-making when awake, the thoughts saved us as surplus from the day only, reaches presentation in dreams with the help of repressed erotic desires.

Towards the explanation of this statement, which is no theoretical postulate, it must be remembered that no other class of instincts has required so vast a suppression at the behest of civilisation as the sexual, whilst their mastery by the highest psychical processes are in most persons soonest of all relinquished. Since we have learnt to understand *infantile sexuality*, often so vague in its expression, so invariably overlooked and misunderstood, we are justified in saying that nearly every civilised person has retained at some point or other the infantile type of sex life; thus we understand that repressed infantile sex desires furnish the most frequent and most powerful impulses for the formation of dreams.

If the dream, which is the expression of some erotic desire, succeeds in making its manifest content appear innocently asexual, it is only possible in one way. The matter of these sexual presentations cannot be exhibited as such, but must be replaced by allusions, suggestions, and similar indirect means; differing from other cases of indirect presentation, those used in dreams must be deprived of direct understanding. The means of presentation which answer these requirements are commonly termed "symbols." A special interest has been directed towards these, since it has been observed that the dreamers of the same language use the like symbols—indeed, that in certain cases community of symbol is greater than community of speech. Since the dreamers do not themselves know the meaning of the symbols they use, it remains a puzzle whence arises their relationship with what they replace and denote. The fact itself is undoubted, and becomes of importance for the technique of the interpretation of dreams, since by the aid of a knowledge of this symbolism it is possible to understand the meaning of the elements of a dream, or parts of a dream, occasionally even the whole dream itself, without having to question the dreamer as to his own ideas. We thus come near to the popular idea of an interpretation of dreams, and, on the other hand, possess again the technique of the ancients, among whom the interpretation of dreams was identical with their explanation through symbolism.

Though the study of dream symbolism is far removed from finality, we now possess a series of general statements and of particular observations which are quite certain. There are symbols which practically always have the same meaning: Emperor and Empress (King and Queen) always mean the parents; room, a woman, and so on. The sexes are represented by a great variety of symbols, many of which would be at first quite incomprehensible had not the clues to the meaning been often obtained through other channels.

There are symbols of universal circulation, found in all dreamers, of one range of speech and culture; there are others of the narrowest individual significance which an individual has built up out of his own material. In the first class those can be differentiated whose claim can be at once recognised by the replacement of sexual things in common speech (those, for instance, arising from agriculture, as reproduction, seed) from others whose sexual references appear to reach back to the earliest times and to the obscurest depths of our image-building. The power of building symbols in both these special forms of symbols has not died out. Recently discovered things, like the airship, are at once brought into universal use as sex symbols.

It would be quite an error to suppose that a profounder knowledge of dream symbolism (the "Language of Dreams") would make us independent of questioning the dreamer regarding his impressions about the dream, and would give us back the whole technique of ancient dream interpreters. Apart from individual symbols and the variations in the use of what is general, one never knows whether an element in the dream is to be understood symbolically or in its proper meaning; the whole content of the dream is certainly not to be interpreted symbolically. The knowledge of dream symbols will only help us in understanding portions of the dream content, and does not render the use of the technical rules previously given at all superfluous. But it must be of the greatest service in interpreting a dream just when the impressions of the dreamer are withheld or are insufficient.

Dream symbolism proves also indispensable for understanding the so-called "typical" dreams and the dreams that "repeat themselves." If the value of the symbolism of dreams has been so incompletely set out in this brief portrayal, this attempt will be corrected by reference to a point of view which is of the highest import in this connection. Dream symbolism leads us far beyond the dream; it does not belong only to dreams, but is likewise dominant in legend, myth, and saga, in wit and in folklore. It compels us to pursue the inner meaning of the dream in these productions. But we must acknowledge that symbolism is not a result of the dream work, but is a peculiarity probably of our unconscious thinking, which furnishes to the dream work the matter for condensation, displacement, and dramatisation.

Glossary

A PRIORI: an assertion based on theoretical assumption rather than on experimentation or observation.

ALLEGORIES: stories or visual presentation with symbolic meaning, often used to teach a moral lesson.

ANTHROPOMORPHIC: of, having, or presented as having human characteristics.

CONCATENATION: a series of related or connected items or situations; list or series.

INTERPOLATIONS: interruptions or insertions into a narrative or statement.

NOMENCLATURE: terms or names for items or processes, often considered "official" or accepted.

PARANOIACS: those who suffer from delusions that they are being persecuted.

PANTOMIME: performance or presentation of meaning without the use of words or sounds.

PARNASSUS: mountain in central Greece considered to have been sacred to several figures in Greek mythology, including Dionysus, Apollo, and the Muses.

PHOBIAS: persistent fears of items (animal, material item) or situations (heights, ledges, confined spaces, etc.).

REGRESSION: return to an original or lesser state of being.

SYLLOGISM: a reasoned argument of linked assertions to a logical conclusion.

Questions for Conversation

Freud argues that mythologies and religions are, deep down, "*psychology projected into the outer world*." Does this mean that they are not real?

Freud agrees with the popular view that "dreams have got to have a meaning" and that this meaning "can be unraveled from their bizarre and enigmatical content." How does he use his "dream work" analysis (condensation, displacement, dramatization, symbolization) to assert the meaningfulness of dreams?

Freud's suggests that dream symbolism extends into popular culture—including fairy tales, myths and legends, jokes and folklore. Does it follow that these have meaning, and are not, as some critics would assert, meaningless "sea foam"?

For Freud, how does the mind act as a kind of censor on its own capacities? Does this self-censorship have anything to do with the way societies control information (e.g., the way societies often act to censor extreme forms of popular culture, like pornography or depictions of violence)?

Suggestions for Additional Reading

The following is a list of supplemental readings that provide additional information about, apply, or respond critically to the ideas presented in this chapter.

Anker, Roy. *Self-Help and Popular Religion in Early American Culture: An Interpretive Guide*. Westport, CT: Greenwood Press, 1999.

Apostolidis, Paul. *Stations of the Cross: Adorno and Christian Right Radio*. Durham, NC: Duke University Press, 2000.

Bettelheim, Bruno. *The Uses of Enchantment: The Meaning and Importance of Fairy Tales*. New York: Vintage Books, 1975.

Brickman, Celia. *Aboriginal Populations in the Mind: Race and Primitivity in Psychoanalysis*. New York: Columbia University Press, 2003.

Caplan, Eric. "Popularizing American Psychotherapy: The Emmanuel Movement, 1906–1910," *History of Psychology* 1, no. 4 (1998): 289–314.

Capps, Donald, ed. *Freud and Freudians on Religion: A Reader*. New Haven, CT: Yale University Press, 2001.

Dodes, Lance, and Zachary Dodes. *The Sober Truth*. Boston, MA: Beacon Press, 2015.

Freud, Sigmund. *Civilization and Its Discontents*, trans. James Strachey. New York: Norton & Company, 2010.

Freud, Sigmund. *Future of an Illusion*, trans. James Strachey. New York: Norton, 1961.

Freud, Sigmund. *Moses and Monotheism*, trans. Katherine Jones. New York: Knopf, 1939.

Freud, Sigmund. *Totem and Taboo: Resemblances between the Psychic Lives of Savages and Neurotics*, trans. A. A. Brill. Amherst, NY: Prometheus Books, 2000.

Homans, Peter. "Toward a Psychology of Religion: By Way of Freud and Tillich," *Zygon* 2, no. 1 (1967): 97–119.

Idema, Henry. *Freud, Religion, and the Roaring Twenties: A Psychoanalytic Theory of Secularization in Three Novelists: Anderson, Hemingway, and Fitzgerald*. Savage, MD: Rowman and Littlefield, 1990.

James, William. *The Varieties of Religious Experience*. New York: Random House, 1929. [1902]

Küng, Hans. *Freud and the Problem of God*. New Haven, CT: Yale University Press, 1990.

Lasch, Christopher. *The Culture of Narcissism*. New York: W. W. Norton & Company, 1979.

Lofton, Kathryn. *Oprah: The Gospel of an Icon*. Berkeley: University of California Press, 2011.

Matory, J. Lorand. *The Fetish Revisited: Marx, Freud, and the Gods Black People Make*. Durham, NC: Duke University Press, 2018.

McBride, James. "Symptomatic Expression of Male Neuroses: Collective Effervescence, Male Gender Performance, and the Ritual of Football," in *God in the Details: American Religion in Popular Culture*, ed. Eric Michael Mazur and Kate McCarthy, 123–38. New York: Routledge, 2001.

Nolan, Steve. *Film, Lacan and the Subject of Religion: A Psychoanalytic Approach to Religious Film Analysis*. New York: Continuum Books, 2009.

Peale, Norman Vincent. *The Power of Positive Thinking*. New York: Prentice Hall, Inc., 1952.

Trine, Ralph Waldo. *In Tune With the Infinite, or Fullness of Peace, Power and Plenty*. New York: Dodd, Mead & Company, 1897.

W, Bill. *Alcoholics Anonymous: The Story of How More Than One Hundred Men Have Recovered from Alcoholism*. New York: Works Publishing Company, 1939.

3 Emile Durkheim

Emile Durkheim (1858–1917) was one of the great figures in the early development of sociology, and his ideas and methods have influenced other disciplines as well, especially anthropology and religious studies. Durkheim held a series of influential academic positions in his native France, founded the journal *Année sociologique*, and, most importantly, wrote a number of highly influential articles and books advocating the scientific study of human societies. In these, Durkheim argued that groups, from tribal societies to modern industrialized cities, could be studied with the same empirical dedication to facts and data, statistical rigor, and disinterested objectivity that were found in the natural sciences. His scholarly output addressed subjects that are still central concerns for social scientists, including work, class, family, crime, law, and education. His classic work on religion, *The Elementary Forms of the Religious Life* (1912), built a general sociological theory of human religiosity by looking in-depth at the basic elements of one particular group, the Australian Aborigines. The text included Durkheim's famous definition:

> A religion is a unified system of beliefs and practices relative to sacred things, that is to say, things set apart and forbidden—beliefs and practices which unite into one single moral community called a Church, all those who adhere to them. (47)

His analysis focused on concepts like totemism, beliefs in the soul, spirits and gods, the sacred and profane, asceticism and sacrifice, and most especially, group solidarity created by collective ritual.

The excerpt below summarizes the core argument and highlights Durkheim's still-potent insight that religion should be analyzed as a social phenomenon; that it serves an essential social function—group solidarity. Durkheim's critics argued that his views "reduced" religion to social need and perhaps brought a critical and scientific way of thinking into a realm of thought and action that were better approached using other qualities: metaphysics, mysticism, empathy. He is often grouped with other social theorists of the nineteenth and early twentieth centuries in that he predicted broader secularization as societies modernized. And yet, in a paradoxical way, his theories in *Elementary Forms* can be read as explanation for the durability and broad historical scope of religion. Assuming all societies, in any era, need to sustain and reinforce their basic sense of collective identity, they will cultivate the "elementary forms" of religion—totemism, ritual, sacredness—or at least thoughts and actions that look and feel like religion. Some of Durkheim's heirs have found this insight a useful strategy for the study of religion in popular culture. Thus holiday celebrations and festivals, celebrity, sport, and media can be scrutinized as rich sources of "totemic" symbols and exuberant ritual expression. Per Durkheim, "now as in the past, we see that society never stops creating new sacred things."

"Origins of These Beliefs" (1915)[1]

The proposition established in the preceding chapter determines the terms in which the problem of the origins of **totemism** should be posed. Since totemism is everywhere dominated by the idea of a quasi-divine principle, imminent in certain categories of men and things and thought of under the form of an animal or vegetable, the explanation of this religion is essentially the explanation of this belief; to arrive at this, we must seek to learn how men have been led to construct this idea and out of what materials they have constructed it.

I

It is obviously not out of the sensations which the things serving as totems are able to arouse the mind; we have shown that these things are frequently insignificant. The lizard, the caterpillar, the rat, the ant, the frog, the turkey, the bream-fish, the plum-tree, the cockatoo, etc., to cite only those names which appear frequently in the lists of Australian totems, are not of a nature to produce upon men these great and strong impressions which in a way resemble religious emotions and which impress a sacred character upon the objects they create. It is true that this is not the case with the stars and the great atmospheric phenomena, which have, on the contrary, all that is necessary to strike the imagination forcibly; but as a matter of fact, these serve only very exceptionally as totems. So it is not the intrinsic nature of the thing whose name the clan bears that marked it out to become the object of a cult. Also, if the sentiments which it inspired were really the determining cause of the totemic rights and beliefs, it would be the pre-eminently sacred thing; the animals or plants employed as totems would play an eminent part in the religious life. But we know that the centre of the cult is actually elsewhere. It is the figurative representations of this plant or animal and the totemic emblems and symbols of every sort, which have the greatest sanctity; so it is in them that is found the source of that religious nature, of which the real objects represented by these emblems receive only a reflection.

Thus the totem is before all a symbol, a material expression of something else. But of what?

From the analysis to which we have been giving our attention, it is evident that it expresses and symbolizes two different sorts of things. In the first place, it is the outward and visible form of what we have called the totemic principle or god. But it is also the symbol of the determined society called the clan. It is its flag; it is the sign by which each clan distinguishes itself from the others, the visible mark of its personality, a mark borne by everything which is a part of the clan under any title whatsoever, men, beasts or things. So if it is at once the symbol of the god and of the society, is that not because the god and the society are only one? How could the emblem of the group have been able to become the figure of this quasi-divinity, if the group and the divinity were two distinct realities? The god of the clan, the totemic principle, can therefore be nothing else than the clan itself, personified

---

[1]Emile Durkheim, excerpt from "Origins of These Beliefs," in *The Elementary Forms of the Religious Life*, trans. Joseph Ward Swain (London: George Allen and Unwin Ltd., 1915), 205–14. [Originally published as *Formes élémentaires de la vie religieuse* (1912).]

and represented to the imagination under the visible form of the animal or vegetable which serves as totem.

But how has this **apotheosis** been possible, and how did it happen to take place in this fashion?

II

In a general way, it is unquestionable that a society has all that is necessary to arouse the sensation of the divine in minds, merely by the power that it has over them; for to its members it is what a god is to his worshippers. In fact, a god is, first of all, a being whom men think of as superior to themselves, and upon whom they feel that they depend. Whether it be a conscious personality, such as Zeus or **Jahveh**, or merely abstract forces such as those in play in totemism, the worshipper, in the one case as in the other, believes himself held to certain manners of acting which are imposed upon him by the nature of the sacred principle with which he feels that he is in communion. Now society also gives us the sensation of a perpetual dependence. Since it has a nature which is peculiar to itself and different from our individual nature, it pursues ends which are likewise special to it; but, as it cannot attain them except through our intermediacy, it imperiously demands our aid. It requires that, forgetful of our own interests, we make ourselves its servitors, and it submits us to every sort of inconvenience, privation and sacrifice, without which social life would be impossible. It is because of this that at every instant we are obliged to submit ourselves to rules of conduct and of thought which we have neither made nor desired, and which are sometimes even contrary to our most fundamental inclinations and instincts.

Even if society were unable to obtain these concessions and sacrifices from us except by a material constraint, it might awaken in us only the idea of a physical force to which we must give way of necessity, instead of that of a moral power such as religions adore. But as a matter of fact, the empire which it holds over consciences is due much less to the physical supremacy of which it has the privilege than to the moral authority with which it is invested. If we yield to its orders, it is not merely because it is strong enough to triumph over our resistance; it is primarily because it is the object of a venerable respect.

We say that an object, whether individual or collective, inspires respect when the representation expressing it in the mind is gifted with such a force that it automatically causes or inhibits actions, *without regard for any consideration relative to their useful or injurious effects*. When we obey somebody because of the moral authority which we recognize in him, we follow out his opinions, not because they seem wise, but because a certain sort of physical energy is imminent in the idea that we form of this person, which conquers our will and inclines it in the indicated direction. Respect is the emotion which we experience when we feel this interior and wholly spiritual pressure operating upon us. Then we are not determined by the advantages or inconveniences of the attitude which is prescribed or recommended to us; it is by the way in which we represent to ourselves the person recommending or prescribing it. This is why commands generally take a short, peremptory form leaving no place for hesitation; it is because, in so far as it is a command and goes by its own force, it excludes all ideas of deliberation or calculation; it gets its efficacy from the intensity of the mental state in which it is placed. It is this intensity which creates what is called a moral ascendancy.

Now the ways of action to which society is strongly enough attached to impose them upon its members, are, by that very fact, marked with a distinctive sign provocative of respect. Since they are elaborated in common, the vigour with which they have been thought of by each particular mind is retained in all the other minds, and reciprocally. The representations which express them within each of us have an intensity which no purely private states of consciousness could ever attain; for they have the strength of the innumerable individual representations which have served to form each of them. It is society who speaks through the mouths of those who affirm them in our presence; it is society whom we hear in hearing them; and the voice of all has an accent which that of one alone could never have. The very violence with which society reacts, by way of blame or material suppression, against every attempted dissidence, contributes to strengthening its empire by manifesting the common conviction through this burst of ardour. In a word, when something is the object of such a state of opinion, the representation which each individual has of it gains a power of action from its origins and the conditions in which it was born, which even those feel who do not submit themselves to it. It tends to repel the representations which contradict it, and it keeps them at a distance; on the other hand, it commands those acts which will realize it, and it does so, not by a material coercion or by the perspective of something of this sort, but by the simple radiation of the mental energy which it contains. It has an efficacy coming solely from its physical properties, and it is by just this sign that moral authority is recognized. So opinion, primarily a social thing, is a source of authority, and it might even be asked whether all authority is not the daughter of opinion. It may be objected that science is often the antagonist of opinion, whose errors it combats and rectifies. But it cannot succeed in this task if it does not have sufficient authority, and it can obtain this authority only from opinion itself. If a people did not have faith in science, all the scientific demonstrations in the world would be without any influence whatsoever over their minds. Even to-day, if science happened to resist a very strong current of public opinion, it would risk losing its credit there.

Connections 3a: Durkheim, Memorial Day, and Civil Religion

Sociologists of religion in the Durkheimian tradition hold that much of what is classified as patriotism and ritual expressions of nationalism should be understood as religious in character. Thus anthems and pledges of allegiance to the flag, national holiday celebrations, and sites devoted to fallen soldiers or key national figures should be regarded, a la Durkheim, as "totemic" and expressive of a collective sense of the sacred. All engender deep feelings of joy and sorrow through participation in public devotional acts. In à famous study from the 1950s, sociologist W. Lloyd Warner showed how Memorial Day celebrations in the United States had become, in the wake of the Second World War, an elaborate "cult of the dead" centered on the sacralized bodies of dead soldiers. The various ritual activities of Memorial Day, parades, music, oratory, and solemn ceremonies at gravesites, all suggested that "the deaths of such men [had] become powerful sacred symbols which organize, direct, and constantly revive the collective ideals of the community and the nation" (Warner 1953: 26). Using a similar argument in the late 1960s, sociologist Robert Bellah revived the concept of "civil religion" (first developed by the philosopher Jean-Jacques Rousseau) as a way of theorizing a "religious dimension" of modern life with "seriousness and integrity" that exists "alongside of and rather clearly differentiated from the churches." Like Warner, Bellah built upon Durkheim's core insight into the ways that participatory ritual binds together diverse people, even if they are not fully conscious of the fact that they are "worshipping" their collective need for unity.

While Bellah's article sparked significant debate over the use of the term and the existence of the phenomenon, it also served as a foundation for an entire library of work examining the emotional and spiritual power citizens feel in connection with their sense of patriotism. Even historians such as Catherine Albanese and Charles Reagan Wilson employed Durkheim's model to examine how Colonists involved in the American Revolution and Confederates who survived the American Civil War (respectively) felt and conceptualized their experiences.

Since it is in spiritual ways that social pressure exercises itself, it could not fail to give men the idea that outside themselves there exist one or several powers, both moral and, at the same time, efficacious, upon which they depend. They must think of these powers, at least in part, as outside themselves, for these address them in a tone of command and sometimes even order them to do violence to their most natural inclinations. It is undoubtedly true that if they were able to see that these influences which they feel emanate from society, then the mythological system of interpretations would never be born. But social action follows ways that are too circuitous and obscure and employs psychical mechanisms that are too complex to allow the ordinary observer to see whence it comes. As long as scientific analysis does not come to teach it to them, men know well that they are acted upon, but they do not know by whom. So they must invent by themselves the idea of these powers with which they feel themselves in connection, and from that, we are able to catch a glimpse of the way by which they were led to represent them under forms that are really foreign to their nature and to transfigure them by thought.

But a god is not merely an authority upon whom we depend; it is a force upon which our strength relies. The man who has obeyed his god and who, for this reason, believes the god is with him, approaches the world with confidence and with the feeling of an increased energy. Likewise, social action does not confine itself to demanding sacrifices, privations and efforts from us. For the collective force is not entirely outside of us; it does not act upon us wholly from without; but rather, since society cannot exist except in and through individual consciousnesses, this force must also penetrate us and organize itself within us; it thus becomes an integral part of our being and by that very fact this is elevated and magnified.

There are occasions when this strengthening and vivifying action of society is especially apparent. In the midst of an assembly animated by a common passion, we become susceptible of acts and sentiments of which we are incapable when reduced to our own forces; and when the assembly is dissolved and when, finding ourselves alone again, we fall back to our ordinary level, we are then able to measure the height to which we have been raised above ourselves. History abounds in examples of this sort. It is enough to think of the night of the **Fourth of August, 1789**, when an assembly was suddenly led to an act of sacrifice and abnegation which each of its members had refused the day before, and at which they were all surprised the day after. This is why all parties, political, economic, or confessional, are careful to have periodical reunions where their members may revivify their common faith by manifesting it in common. To strengthen those sentiments which, if left to themselves, would soon weaken, it is sufficient to bring those who hold them together and to put them into closer and more active relations with one another. This is the explanation of the particular attitude of a man speaking to a crowd, at least if he has succeeded in entering into communion with it. His language has a grandiloquence that would be ridiculous in ordinary circumstances; his gestures show a certain domination; his very thought is impatient of all rules, and easily falls into all sorts of excesses. It is because he feels within him an abnormal over-supply of force which overflows and tries to burst out from him; sometimes he even has the feeling that he is dominated by a moral force which is greater than he and of which he is only the interpreter. It is by this trait that we are able to recognize what has often been called the demon of oratorical inspiration. Now this exceptional increase of force is something very real; it comes to him from the very group which he addresses. The sentiments provoked by his words come back to him, but enlarged and amplified, and to this degree they strengthen his own sentiment. The passionate energies he arouses re-echo within him and quicken his vital tone. It is no longer a simple individual who speaks; it is a group incarnate and personified.

Beside these passing and intermittent states, there are other more durable ones, where this strengthening influence of society makes itself felt with greater consequences and frequently even with greater brilliancy. There are periods in history when, under the influence of some great collective shock, social interactions have become much more frequent and active. Men look for each other and assemble together more than ever. That general **effervescence** results which is characteristic of revolutionary or creative epochs. Now this greater activity results in a general stimulation of individual forces. Men see more and differently now than in normal times. Changes are not merely of shades and degrees; men become different. The passions moving them are of such an intensity that they cannot be satisfied except by violent and unrestrained actions, actions of superhuman heroism or of bloody barbarism. This is what explains the Crusades, for example, or many of the scenes, either sublime or savage, of the French Revolution. Under the influence of the general exaltation, we see the most mediocre and inoffensive bourgeois become either a hero or a butcher. And so clearly are all these mental processes the ones that are also at the root of religion that the individuals themselves have often pictured the pressure before which they thus gave way in a distinctly religious form. The Crusaders believed that they felt God present in the midst of them, enjoining them to go to the conquest of the Holy Land; Joan of Arc believed that she obeyed celestial voices.

But it is not only in exceptional circumstances that this stimulating action of society makes itself felt; there is not, so to speak, a moment in our lives when some current of energy does not come to us from without. The man who has done his duty finds, in the manifestations of every sort expressing the sympathy, esteem or affection which his fellows have for him, a feeling of comfort, of which he does not ordinarily take account, but which sustains him, nonetheless. The sentiments which society has for him raise the sentiments which he has for himself. Because he is in moral harmony with his comrades, he has more confidence, courage, and boldness in action, just like the believer who thinks that he feels the regard of his god turned graciously towards him. It thus produces, as it were, a perpetual sustenance for our moral nature. Since this varies with a multitude of external circumstances, as our relations with the groups about us are more or less active and as these groups themselves vary, we cannot fail to feel that this moral support depends upon an external cause; but we do not perceive where this cause is nor what it is. So we ordinarily think of it under the form of a moral power which, though immanent in us, represents within us something not ourselves: this is the moral conscience, of which, by the way, men have never made even a slightly distinct representation except by the aid of religious symbols.

In addition to these free forces which are constantly coming to renew our own, there are others which are fixed in the methods and traditions which we employ. We speak a language that we did not make; we use instruments that we did not invent; we invoke rights that we did not found; a treasury of knowledge is transmitted to each generation that it did not gather itself, etc. It is to society that we owe these varied benefits of civilization, and if we do not ordinarily see the source from which we get them, we at least know that they are not our own work. Now it is these things that give man his own place among things; a man is a man only because he is civilized. So he could not escape the feeling that outside of him there are active causes from which he gets the characteristic attributes of his nature and which, as benevolent powers, assist him, protect him, and assure him of a privileged fate. And of course he must attribute to these powers a dignity corresponding to the great value of the good things he attributes to them.

Connections 3b: Durkheim and Totemism at the Stadium

Durkheim's interest in Aboriginal religions gave much attention to totems—animals, plants, and objects that were central to the ritual life and identity of particular clans. These totems varied and could be found in the natural environment of Australia: "the lizard, the caterpillar, the rat, the ant, the frog, the turkey, the bream-fish, the plum-tree, [and] the cockatoo" (1915: 205). And yet for the clan they took on a particular symbolic meaning that Durkheim thought was essential to understanding the social nature of religion—to worship the totem and treat it with special rules and ceremonies helps sustain the group. The totem's sacredness is likewise immersive, infusing language, behavior, adornment, and demanding exclusion of that which is profane (including the "totems" of others). Does something similar happen in contemporary sports? Consider the widespread use of animals as mascots for sports teams and their particular role on game day when the emotional energy of players and fans alike becomes, to use Durkheim's potent adjectives, "effervescent" and "contagious." One fan of the long-suffering Cleveland Browns franchise explains his dedication, "This is like church for me" (Cucuza and Cline).

Ironically, in part it may be the "power" invested in the totem that has given rise to more recent conflicts over the use of certain mascots in college and professional sports. While there may be those who object to the use of animals (and a few plants) as mascots, most of the objections have come from the use of groups of people, almost all of them based on negative stereotypes, or pejorative, demeaning, or dismissive terms ("chiefs," "braves") or images. Recently, both the Washington, DC-based professional football team and the Cleveland-based professional baseball team (as well as assorted college sports teams) have announced plans to drop names based on terms considered offensive to Native Americans. While there remain teams on both the professional and college level named for categories of people ("Forty-niners," "Brewers," "Yankees," etc.), it is the historic treatment of Native Americans that has informed the debate; while some have argued that the use of Native American terms and images is meant as an honorific, those who oppose them have noted the de-humanizing impact of using a subjugated people as a totem for a team.

Thus the environment in which we live seems to us to be peopled with forces that are at once imperious and helpful, august and gracious, and with which we have relations. Since they exercise over us a pressure of which we are conscious, we are forced to localize them outside ourselves, just as we do for the objective causes of our sensations. But the sentiments which they inspire in us differ in nature from those which we have for simple visible objects. As long as these latter are reduced to their empirical characteristics as shown in ordinary experience, and as long as the religious imagination has not metamorphosed them, we entertain for them no feeling which resembles respect, and they contain within them nothing that is able to raise us outside ourselves. Therefore, the representations which express them appear to us to be very different from those aroused in us by collective influences. The two form two distinct and separate mental states in our consciousness, just as do the two forms of life to which they correspond. Consequently, we get the impression that we are in relations with two distinct sorts of reality and that a sharply drawn line of demarcation separates them from each other: on the one hand is the world of **profane** things, on the other, that of sacred things.

Also, in the present day just as much as in the past, we see society constantly creating sacred things out of ordinary ones. If it happens to fall in love with a man and if it thinks it has found in him the principal aspirations that move it, as well as the means of satisfying them, this man will be raised above the others and, as it were, deified. Opinion will invest him with a majesty exactly analogous to that protecting the gods. This is what has happened to so many sovereigns in whom their age had faith: if they were not made gods, they were at least regarded as direct representatives of the deity. And the fact that it is society alone which is the author of these varieties of apotheosis, is evident since it frequently chances to consecrate men thus who have no right to it from their own merit. The simple deference inspired by men invested with high social functions is not different in nature from religious respect. It is expressed by the same movements: a man keeps at a distance from a high personage; he approaches him only with precautions; in conversing with him, he uses other gestures and language than those used with ordinary mortals. The sentiment felt on these occasions is so closely related to the religious sentiment that many peoples have confounded the two. In order to explain the consideration accorded to princes, nobles, and political chiefs, a sacred character has been attributed to them. In **Melanesia** and Polynesia, for example, it is said that an influential man has *mana*, and that his influence is due to this *mana*. However, it is evident that his situation is due solely to the importance attributed to him by public opinion. Thus the moral power conferred by opinion and that with which sacred being are invested are at bottom of a single origin and made up of the same elements. That is why a single word is able to designate the two.

In addition to men, society also consecrates things, especially ideas. If a belief is unanimously shared by a people, then, for the reason which we pointed out above, it is forbidden to touch it, that is to say, to deny it or to contest it. Now the prohibition of criticism is an interdiction like the others and proves the presence of something sacred. Even to-day, howsoever great may be the liberty which we accord to others, a man who should totally deny progress or ridicule the human ideal to which modern societies are attached would produce the effect of a sacrilege. There is at least one principle which those the most devoted to the free examination of everything tend to place above discussion and to regard as untouchable, that is to say, as sacred: this is the very principle of free examination.

This aptitude of society for setting itself up as a god or for creating gods was never more apparent than during the first years of the French Revolution. At this time, in fact, under the influence of the general enthusiasm, things purely laical by nature were transformed by public opinion into sacred things: these were the Fatherland, Liberty, Reason. A religion tended to become established which had its dogmas, symbols, altars and feasts. It was to these spontaneous aspirations that the cult of Reason and the Supreme Being attempted to give a sort of official satisfaction. It is true that this religious renovation had only an ephemeral duration. But that was because the patriotic enthusiasm which at first transported the masses soon relaxed. The cause being gone, the effect could not remain. But this experiment, though short-lived, keeps all its sociological interest. It remains true that in one determined case we have seen society and its essential ideas become, directly and with no transfiguration of any sort, the object of a veritable cult.

All these facts allow us to catch glimpses of how the clan was able to awaken within its member the idea that outside of them there exist forces which dominate them and at the same time sustain them, that is to say in fine, religious forces: it is because there is no society with which the primitive is more directly and closely connected. The bonds uniting him to the tribe are much more lax and more feebly felt. Although this is not at all strange or foreign to him, it is with the people of his own clan that he has the greatest number of things in common; it is the action of this group that he feels the most directly; so it is this also which, in preference to all others, should express itself in religious symbols.

Glossary

APOTHEOSIS: the culmination or climax of development; glorification to a divine level.

EFFERVESCENCE: often used to describe the carbonation in drinks, in this case it is the enthusiasm or vitality felt by people when they are accepted by, and participate in the activities of, a large or like-minded group.

FOURTH OF AUGUST, 1789: Date on which the French National Assembly abolished feudalism.

JAHVEH: often spelled "Yahweh," refers to the god of the ancient Hebrews, derived from four letters that are presumed to correspond roughly to the sounds of the letters "YHWH."

MANA: pervasive supernatural power or spirit in the material world.

MELANESIA: the collection of islands in the southwestern portion of the South Pacific, northeast of Australia and west of Polynesia.

PROFANE: often used to suggest coarse or dirty, in this case it is that which is not sacred; mundane, everyday.

TOTEMISM: a nature-based belief system that stresses kinship to—and special, supernatural powers in—nonhuman elements (symbolically represented by a **TOTEM**) which are not themselves the object of worship but which serve as physical surrogates for the powers they convey or represent.

Questions for Conversation

What is totemism and how is it important to Durkheim's general social theory of religion?

Durkeim stresses how gods and totemism work through "moral influence" and not physical force. How and why do they work this way?

For religious persons, sacred things are thought to be external to and greater than the individual. Does Durkheim agree?

Why are large collective events, like conventions and group rituals, so important to Durkheim's theory?

Durkheim suggests that like persons and things, ideas can be made sacred. He also suggests that in his own era that the idea of progress had become so widely accepted that it was "untouchable." Can you think of any ideas with similar standing today?

How might Durkheim's theories be applied to the study of popular culture?

Suggestions for Additional Reading

The following is a list of supplemental readings that provide additional information about, apply, or respond critically to the ideas presented in this chapter.

Ahmed, Sara. "Collective Feelings: Or, the Impressions Left by Others," *Theory, Culture & Society* 21 (2004): 25–42.

Albanese, Catherine L. *Sons of the Fathers: The Civil Religion of the American Revolution*. Philadelphia, PA: Temple University Press, 1976.

Bain-Selbo, Eric, and D. Gregory Sapp. *Understanding Sport as a Religious Phenomenon*. London: Bloomsbury Academic, 2016.

Bellah, Robert N. "Civil Religion in America," *Dædalus* 96, no. 1 (1967): 1–21.

Birrell, Susan. "Sport as Ritual: Interpretations from Durkheim to Goffman," *Social Forces* 60, no. 2 (1981): 354–76.

Cucuza, Nick, and Nathaniel Cline. "Why Am I a Cleveland Browns Fan? Watch This Video to Get Reminded," Cleveland.com. (November 16, 2016). Available online: https://www.youtube.com/watch?v=XF5ZYlFiLTs (accessed November 29, 2019).

Durkheim, Emile. *The Elementary Forms of the Religious Life*, trans. Joseph Ward Swain. London: George Allen and Unwin Ltd., 1915. [Originally published as *Les Formes élémentaires de la vie religieuse: le système totémique en Australie*, 1912.]

Durkheim, Emile. *The Elementary Forms of Religious Life*, trans. Karen E. Fields. New York: Free Press, 1995.

Erickson, Victoria Lee. "Back to the Basics: Feminist Social Theory, Durkheim and Religion," *Journal of Feminist Studies in Religion* 8 (1992): 35–46.

Giddens, Anthony. "Classical Social Theory and the Origins of Modern Sociology," *American Journal of Sociology* 81, no. 4 (1976): 703–29.

Kidd, Dustin. "Harry Potter and the Functions of Popular Culture," *Journal of Popular Culture* 40, no. 1 (2007): 69–89.

Kurasawa, Fuyuki. "The Durkheimian School and Colonialism: Exploring the Constitutive Paradox," in *Sociology and Empire: The Imperial Entanglements of a Discipline*, ed. George Steinmetz, 188–210. Durham, NC: Duke University Press, 2013.

Levine, Nancy. *Powers of Distinction: On Religion and Modernity*. Chicago: The University of Chicago Press, 2017 (particularly chapter 3).

Marvin, Carolyn, and David W. Ingle. *Blood Sacrifice and the Nation: Totem Rituals and the American Flag*. New York: Cambridge University Press, 1999.

Pals, Daniel. "Society as Sacred: Emile Durkheim," in *Nine Theories of Religion*, 3rd ed., 81–112. New York: Oxford University Press, 2015.

Parsons, Talcott. "Durkheim on Religion Revisited: Another Look at the Elementary Forms of the Religious Life," in *Beyond the Classics? Essays in the Scientific Study of Religion*, ed. Charles Y. Glock and Phillip E. Hammond, 156–80. New York: Harper and Row, 1973.

Pickering, W. S. F., ed. *Durkheim on Religion*. Atlanta, GA: Scholars Press, 1994.

Pogačnik, Anja, and Aleš Črnič. "iReligion: Religious Elements of the Apple Phenomenon," *Journal of Religion & Popular Culture* 26, no. 3 (2014): 353–64.

Warner, W. Lloyd. *American Life: Dream and Reality*. Chicago: The University of Chicago Press, 1953.

Wilson, Charles Reagan. *Baptized in Blood: The Religion of the Lost Cause, 1865–1920*. Athens: University of Georgia Press, 1983.

4   Max Horkheimer and Theodor Adorno

Max Horkheimer (1895–1973) and Theodor Adorno (1903–69) were foundational members of the Frankfurt School of cultural analysis and social theory, associated with the Institute for Social Research at Goethe University in Frankfurt, Germany.

Max Horkheimer was born to a wealthy family in Stuttgart. He worked in his family's textile business as a manager until the First World War, when he entered university after failing a physical and being unable to join the military. He studied psychology and philosophy and received a PhD from the University of Frankfurt. In 1930 he became the director of the Institute for Social Research.

Theodor Adorno was the son of a wine merchant and a singer. A gifted pianist, he studied music composition before becoming interested in philosophy, psychology, and sociology at the University of Frankfurt, where he met Horkheimer (and Walter Benjamin). Paul Tillich (also excerpted in this volume), who was a philosophy professor at the university, directed Adorno's dissertation on Soren Kierkegaard. Adorno continued his interests in music alongside his work in critical theory at the institute, writing many opera and concert reviews, as well as musical compositions.

Horkheimer and Adorno were two of the most recognizable and influential members of the Frankfurt School. The scholars, which also included Herbert Marcuse, Erich Fromm, Jurgen Habermas, and Walter Benjamin, among others, devoted their energies to understanding the economic, political, social, and cultural forces at play in the European and American world emerging after the First World War. Revising Marxist political analysis with psychoanalysis, existentialism, and sociology, the Frankfurt School sought to critique and transform modern capitalist society.

Together, these thinkers are central to an approach to cultural studies that is known as *critical theory*. The purpose of critical theory is to analyze and critique the ruling ideologies of society by showing how people's understandings of social relations, material value, political truth, and the nature of reality are shaped by the economic and political interests of those in power.

Members of the Institute were forced to leave Germany when Adolf Hitler became Chancellor in 1933. Several relocated to the United States where they resumed their critical studies of capitalism and culture, primarily at Columbia University. In the United States, Adorno and Horkheimer, along with Columbia sociologist Paul Lazarsfeld, initiated the Princeton Radio Research Project, an important study of the social impact of new forms of mass media. This project studied such phenomena as soap operas and Orson Welles's 1938 broadcast adaptation of *The War of the Worlds*. Adorno left the project in 1941, but his research had convinced him of the importance of recognizing the relationship between mass media, advertising, and commercialized popular culture in producing and maintaining hierarchies of power in a capitalist society.

In 1947, Adorno and Horkheimer published *The Dialectic of Enlightenment: Philosophical Fragments*, in which they introduced the idea of the "culture industry." In short, the concept named the process in mass-mediated capitalist society whereby cultural products were created for mass consumption and carried within them—in content and form—ideological perspectives and influences. The effect was a public whose desires and interests were shaped by an overwhelming ideological system that people did not see. What members of that public took to be "natural" or "the way things are" was, in fact, produced by the culture industry from which they received their views of the world. Horkheimer and Adorno distinguished popular culture produced by the culture industry, which was a consumer product, from authentic art, which Adorno found to be more serious and opposed to the ideologies of capitalism. While Horkheimer and Adorno did not discuss religion at length, their analysis of popular culture, power, and ideology has important application to scholarship on the intersections of popular culture and religion.

Upon its translation into English in 1972 *The Dialectic of Enlightenment* had a profound impact on the study of popular culture in Britain and the United States. It provided a language for critical analysis of power and ideology in popular culture, but it was also criticized for assuming that audiences were such dupes to the overwhelming power of the culture industry. Subsequent critical analysis of the role of power, ideology, and popular culture by members of the Birmingham School, for instance (see the excerpt from Stuart Hall), explored the audience's ability to interpret, and even subvert, popular culture texts, placing more emphasis on the entire circuit of production and reception to understand the dynamics of power and resistance in popular culture.

"The Culture Industry: Enlightenment as Mass Deception" (1944)[1]

The sociological view that the loss of support from objective religion and the disintegration of the last precapitalist residues, in conjunction with technical and social differentiation and specialization, have given rise to cultural chaos is refuted by daily experience. Culture today is infecting everything with sameness. Film, radio, and magazines form a system. Each branch of culture is unanimous within itself and all are unanimous together. [...] The decorative administrative and exhibition buildings of industry differ little between authoritarian and other countries. The bright monumental structures shooting up on all sides show off the systematic ingenuity of the state-spanning combines, toward which the unfettered entrepreneurial system, whose monuments are the dismal residential and commercial blocks in the surrounding areas of desolate cities, was already swiftly advancing. [...] But the town-planning projects, which are supposed to perpetuate individuals as autonomous units in hygienic small apartments, subjugate them only more completely to their adversary, the

---

[1]Max Horkheimer and Theodor Adorno, excerpt from "The Culture Industry: Enlightenment as Mass Deception," in *Dialectic of Enlightenment: Philosophical Fragments*, ed. Gunzelin Schmid Noerr, trans. Edmund Jephcott (Stanford: Stanford University Press, 2002), 94–136. [Originally published as *Dialektik der Aufklarung* (1944).]

total power of capital. Just as the occupants of city centers are uniformly summoned there for purposes of work and leisure, as producers and consumers, so the living cells crystallize into homogenous, well-organized complexes. The conspicuous unity of macrocosm and microcosm confronts human beings with a model of their culture: the false identity of universal and particular. All mass culture under monopoly is identical, and the contours of its skeleton, the conceptual armature fabricated by monopoly, are beginning to stand out. Those in charge no longer take much trouble to conceal the structure, the power of which increases the more bluntly its existence is admitted. Films and radio no longer need to present themselves as art. The truth that they are nothing but business is used as an ideology to legitimize the trash they intentionally produce. They call themselves industries, and the published figures for their directors' incomes quell any doubts about the social necessity of their finished products.

Interested parties like to explain the culture industry in technological terms. Its millions of participants, they argue, demand reproduction processes which inevitably lead to the use of standard products to meet the same needs at countless locations. The technical antithesis between few production centers and widely dispersed reception necessitates organization and planning by those in control. The standardized forms, it is claimed, were originally derived from the needs of the consumers: that is why they are accepted with so little resistance. In reality, a cycle of manipulation and retroactive need is unifying the system ever more tightly. What is not mentioned is that the basis on which technology is gaining power over society is the power of those whose economic position in society is strongest. Automobiles, bombs, and films hold the totality together until their leveling element demonstrates its power against the very system of injustice it served. For the present the technology of the culture industry confines itself to standardization and mass production and sacrifices what once distinguished the logic of the work from that of society. Any trace of spontaneity in the audience of the official radio is steered and absorbed into a selection of specializations by talent-spotters, performance competitions, and sponsored events of every kind. The talents belong to the operation long before they are put on show; otherwise they would not conform so eagerly. The mentality of the public, which allegedly and actually favors the system of the culture industry, is a part of the system, not an excuse for it. [...] An explanation in terms of the specific interests of the technical apparatus and its personnel would be closer to the truth, provided that apparatus were understood in all its details as a part of the economic mechanism of selection. Added to this is the agreement, or at least the common determination, of the executive powers to produce or let pass nothing which does not conform to their tables, to their concept of the consumer, or, above all, to themselves.

[...]

The relentless unity of the culture industry bears witness to the emergent unity of politics. Sharp distinctions like those between A and B films, or between short stories published in magazines in different price segments, do not so much reflect real differences as assist in the classification, organization, and identification of consumers. Something is provided for everyone so that no one can escape; differences are hammered home and propagated. The hierarchy of serial qualities purveyed to the public serves only to quantify it more completely. Everyone is supposed to behave spontaneously according to a "level" determined by indices and to select the category of mass product manufactured for their type. On the charts of research organizations, indistinguishable from those of political propaganda, consumers are divided up as statistical material into red, green, and blue areas according to income group.

[…] The technical media, too, are being engulfed by an insatiable uniformity. Television aims at a synthesis of radio and film, delayed only for as long as the interested parties cannot agree. Such a synthesis, with its unlimited possibilities, promises to intensify the impoverishment of the aesthetic material so radically that the identity of all industrial cultural products, still scantily disguised today, will triumph openly tomorrow in a mocking fulfillment of **Wagner**'s dream of the total art work. The accord between word, image, and music is achieved so much more perfectly than in **Tristan** because the sensuous elements, which compliantly document only the surface of social reality, are produced in principle within the same technical work process, the unity of which they express as their true content. This work process integrates all the elements of production, from the original concept of the novel, shaped by its sidelong glance at film, to the last sound effect. It is the triumph of invested capital. To impress the omnipotence of capital on the hearts of expropriated job candidates as the power of their true master is the purpose of all films, regardless of the plot selected by the production directors.

Even during their leisure time, consumers must orient themselves according to the unity of production. The active contribution which **Kantian schematism** still expected of subjects—that they should, from the first, relate sensuous multiplicity to fundamental concepts—is denied to the subject by industry. It purveys schematism as its first service to the customer. According to Kantian schematism, a secret mechanism within the psyche preformed immediate data to fit them into the system of pure reason. That secret has now been unraveled. Although the operations of the mechanism appear to be planned by those who supply the data, the culture industry, the planning is in fact imposed on the industry by the inertia of a society irrational despite all its rationalization, and this calamitous tendency, in passing through the agencies of business, takes on the shrewd intentionality peculiar to them. For the consumer there is nothing left to classify, since the classification has already been preempted by the schematism of production. This dreamless art for the people fulfills the dreamy idealism which went too far for idealism in its critical form. Everything comes from consciousness—from that of God for **Malebranche** and **Berkeley**, and from earthly production management for mass art. Not only do hit songs, stars, and soap operas conform to types recurring cyclically as rigid invariants, but the specific content of productions, the seemingly variable element, is itself derived from those types. The details become interchangeable. The brief interval sequence which has proved catchy in a hit song, the hero's temporary disgrace which he accepts as a "good sport," the wholesome slaps the heroine receives from the strong hand of the male star, his plain-speaking abruptness toward the pampered heiress, are, like all the details, ready-made clichés, to be used here and there as desired and always completely defined by the purpose they serve within the schema. To confirm the schema by acting as its constituents is their sole *raison d'être*. In a film, the outcome can invariably be predicted at the start—who will be rewarded, punished, forgotten—and in light music the prepared ear can always guess the continuation after the first bars of a hit song and is gratified when it actually occurs. The average choice of words in a short story must not be tampered with. The gags and effects are no less calculated than their framework. They are managed by special experts, and their slim variety is specifically tailored to the office pigeonhole. [...]

Connections 4a: Horkheimer, Adorno, Religion, Consumer Culture, and Advertising

Horkheimer and Adorno cast advertising as one of the main agents of the culture industry, having pervasive influence over both public life and the inner lives of modern individuals. Repetitious, uniform, insidious, armed with a variety of communication styles and attention-grabbing techniques, advertisers manipulated the supposedly "free" choices of consumers. By the mid-twentieth century professional agencies and marketers had created a culture where ads had all but taken over media, the arts, and everyday life. To borrow the language of older forms of religion, advertising did the culture industry's missionizing and pastoral work, inspiring, explaining, counseling, cajoling, and consoling the modern consumer. At the same time, the consumer was, paradoxically, strangely dissatisfied and vaguely aware that much of the heavily advertised world was superficial and false, a sentiment voiced in the Rolling Stones' popular 1965 song, "(I Can't Get No) Satisfaction." Thus for all its enticement and manipulation of desire, advertising prompted an inner longing for something deeper and more meaningful. But just what would that be? The Frankfort School hoped their critiques would contribute to an unmasking of the ways big businesses used advertising to solidify their social and economic power, and possibly to some kind of revolutionary actions. They also recognized, however, that this longing made modern societies susceptible to propaganda and authoritarian political movements.

Other scholars have explored the connections between religion, consumerism, and advertising. Cultural and religious historians, for example, have explored the emergence of "consumer culture" in the nineteenth and early twentieth century, a process intimately interwoven with the rise of the modern advertising. What did the consumer culture mean, especially for societies that had previously focused on agricultural and industrial production? How did it transform the sense of self and personal identity? Did consumerism secularize modern societies, or was it interwoven with religion? Scholars who root consumer culture in religious trends have examined nineteenth-century evangelical revivals that pioneered modern marketing techniques (see McLoughlin 2004), Victorian era "feminized" forms of Christianity which emphasized domestic comforts (see Douglas 1977), and the anti-poverty social gospel movement which, according to historian Susan Curtis, created "not a critique of modern capitalism, but rather a consuming faith in the material abundance it promised" (2001: 278). In *Consuming Religion*, religion scholar Kathryn Lofton argues, "much of consumer life is a religious enterprise, religious in the sense of enshrining certain commitments stronger than almost any other acts of social participation" (2017: 6). Case studies that explore things such as the marketing of soap, the complexities of celebrity in the Internet age, parenting, and corporate culture, support a highly nuanced understanding of how religion and consumption are intertwined.

How did advertisers themselves incorporate religious content into their work? Jackson Lears's *Fables of Abundance* explores the early history of advertising as a profession and argues that it was built upon a fundamental tension between "carnivalesque sensuality" animated by magic, wonder, and "fabulous visions of excess" over and against "managerial rationality" which preferred applied social scientific techniques. Other studies explore the content of ads themselves. Roland Marchand's *Advertising the American Dream* shows how advertisements in magazines told parable-like stories and used visual strategies that echoed religious art. Thus using parables like "the first impression" and "the democracy of goods" advertisers prompted consumers "to draw practical moral lessons from everyday life" and "employed stark contrasts and exaggeration to drama-tize a central message." Although more "melodramatic" than confrontational (which con-trasts with the use of parables by religious figures like Jesus), those of advertising aimed to "provoke immediate decision for action"—the purchase of a product (1985: 207). Finally, media scholar Sut Jhally asserts that in advertising the most fundamental rela-tions between the human world and modern systems of commodities are established. This is religious work in that advertising "performs magical feats of transformation and bewitchment, brings instant happiness and gratification, captures the forces of nature, and holds within itself the essence of important social relationships" (1989: 218).

The whole world is passed through the filter of the culture industry. The familiar experience of the moviegoer, who perceives the street outside as a continuation of the film he has just left, because the film seeks strictly to reproduce the world of everyday perception, has become the guideline of production. The more densely and completely its techniques duplicate empirical objects, the more easily it creates the illusion that the world outside is a seamless extension of the one which has been revealed in the cinema. Since the abrupt introduction of the sound film, mechanical duplication has become entirely subservient to this objective. [...] The withering of imagination and spontaneity in the consumer of culture today need not be traced back to psychological mechanisms. The products themselves, especially the most characteristic, the sound film, cripple those faculties through their objective makeup. They are so constructed that their adequate comprehension requires a quick, observant, knowledgeable cast of mind but positively debars the spectator from thinking, if he is not to miss the fleeting facts. This kind of alertness is so ingrained that it does not even need to be activated in particular cases, while still repressing the powers of imagination. Anyone who is so absorbed by the world of the film, by gesture, image, and word, that he or she is unable to supply that which would have made it a world in the first place, does not need to be entirely transfixed by the special operations of the machinery at the moment of the performance. The required qualities of attention have become so familiar from other films and other culture products already known to him or her that they appear automatically. The power of industrial society is imprinted on people once and for all. The products of the culture industry are such that they can be alertly consumed even in a state of distraction. But each one is a model of the gigantic economic machinery, which, from the first, keeps everyone on their toes, both at work and in the leisure time which resembles it. In any sound film or any radio broadcast something is discernible which cannot be attributed as a social effect to any one of them, but to all together. Each single manifestation of the culture industry inescapably reproduces human beings as what the whole has made them. And all its agents, from the producer to the women's organizations, are on the alert to ensure that the simple reproduction of mind does not lead on to the expansion of mind. [...]

[...] the inferior work has relied on its similarity to others, the surrogate of identity. The culture industry has finally posited this imitation as absolute. Being nothing other than style, it divulges style's secret: obedience to the social hierarchy. Aesthetic barbarism today is accomplishing what has threatened intellectual formations since they were brought together as culture and neutralized. To speak about culture always went against the grain of culture. The general designation "culture" already contains, virtually, the process of identifying, cataloging, and classifying which imports culture into the realm of administration. Only what has been industrialized, rigorously subsumed, is fully adequate to this concept of culture. Only by subordinating all branches of intellectual production equally to the single purpose of imposing on the senses of human beings, from the time they leave the factory in the evening to the time they clock on in the morning, the imprint of the work routine which they must sustain throughout the day, does this culture mockingly fulfill the notion of a unified culture which the philosophers of the individual personality held out against mass culture.

The culture industry, the most inflexible style of all, thus proves to be the goal of the very liberalism which is criticized for its lack of style. Not only did its categories and contents originate in the liberal sphere, in domesticated naturalism no less than in the operetta and the revue, but the modern culture combines are the economic area in which a piece of the circulation sphere otherwise in the process of disintegration, together with the corresponding entrepreneurial types, still tenuously survives. In that area people can still make their way, provided they do not look too closely at their true purpose and are willing to be compliant. Anyone who resists can survive only by being incorporated. Once registered as diverging from the culture industry, they belong to it as the land reformer does to capitalism. Realistic indignation is the trademark of those with a new idea to sell. Public authority in the present society allows only those complaints to be heard in which the attentive ear can discern the prominent figure under whose protection the rebel is suing for peace. The more immeasurable the gulf between chorus and leaders, the more certainly is there a place among the latter for anyone who demonstrates superiority by well-organized dissidence. In this way liberalism's tendency to give free rein to its ablest members survives in the culture industry. […]

The analysis offered by **de Tocqueville** a hundred years ago has been fully borne out in the meantime. Under the private monopoly of culture tyranny does indeed "leave the body free and sets to work directly on the soul. The ruler no longer says: 'Either you think as I do or you die.' He says: 'You are free not to think as I do; your life, your property—all that you shall keep. But from this day on you will be a stranger among us.'" Anyone who does not conform is condemned to an economic impotence which is prolonged in the intellectual powerlessness of the eccentric loner. Disconnected from the mainstream, he is easily convicted of inadequacy.

[…] the culture industry remains the entertainment business. Its control of consumers is mediated by entertainment, and its hold will not be broken by outright dictate but by the hostility inherent in the principle of entertainment to anything which is more than itself. Since the tendencies of the culture industry are turned into the flesh and blood of the public by the social process as a whole, those tendencies are reinforced by the survival of the market in the industry. Demand has not yet been replaced by simple obedience.

[…] Entertainment is the prolongation of work under late capitalism. It is sought by those who want to escape the mechanized labor process so that they can cope with it again. At the same time, however, mechanization has such power over leisure and its happiness, determines so thoroughly the fabrication of entertainment commodities, that the off-duty worker can experience nothing but after-images of the work process itself. The ostensible content is merely a faded foreground; what is imprinted is the automated sequence of standardized tasks. The only escape from the work process in factory and office is through adaptation to it in leisure time. This is the incurable sickness of all entertainment. Amusement congeals into boredom, since, to be amusement, it must cost no effort and therefore moves strictly along the well-worn grooves of association. The spectator must need no thoughts of his own: the product prescribes each reaction, not through any actual coherence—which collapses once exposed to thought—but through signals. Any logical connection presupposing mental capacity is scrupulously avoided. Developments are to emerge from the directly preceding situation, not from the idea of the whole. There is no plot which could withstand the screenwriters' eagerness to extract the maximum effect from the individual scene. Finally, even the schematic formula seems dangerous, since it provides some coherence of meaning, however meager, when only meaninglessness is acceptable. Often the plot is willfully denied the development called for by characters and theme under the old schema. Instead, the next step is determined by what the writers take to be their most effective idea. Obtusely ingenious surprises disrupt the plot. The product's tendency to fall back perniciously on the pure nonsense which, as buffoonery and clowning, was a legitimate part of popular art up to **Chaplin** and the **Marx brothers**, emerges most strikingly in the less sophisticated genres.

[…]

Connections 4b: Horkheimer, Adorno, and Selling Religion

In a society, and ultimately a world system, that is dominated by capitalism, religion is shaped by the culture industry no less than any other aspect of culture. One of the best-selling non-fiction books of the twentieth century, advertising executive Bruce Barton's 1925 *The Man Nobody Knows*, portrayed Jesus as the "founder of modern business," and Christianity's global growth as the result of extremely successful marketing strategies. If one of the goals of Christianity, especially in its evangelical form, is to spread the word of Christ, then it shared a common goal with selling products in the capitalist marketplace. Evangelists quickly adopted new communication and advertising technologies like billboards, radio, television, and the Internet to their cause as soon as they were developed. In consumer culture, not only did advertising and consumption take on religious significance; religion itself became a commodity to be marketed.

R. Laurence Moore's *Selling God: American Religion in the Marketplace of Culture* is a historical survey of the use of commercial practices for the promotion of religion from America's Early Republic to the late twentieth century; from the use of entertainment idioms by revivalists like George Whitefield and Dwight Moody to Jim and Tammy Faye Bakker's Christian theme park, Heritage USA; from Bible-based diets to L. Ron Hubbard's Scientology-based science fiction. While Moore's approach provides material evidence that could be interpreted through the perspective of Adorno and Horkheimer's critical theory, in *Stations of the Cross: Adorno and Christian Right Radio*, Paul Apostolidis moves directly into this form of analysis through an examination of contemporary influential conservative Christian James Dobson's hugely influential radio program, *Focus on the Family*.

While Apostolidis finds that *Focus on the Family* represents Christian values as ideologically matched to conservative politics, Heather Hendershot's *Shaking the World for Jesus: Media and Conservative Evangelical Culture* finds that this is not always the case in conservative evangelical media. "Although some Christian media are designed for overtly political and sometimes incendiary purposes . . . the majority of Christian media does not have over political intentions," she writes (2004: 9). Nevertheless, participation in the culture industry has shaped evangelical culture, producing a consumer-oriented conservative Christianity that is itself struggling with its place in the marketplace of culture. Mara Einstein's *Brands of Faith: Marketing Religion in a Commercial Age* similarly shows how contemporary "faith brands, like their secular counterparts, exist to aid consumers in making and maintaining a personal connection to a commodity product" (2008: xi). These strategies are crucial to their survival and flourishing in a highly competitive marketplace.

The influence of global capitalism and ever-expanding technologies of communication and transportation has meant that particularly American forms of religious commodification and consumption extend far beyond American geographic space. In *Colored Television: American Religion Gone Global*, a recent study of the globalization of televised gospels of prosperity and gospels of sexual redemption that stem from the ministries of American women and African American televangelists, Marla F. Frederick traces the effects of such products of this element of the American religious culture industry on the personal lives, political views, and economic practices of people of color outside of the United States. In doing so, she reveals the complex relationships between race, gender, and economic inequality in the social realities of global capitalism.

Cartoon and stunt films were once exponents of fantasy against rationalism. They allowed justice to be done to the animals and things electrified by their technology, by granting the mutilated beings a second life. Today they merely confirm the victory of technological reason over truth. A few years ago they had solid plots which were resolved only in the whirl of pursuit of the final minutes. In this their procedure resembled that of slapstick comedy. But now the temporal relations have shifted. The opening sequences state a plot motif so that destruction can work on it throughout the action: with the audience in gleeful pursuit the protagonist is tossed about like a scrap of litter. The quantity of organized amusement is converted into the quality of organized cruelty. The self-elected censors of the film industry, its accomplices, monitor the duration of the atrocity prolonged into a hunt. The jollity dispels the joy supposedly conferred by the sight of an embrace and postpones satisfaction until the day of the **pogrom**. To the extent that cartoons do more than accustom the senses to the new tempo, they hammer into every brain the old lesson that continuous attrition, the breaking of all individual resistance, is the condition of life in this society. Donald Duck in the cartoons and the unfortunate victim in real life receive their beatings so that the spectators can accustom themselves to theirs.

The enjoyment of the violence done to the film character turns into violence against the spectator; distraction becomes exertion. No stimulant concocted by the experts may escape the weary eye; in face of the slick presentation no one may appear stupid even for a moment; everyone has to keep up, emulating the smartness displayed and propagated by the production. This makes it doubtful whether the culture industry even still fulfils [sic] its self-proclaimed function of distraction. If the majority of radio stations and cinemas were shut down, consumers probably would not feel too much deprived. In stepping from the street into the cinema, they no longer enter the world of dream in any case, and once the use of these institutions was no longer made obligatory by their mere existence, the urge to use them might not be so overwhelming. Shutting them down in this way would not be reactionary machine-wrecking. Those who suffered would not be the film enthusiasts but those who always pay the penalty in any case, the ones who had lagged behind. For the housewife, despite the films which are supposed to integrate her still further, the dark of the cinema grants a refuge in which she can spend a few unsupervised hours, just as once, when there were still dwellings and evening repose, she could sit gazing out of the window. The unemployed of the great centers find freshness in summer and warmth in winter in these places of regulated temperature. Apart from that, and even by the measure of the existing order, the bloated entertainment apparatus does not make life more worthy of human beings. The idea of "exploiting" the given technical possibilities, of fully utilizing the capacities for aesthetic mass consumption, is part of an economic system which refuses to utilize capacities when it is a question of abolishing hunger.

The culture industry endlessly cheats its consumers out of what it endlessly promises. The promissory note of pleasure issued by plot and packaging is indefinitely prolonged: the promise, which actually comprises the entire show, disdainfully intimates that there is nothing more to come, that the diner must be satisfied with reading the menu. The desire inflamed by the glossy names and images is served up finally with a celebration of the daily round it sought to escape. Of course, genuine works of art were not sexual exhibitions either. But by presenting denial as negative, they reversed, as it were, the debasement of the drive and rescued by mediation what had been denied. That is the secret of aesthetic **sublimation**: to present fulfillment in its brokenness. The culture industry does not sublimate: it suppresses. By constantly exhibiting the object of desire, the breasts beneath the sweater, the naked torso of the sporting hero, it merely goads the unsublimated anticipation of pleasure, which through the habit of denial has long since been mutilated as masochism. There is no erotic situation in which innuendo and incitement are not accompanied by the clear notification that things will never go so far. The **Hays Office** merely confirms the ritual which the culture industry has staged in any case: that of **Tantalus**. Works of art are ascetic and shameless; the culture industry is pornographic and prudish. It reduces love to romance. And, once reduced, much is permitted, even libertinage as a marketable specialty, purveyed by quota with the trade description "daring." The mass production of sexuality automatically brings about its repression. Because of his ubiquity, the film star with whom one is supposed to fall in love is, from the start, a copy of himself. Every tenor now sounds like a **Caruso** record, and the natural faces of Texas girls already resemble those of the established models by which they would be typecast in Hollywood. The mechanical reproduction of beauty — which, admittedly, is made only more inescapable by the reactionary culture zealots with the methodical idolization of individuality — no longer leaves any room for the unconscious idolatry with which the experience of beauty has always been linked.

Culture is a paradoxical commodity. It is so completely subject to the law of exchange that it is no longer exchanged; it is so blindly equated with use that it can no longer be used. For this reason it merges with the advertisement. The more meaningless the latter appears under monopoly, the more omnipotent culture becomes. Its motives are economic enough.

That life could continue without the whole culture industry is too certain; the satiation and apathy it generates among consumers are too great. It can do little to combat this from its own resources. Advertising is its elixir of life. But because its product ceaselessly reduces the pleasure it promises as a commodity to that mere promise, it finally coincides with the advertisement it needs on account of its own inability to please. In the competitive society advertising performed a social service in orienting the buyer in the market, facilitating choice and helping the more efficient but unknown supplier to find customers. It did not merely cost labor time, but saved it. [...] The costs of advertising, which finally flow back into the pockets of the combines, spare them the troublesome task of subduing unwanted outsiders; they guarantee that the wielders of influence remain among their peers, not unlike the resolutions of economic councils which control the establishment and continuation of businesses in the totalitarian state. [...] Through their ubiquitous use under the pressure of the system, advertising techniques have invaded the idiom, the "style" of the culture industry. So complete is their triumph that in key positions it is no longer even explicit: the imposing buildings of the big companies, floodlit advertisements in stone, are free of advertising, merely displaying the illuminated company initials on their pinnacles, with no further need of self-congratulation. [...] The montage character of the culture industry, the synthetic, controlled manner in which its products are assembled—factory-like not only in the film studio but also, virtually, in the compilation of the cheap biographies, journalistic novels, and hit songs—predisposes it to advertising. [...] The special effect, the trick, the isolated and repeatable individual performance have always conspired with the exhibition of commodities for advertising purposes, and today every close-up of a film actress is an advert for her name, every hit song a plug for its tune. Advertising and the culture industry are merging technically no less than economically. In both, the same thing appears in countless places, and the mechanical repetition of the same culture product is already that of the same propaganda slogan. [...] In both, the norms of the striking yet familiar, the easy but catchy, the worldly wise but straightforward hold good; everything is directed at overpowering a customer conceived as distracted or resistant.

[...]

Today the culture industry has taken over the civilizing inheritance of the frontier and entrepreneurial democracy, whose receptivity to intellectual deviations was never too highly developed. All are free to dance and amuse themselves, just as, since the historical neutralization of religion, they have been free to join any of the countless sects. But freedom to choose an ideology, which always reflects economic coercion, everywhere proves to be freedom to be the same. The way in which the young girl accepts and performs the obligatory date, the tone of voice used on the telephone and in the most intimate situations, the choice of words in conversation, indeed, the whole inner life compartmentalized according to the categories of vulgarized **depth psychology**, bears witness to the attempt to turn oneself into an apparatus meeting the requirements of success, an apparatus which even in its unconscious impulses, conforms to the model presented by the culture industry. The most intimate reactions of human beings have become so entirely **reified**, even to themselves, that the idea of anything peculiar to them survives only in extreme abstraction: personality means hardly more than dazzling white teeth and freedom from body odor and emotions. That is the triumph of advertising in the culture industry; the compulsive imitation by consumers of cultural commodities which, at the same time, they recognize as false.

Glossary

BERKELEY, George (1685–1753): Irish philosopher and Anglican bishop.

CARUSO, Enrico (1873–1921): Italian operatic tenor.

CASINO DE PARIS: Music hall in Paris, France, built in the 1770s.

CHAPLIN, Charlie (1889–1977): British actor, director.

DEPTH PSYCHOLOGY: Form of psychological analysis that takes into account both the conscious and the unconscious mind.

HAYS OFFICE: referring to the Production Code Administration, instituted by Will Hays (1879–1954; president of the Motion Picture Producers and Distributors of America), which administered the Motion Picture Production Code to monitor American film content.

KANTIAN SCHEMATISM: referring to philosopher Emmanuel Kant's idea that knowledge is constituted by both empirical sense data and mental categories, or schema, that organize that data.

MALEBRANCHE, Nicolas (1638–1715): French Roman Catholic priest, theologian, and philosopher.

MARX brothers: American comedic actors Leonard "Chico" Marx (1887–1961), Adolph/Arthur "Harpo" Marx (1888–1964), Julius "Groucho" Marx (1890–1977), Milton "Gummo" Marx (1892–1977), and Herbert "Zeppo" Marx (1901–79).

POGROM: Government sanctioned mob action against a targeted community; used by the Russian government against resident Jews in the late 1800s and early 1900s.

REIFIED: something made real, material.

SUBLIMATION: The psychological process whereby undesirable impulses are unconsciously redirected and transformed into acceptable behaviors.

TANTALUS: Greek mythical figure, punished by being forced to stand neck-deep in water that he could not drink, under fruit he could not reach.

de TOCQUEVILLE, Alexis (1805–59): French historian, writer, author of *Democracy in America* (1835–40).

TRISTAN: Refers to Richard Wagner's opera *Tristan and Isolde*, composed between 1857 and 1859 and first performed in 1865. It is noted as a new direction in classical music and opera style.

WAGNER, Richard (1813–83): German composer

Questions for Conversation

The culture industry, according to Horkheimer and Adorno, establishes and maintains unity, uniformity, and wields "totaling" and "leveling" effects on everyday life. How does it do this?

Horkheimer and Adorno have withering criticism of modern forms of media, including radio, TV, films, music, and magazines (the Internet had not yet been invented). Why are they so disdainful of these modern forms of media?

Horkheimer and Adorno make occasional references to religion in this excerpt—"God," "soul," "Idealism," "countless sects"—but they also suggest that religion has lost support or been "neutralized" in the modern era. How does the culture industry relate to religion?

What is the role of the consumer in the society created by the culture industry? What choices do they have? Why do Horkheimer and Adorno suggest consumers are being "cheated"?

Why is the culture industry so preoccupied with sorting, classifying, and ranking?

Given the power of the culture industry, what is the problem with cartoons? (At the time of writing, Horkheimer and Adorno probably were watching early ones by Disney and Warner Brothers.)

How powerful is the culture industry and what is the source of its power? Can one resist, live as a non-conformist, or escape into a life of leisure?

What do the authors mean by the phrase, "The culture industry does not sublimate: it suppresses"?

What is the role of advertising in the culture industry?

Suggestions for Additional Reading

The following is a list of supplemental readings that provide additional information about, apply, or respond critically to the ideas presented in this chapter.

Apostolidis, Paul. *Stations of the Cross: Adorno and Christian Right Radio*. Durham, NC: Duke University Press, 2000.

Baum, Bruce. "Decolonizing Critical Theory," *Constellations* 22 (2015): 420–34.

Bowman, Marion. "Healing in the Spiritual Marketplace: Consumers, Courses and Credentialism," *Social Compass* 46, no. 2 (1999): 181–9.

Clark, Lynn Schofield. "Identity, Belonging, and the Emergence of Religious Lifestyle Branding: Fashion Bibles, Bhangra Parties, and Muslim Pop," in *Religion, Media, and the Marketplace*, ed. Lynn Schofield Clark, 1–33. New Brunswick, NJ: Rutgers University Press, 2007.

Crook, Stephen, ed. *Theodor Adorno: The Stars Down to Earth and Other Essays on the Irrational in Culture*. New York: Routledge, 1994.

Curtis, Susan. *A Consuming Faith: The Social Gospel and Modern American Culture*. Columbia: University of Missouri Press, 2001.

Douglas, Anne. *The Feminization of American Culture*. New York: Farrar, Strauss, and Giroux, 1977.

Einstein, Mara. *Brands of Faith: Marketing Religion in a Commercial Age*. New York: Routledge, 2008.

Frederick, Marla F. *Colored Television: American Religion Gone Global*. Redwood City, CA: Stanford University Press, 2015.

Hansen, Miriam. "Of Mice and Ducks: Benjamin and Adorno on Disney," *The South Atlantic Quarterly* 92 (1993): 27–61.

Heberle, Renee J. *Feminist Interpretations of Theodor Adorno*. University Park: Pennsylvania State University Press, 2010.

Hendershot, Heather. *Shaking the World for Jesus: Media and Conservative Evangelical Culture*. Chicago: The University of Chicago Press, 2004.

Jhally, Sut. "Advertising as Religion: The Dialectic of Technology and Magic," in *Cultural Politics in Contemporary America*, ed. Ian Angus and Sut Jhally, 217–29. New York: Routledge, 1989.

Jones, Carla. "Images of Desire: Creating Virtue and Value in an Indonesian Islamic Lifestyle Magazine," *Journal of Middle Eastern Women's Studies* 6 (2010): 91–117.

Lears, Jackson. *Fables of Abundance: A Cultural History of Advertising in America*. New York: Basic Books, 1995.

Lofton, Kathryn. *Consuming Religion*. Chicago: The University of Chicago Press, 2017.

Lofton, Kathryn. *Oprah: The Gospel of an Icon*. Berkeley: The University of California Press, 2011.

Marchand, Roland. *Advertising the American Dream: Making Way for Modernity, 1920–1940*. Berkeley: University of California Press, 1985.

McLoughlin, William. *Modern Revivalism: Charles Grandison Finney to Billy Graham*. Eugene, OR: Wipf and Stock Publishers, 2004.

McMullen, Josh. *Under the Big Top: Big Tent Revivalism and American Culture, 1885–1925*. Oxford: Oxford University Press, 2015.

Mendieta, Eduardo. *The Frankfurt School on Religion: Key Writings by the Major Thinkers*. New York: Routledge, 2004.

Mignolo, Walter D. "Epistemic Disobedience and the Decolonial Option: A Manifesto," *Transmodernity* 1 (2011): 44–66.

Moore, R. Laurence. *Selling God: American Religion in the Marketplace of Culture*. Oxford: Oxford University Press, 1995.

Nederman, Cary J., and James Wray Goulding. "Popular Occultism and Critical Social Theory: Exploring some Themes in Adorno's Critique of Astrology and the Occult," *Sociology of Religion* 42 (1981): 325–32.

Rolsky, L. Benjamin. *The Rise and Fall of the Religious Left: Politics, Television, and Popular Culture in the 1970s and Beyond*. New York: Columbia University Press, 2019.

Sheffield, Tricia. *The Religious Dimensions of Advertising*. New York: Palgrave Macmillan, 2006.

Thomas, Pradip. "Selling God/Saving Souls: Religious Commodities, Spiritual Markets, and the Media," *Global Media and Communication* 5 (2009): 57–76.

Winston, Diane, and John M. Giggie, eds. *Faith in the Market: Religion and the Rise of Urban Commercial Culture*. New Brunswick, NJ: Rutgers University Press, 2002.

5   Paul Tillich

Paul Tillich (1886–1965) was born in Prussia and studied in Berlin, Tubingen, Breslau (where he earned a PhD), and Halle (where he earned a degree in theology). Following in the footsteps of his father, he became an ordained Lutheran minister in 1912 and served as a chaplain for the German army during the First World War. After the war, he taught in Berlin, Marburg, Dresden, Leipzig, and Frankfurt, where in 1933 he was dismissed for defending students who had been persecuted for their politics. On an invitation from Reinhold Niebuhr, Tillich came to the United States and joined the faculty at Union Theological Seminary in New York, where he remained until 1955 when he relocated to Harvard. In 1962, he joined the faculty at the University of Chicago Divinity School.

Considered one of the most influential Christian thinkers of the period, Tillich had appeal across professional and academic lines. A prolific author, Tillich enjoyed popular appeal for a number of his works—including *The Courage to Be*, *Dynamics of Faith*, and *The Protestant Era*—in part because his work was considered accessible and current. A large part of this appeal was based on Tillich's argument that religion and culture were closely linked. It was not the cultural product but the process of cultural production that revealed the religious; any expression of culture was worthy of deep theological or existential analysis. Art that sought answers or was critical of the human condition—particularly avant-garde or revolutionary art—was religious. "Doubt," noted Tillich in a 1959 interview in *Time* titled "To Be or Not To Be," was "an inevitable part of faith," and the "ultimate concern"' was the inevitable "combination of longing and frustration" In a post-Hiroshima world, Tillich's inquiries also gave theology a voice while maintaining the era's increasing difficulty with moral certitude. Tillich was even admired by "Death of God" theologians, who may have disagreed with his conclusions but who respected his courage to address growing post-War secularism.

Tillich's theory—particularly his notion of "ultimate concern"—has been misused by those, including students and scholars in the area of religion and popular culture, who have focused on "concern" as "object of thought" rather than as "cause of dilemma." This may be why, in his own work, he avoided any serious discussion of popular culture. Not surprisingly, scholars of religion have expressed concern, arguing that, in the wrong hands, Tillich's approach could seem to justify the investigation of almost anything as "religion."

Nonetheless, Tillich has provided Christian theology—and for some, all of religion—with a language that is broader than the kind of "God talk" that is traditional among theologians and which shifted the conversation from God's vantage point to one with a more human perspective, particularly in terms of the interpretation of symbols and the relationship of religion to culture more broadly understood. By downplaying the "God talk" and instead focusing on the human aspect of the encounter with sacred powers, Tillich's theory—like that of many anthropologists and sociologists before it—also facilitated the emergence of the academic study of religion as an acceptable field in American public universities that were restricted by presumptions of a separation of church and state.

"Aspects of a Religious Analysis of Culture" (1959)[1]

If we abstract the concept of religion from the great commandment, we can say that religion is being ultimately concerned about that which is and should be our ultimate concern. This means that faith is the state of being grasped by an ultimate concern, and God is the name for the content of the concern. Such a concept of religion has little in common with the description of religion as the belief in the existence of a highest being called God, and the theoretical and practical consequences of such a belief. Instead, we are pointing to an **existential**, not a theoretical, understanding of religion. Christianity claims that the God who is manifest in Jesus the Christ is the true God, the true subject of an ultimate and unconditional concern. Judged by him, all other gods are less than valid objects of an ultimate concern, and if they are made into one, become idols. Christianity can claim this extraordinary character because of the extraordinary character of the events on which it is based, namely, the creation of a new reality within and under the conditions of man's predicament. Jesus as the bringer of this new reality is subject to those conditions, to finitude and anxiety, to law and tragedy, to conflicts and death. But he victoriously keeps the unity with God, sacrificing himself as Jesus to himself as the Christ. In doing so he creates the new reality of which the Church is the communal and historical embodiment.

From this it follows that the unconditional claim made by Christianity is not related to the Christian Church, but to the event on which the Church is based. If the Church does not subject itself to the judgment which is pronounced by the Church, it becomes idolatrous towards itself. Such idolatry is its permanent temptation, just because it is the bearer of the New Being in history. As such it judges the world by its very presence. But the Church is also of the world and included under the judgment with which it judges the world. A Church which tries to exclude itself from such a judgment loses its right to judge the world and is rightly judged by the world. This is the tragedy of the Roman Catholic Church. Its way of dealing with culture is dependent upon its unwillingness to subject itself to the judgment pronounced by itself. Protestantism, at least in principle, resists this temptation, though actually it falls into it in many ways, again and again.

A second consequence of the existential concept of religion is the disappearance of the gap between the sacred and secular realm. If religion is the state of being grasped by an ultimate concern, this state cannot be restricted to a special realm. The unconditional character of this concern implies that it refers to every moment of our life, to every space and every realm. The universe is God's sanctuary. Every work day is a day of the Lord, every supper a Lord's supper, every work the fulfillment of a divine task, every joy a joy in God. In all preliminary concerns, ultimate concern is present, consecrating them. Essentially the religious and the secular are not separated realms. Rather they are within each other.

---

[1]Paul Tillich, excerpt from "Aspects of a Religious Analysis of Culture," in *Theology of Culture*, ed. Robert C. Kimball (New York: Oxford University Press, 1959), 40–51.

But this is not the way things actually are. In actuality, the secular element tends to make itself independent and to establish a realm of its own. And in opposition to this, the religious element tends to establish itself also as a special realm. Man's predicament is determined by this situation. It is the situation of the estrangement of man from his true being. One could rightly say that the existence of religion as a special realm is the most conspicuous proof of man's fallen state. This does not mean that under the conditions of estrangement which determine our destiny the religious should be swallowed by the secular, as secularism desires, nor that the secular should be swallowed by the religious, as **ecclesiastic** imperialism desires. But it does mean that the inseparable division is a witness to our human predicament.

The third consequence following from the existential concept of religion refers to the relation of religion and culture. Religion as ultimate concern is the meaning-giving substance of culture, and culture is the totality of forms in which the basic concern of religion expresses itself. In abbreviation: religion is the substance of culture, culture is the form of religion. Such a consideration definitely prevents the establishment of a **dualism** of religion and culture. Every religious act, not only in organized religion, but also in the most intimate movement of the soul, is culturally formed.

The fact that every act of man's spiritual life is carried by language, spoken or silent, is proof enough for this assertion. For language is the basic cultural creation. On the other hand, there is no cultural creation without an ultimate concern expressed in it. This is true of the theoretical functions of man's spiritual life, e.g. artistic intuition and cognitive reception of reality, and it is true of the practical functions of man's spiritual life, e.g. personal and social transformation of reality. In each of these functions in the whole of man's cultural creativity, an ultimate concern is present. Its immediate expression is the style of a culture. He who can read the style of a culture can discover its ultimate concern, its religious substance. This we will now try to do in relation to our present culture.

The Special Character of Contemporary Culture

Our present culture must be described in terms of one predominant movement and an increasingly powerful protest against this movement. The spirit of the predominant movement is the spirit of industrial society. The spirit of the protest is the spirit of the existentialist analysis of man's actual predicament. The actual style of our life, as it was shaped in the 18th and 19th centuries, expresses the still unbroken power of the spirit of industrial society. There are numerous analyses of this style of thought, life, and artistic expression. One of the difficulties in analyzing it is its dynamic character, its continuous change, and the influence the protest against it has already had upon it. We may nevertheless elaborate two main characteristics of man in industrial society.

The first of these is the concentration of man's activities upon the methodical investigation and technical transformation of his world, including himself, and the consequent loss of the dimension of depth in his encounter with reality. Reality has lost its inner **transcendence** or, in another metaphor, its transparency for the eternal. The system of finite inter-relations which we call the universe has become self-sufficient. It is calculable and manageable and can be improved from the point of view of man's needs and desires. Since the beginning of the 18th century God has been removed from the power field of man's activities. He has been put alongside the world without permission to interfere with it because every interference would disturb man's technical and business calculations. The result is that God has become superfluous and the universe left to man as its master. This situation leads to the second characteristic of industrial society.

In order to fulfill his destiny, man must be in possession of creative powers, analogous to those previously attributed to God, and so creativity must become a human quality. The conflict between what man essentially is and what he actually is, his estrangement, or in traditional terms his fallen state, is disregarded. Death and guilt disappear even in the preaching of early industrial society. Their acknowledgment would interfere with man's progressive conquest of nature, outside and inside himself. Man has shortcomings, but there is no sin and certainly no universal sinfulness. The bondage of the will, of which the **Reformer** spoke, the demonic powers which are central for the New Testament, the structures of destruction in personal and communal life, are ignored or denied. Educational processes are able to adjust the large majority of men to the demands of the system of production and consumption. Man's actual state is hence mistakenly regarded as his essential state, and he is pictured in a position of progressive fulfillment of his potentialities.

This is supposed to be true not only of man as an individual personality, but also of man as community. The scientific and technical conquest of time and space is considered as the road to the reunion of mankind. The demonic structures of history, the conflicts of power in every realization of life are seen as preliminary impediments. Their tragic and inescapable character is denied. As the universe replaces God, as man in the center of the universe replaces the Christ, so the expectation of peace and justice in history replaces the expectation of the Kingdom of God. The dimension of depth in the divine and demonic has disappeared. This is the spirit of industrial society manifest in the style of its creations.

Connections 5a: Tillich, Theology, and Culture

After the Second World War, there was a shift in how theologians understood religion—their own as well as that of others. On the one hand, the carnage of the Nazi death camps, the firebombing of Dresden, and the atomic blasts at Hiroshima and Nagasaki led some to question the nature of the Divine, its presence and action in the world, and the possibility of human perfection. On the other hand, the seeming triumph of "good" over the forces of "evil"—as well as increased exposure of those from the Western dominant cultures to long-segregated religious communities across the religious spectrum—led others to seek the Divine not in the skies but among the people.

These shifts were particularly noticeable in the United States, where religious thinkers like Thomas J. J. Altizer, Richard Rubenstein, Paul van Buren, and Gabriel Vahanian (among others) became associated with "Death of God" theology. The name was a misnomer based (in part) on the wildly popular cover of the April 8, 1966, issue of *Time* magazine, which—in bold letters (and, for the first time in the magazine's history, no accompanying image)—asked: "Is God Dead?"; the article within the magazine's covers ("Theology Toward a Hidden God," by John Elson) more accurately represented the philosophers' works. They were not convinced that God had died; rather, they were concerned that, in a popular expression of the time, "God isn't dead, He just got the hell out of here." Challenged by competing forces of theological questioning, the effects of exposure to non-Western religious traditions, and the growing voice of an increasingly anti-establishment youth culture, many more traditional philosophers and theologians feared that traditional religion that had been at the core of Western civilization was failing.

Two years after *Time* magazine published its provocative cover, however, the *New York Times* declared in 1968 that the "God is Dead" doctrine was dying, "losing ground," it seemed, to a "theology of hope." This new theological approach was grounded in the popular work of Paul Tillich, but also in Harvey Cox's *The Secular City* (1965), which opened doors for less traditional voices—some of whom presented less hope than challenge—like James Cone (*Black Theology and Black Power*, 1969), Gustavo Gutiérrez (*A Theology of Liberation*, 1973), and Mary Daly (*Beyond God the Father*, 1973), among others. Those who were coming of age in the late 1960s—the so-called baby boomers—would transform theological impulses from institutional to personal foundations, opening the way for them (and others) to find deep meaning in the world around them.

The attitude of the churches toward this situation was contradictory. Partly they defended themselves by retiring to their traditional past in doctrine, cult, and life. But in so doing, they used the categories created by the industrial spirit against which they were fighting. They drew the symbols in which the depth of being expresses itself down to the level of ordinary, so to speak, two-dimensional experiences. They understood them literally and defended their validity by establishing a supranatural above the natural realm. But supranaturalism is only the counterpart of naturalism and vice versa. They produce each other in never-ending fights against each other. Neither could live without its opposite.

The impossibility of this kind of defense of the tradition was recognized by the other way in which the churches reacted to the spirit of industrial society. They accepted the new situation and tried to adapt themselves to it by reinterpreting the traditional symbols in contemporary terms. This is the justification and even the glory of what we call today "liberal theology." But it must also be stated that in its theological understanding of God and man, liberal theology paid the price of adjustment by losing the message of the new reality which was preserved by its supranaturalistic defenders. Both ways in which the churches dealt with the spirit of industrial society proved to be inadequate.

While naturalism and supranaturalism, liberalism and orthodoxy were involved in undecisive struggles, historical providence prepared another way of relating religion to contemporary culture. This preparation was done in the depth of industrial civilization, sometimes by people who represented it in its most anti-religious implications. This is the large movement known as existentialism which started with **Pascal**, was carried on by a few prophetic minds in the 19th century and came to a full victory in the 20th century.

Existentialism, in the largest sense, is the protest against the spirit of industrial society within the framework of industrial society. The protest is directed against the position of man in the system of production and consumption of our society. Man is supposed to be the master of his world and of himself. But actually he has become a part of the reality he has created, an object among objects, a thing among things, a cog within a universal machine to which he must adapt himself in order not to be smashed by it. But this adaptation makes him a means for ends which are means themselves, and in which an ultimate end is lacking.

Out of this predicament of man in the industrial society the experiences of emptiness and meaninglessness, of dehumanization and estrangement have resulted. Man has ceased to encounter reality as meaningful. Reality in its ordinary forms and structures does not speak to him any longer.

One way out is that man restricts himself to a limited section of reality and defends it against the intrusion of the world into his castle. This is the neurotic way out which becomes psychotic if reality disappears completely. It involves subjection to the demands of culture and repression of the question of meaning. Or some may have the strength to take anxiety and meaninglessness courageously upon themselves and live creatively, expressing the predicament of the most sensitive people in our time in cultural production. It is the latter way to which we owe the artistic and philosophical works of culture in the first half of the 20th century. They are creative expressions of the destructive trends in contemporary culture. The great works of the visual arts, of music, of poetry, of literature, of architecture, of dance, of philosophy, show in their style both the encounter with non-being, and the strength which can stand this encounter and shape it creatively. Without this key, contemporary culture is a closed door. With this key, it can be understood as the revelation of man's predicament, both in the present world and in the world universally. This makes the protesting element in contemporary culture theologically significant.

The Cultural Forms in Which Religion Actualizes Itself

The form of religion is culture. This is especially obvious in the language used by religion. Every language, including that of the Bible, is the result of innumerable acts of cultural creativity. All functions of man's spiritual life are based on man's power to speak vocally or silently. Language is the expression of man's freedom from the given situation and its concrete demands. It gives him universals in whose power he can create worlds above the given world of technical civilization and spiritual content.

Conversely, the development of these worlds determines the development of language. There is no sacred language which has fallen from a supranatural heaven and been put between the covers of a book. But there is human language, based on man's encounter with reality, changing through the millenia, used for the needs of daily life, for expression and communication, for literature and poetry, and used also for the expression and communication of our ultimate concern. In each of these cases the language is different. Religious language is ordinary language, changed under the power of what it expresses, the ultimate of being and meaning. The expression of it can be narrative (mythological, legendary, historical), or it can be prophetic, poetic, **liturgical**. It becomes holy for those to whom it expresses their ultimate concern from generation to generation. But there is no holy language in itself, as translations, retranslations and revisions show.

Connections 5b: Tillich and "The Gospel According to . . ."

While Tillich's work popularized theological inquiry, a small book by Presbyterian minister Robert Short—The Gospel According to Peanuts—made theology accessible to all. The little volume—published in 1965 by John Knox Press, the official publisher of the Presbyterian movement—was produced with the blessing of *Peanuts* creator Charles Schulz and included a foreword by respected religion and literature scholar Nathan Scott.

Using child characters and their various adventures to examine basic Christian principles, the book was an enormous hit, eventually selling more than ten million copies globally and translated into eleven languages. Its popularity tapped into an interest generally in reading religion into nontraditional forms of cultural expression. From 1965 to 2011, interest in the traditional (canonical) Gospels—as measured solely in terms of books published using as part of the title the phrase "Gospel According to . . ."—increased 100 percent, as did interest in noncanonical gospels (Thomas, Mary, Peter, etc.) and more creative "Bible-related" gospels (of Abraham, Isaac, Moses, etc.). Over the same period of time, however, the rate of publication of "popular" (non-religious) gospels—according to such things as Madison Avenue, Harvard Business School, Superman, Casey Stengel, Disney, and the *New York Times*—increased over 1,200 percent. Short's original *Gospel According to Peanuts* was rereleased in 2000 on the occasion of its thirty-fifth anniversary, this time with the foreword written by respected American Protestant historian Martin Marty and sparking a wave of similar ventures, including "gospels" according to Winnie the Pooh, Bob Dylan, *Star Wars*, Harry Potter, Oprah Winfrey, *The Simpsons*, Bruce Springsteen, the Beatles, and J.R.R. Tolkien. Many of these were produced by religiously affiliated publishing houses, some were written by well-known religious authors. All of them were taking their cues from the introduction provided by Short, who was inspired by the same line of reasoning as Tillich: that deep theological concepts could be plumbed from the depths of any human endeavor, even those of Charlie Brown.

This leads to a second example of the use of cultural creations within religion: religious art. One principle which must be emphasized again and again in religious art is the principle of artistic honesty. There is no sacred artistic style in Protestant, in contrast, for example, to Greek-Orthodox doctrine. An artistic style is honest only if it expresses the real situation of the artist and the cultural period to which he belongs. We can participate in the artistic styles of the past in so far as they were honestly expressing the encounter which they had with God, man, and world. But we cannot honestly imitate them and produce for the cult of the Church works which are not the result of a creating ecstasy, but which are learned reproductions of creative ecstasies of the past. It was a religiously significant achievement of modern architecture that it liberated itself from traditional forms which, in the context of our period, were nothing but trimmings without meaning and, therefore, neither aesthetically valuable nor religiously expressive.

A third example is taken from the cognitive realm. It is the question: what elements of the contemporary philosophical consciousness can be used for the theological interpretation of the Christian symbols? If we take the existentialist protest against the spirit of industrial society seriously, we must reject both naturalism and idealism as tools for theological self-expression. Both of them are creations of that spirit against which the protest of our century is directed. Both of them have been used by theology in sharply conflicting methods, but neither of them expresses the contemporary culture.

Instead, theology must use the immense and profound material of the existential analysis in all cultural realms, including therapeutic psychology. But theology cannot use it by simply accepting it. Theology must confront it with the answer implied in the Christian message. The confrontation of the existential analysis with the symbol in which Christianity has expressed its ultimate concern is the method which is adequate both to the message of Jesus as the Christ and to the human predicament as rediscovered in contemporary culture. The answer cannot be derived from the question. It is said *to* him who asks, but it is not taken *from* him. Existentialism cannot give answers. It can determine the form of the answer, but whenever an existentialist artist or philosopher answers, he does so through the power of another tradition which has revelatory sources. To give such answers is the function of the Church not only to itself, but also to those outside the Church.

The Influences of the Church on Contemporary Culture

The Church has the function of answering the question implied in man's very existence, the question of the meaning of this existence. One of the ways in which the Church does this is **evangelism**. The principle of evangelism must be to show to the people outside the Church that the symbols in which the life of the Church expresses itself are answers to the questions implied in their very existence as human beings. Because the Christian message is the message of salvation and because salvation means healing, the message of healing in every sense of the word is appropriate to our situation. This is the reason why movements at the fringe of the Church, sectarian and evangelistic movements of a most primitive and unsound character, have such great success. Anxiety and despair about existence itself induces millions of people to look out for any kind of healing that promises success.

The Church cannot take this way. But it must understand that the average kind of preaching is unable to reach the people of our time. They must feel that Christianity is not a set of doctrinal or ritual or moral laws, but is rather the good news of the conquest of the law by the appearance of a new healing reality. They must feel that the Christian symbols are not absurdities, unacceptable for the questioning mind of our period, but that they point to that which alone is of ultimate concern, the ground and meaning of our existence and of existence generally.

There remains a last question, namely, the question of how the Church should deal with the spirit of our society which is responsible for much of what must be healed by the Christian message. Has the Church the task and the power to attack and to transform the spirit of industrial society? It certainly cannot try to replace the present social reality by another one, in terms of a progress to the realized Kingdom of God. It cannot sketch perfect social structures or suggest concrete reforms. Cultural changes occur by the inner dynamics of culture itself. The Church participates in them, sometimes in a leading role, but then it is a cultural force beside others and not the representative of the new reality in history.

In its prophetic role the Church is the guardian who reveals dynamic structures in society and undercuts their demonic power by revealing them, even within the Church itself. In so doing the Church listens to prophetic voices outside itself, judging both the culture and the Church in so far as it is a part of the culture. We have referred to such prophetic voices in our culture. Most of them are not active members of the manifest Church. But perhaps one could call them participants of a "latent Church," a Church in which the ultimate concern which drives the manifest Church is hidden under cultural forms and deformations.

Sometimes this latent Church comes into the open. Then the manifest Church should recognize in these voices what its own spirit should be and accept them even if they appear hostile to the Church. But the Church should also stand as a guardian against the demonic distortions into which attacks must fall if they are not grasped by the right subject of our ultimate concern. This was the fate of the **communist movement**. The Church was not sufficiently aware of its function as guardian when this movement was still undecided about its way. The Church did not hear the prophetic voice in communism and therefore did not recognize its demonic possibilities.

Judging means seeing both sides. The Church judges culture, including the Church's own forms of life. For its forms are created by culture, as its religious substance makes culture possible. The Church and culture are within, not alongside, each other. And the Kingdom of God includes both while transcending both.

Glossary

COMMUNIST MOVEMENT: A form of governance in which all is owned equally by the citizens; here a reference to a more dictatorial form of governance popular starting in the early twentieth century (in the Soviet Union, many countries of eastern Europe, and China) in which religious adherence was seen as an illusion designed to keep the economically disadvantaged in a politically marginal position.

DUALISM: a pairing, often implying a necessary relationship of opposites (right/wrong, good/bad, etc.).

ECCLESIASTIC: of (or related to) the clergy.

EVANGELISM: the spreading of Christianity by means of preaching or personal witness; also used (more generally) to refer to any enthusiastic promotion.

EXISTENTIAL: related to existence, or to the reality of the existence of something.

LITURGICAL: related to the ritual and pattern of public worship.

PASCAL, Blaise (1623–62): French philosopher, scientist.

REFORMER: referring to Martin Luther (1483–1546), German theologian identified as the founder of the Protestant Reformation.

TRANSCENDENCE: existing in but also beyond the physical world.

Questions for Conversation

Tillich defines religion as being "grasped by ultimate concern." How might this provide an opening for a theological study of culture, including popular culture?

Why might Tillich argue that the gap between sacred and secular disappears if religion is understood as "ultimate concern"? Or put another way, why is there no strict dualism of religion and culture?

According to Tillich, how does industrial society suppress and deemphasize religion (or at least the traditional modes of religion)?

How might existential analysis protest against industrial society?

According to Tillich, how were the initial church responses to industrial society inadequate? If he's correct, how might the church sharpen its critical role?

What role do the arts play in the responses to industrial society, especially the best and most creative arts?

Why are religious language and religious art important for Tillich?

How does popular culture express the themes outlined by Tillich? How do they express Ultimate concern? Existential protest? Prophetic judgment?

Suggestions for Additional Reading

The following is a list of supplemental readings that provide additional information about, apply, or respond critically to the ideas presented in this chapter.

Beaudoin, Tom. *Virtual Faith: The Irreverent Spiritual Quest of Generation X*. San Francisco, CA: Jossey-Boss, 1998.

Brant, Jonathan. *Paul Tillich and the Possibility of Revelation Through Film*. New York: Oxford University Press, 2012.

Cobb, Kelton. *The Blackwell Guide to Theology and Popular Culture*. Malden, MA: Blackwell Publishing, 2005.

Cobb, Kelton. "Reconsidering the Status of Popular Culture in Tillich's Theology of Culture," *Journal of the American Academy of Religion* 63, no. 1 (1995): 53–84.

Deacy, Christopher, and Gaye Williams Ortiz. *Theology and Film: Challenging the Sacred/Secular Divide*. Malden, MA: Blackwell Publishers, 2008.

Detweiler, Craig, and Barry Taylor. *A Matrix of Meanings: Finding God in Pop Culture*. Grand Rapids, MI: Baker Publishing Group, 2003.

Fessenden, Tracy. "'Woman' and the 'Primitive' in Paul Tillich's Life and Thought: Some Implications for the Study of Religion," *Feminist Studies in Religion* 14 (1998): 45–76.

Fillingim, David. *Redneck Liberation: Country Music as Theology*. Macon, GA: Mercer University Press, 2003.

Finstuen, Andrew S. *Original Sin and Everyday Protestants: The Theology of Reinhold Niebuhr, Billy Graham, and Paul Tillich in an Age of Anxiety*. Chapel Hill: University of North Carolina Press, 2009.

Gudmarsdottir, Sigridur. *Tillich and the Abyss: Foundations, Feminism, and Theology of Praxis*. London: Palgrave Macmillan, 2016.

Lynch, Gordon. *Understanding Theology and Popular Culture*. Malden, MA: Blackwell Publishing, 2005.

"A Man of Ultimate Concern," *Time* (October 29, 1965): 90+.

Manning, Russell R. E. "The Religious Meaning of Culture: Paul Tillich and Beyond," *International Journal of Systematic Theology* 15, no. 4 (2013): 437–52.

Marsh, Clive, and Gaye Ortiz, eds. *Explorations in Theology and Film: Movies and Meaning*. Malden, MA: Blackwell, 1998.

Mazur, Eric Michael. "The Gospel According to Comic Strips: On *Peanuts* and *The Far Side*," in *Godly Heretics: Essays on Alternative Christianity in Literature and Popular Culture*, ed. Marc Dipaolo, 143–61. Jefferson, NC: McFarland, 2013.

Plaskow, Judith. *Sex, Sin, and Grace: Women's Experiences and the Theologies of Reinhold Niebuhr and Paul Tillich*. Washington, DC: University Press of America, 1980.

Short, Robert L. *Gospel According to Peanuts*. Richmond, VA: John Knox Press, 1965; reprint, Louisville, KY: Westminster John Knox Press, 2000.

Smith, Jonathan Z. "Tillich['s] Remains," *Journal of the American Academy of Religion* 78, no. 4 (2010): 1139–70.

Tillich, Paul. "Aspects of a Religious Analysis of Culture," in *Theology of Culture*, ed. Robert C. Kimball, 40–51. New York: Oxford University Press, 1959.

Tillich, Paul. *The Courage to Be*. New Haven, CT: Yale University Press, 1952.

Tillich, Paul. *Dynamics of Faith*. New York: Harper, 1957.

Tillich, Paul. *The Protestant Era*. Chicago: The University of Chicago Press, 1957.

"To Be or Not to Be," *Time* (March 16, 1959): 46+.

Yip, Francis Ching-Wah. *Capitalism as Religion? A Study of Paul Tillich's Interpretation of Modernity*. Cambridge, MA: Harvard University Press, 2010.

6   Roland Barthes

In the middle decades of the twentieth century, French literary theorist, linguist, philosopher, and writer Roland Barthes (1915–80) contributed to various forms of literary interpretation, including semiology, structuralism, and later, post-structuralism. Despite suffering from tuberculosis, he showed academic promise as a youth and eventually studied a wide range of subjects, including classics, philology, sociology, and lexicology. His early professional career was peripatetic, moving among positions in various regional French colleges and universities, as well as brief stints in other European centers, Egypt, and the United States, eventually being awarded a prestigious chair at the College de France in Paris. Nonetheless, all the while he was very productive and, starting in the 1950s, he produced a stream of literary criticism, academic papers, and popular magazine articles that would eventually make him a leading figure among the French intelligentsia.

Barthes's wide range of academic influences and interests makes him hard to summarize. He could masterfully analyze dense literary texts and subtle philosophical debates, but he could also find meaning in professional wrestling bouts, plastics exhibitions, and margarine ads. His published works include studies of famous French writers, the use of language by the fashion industry, the complexities of literary authorship, the use of signs and symbols in Japanese culture, and the pleasurable experiences of readers. In the area of the study of religion and popular culture, his early work that applied the discipline of semiotics to the study of myth, collected in his celebrated 1957 volume *Mythologies*, is perhaps the best introduction to his thought. A series of short articles originally written for popular magazines, the pieces in *Mythologies* sought to expand the understanding of what comprised "myth" in modern societies. These included brief but illuminating studies of ordinary objects, food, sports, celebrity, photography, and other commonplace experiences. In the first excerpt, Barthes makes the case for a generalized understanding of myth—potentially applicable to any aspect of popular culture—and introduces to his readers concepts from semiotics to analyze these myths. Following it are two short examples from Barthes's *Mythologies*, wherein he applies his theories of myth to explore the inner meanings of everyday objects and events. The first, inspired by an article on jet pilots in the magazine *Match*, looks at how even in the most modern of activities—jet airline flight—there are lingering traces of religious devotion and self-discipline (asceticism). The last excerpt was inspired by a visit to a plastics exhibition in the mid-1950s. In it, Barthes is able to use critical notions of semiotics to look beyond the superficial form of plastic and plumb its various inner meanings, suggesting that for all its ordinariness and functionality, plastic is really quite magical.

"Myth Today" (1957)[1]

What is a myth, today? I shall give at the outset a first, very simple answer, which is perfectly consistent with **etymology**: myth is a type of speech.

Myth is a Type of Speech

Of course, it is not any type: language needs special conditions in order to become myth: we shall see them in a minute. But what must be firmly established at the start is that myth is a system of communication, that it is a message. This allows one to perceive that myth cannot possibly be an object, a concept, or an idea; it is a mode of **signification**, a form. Later, we shall have to assign to this form historical limits, conditions of use, and reintroduce society into it: we must nevertheless first describe it as a form.

It can be seen that to purport to discriminate among mythical objects according to their substance would be entirely illusory: since myth is a type of speech, everything can be a myth provided it is conveyed by a **discourse**. Myth is not defined by the object of its message, but by the way in which it utters this message: there are formal limits to myth, there are no "substantial" ones. Everything, then, can be a myth? Yes, I believe this, for the universe is infinitely fertile in suggestions. Every object in the world can pass from a closed, silent existence to an oral state, open to appropriation by society, for there is no law, whether natural or not, which forbids talking about things. A tree is a tree. Yes, of course. But a tree as expressed by **Minou Drouet** is no longer quite a tree, it is a tree which is decorated, adapted to a certain type of consumption, laden with literary self-indulgence, revolt, images, in short with a type of social usage which is added to pure matter.

Naturally, everything is not expressed at the same time: some objects become the prey of mythical speech for a while, then they disappear, others take their place and attain the status of myth. Are there objects which are inevitably a source of suggestiveness, as **Baudelaire** suggested about Woman? Certainly not: one can conceive of very ancient myths, but there are no eternal ones; for it is human history which converts reality into speech, and it alone rules the life and the death of mythical language. Ancient or not, mythology can only have an historical foundation, for myth is a type of speech chosen by history: it cannot possibly evolve from the "nature" of things.

Speech of this kind is a message. It is therefore by no means confined to oral speech. It can consist of modes of writing or of representations; not only written discourse, but also photography, cinema, reporting, sport, shows, publicity, all these can serve as a support to mythical speech. Myth can be defined neither by its object nor by its material, for any material can arbitrarily be endowed with meaning: the arrow which is brought in order to signify a challenge is also a kind of speech. True, as far as perception is concerned, writing and pictures, for instance, do not call upon the same type of consciousness; and even with pictures, one can use many kinds of reading: a diagram lends itself to signification more than a drawing, a copy more than an original, and a caricature more than a portrait. But this is the point: we are no longer dealing here with a theoretical mode of representation: we

---

[1] Roland Barthes, excerpts from *Mythologies*, trans. Annette Lavers (New York: Hill and Wang, 1972), 71–3; 97–9; 107–14. [Originally published in French (1957).]

are dealing with this particular image, which is given for this particular signification. Mythical speech is made of a material which has already been worked on so as to make it suitable for communication: it is because all the materials of myth (whether pictorial or written) presuppose a **signifying** consciousness, that one can reason about them while discounting their substance. This substance is not unimportant: pictures, to be sure, are more imperative than writing, they impose meaning at one stroke, without analysing or diluting it. But this is no longer a constitutive difference. Pictures become a kind of writing as soon as they are meaningful: like writing, they call for a **lexis**.

We shall therefore take language, discourse, speech, etc., to mean any significant unit or synthesis, whether verbal or visual: a photograph will be a kind of speech for us in the same way as a newspaper article; even objects will become speech, if they mean something. This generic way of conceiving language is in fact justified by the very history of writing: long before the invention of our alphabet, objects like the Inca *quipu*, or drawings, as in pictographs, have been accepted as speech. This does not mean that one must treat mythical speech like language; myth in fact belongs to the province of a general science, coextensive with linguistics, which is **semiology**.

Myth as a Semiological System

For mythology, since it is the study of a type of speech, is but one fragment of this vast science of signs which **Saussure** postulated some forty years ago under the name of semiology. Semiology has not yet come into being. But since Saussure himself, and sometimes independently of him, a whole section of contemporary research has constantly been referred to the problem of meaning: psycho-analysis, **structuralism**, **eidetic** psychology, some new types of literary criticism of which **Bachelard** has given the first examples, are no longer concerned with facts except inasmuch as they are endowed with significance. Now to postulate a signification is to have recourse to semiology. I do not mean that semiology could account for all these aspects of research equally well: they have different contents. But they have a common status: they are all sciences dealing with values. They are not content with meeting the facts: they define and explore them as tokens for something else.

Semiology is a science of forms, since it studies significations apart from their content. I should like to say one word about the necessity and the limits of such a formal science. The necessity is that which applies in the case of any exact language. **Zhdanov** made fun of **Alexandrov** the philosopher, who spoke of "*the spherical structure of our planet.*" "*It was thought until now*", Zhdanov said, "*that form alone could be spherical.*" Zhdanov was right: one cannot speak about structures in terms of forms, and vice versa. It may well be that on the plane of "life", there is but a totality where structures and forms cannot be separated. But science has no use for the ineffable: it must speak about "life" if it wants to transform it. Against a certain **quixotism** of synthesis, quite platonic incidentally, all criticism must consent to the **ascesis**, to the artifice of analysis; and in analysis, it must match method and language. Less terrorized by the spectre of "formalism", historical criticism might have been less sterile; it would have understood that the specific study of forms does not in any way contradict the necessary principles of totality and History. On the contrary: the more a system is specifically defined in its forms, the more amenable it is to historical criticism. To parody a well-known saying, I shall say that a little formalism turns one away from History, but that a lot brings one back to it. Is there a better example of total criticism than the description of saintliness, at once formal and historical, semiological and ideological, in **Sartre's *Saint-Genet***? The danger, on the contrary, is to consider forms as ambiguous objects, half form and half substance, to endow form with a substance of form, as was done, for instance, by Zhdanovian realism. Semiology, once its limits are settled, is not a metaphysical trap: it is a science among others, necessary but not sufficient. The important thing is to see that the unity of an explanation cannot be based on the amputation of one or other of its approaches, but, as **Engels** said, on the dialectical co-ordination of the particular sciences it makes use of. This is the case with mythology: it is a part both of semiology inasmuch as it is a formal science, and of ideology inasmuch as it is an historical science: it studies ideas-in-form.

Connections 6a: Barthes, Poaching, and Fandom

Roland Barthes's semiotic mining of ordinary things looking for the mythological nuggets inspired later generations of scholars to look more deeply into how people navigate the "everyday" in modern life. Among the most influential of these was sociologist Michel de Certeau, whose *The Practice of Everyday Life* (1984) examined things done repeatedly and largely unconsciously, like walking, talking, reading, cooking, and traversing public spaces. De Certeau sought to understand both the strategies used by powerful social interests (governments, corporations, religions, etc.) to shape and control the ways people thought and acted, as well as how people responded to these repressive controls with varied tactics of selective conformity, reinterpretation, dialogue, and resistance. Among his significant findings was that individuals often developed their own way of "reading" texts (or other media like TV and film), imaginatively reshaping them to their own desires and purposes. Thus the reader

insinuates into another person's text the ruses of pleasure and appropriation: he poaches on it, is transported into it, pluralizes himself in it like the internal rumblings of one's body. . . . A different world (the reader's) slips into the author's place. . . . Reading thus introduces an 'art' which is anything but passive. (de Certeau 1984: xxi–xxii)

Other scholars, like media studies theorist Harry Jenkins, enlarged this notion of textual poaching into a more elaborate study of fans and fandom. Novels, TV series, films, and more recently computer gaming develop fan cultures and subcultures that use newsletters, fan magazines, conventions, online forums, social media, and other means to share their ideas. Prominent among these are interpretations that stress the original text has hidden meanings available only to the most dedicated or insightful, and fan-generated side stories that play around with "canonical" characters by putting them into new situations. The main point, reinforced by many additional studies of fan cultures, is that fans are not passive consumers who accept the "message" of popular narratives as given by the artists and producers. Rather, they are active participants in creating their own subcultures and communities, reshaping and reinterpreting their lives and stories, "built from the semiotic raw materials the media provides" (Jenkins 1992: 49).

Let me therefore restate that any semiology postulates a relation between two terms, a signifier and a **signified**. This relation concerns objects which belong to different categories, and this is why it is not one of equality but one of equivalence. We must here be on our guard for despite common parlance which simply says that the signifier expresses the signified, we are dealing, in any semiological system, not with two, but with three different terms. For what we grasp is not at all one term after the other, but the correlation which unites them: there are, therefore, the signifier, the signified and the sign, which is the associative total of the first two terms. Take a bunch of roses: I use it to signify my passion. Do we have here, then, only a signifier and a signified, the roses and my passion? Not even that: to put it accurately, there are here only "passionified" roses. But on the plane of analysis, we do have three terms; for these roses weighted with passion perfectly and correctly allow themselves to be decomposed into roses and passion: the former and the latter existed before uniting and forming this third object, which is the sign. It is as true to say that on the plane of experience I cannot dissociate the roses from the message they carry, as to say that on the plane of analysis I cannot confuse the roses as signifier and the roses as sign: the signifier is empty, the sign is full, it is a meaning. Or take a black pebble: I can make it signify in several ways, it is a mere signifier; but if I weigh it with a definite signified (a death sentence, for instance, in an anonymous vote), it will become a sign. Naturally, there are between the signifier, the signified and the sign, functional implications (such as that of the part to the whole) which are so close that to analyse them may seem futile; but we shall see in a moment that this distinction has a capital importance for the study of myth as semiological schema.

Naturally these three terms are purely formal, and different contents can be given to them. Here are a few examples: for Saussure, who worked on a particular but methodologically exemplary semiological system—the language or *langue*—the signified is the concept, the signifier is the acoustic image (which is mental) and the relation between concept and image is the sign (the word, for instance), which is a concrete entity. For Freud, as is well known, the human psyche is a stratification of tokens or representatives. One term (I refrain from giving it any precedence) is constituted by the manifest meaning of behaviour, another, by its latent or real meaning (it is, for instance, the substratum of the dream); as for the third term, it is here also a correlation of the first two: it is the dream itself in its totality, the **parapraxis** (a mistake in speech or behaviour) or the neurosis, conceived as compromises, as economies effected thanks to the joining of a form (the first term) and an intentional function (the second term). We can see here how necessary it is to distinguish the sign from the signifier: a dream, to Freud, is no more its manifest datum than its latent content: it is the functional union of these two terms. In Sartrean criticism, finally (I shall keep to these three well-known examples), the signified is constituted by the original crisis in the subject (the separation from his mother for Baudelaire, the naming of the theft for **Genet**); Literature as discourse forms the signifier; and the relation between crisis and discourse defines the work, which is a signification. Of course, this tri-dimensional pattern, however constant in its form, is actualized in different ways: one cannot therefore say too often that semiology can have its unity only at the level of forms, not contents; its field is limited, it knows only one operation: reading, or deciphering.

In myth, we find again the tri-dimensional pattern which I have just described: the signifier, the signified and the sign. But myth is a peculiar system, in that it is constructed from a semiological chain which existed before it: it is a second-order semiological system. That which is a sign (namely the associative total of a concept and an image) in the first system, becomes a mere signifier in the second. We must here recall that the materials of mythical speech (the language itself, photography, painting, posters, rituals, objects, etc.), however different at the start, are reduced to a pure signifying function as soon as they are caught by myth. Myth sees in them only the same raw material; their unity is that they all come down to the status of a mere language. Whether it deals with alphabetical or pictorial writing, myth wants to see in them only a sum of signs, a global sign, the final term of a first semiological chain. And it is precisely this final term which will become the first term of the greater system which it builds and of which it is only a part. Everything happens as if myth shifted the formal system of the first significations sideways. As this lateral shift is essential for the analysis of myth, I shall represent it in the following way, it being understood, of course, that the spatialization of the pattern is here only a metaphor.

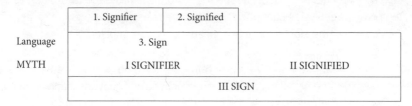

It can be seen that in myth there are two semiological systems, one of which is staggered in relation to the other: a linguistic system, the language (or the modes of representation which are assimilated to it), which I shall call the language-object, because it is the language which myth gets hold of in order to build its own system; and myth itself, which I shall call **metalanguage**, because it is a second language, in which one speaks about the first. When he reflects on a metalanguage, the semiologist no longer needs to ask himself questions about the composition of the language object, he no longer has to take into account the details of the linguistic schema; he will only need to know its total term, or global sign, and only inasmuch as this term lends itself to myth. This is why the semiologist is entitled to treat in the same way writing and pictures: what he retains from them is the fact that they are both signs, that they both reach the threshold of myth endowed with the same signifying function, that they constitute, one just as much as the other, a language-object.

Connections 6b: Barthes and Religion as Critique

One thing we learn from reading scholars like Barthes is that nothing is beyond critique. The broader acceptance of this position by public culture has meant that long power-ful but rarely challenged aspects of our society have come under increased scrutiny. Wrote Sam Anderson on the occasion of the rerelease of Barthes's *Mythologies*, "the thing that's exploding into relevance in our era is not mass culture but the critique of mass culture—the Barthesian dissection of everything, no matter how trivial." But there is more going on here than just critique, he notes. Indeed, "this critical analysis is often as vital and interesting and consumable as the culture it discusses. . . . We seem to be approaching some kind of singularity—a collapse of creativity and criticism into one" (Anderson 2012).

No social institution has been immune. Even as Barthes was writing his analyses, the monopoly on the construction and maintenance of meaning and power enjoyed by institutional religion—in general, and not just one religion in particular—was coming into question. In part due to the horrors of the Second World War, in part because of growing pluralism in Western society, and in part because of the rise of competing sources such as the media-entertainment complex, religious institutions were forced to yield to a growing number of people who were choosing to disaffiliate with religion, as well as a growing critique of religious institutions. Public debates over the very presence of religion in public, engaged by Madalyn Murray O'Hair and American atheists starting in the 1960s and the Freedom From Religion Foundation starting in the late 1970s, were eventually joined by more aggressive anti-religion public intellectuals such as Sam Harris (*End of Faith*, 2004), Richard Dawkins (*The God Delusion*, 2006), and Christopher Hitchens (*God is Not Great*, 2007).

With the beginning of the twenty-first century, a new phenomenon registered on the cultural radar: movements (themselves identified as religions) that sprang—at least in part—from a critique of religion. In 2001, nearly half a million citizens of Australia, Canada, Great Britain, and New Zealand identified themselves as "Jediist" (derived from the *Star Wars* films), many protesting what they considered to be an inappropriate question concerning their religious identity on a Commonwealth census (likely to affirm the status of the national church). Today, "Jediists" are among those who identify themselves as a religion, and for whom governments have made religion-like accommodations. From the biblical prophets to the modern sermon, critique of culture is not new. But these new forms—identified variously by scholars as artificial, farcical, fictitious, or satirical—not only don't seek to be like "real" religions, but they seem to thrive on their novelty.

Over the past few decades, other groups such as Matrixists (derived from the *Matrix* films) and Dudeists (from *The Big Lebowski*, 1998) have emerged, mostly as Internet phenomena, but often with accompanying texts and merchandise, and occasional media-related events. Likely one of the most obviously grounded in cultural critique is the Church of the Flying Spaghetti Monster, founded unintentionally when Bobby Henderson protested the decision of the Kansas State Board of Education to include in the state school curriculum the teaching of Intelligent Design (the notion that the universe's complexities could not possibly have come about by chance or evolution, and needed an intelligence to orchestrate it). Henderson offered to Kansas his own alternative creation narrative: the cosmos had been created by the Flying Spaghetti Monster—a cosmic being evolved from a single-celled organism—and pirates, who were then subjugated by Christian missionaries. Striking a chord, the idea—and the critique it embodied—grew quite popular. Today, several US states (and a few foreign nations) have granted "Pastafarians" the right to perform weddings or wear religious headgear (a colander) in official photos; one man in western New York wore one while taking an oath of office for an elected municipal position.

With the Church of the Flying Spaghetti Monster, as with others, it may no longer be worthwhile to ask whether or not they are "real" religions, a category that is itself subject to critique.

"The Jet-Man"

The jet-man is a jet-pilot. *Match* has specified that he belongs to a new race in aviation, nearer to the robot than to the hero. Yet there are in the jet-man several **Parsifalian** residues, as we shall see shortly. But what strikes one first in the mythology of the jet-man is the elimination of speed: nothing in the legend alludes to this experience. We must here accept a paradox, which is in fact admitted by everyone with the greatest of ease, and even consumed as a proof of modernity. This paradox is that an excess of speed turns into repose. The pilot-hero was made unique by a whole mythology of speed as an experience, of space devoured, of intoxicating motion; the jet-man, on the other hand, is defined by a **coenaesthesis** of motionlessness ("at 2,000 km per hour, in level flight, no impression of speed at all"), as if the extravagance of his vocation precisely consisted in overtaking motion, in going faster than speed. Mythology abandons here a whole imagery of exterior friction and enters pure coenaesthesis: motion is no longer the optical perception of points and surfaces; it has become a kind of vertical disorder, made of contractions, black-outs, terrors and faints; it is no longer a gliding but an inner devastation, an unnatural perturbation, a motionless crisis of bodily consciousness. No wonder if, carried to such a pitch, the myth of the aviator loses all humanism. The hero of classical speed could remain a "gentleman," inasmuch as motion was for him an occasional exploit, for which courage alone was required: one went faster in bursts, like a daring amateur, not like a professional, one sought an 'intoxication,' one came to motion equipped with an age-old moralizing which made its perception keener and enabled one to express its philosophy. It is inasmuch as speed was an adventure that it linked the airman to a whole series of human roles.

The jet-man, on the other hand, no longer seems to know either adventure or destiny, but only a condition. Yet this condition is at first sight less human than anthropological: mythically, the jet-man is defined less by his courage than by his weight, his diet and his habits (temperance, frugality, continence). His racial apartness can be read in his **morphology**: the anti-G suit of inflatable nylon, the shiny helmet, introduce the jet-man into a novel type of skin in which "even his mother would not know him". We are dealing with a true racial conversion, all the more credible since science-fiction has already largely substantiated this metamorphosis of species: everything happens as if there had been a sudden mutation between the earlier creatures of propeller-mankind and the later ones of jet-mankind.

In fact, and in spite of the scientific garb of this new mythology, there has merely been a displacement of the sacred: after the **hagiographic** era (Saints and Martyrs of propeller-aviation) there follows a monastic period; and what passes at first for mere dietetic prescriptions soon appears invested with a **sacerdotal** significance: continence and temperance, abstention and withdrawal from pleasures, community life, uniform clothing— everything concurs, in the mythology of the jet-man, to make manifest the plasticity of the flesh, its submission to collective ends (chastely undefined, by the way), and it is this submission which is offered as a sacrifice to the glamorous singularity of an inhuman condition. Society eventually recognizes, *a propos* of the jet-man, the old **theosophical** pact, which has always compensated power by an ascetic life, paid for semi-divinity in the coin of human "happiness." So truly does the situation of the jet-man comprise the sense of a religious call, that it is itself the reward of previous austerities, of initiatory proceedings, meant to test the **postulant** (passage through the altitude chamber and in the centrifugal machine). Right down to the Instructor, greying, anonymous and inscrutable, who is perfectly suited to the part of the necessary **mystagogue**. As for endurance, we are definitely told that, as is the case in all initiations, it is not physical in nature: triumph in preliminary ordeals is, truth to tell, the fruit of a spiritual gift, one is gifted for jet-flying as others are called to God.

All this would be commonplace if we were dealing with the traditional hero, whose whole value was to fly without forgoing his humanity (like **Saint-Exupéry** who was a writer, or **Lindbergh** who flew in a lounge-suit). But the mythological peculiarity of the jet-man is that he keeps none of the romantic and individualistic elements of the sacred role, without nevertheless forsaking the role itself. Assimilated by his name to pure passivity (what is more inert and more dispossessed than an object expelled in jet form?), he reintegrates the ritual nevertheless, thanks to the myth of a fictitious, celestial race, which is said to derive its peculiarities from its ascetic life, and which effects a kind of anthropological compromise between humans and Martians. The jet-man is a reified hero, as if even today men could conceive the heavens only as populated with semi-objects.

"Plastic"

Despite having names of Greek shepherds (Polystyrene, Polyvinyl, Polyethylene), plastic, the products of which have just been gathered in an exhibition, is in essence the stuff of alchemy. At the entrance of the stand, the public waits in a long queue in order to witness the accomplishment of the magical operation par excellence: the transmutation of matter. An ideally-shaped machine, tubulated and oblong (a shape well suited to suggest the secret of an itinerary) effortlessly draws, out of a heap of greenish crystals, shiny and fluted dressing-room tidies. At one end, raw, **telluric** matter, at the other, the finished, human object; and between these two extremes, nothing; nothing but a transit, hardly watched over by an attendant in a cloth cap, half-god, half-robot.

So, more than a substance, plastic is the very idea of its infinite transformation; as its everyday name indicates, it is ubiquity made visible. And it is this, in fact, which makes it a miraculous substance: a miracle is always a sudden transformation of nature. Plastic remains impregnated throughout with this wonder: it is less a thing than the trace of a movement.

And as the movement here is almost infinite, transforming the original crystals into a multitude of more and more startling objects, plastic is, all told, a spectacle to be deciphered: the very spectacle of its end-products. At the sight of each terminal form (suitcase, brush, car-body, toy, fabric, tube, basin or paper), the mind does not cease from considering the original matter as an enigma. This is because the quick-change artistry of plastic is absolute: it can become buckets as well as jewels. Hence a perpetual amazement, the reverie of man at the sight of the proliferating forms of matter, and the connections he detects between the singular of the origin and the plural of the effects. And this amazement is a pleasurable one, since the scope of the transformations gives man the measure of his power, and since the very itinerary of plastic gives him the euphoria of a prestigious free-wheeling through Nature.

But the price to be paid for this success is that plastic, sublimated as movement, hardly exists as substance. Its reality is a negative one: neither hard nor deep, it must be content with a 'substantial' attribute which is neutral in spite of its utilitarian advantages: resistance, a state which merely means an absence of yielding. In the hierarchy of the major poetic substances, it figures as a disgraced material, lost between the effusiveness of rubber and the flat hardness of metal; it embodies none of the genuine produce of the mineral world: foam, fibres, strata. It is a "shaped" substance: whatever its final state, plastic keeps a **flocculent** appearance, something opaque, creamy and curdled, something powerless ever to achieve the triumphant smoothness of Nature. But what best reveals it for what it is is the sound it gives, at once hollow and flat; its noise is its undoing, as are its colors, for it seems capable of retaining only the most chemical looking ones. Of yellow, red and green, it keeps only the aggressive quality, and uses them as mere names, being able to display only concepts of colors.

The fashion for plastic highlights an evolution in the myth of "imitation" materials. It is well known that their use is historically **bourgeois** in origin (the first **vestimentary postiches** date back to the rise of capitalism). But until now imitation materials have always indicated pretension, they belonged to the world of appearances, not to that of actual use; they aimed at reproducing cheaply the rarest substances, diamonds, silk, feathers, furs, silver, all the luxurious brilliance of the world. Plastic has climbed down, it is a household material. It is the first magical substance which consents to be prosaic. But it is precisely because this prosaic character is a triumphant reason for its existence: for the first time, artifice aims at something common, not rare. And as an immediate consequence, the age-old function of nature is modified: it is no longer the Idea, the pure Substance to be regained or imitated: an artificial Matter, more bountiful than all the natural deposits, is about to replace her, and to determine the very invention of forms. A luxurious object is still of this earth, it still recalls, albeit in a precious mode, its mineral or animal origin, the natural theme of which it is but one actualization. Plastic is wholly swallowed up in the fact of being used: ultimately, objects will be invented for the sole pleasure of using them. The hierarchy of substances is abolished: a single one replaces them all: the whole world can be plasticized, and even life itself since, we are told, they are beginning to make plastic aortas.

Glossary

BACHELARD, Gaston (1884–1962): French philosopher interested in history and the philosophy of science.

ASCESIS: the practice of strict self-discipline, often for religious reasons.

ALEXANDROV, Georgy (1908–61): Soviet propagandist in the years leading up to the Second World War.

BAUDELAIRE, Charles: (1821–67): French poet and writer.

BOURGEOIS: referring to the economic middle-class, often with disdain for its members' ethics and social practices.

COENAESTHESIS: full integration of the senses, a total awareness of one's own body.

DIALECTICAL: often meant to imply the relation of opposites, it also suggests their related interaction.

DISCOURSE: communication beyond simple conversation, which may include language, signs, or symbols.

DROUET, Marie-Noëlle "Minou" (1947–): French poet and writer.

EIDETIC: referring to strong, realistic mental images.

ENGELS, Friedrich (1820–95): German philosopher, cofounder (with Karl Marx [1818–83]) of modern communism, coauthor (with Marx) of *The Communist Manifesto* (1869).

ETYMOLOGY: the study of word origins and changing meanings.

FLOCCULENT: loosely clumped, like tufts of wool or cotton bolls.

GENET, Jean (1910–86): French author and playwright.

HAGIOGRAPHIC: traditionally a saint's biography, often used to describe uncritically admiring accounts or descriptions.

LEXIS: a complete vocabulary.

LINDBERGH, Charles (1902–74): American pilot, first to fly non-stop from Long Island, New York, to Paris, France (1927).

METALANGUAGE: a language or terminology used to describe other languages.

METAPHYSICAL: related to or referring to the supernatural, or to a reality beyond the known or perceived.

MORPHOLOGY: the study of the form and structure of things.

MYSTAGOGUE: one who teaches or endorses the mystical.

PARAPRAXIS: a written, spoken, or behavioral error thought to reveal unconscious intention.

PARSIFALIAN: referring to *Parsifal*, the 1882 opera by German composer Richard Wagner (1813–83), and the quest for the Holy Grail by Percival, a knight of King Arthur's court, upon which it is loosely based.

POSTICHES: additional, as to excess.

POSTULANT: an initiate into a religious order.

QUIPU: knotted cords used as method of recording information or narratives.

QUIXOTISM: practice of impulsive or impractical acts.

SACERDOTAL: of or relating to the priesthood, their doctrine, or practices.

SAINT-EXUPÉRY, Antoine de (1900–44): French pilot and writer, author of *Le Petit Prince* (*The Little Prince*, 1943).

SAINT-GENET: Play written by Jean-Paul Sartre about Jean Genet.

SARTRE, Jean-Paul (1905–80): French philosopher and writer.

SAUSSURE, Ferdinand de (1857–1913): Swiss linguist.

SEMIOLOGY: The analysis of systems of signs or symbols as conveyors of meaning.

SIGNIFICATION/SIGNIFYING/SIGNIFIER/SIGNIFIED: The process by which people create signs to convey meaning by bringing together a **SIGNIFIER** (an image, symbol, or representative form that stands for something else) and a **SIGNIFIED** (that for which the signifier stands), as with language, images, or objects.

STRUCTURALISM: a method for understanding the meaning of cultural elements by examining their relationships to other elements within a larger system of meaning creation.

TELLURIC: earthy, from the earth.

THEOSOPHICAL: referring to a form of special or divine knowledge or relationship.

VESTIMENTARY: related to clothing, often of a ritual sort.

ZHDANOV, Andrei Alexandrovich (1896–1948): Soviet leader of ideological purges after the Second World War.

Questions for Conversation

Barthes boldly asserts that potentially "everything is a myth" and thus the universe is "infinitely fertile." What might he mean by this?

What does Barthes mean by asserting that "myth" and "meaning" are chosen by history and thus do not arise from nature?

Why does Barthes call myth a "second order" semiological system?

What are signifier, signified, and sign in Barthes's semiological system? How do they relate to his notion of "myth"?

How is the Jet-Man a myth? What does this myth have to do with religion?

How is plastic like "alchemy"? What powers does it give to humanity?

What is the price of plastic? What is threatened or lost by the increasing use of plastic products and building materials?

Suggestions for Additional Reading

The following is a list of supplemental readings that provide additional information about, apply, or respond critically to the ideas presented in this chapter.

Alderton, Zoe. "'Snapewives' and 'Snapeism': A Fiction-Based Religion within the Harry Potter Fandom," *Religions* 5, no. 1 (2014): 219–67.

Anderson, Sam. "No Power, a Little Knowledge, a Little Wisdom and as Much Flavor as Possible," *New York Times* (May 27, 2012): Sunday Magazine 44.

Barthes, Roland. *Elements of Semiology*. New York: Hill and Wang, 1968.

Barthes, Roland. *Mythologies*, trans. Annette Lavers. New York: Hill and Wang, 1972.

Barthes, Roland, and Lionel Duisit. "An Introduction to the Structural Analysis of Narrative," *New Literary History* 6, no. 2 (Winter 1975): 237–72.

Beller, Jonathan. "*Camera Obscura* After All: The Racist Writing with Light," *The Scholar and Feminist Online* 10 (2012). Available online: http://sfonline.barnard.edu/feminist-media-theory/camera-obscura-after-all-the-racist-writing-with-light/0/ (accessed January 14, 2021).

Broadfoot, Keith. "Barthes Religious Substance: Photography and Acheiropoietos," *Image and Narrative* 13, no. 3 (2012): 141–54.

Brody, Richard. "The Uses of *Mythologies*," *New Yorker* (April 19, 2012). Available online: https://www.newyorker.com/culture/richard-brody/the-uses-of-mythologies (accessed October 29, 2017).

de Certeau, Michel. *The Practice of Everyday Life*, trans. Steven Rendall. Berkeley: University of California Press, 1984.

Grad, Iulia. "Religion, Advertising and Production of Meaning," *Journal for the Study of Religions and Ideologies* 13 (2014): 137–54.

Hardin, Michael. "Was the Killing of the Queer Author Necessary to Liberate the Queer Text?: The Case of Andy Warhol's *A: A Novel*," *Journal of Homosexuality* 56 (2009): 218–32.

Jenkins, Henry. *Textual Poachers: Television Fans and Participatory Culture*. New York: Routledge, 1992.

Jindra, Michael. "Star Trek Fandom as a Religious Phenomenon," *Sociology of Religion* 55, no. 1 (1994): 27–51.

Knight, Diana. "Barthes and Orientalism," *New Literary History* 24 (1993): 617–33.

Murphy, Tim. "Elements of a Semiotic Theory of Religion," *Method & Theory in the Study of Religion* 15 (2003): 48–67.

Thompson, Craig, and Kelly Tian. "Reconstructing the South: How Commercial Myths Compete for Identity Value through the Ideological Shaping of Popular Memories and Countermemories," *Journal of Consumer Research* 34 (2008): 595–613.

7   Victor W. Turner

Victor Turner (1920–83) was a British anthropologist best known for interpreting and theorizing ritual processes, most especially rites of passage undertaken by social groups at crucial periods of life-cycle transition. Born in Scotland, Turner studied poetry and classics as an undergraduate at University College London before service in the Second World War. Later he pursued graduate study in social anthropology, eventually landing at the University of Manchester, where his notable influences included the structural-functionalist orientation of British anthropology, his mentor Max Gluckman, and the ritual studies of ethnographer and folklorist, Arnold van Gennep. Turner's early field work focused on the Ndembu tribe found in present-day Zambia. This eventually resulted in two monographs, *The Forest of Symbols: Aspects of Ndembu Ritual* (1967) and *Schism and Continuity in an African Society* (1968), plus the theoretical work that would become his most influential, *The Ritual Process: Structure and Anti-Structure* (1969).

Turner spent most of his professional career in the United States, including professorships at Cornell and the University of Chicago, where he often worked in tandem with his wife Edith. He was an excellent lecturer known for his ability to make connections between diverse topics across academic disciplines. He regularly included philosophical content and literary references in his teaching of social anthropology. A convert to Catholicism, he eventually extended his fieldwork to Mexico, Ireland, Japan, Brazil, and the experimental theater groups in New York City, focusing on ritual processes, pilgrimages, carnivals, and varied forms of theatrical performance. These resulted in numerous essays and books, including *Dramas, Fields, and Metaphors: Symbolic Action in Human Society* (1974) and *From Ritual to Theatre: The Human Seriousness of Play* (1982).

The following excerpt, from *The Forest of Symbols*, outlines Turner's expansive understanding of the rites of passage, most especially his detailed interpretation of the middle, or "liminal," phase, as a rejection of normal social structures (which later he would call "anti-structure") that in so doing created a powerful sense of community bonding (later called "communitas") and facilitated the learning of religious knowledge ("communication of the sacra"). Some critics later questioned whether or not Turner had overextended his model by making rites of passage into a kind of universal archetype, applicable almost everywhere, and thus was neglectful of particular political and historical forces. Others, like John Eade and Michael Sallnow (1991), challenged his rather idealistic reading of the enthusiastic social bonding of ritual processes, finding in many situations a far messier reality that often creates divisions and conflicts. Nonetheless, Turner's ideas have been and remain generative, most especially as they have shaped the interpretation of broadly "liminal" forms of popular culture in which there is a conspicuous element of "anti-structure," as with carnivals and festivals.

In more subtle ways his work also suggests that some forms of popular culture can be interpreted as vicarious modes of accessing the liminal. Thus folkloric stories, character arcs in dramas and films, and a wide range of live performances, evoke in readers, watchers, and live audiences something akin to the experiences of initiands in rites of passage.

"Betwixt and Between: The Liminal Period in *Rites De Passages*" (1967)[1]

Rites de passage are found in all societies but tend to reach their maximal expression in small-scale, relatively stable and cyclical societies, where change is bound up with biological and meteorological rhythms and recurrences rather than with technological innovations. Such rites indicate and constitute *transitions between states*. By "state" I mean here "a relatively fixed or stable condition," and would include in its meaning such social constancies as legal status, profession, office or calling, rank or degree. I also hold it to designate the condition of a person as determined by his culturally recognized degree of maturation as when one speaks of "the married or single state" or the "state of infancy." The term "state" may also be applied to ecological condition, or to the physical, mental or emotional condition in which a person or group may be found at a particular time. Thus a man may be in a state of good or bad health; a society in a state of war or peace or a state of famine or of plenty. State, in short, is a more inclusive concept than status or office, and refers to any type of stable or recurrent condition that is culturally recognized. [...]

[...] **Van Gennep** has shown that all rites of transition are marked by three phases: separation, margin (or *limen*), and aggregation. The first phase of separation comprises symbolic behavior signifying the detachment of the individual or group either from an earlier fixed point in the social structure or a set of cultural conditions (a "state"); during the intervening "liminal" period the state of the ritual subject (the "passenger") is ambiguous; he passes through a realm which has few or none of the attributes of the past or coming state; in the third phase the passage is consummated. The ritual subject, individual or corporate, is in a stable state once more and, by virtue of this has rights and obligations of a clearly defined and "structural" type, and is expected to behave in accordance with certain customary norms and ethical standards. The most prominent type of *rites de passage* tends to accompany what **Lloyd Warner** has called "the movement of a man through his lifetime, from a fixed placental placement within the mother's womb to his death and ultimate fixed point of his tombstone and final containment in his grave as a dead organism—punctuated by a number of critical moments of transition which all societies ritualize and publicly mark with suitable observances to impress the significance of the individual and the group on living members of the community. These are the important time of birth, puberty, marriage, and death." But as van Gennep, [...] and others have shown, *rites de passage* are not confined to culturally defined life-crises but may accompany any change from one state to another, as when a whole tribe goes to war, or when it attests to the passage from scarcity to plenty by performing a first-fruits or

[1]Victor W. Turner, excerpt from "Betwixt and Between: The Liminal Period in *Rites de Passage*," *The Proceedings of the American Ethnological Society* (1964): 4–17.

a harvest festival. *Rites de passage*, too, are not restricted, sociologically speaking, to movements between *ascribed* statuses. They also concern entry into a new *achieved* status, whether this be a political office or membership of an exclusive club or secret society. Or they may admit persons into membership of a religious group where such a group does not include the whole society, or qualify them for the official duties of a cult, sometimes in a graded series of rites.

[...]

The subject of passage ritual is, in the liminal period, structurally, if not physically, "invisible." As members of society most of us only see what we expect to see, and what we expect to see is what we are conditioned to see when we have learned the definitions and classifications of our culture. A society's secular definitions do not allow for the existence of a not-boy-not-man, which is what a novice in a male puberty rite is (if he can be said to *be* anything). But a set of essentially *religious* definitions co-exist with these, which *do* set out to define the structurally indefinable "transitional-being." The transitional-being or "liminal *persona*" is defined by a name and by a set of symbols. The same name is very frequently employed to designate those who are being initiated into very different states of life. [...] Our own terms "initiate" and "**neophyte**" have a similar breadth of reference. It would seem from this that emphasis tends to be laid on the transition itself, rather than on the particular states between which it is taking place.

The symbolism attached to and surrounding the liminal *persona* is complex and bizarre. Much of it is modeled on human biological processes, which are conceived to be what **Levi-Strauss** might call "**isomorphic**" with structural and cultural processes. They give an outward and visible form to an inward and conceptual process. The structural "invisibility" of liminal *personae* has a twofold character. They are at once *no longer* classified *and not* yet classified. In so far as they are no longer classified the symbols that represent them are, in many societies, drawn from the biology of death, decomposition, **katabolism**, and other physical processes which have a negative tinge, such as menstruation (frequently regarded as the absence or loss of a fetus). [...] The metaphor of dissolution is often applied to neophytes—they are allowed to go filthy and identified with the earth, the generalized matter into which every specific individual is rendered down. Particular form here becomes general matter—often their very names are taken from them and each is called solely by the generic term for "neophyte" or "**initiand**."

The other aspect, that they are *not yet* classified, is often expressed in symbols modeled on processes of gestation and **parturition**. The neophytes are likened to or treated as embryos, new-born infants, or sucklings by symbolic means which vary from culture to culture. I shall return to this theme presently.

But the essential feature of these symbolizations is that the neophytes are *neither* living *nor* dead from one aspect and *both* living *and* dead from another. Their condition is one of ambiguity and paradox, a confusion of all the customary categories. **Jakob Boehme**, the German mystic whose obscure writings gave **Hegel** his celebrated dialectical "triad," liked to say that "In Yea and Nay all things consist." Liminality may perhaps be regarded as the Nay to all positive structural assertions, but as in some sense the source of them all, and, more than that, as a realm of pure possibility whence *novel* configurations of ideas and relations may arise. [...]

Dr. **Mary Douglas**, of University College, London, has recently advanced (in an as yet unpublished book on pollution notions) the very interesting and illuminating view that the concept of pollution "is a reaction to protect cherished principles and categories from contradiction." She holds that, in effect, what is unclear and contradictory (from the perspective of social definition) tends to be regarded as (ritually) unclean. The unclear is the unclean: e.g., she examines the prohibitions on eating certain animals and crustaceans in Leviticus in the light of this hypothesis (these being creatures that cannot be unambiguously classified in terms of traditional criteria). From this standpoint, one would expect to find that transitional-beings are particularly polluting, since they are neither one thing nor another, or may be both, or neither here nor there and may even be nowhere (in terms of any recognized cultural **topography**), and are at the very least "betwixt and between" all the recognized fixed points in space-time of structural classification. And in fact, in confirmation of Dr. Douglas's hypothesis, liminal *personae* nearly always and everywhere are regarded as polluting to those who have never been, so to speak, "inoculated" against them, through having been themselves initiated into the same state. I think that we may perhaps usefully discriminate here between the Statics and Dynamics of pollution situations. In other words, we may have to distinguish between pollution notions which concern *states* that have been ambiguously or contradictorily *defined*, and those which derive from ritualized *transitions* between states. In the first case, we are dealing with what has been defectively defined or ordered, in the second with what cannot be defined in static terms. We are not dealing with structural *contradictions* when we discuss liminality, but with the essentially unstructured (which is at once *de*structured and *pre*-structured) and often the people themselves see this in terms of bringing neophytes into close connection with deity or with superhuman power, with what is, in fact, often regarded as the *un*bounded, the *in*finite, the limit*less*. Since neophytes are not only structurally "invisible" (though physically visible) and ritually polluting, they are very commonly *secluded*, partially or completely, from the realm of culturally defined and ordered states and statuses. Often the indigenous term for the liminal period is [...] the *locative* form of a noun meaning "seclusion site" [...]. The are sometimes said to "be in another place." Neophytes have physical but not social "reality," hence they have to be hidden, since it is a paradox, a scandal, to see what ought not to be there! Where they are not removed to a sacred place of concealment they are often *disguised*—in masks or grotesque costumes or striped with white, red or black clay and the like. [...]

Connections 7a: Turner and Liminal Raving

Victor Turner's theorizing of ritual processes in his anthropological work in small-scale societies led him to later explore how "liminoid" qualities can be found in things like Christian pilgrimages (see Chapter 18 ["Where We Go"]) and theatrical dramas. This work would inform a field called *performance studies*, which explores the sources, contents, and sociopolitical implications of varied types of performances, including those from religion, arts, political movements, sports, and other forms of collective activity involving dramatic actions, play, and dynamic interactions between performers and audiences. Turner and other performance scholars recognized that for many modern societies, play had become a very serious matter, often revealing more about a culture than its economic activities or traditional social institutions. Among the scholars who have taken up Turner's theories and applied them to contemporary cultural movements is Graham St John who studies electronic dance music culture (EDMC) found at raves, clubs, music festivals, and other collective music "scenes." These events can be quite ephemeral, often "popping up" and dissolving quite quickly, as musical tastes shift and participants push the limits of licit activities. Nonetheless, there seems to be a core set of characteristics—young people coming together to dance and party to music with a strong beat overseen by a DJ who creatively mixes musical genres to sustain positive emotions and communal feelings of connection. Also, although some scenes are quite localized and self-consciously "tribal" in character, the overarching trend has been toward globalization, particularly with the advent of social media platforms that allow sharing of ideas and musical forms. In one of his studies of "trance tribes" that emerged in the 1990s around a particular genre of dance music, St John finds Turner's theories still potent:

> [T]he ethnography of those moments beyond, beneath, and between the fixed, the finished, and the predictable lends great insight into culture in its moments of (re)constitution. As a recreational pursuit enabling participants to be "out there," "loved up," or "in the zone," EDMCs are intriguing manifestations of liminality in the present. (St John 2008: 150)

St John goes on to explore how these "highly mobile and technologically savvy spiritual counterculture[s]" reflect ambivalences about freedom and identity in late capitalist societies, particularly those related to the tension between work and leisure. As more people, particularly those coming into adulthood, have time and resources to explore experimental lifestyles and fluid identities, EDMCs emerge as a collective form of ritual in which participants hope to (in Turner's words) "obtain a flash of lucid mutual understanding on the existential level, when they feel that all problems, not just their problems, could be resolved" (quoted in St John 2008: 149).

Already we have noted how certain liminal processes are regarded as analogous to those of gestation, parturition, and suckling. Undoing, dissolution, decomposition are accompanied by processes of growth, transformation and the reformulation of old elements in new patterns. It is interesting to note how by the principle of the *economy (or **parsimony**) of symbolic reference* logically antithetical processes of death and growth may be represented by the *same* tokens—e.g. by huts and tunnels which are at once tombs and wombs, by lunar symbolism (for the same moon waxes and wanes), by snake symbolism (for the snake appears to die, but only to shed its old skin and appear in a new one), by bear symbolism (for the bear "dies" in autumn and is "reborn" in spring), by nakedness (which is at once the mark of a new-born infant and a corpse prepared for burial) and by innumerable other symbolic formations and actions. This coincidence of opposite processes and notions in a single representation characterizes the peculiar unity of the liminal: that which is *neither* this *nor* that, and yet is *both*.

I have spoken of the *inter*-structural character of the liminal. But, in fact, between neophytes and their instructors (where these exist), and connecting neophytes with one another, exists a set of relations which compose a "social structure" of highly specific type.

It is a structure of a very simple kind: *between* instructors and neophytes there is often complete authority and complete submission; *among* neophytes there is often complete equality. Between incumbents of positions in secular politico-jural systems there exist intricate and situationally shifting networks of rights and duties proportioned to their rank, status and corporate affiliation. There are many different *kinds* of privileges and obligations; many *degrees* of *super*ordination and *sub*ordination. In the liminal period such distinctions and gradations tend to be eliminated. But it must be understood that the authority of the elders over the neophytes is not based on legal sanctions; it is in a sense the personification of the self-evident authority of tradition. The authority of the elders is absolute because it represents the absolute, the axiomatic values of society in which are expressed the "common good" and the common interest. And the essence of the complete obedience of the neophytes is to submit to the elders but only in so far as they are in charge, so to speak, of *the common good* and represent in their persons the total community. That the authority in question is really quintessential tradition emerges clearly in societies where initiations are not collective but individual and where there are no instructors or *gurus*. [...] A normal man acts abnormally because he is obedient to tribal tradition, not out of disobedience to it. He does not evade but fulfills his duties as a citizen.

But if complete obedience characterizes the relationship of neophyte to elder, complete equality usually characterizes the relationship of neophyte to neophyte, where the rites are collective. This *comradeship* must be distinguished from *brotherhood* or *sibling-ship*, since in the latter relation there is always the inequality of older and younger, which often achieves linguistic representation and may be maintained by legal sanctions. The liminal group is a community or **comity** of comrades and not a structure of hierarchically arrayed positions. This comradeship transcends distinctions of rank, age, kinship position, and, in some kinds of cultic group, even of sex. [...]

This comradeship, with its familiarity, ease and, I would add, mutual outspokenness, is once more the product of inter-structural liminality, with its scarcity of jurally-sanctioned relationships and its emphasis on axiomatic values expressive of the **common weal**. People can "be themselves" it is frequently said, when they are not acting institutionalized roles. Roles, too, carry responsibilities and in the liminal situation the main burden of responsibility is borne by the elders, leaving the neophytes free to develop interpersonal relationships as they will. They confront one another, as it were, integrally and not in compartmentalized fashion as actors of roles.

The passivity of neophytes to their instructors, their malleability, which is increased by submission to ordeal, their reduction to a uniform condition, are signs of the process whereby they are ground down to be fashioned anew and endowed with additional powers to cope with their new station in life. [...] The arcane knowledge or "*gnosis*" obtained in the liminal period is felt to change the inmost nature of the neophyte, impressing him, as a seal impresses wax, with the characteristics of his new state. It is not a mere acquisition of knowledge, but a change in being. His apparent passivity is revealed as an *absorption* of powers which will become active after his social status has been redefined in the aggregation rites.

The structural simplicity of the liminal situation in many initiations is offset by its cultural complexity. I can only touch on one aspect of this vast subject matter here and raise three problems in connection with it. This aspect is the vital one of the *communication of the sacra*, the heart of the liminal matter.

[…T]his communication of the *sacra* has three main components. By and large this threefold classification holds good for initiation rites all over the world. *Sacra* may be communicated as: (1) exhibitions, "what is shown"; (2) actions, "what is done"; and (3) instructions, "what is said."

Connections 7b: Turner, Religion, Sports, and Digital Gaming

Turner's efforts to find modern parallels to the ritual processes of traditional societies led him to develop an elaborate theory of the "liminoid," or the ways that liminal activities survive (even prosper) in modern societies. For Turner, liminoid activities are interwoven with work, play, and leisure, often in ways that emphasize public spectacles. Akin to liminal rituals, these can defy normalcy, invert expectations and hierarchies, and yet they retain a sense of overall direction or ritual purpose. Very importantly, they create a powerful sense of union among the participants (often strangers) that can be compared to the "communitas" found in rites of passage. Turner explored how the liminoid infuses theatrical productions, modern forms of art, and, perhaps most influential to popular culture, various forms of play like sports and gaming.

The study of play has a long history. In his classic work, *Homo Ludens* (1938), cultural theorist Johan Huizinga argued that play deeply influences human culture, including things such as language, poetry, art, law, warfare, and philosophical debate. In general terms, play is about freedom, can be distinguished from ordinary life, is governed by rules, and is not apparently done for material or economic benefits. Later thinkers noted that many games seem to create their own imagined worlds, set apart from everyday life, and governed by their own rules. These, of course, suggest a kind of religious character to games, as playing them compares to the rules and rituals enacted by groups in devotion to their sacred ideals or totems.

Building upon these basic insights, many scholars have explored the varied relationships between religion and modern sports. These include studies of the ascetic and magical practices done to secure better performances, the quasi-mystical "flow" experiences achieved by some athletes while training or competing, ethical considerations of sports arising from various religious traditions, the powerful sense of community and identity created by fans routing for their favorite teams, the hero-worship of famous athletes, the pastoral dimensions of coaching, the fervent nationalism inspired by international competitions like the Olympics and the World Cup, and many, many other topics. Theories and methods used by these scholars vary, but all challenge the general notion that modern sports are resolutely secularized. Instead, they find varieties of religious experiences shaping the preparations, performances, and spectatorship of modern sports.

The rise of digital gaming as a major dimension of popular culture has also been of interest to scholars of religion, who have documented a rich arena with all manner of liminoid activities including play, myth, magic, ritual, gods, and monsters. Some games are explicitly designed to recreate worlds with religious content, including imaginative historical landscapes infused with magical forces, post-apocalyptic dystopias, journeys to heaven or hell, and many others. Players in many of the most popular games create "avatars" or other enhanced characters that have superhuman powers in the context of the games. Many of these powers echo the supernaturalism in more traditional folklore and religious myth—flight, strength, battle skill, rapid healing, spell-casting, bodily transformations, etc. To study these things, scholars have looked at the content of games, noting where they employ symbols or narratives found in religious traditions, as well as the experiences of players who follow rules to gain mastery over successive layers of complexity. Often this means battling against antagonists, figuring out puzzles, mastering complex maneuvers, collaborating with other players, or other challenges. Because the violence is pervasive in many games, they have been controversial and have elicited calls for ethical oversight, including legal regulation and content ratings comparable to other modern media. Various studies have also examined the communities that formed in connection with some of the more popular games, and the social dynamics of the burgeoning interest in formalized competitions, or eSports. Of particular interest are religious groups that now encourage the creation of games that teach their values, often by virtually reconstructing scenes from scriptures.

"Exhibitions" would include *evocatory instruments* or *sacred articles*, such as relics of deities, heroes or ancestors, aboriginal *churingas*, sacred drums or other musical instruments, the contents of Amerindian medicine bundles, and the fan, **cist** and **tympanum** of Greek and Near Eastern mystery cults. [...] Other *sacra* include *masks*, *images*, *figurines*, and *effigies*; [...] In some kinds of initiation [...], *pictures* and *icons* representing the journeys of the dead or the adventures of supernatural beings may be shown to the initiands. A striking feature of such *sacred articles* is often their formal simplicity. It is their interpretation which is complex, not their outward form.

Among the "instructions" received by neophytes may be reckoned such matters as the *revelation of the real*, but secularly secret, *names of the deities* or spirits believed to preside over the rites [...] They are also taught the main outlines of the **theogony**, **cosmogony** and mythical history of their societies or cults, usually with reference to the *sacra* exhibited. Great importance is attached to keeping secret the nature of the *sacra*, the formulae chanted and instructions given about them. These constitute the crux of liminality, for while instruction is also given in ethical and social obligations, in law and in kinship rules, and in technology to fit neophytes for the duties of future office, no interdiction is placed on knowledge thus imparted since it tends to be current among uninitiated persons only.

[...]

In discussing the structural aspect of liminality I mentioned how neophytes are withdrawn from their structural positions and consequently from the values, norms, sentiments and techniques associated with those positions. They are also divested of their previous habits of thought, feeling and action. During the liminal period neophytes are alternately forced and encouraged to think about their society, their cosmos and the powers that generate and sustain them. Liminality may be partly described as a stage of reflection. In it those ideas, sentiments and facts that had been hitherto for the neophytes bound up in configurations and accepted unthinkingly are, as it were, resolved into their constituents. These constituents are isolated and made into objects of reflection for the neophytes by such processes as *componential exaggeration* and *dissociation by varying concomitants*. The communication of *sacra* and other forms of **esoteric** instruction really involve three processes, though these should not be regarded as in series but as in parallel. The first is *the reduction of* *culture into recognized components or factors*; the second is their *recombination in fantastic or monstrous patterns and shapes*; and the third is their *recombination in ways that make sense with regard to the new state and status* which the neophytes will enter.

The second process, monster- or fantasy-making, focuses attention on the components of the masks and effigies, which are so radically ill-assorted that they stand out and can be thought about. The monstrosity of the configuration throws its elements into relief. Put a man's head on a lion's body and you think about the human head in the abstract. Perhaps it becomes for you, as a member of a given culture and with the appropriate guidance, an emblem of chieftanship. Or it may be explained as representing the soul as against the body. Or intellect as contrasted with brute force. Or innumerable other things. But there could be less encouragement to reflect on heads and headship if that same head were firmly ensconced on its familiar, its all too familiar, human body. The man-lion monster also encourages the observer to think about *lions*, their habits, qualities, metaphorical properties, religious significance, and so on. More important than these, the *relation* between man and lion, empirical and metaphorical, may be speculated upon, and *new* ideas developed on this topic. Liminality here breaks, as it were, the cake of custom and enfranchises speculation. [...] Liminality is the realm of primitive hypothesis, where there is a certain freedom to juggle with the factors of existence. As in the works of **Rabelais**, there is a promiscuous intermingling and juxtaposing of the categories of event, experience and knowledge, with a **pedagogic** intention.

But this liberty has fairly narrow limits. The neophytes return to secular society, with more alert faculties perhaps and enhanced knowledge of "how things work," but they have one more to become subject to custom and law. [...] [T]hey are shown that alternative ways of acting and thinking to those laid down by the deities or ancestors are ultimately unworkable and may have disastrous consequences.

Moreover, in initiation, there are usually held to be certain *axiomatic principles* of construction, and certain basic building blocks which make up the cosmos, and into whose nature no neophyte may inquire. Certain *sacra*, usually exhibited in the most arcane episodes of the liminal period, represent, or may be interpreted in terms of these axiomatic principles and primordial constituents. Perhaps we may call these *sacerrima*, "most sacred things." Sometimes they are interpreted by a myth about the world-making activities of supernatural beings "at the beginning of things." Myths may be completely absent, however [...] This use of an aspect of human physiology as a model for social, cosmic, and religious ideas and processes is a variant of a widely distributed initiation theme: that the human body is a microcosm of the universe. The body may be pictured as androgynous, as male or female, or in terms of one or other of its developmental stages, as child, mature adult and elder. On the other hand [...], certain of its properties may be abstracted. Whatever the mode of representation the body is regarded as a sort of symbolic template for the communication of *gnosis*, mystical knowledge, about the nature of things and how they came to be what they are. The cosmos may in some cases be regarded as a vast human body; in other belief systems visible parts of the body may be taken to portray invisible faculties such as reason, passion, wisdom and so on; in others again, the different parts of the social order are arrayed in terms of a human anatomical paradigm.

Whatever the precise mode of explaining reality by the body's attributes, *sacra* which illustrate this are always regarded as absolutely **sacrosanct**, as ultimate mysteries. We are here in the realm of what Warner would call *non-rational or non-logical symbols* which

> arise out of the basic individual and cultural assumptions, more often unconscious than not, from which most social action springs. They supply the solid core of mental and emotional life of each individual and group. This does not mean that they are irrational or maladaptive, or that man cannot often think in a reasonable way about them, but rather that they do not have their source in his rational processes. When they come into play, such factors as data, evidence, proof, and the facts and procedures of rational thought in action are apt to be secondary or unimportant.

The central cluster of non-logical *sacra* is then the symbolic template of the whole system of beliefs and values in a given culture, its archetypal paradigm and ultimate measure. Neophytes shown these are often told that they are in presence of forms established from the beginning of things. [...] I have used the metaphor of a seal or stamp in connection with the **ontological** character ascribed in many initiations to arcane knowledge. The term "archetype" denotes in Greek a master stamp or impress, and these *sacra*, presented with a **numinous** simplicity, stamp into the neophytes the basic assumptions of their culture. The neophytes are told also that they are being filled with mystical power by what they see and what they are told about it. According to the purpose of the initiation this power confers on them capacities to undertake successfully the tasks of their new office, in this world or the next.

Thus, the communication of *sacra* both teaches the neophytes how to think with some degree of abstraction about their cultural milieu and gives them ultimate standards of reference. At the same time it is believed to change their nature, transform them from one kind of human being into another. It intimately united man and office. But for a variable while there was an uncommitted man, an individual rather than a social *persona*, in a sacred community of individuals.

Glossary

BOEHME, Jakob (1575–1624): German mystic.
KATABOLISM: the biological process of the chemical breakdown of organisms.
CHURINGAS: sacred objects, made of wood or stone.
CIST: a coffin or box for sacred objects
COMITY: an association of mutual benefit.
COMMON WEAL: the common good.
CONCOMITANTS: events or phenomena that follow in succession.
COSMOGONY: referring or related to the origin of the universe.
DOUGLAS, MARY (1921–2007): British anthropologist, author of *Purity and Danger* (1966).
ESOTERIC: understood by, or intended for, a select few.
HEGEL, Georg Wilhelm Friedrich (1770–1831): German philosopher of history, argued that progress was the synthesis of dialectical (opposite-yet-related) forces.
INITIAND: a person who is about to be, or is in the process of being, initiated.

ISOMORPHIC: similar or identical in structure or form.

LÉVI-STRAUSS, Claude (1908–2009): French anthropologist, advocate of structuralism, or the notion that shared patterns found across different cultures reflect structures common in the human mind.

NEOPHYTE: a beginner, novice, or one new to a skill or circumstance.

NUMINOUS: of, or containing, sacred powers suggestive of divinity.

ONTOLOGICAL: knowledge of or related to the nature of being.

PARSIMONY: frugality; the lack of willingness to expend financial or material resources.

PARTURITION: childbirth.

PEDAGOGIC: related to teaching or educational purpose.

RABELAIS, François (1494–1553): French author and Catholic priest.

SACROSANCT: an item, place, idea, or action that is too important to be altered or interrupted.

THEOGONY: referring or related to the origin or birth of gods.

TOPOGRAPHY: the physical or figurative features of a place or idea.

TYMPANUM: a hand-drum instrument, similar to the modern tambourine.

VAN GENNEP, Arnold (1873–1957): Franco-German anthropologist, author of *The Rites of Passage* (1909).

WARNER, W. Lloyd (1898–1970): American anthropologist and sociologist, author of *The Living and the Dead* (1959).

Questions for Conversation

What are the three stages of a typical rite of passage, and what characterizes each one?

How do concerns about purity relate to the liminal stage of rites?

How is the liminal stage analogous to natural processes like gestation and growth? How is the liminal stage analogous to educational processes?

How does the *communication of the sacra* unfold in a three-part process in the liminal stage? Why are initiands seen as particularly open to religious instruction at that time?

Why is the symbolism of the liminal stage often "complex and bizarre" and "monstrous"?

Why are some symbols especially "sacrosanct" and thus "nonrational" and "nonlogical"?

What is the role of the "elders" in rites of passage, especially in relation to tradition and social authority?

How does liminality encourage learning, including learning via speculation and creativity?

How does the human body figure into the sacred knowledge imparted via rite of passage?

After completing a rite of passage, what does the participant gain?

How can liminality be both the rejection of structural possibilities and "the source of them all"?

Suggestions for Additional Reading

The following is a list of supplemental readings that provide additional information about, apply, or respond critically to the ideas presented in this chapter.

Alexander, Bobby C. *Victor Turner Revisited: Ritual as Social Change*. New York: Oxford University Press, 1991.

Alpert, Rebecca. *Religion and Sports: An Introduction and Case Studies*. New York: Columbia University Press, 2015.

Ashley, Kathleen, ed. *Victor Turner and the Constructions of Cultural Criticism: Between Literature and Anthropology*. Bloomington: Indiana University Press, 1990.

Bainbridge, William Sims. *EGods: Faith versus Fantasy in Computer Gaming*. New York: Oxford University Press, 2013.

Bynum, Caroline Walker. "Women's Stories, Women's Symbols: A Critique of Victor Turner's Theory of Liminality," in *Fragmentation and Redemption: Essays on Gender and the Human Body in Medieval Religion*, 27–52. New York: Zone Books, 1991.

Campbell, Heidi, and Greg Grieve, eds. *Playing with Religion in Digital Games*. Bloomington: Indiana University Press, 2014.

Csikszentmihalyi, Mihaly. *Flow: The Psychology of Optimal Experience*. New York: Harper and Row, 1990.

Deflem, Mathieu. "Ritual, Anti-Structure, and Religion: A Discussion of Victor Turner's Processual Symbolic Analysis," *Journal for the Scientific Study of Religion* 30, no. 1 (1991): 1–25.

Eade, John, and Michael Sallnow, eds. *Contesting the Sacred: The Anthropology of Pilgrimage*. Urbana: University of Illinois Press, 1991.

Grieve, Gregory Price, and Heidi A. Campbell. "Studying Religion in Digital Gaming: A Critical Review of an Emerging Field," *Online: Heidelberg Journal of Religions on the Internet* 5, no. 1 (2014): 51–67. Available online: https://heiup.uni-heidelberg.de/journals/index.php/religions/article/view/12183/6027 (accessed December 19, 2019).

Huizinga, Johan. *Homo Ludens: A Study of the Play-Element in Culture*. Boston, MA: Beacon, 1955 (1938).

Kwenda, Chirevo Victor. "True Colors: A Critical Assessment of Victor Turner's Study of Ndembu Religion," Ph.D. Dissertation. Syracuse University, 1993.

Price, Joseph L., ed. *From Season to Season: Sports as American Religion*. Macon, GA: Mercer University Press, 2001.

Rogers, Ryan, ed. *Understanding Esports: An Introduction to the Global Phenomenon*. Lanham, MD: Lexington Books, 2019.

St John, Graham, ed. *Victor Turner and Contemporary Cultural Performance*. New York: Berghahn, 2008.

Schechner, Richard. *Performance Studies: An Introduction*. New York: Routledge, 2002.

Turner, Victor. *The Forest of Symbols: Aspects of Ndembu Ritual*. Ithaca, NY: Cornell University Press, 1967.

Turner, Victor. *Schism and Continuity in an African Society*. Manchester: Manchester University Press, 1968.

Turner, Victor. *The Ritual Process: Structure and Anti-Structure*. Ithaca, NY: Cornell University Press, 1969.

Turner, Victor. *Dramas, Fields, and Metaphors: Symbolic Action in Human Society*. Ithaca, NY: Cornell University Press, 1974.

Turner, Victor. *From Ritual to Theatre: The Human Seriousness of Play*. New York: Performing Arts Journal Publications, 1982.

Wagner, Rachel. *Godwired: Religion, Ritual and Virtual Reality*. London: Routledge, 2012.

8 Mircea Eliade

Mircea Eliade (1907–86) was among the most influential scholars of religion of the late twentieth century as founder and main theorist of the "history of religions" school focusing on the comparative study of religious symbolism. His interests were global and diverse, reflecting his life and travels through Europe and Asia. He long held a professorship at the University of Chicago where he helped build the academic study of religion in the United States, training many of the scholars who would define the field in the 1960s and 1970s.

Eliade resisted the notion that religion ultimately could be traced to economic, psychological, or social motives. Rather, it was to be studied as a unique and distinctive category of human life. Accordingly, he was interested in the patterns of religious symbolism across cultures and the fundamental existential questions and philosophical ideas embodied within them. Eliade's most influential works, *Cosmos and History* (1949), *Patterns in Comparative Religion* (1958), and *The Sacred and the Profane* (1959), propounded general theories of religion, myth, ritual, and symbolism that remain influential, although not without controversy.

Akin to Durkheim, Eliade saw religion as fundamentally about how human beings understood the cosmos as two separate realms, the sacred which encompassed the transcendent and eternal, and the profane which encompassed the familiar world in which most of our lives are led. In contrast to Durkheim, Eliade did not trace the sacred to social necessity and solidarity alone but affirmed it as a separate and distinct reality that revealed itself at specific moments ("hierophanies") that transformed those (individuals and communities) who experienced them and their realities.

Eliade's theories were ambitious and in time critics came to see his attempt to develop a universal theory of religion as problematic, citing numerous instances of religious ideas and activities that did not neatly fit into his theoretical model. In practice his application of the "history of religions" method tended to emphasize similarities across time and geography, without the attention to specific conditions and unique contexts that inform most historical studies. Philosophically, Eliade's view of the sacred seemed to some critics a kind of "crypto-theology," advancing a decidedly "Western" framing of religion under the guise of a generally applicable "scientific" theory. Others diminished or dismissed Eliade's ideas after his participation in groups that supported fascism in Romania during the 1930s and 1940s became known.

In spite of these problems, many scholars interested in the intersection of religion and popular culture have found Eliadean ideas about myth, ritual, religious symbolism, sacred time, and sacred space very useful to explore topics as wide ranging as the mythic dimensions of film, the deeper meaning of sports venues, or the sacralization of space at battlefields. Even when they have been critical of his approach, many scholars of religion and popular culture have still started from a position much closer to Eliade's than even they might be willing to admit.

"The Myths of the Modern World" (1967)[1]

Ours is a more modest problem: if the myth is not just an infantile or aberrant creation of "primitive" humanity, but is the expression of *a mode of being in the world*, what has become of myths in the modern world? Or, more precisely, what has taken the *essential* place occupied by the myth in traditional societies? For, if certain "participations" in myths and collective symbols still survive in the modern world, they are far from filling the central part played by the myth in traditional societies; in comparison with these, our modern world seems destitute of myths. It has even been held that the diseases and crises of modern societies are rightly attributable to the absence of a mythology appropriate to them. [...]

It is true that, at least apparently, the modern world is not rich in myths. [...]

* * *

[...] We are thinking of the myth as *a type of human behaviour* and, at the same time, as *an element of civilisation*—that is, of the myth as one finds it in traditional societies. For at the level of *individual experience* it has never completely disappeared: it makes itself felt in the dreams, the fantasies and the longings of the modern man; and an abundant psychological literature has now accustomed us to rediscoveries of both the big and the little mythologies in the unconscious and half-conscious activity of every individual. But what now interests us above all is to find out what it is, in the modern world, that fills the *central* position occupied by the myth in traditional societies. In other words, while recognising that the great mythical themes continue to repeat themselves in the obscure depths of the **psyche**, we still wonder whether the myth, as an exemplary pattern of human behaviour, may not also survive among our contemporaries in more or less degraded forms. It seems that a myth itself, as well as the symbols it brings into play, never quite disappears from the present world of the psyche; it only changes its aspect and disguises its operations. Would it not be instructive to prolong the enquiry and unmask the operations of myths upon the *social plane*?

Here is one example. It is clearly the case that certain festivals observed in the modern world, though apparently secular, still preserve a mythical structure and function: the rejoicings over the New Year, or the festivities following the birth of a child, or the building of a house, or even the removal into a new flat, show the obscurely-felt need for an *entirely new beginning*, of an *incipit vita nova*—that is, of a complete regeneration. Remote as these profane rejoicings may be from their mythic archetype—the periodic repetition of the creation—it is none the less evident that modern man still feels the need for periodic re-enactments of such scenarios, however secularised they have become. There are no means of estimating how far modern man is still aware of any mythological implications of

---

[1]Mircea Eliade, excerpt from "The Myths of the Modern World," in *Myths, Dreams and Mysteries: The Encounter between Contemporary Faiths and Archaic Realities*, trans. Philip Mairet (New York: Harper and Brothers Publishers, 1960), 23–38.

his festivities; what matters to us is that such celebrations still have a resonance, obscure but profound, throughout his being.

That is but one example; it may enlighten us, however, with regard to what appears to be a general situation: that certain mythical themes still survive in modern societies, but are not readily recognisable since they have undergone a long process of **laicisation**. This has long been known: indeed, modern societies might be simply defined as those which have pushed the secularisation of life and of the Cosmos far enough: the novelty of the modern world consists in its revaluation, at the secular level, of the ancient sacred values. What we want to know, however, is whether anything else of the "mythical" survives in the modern world, besides what presents itself merely in the form of procedures and values re-interpreted to fit the secular plane. If all the phenomena were of that description, we should have to agree that the modern world was radically opposed to all the historic forms that had preceded it. But the very presence of Christianity excludes such a hypothesis. Christianity admits none of the secularised views of the Cosmos or of life which are characteristic of all "modern" culture.

The question this raises is not a simple one; but since the Western world, or a great part of it, still claims to be Christian, it cannot be evaded. I shall not insist upon what are at present called the "mythical elements" in Christianity. Whatever may be said about these "mythical elements" it is a long time since they were Christianised, and, in any case, the importance of Christianity must be judged in another perspective. [...]

To us the question presents itself differently: to what extent is Christianity maintaining, in modern secularised and **laicised** society, a spiritual horizon comparable to that of archaic societies, where the myth predominates? Let us say at once that Christianity has nothing to fear from such a comparison: its specificity is assured, it is guaranteed by *faith* as the category *sui generis* of religious experience, and by its valorisation in *history*. With the exception of Judaism, no other pre-Christian religion has set a value on history as a direct and irreversible manifestation of God in the world, nor on faith—in the sense inaugurated by Abraham—as a unique means of salvation. Consequently the Christian polemic against the religious world of paganism is, historically speaking, obsolete: Christianity is no longer in danger of being confused with any other religion or **gnosis** whatsoever. This having been said, and in view of the discovery, which is quite recent, that the myth represents a certain mode of being in the world, it is no less true that Christianity, *by the very fact that it is a religion*, has had to preserve at least one mythic attitude—the attitude towards **liturgical** time; that is, the rejection of profane time and the periodical recovery of the Great Time, *illud tempus* of "the beginnings."

For the Christian, Jesus Christ is not a mythical personage: on the contrary, he is a historical personage; his greatness itself is founded upon that absolute historicity. For the Christ not only made himself man, "man in general," but accepted the historical condition of the people in whose midst he chose to be born; and he had recourse to no miracle to escape from that historicity—although he worked plenty of miracles in order to modify the "historical situations" of others—by curing the paralytic, raising Lazarus, etc. Nevertheless, the religious experience of the Christian is based upon an imitation of the Christ as *exemplary pattern*, upon the liturgical repetition of the life, death and resurrection of the Lord and upon the *contemporaneity* of the Christian with *illud tempus* which begins with the Nativity at Bethlehem and ends, provisionally, with the Ascension. Now, we know that the initiation of a transhuman model, the repetition of an exemplary scenario and the breakaway from profane time through a moment which opens out into the Great Time, are the essential marks of "mythical behaviour"—that is, the behaviour of the man of the archaic societies, who finds the very source of his existence in the myth. One is always *contemporary with a myth*, during the time when one repeats it or imitates the gestures of the mythic personages. **Kierkegaard**'s requirement of the true Christian was that he should be a contemporary of the Christ. But even one who is not a "true Christian" in Kierkegaard's sense still is, and cannot not be, a contemporary of Christ; for the liturgical time in which the Christian *lives* during the divine service is no longer profane duration but is essentially sacred time, the time in which the Word is made flesh, the *illud tempus* of the Gospels. A Christian is not taking part in a commemoration of the Passion of Christ, as he might be joining in the annual celebration of the Fourth of July or the **Eleventh of November**, for example. He is not commemorating an event but re-actualising a mystery. For the Christian, Jesus dies and resurrects before him *hic et nunc*. Through the mystery of the Passion or of the Resurrection, the Christian dispels profane time and is integrated into time primordial and holy.

Connections 8a: Eliade and the Monomyth

Significant work has been done exploring the role of myth in products of popular culture; Joseph Campbell—himself heavily influenced by psychologist Carl Jung—has likely had the greatest impact. A young George Lucas read Campbell's *The Hero with a Thousand Faces* while in college and conducted conversations with him later as he prepared the first installment of the *Star Wars* saga (*Star Wars: A New Hope*, 1977). (He even identifies Campbell in the film credits.) A number of mythic figures and themes run through the film, including many based on films from Lucas's youth—Westerns (the saloon scene), Second World War films (the uniforms of many of the Empire staff), and basic action films. The most significant, however, is the overarching narrative of the hero—a seeming nobody of simple birth, whose destiny it is to achieve his proper station and save the universe. The film begins by taking the viewer back in time, and only once we have experienced this film (and the two that followed it) do we realize how interwoven Luke is in the great conflict that he initially felt had passed him by. Even his name—one who walks the sky, as it were—suggests greatness. Campbell identified this formula as the "monomyth," the foundational myth structure that (he argued) was nearly universal in ancient cultures and therefore formed the foundation of most (if not all) myth in civilization. Not surprisingly, it can be found in many works of culture, virtually any time a hero rises to the occasion.

Robert Jewett and John Shelton Lawrence made popular the notion of an "American monomyth," which focuses less on the hero (and his psycho-spiritual transformation) and more on the location of the heroism. In this version an Edenic community (a small town, for example), set upon by an outside malevolent force, is rescued by a mysterious hero who appears (as if from nowhere) to destroy the evil. Eden is restored, but the hero, now with the blood of vengeance on his hands, must continue on. This model can be found across forms and genres but may be most easily identified in Westerns like *Shane* (1953) and *Pale Rider* (1985). Clint Eastwood, who directed *Pale Rider* as well as other "Eden restored" Westerns like *High Plains Drifter* (1973), upended both the Campbell "monomyth" and the Jewett/Lawrence "American monomyth" with his production of *Unforgiven* (1992), in which the "hero" is a fallen man, the "Eden" he enters is a town populated by fallen people, and the heroine he saves is a working prostitute.

A variation of "American monomyth" model—better suited for serial films as well as radio and television programming—again shifts the focus from the Edenic locale back to the hero. Yet in this version, there is no psycho-spiritual transformation of the hero who initially rejects his (or her) destiny only to accept it in the end. Rather, there is just the continuing saga of the hero traveling to an unending variety of Edens in need of restoration. Television programs like the original *Star Trek* (1966–9), *Kung Fu* (1972–5), *The Incredible Hulk* (1977–82), and others made this pattern a staple.

It is needless to insist upon the radical differences that divide Christianity from the archaic world: they are too obvious to give rise to misunderstandings. But there remains the identity of behaviour that we have just recalled. To the Christian, as to the man of the archaic societies, time is not **homogeneous**: it is subject to periodical ruptures which divide it into "secular duration" and a "sacred time," the latter being indefinitely reversible, in the sense that it repeats itself to infinity without ceasing to be the same time. It is said that Christianity, unlike the archaic religions, proclaims and awaits the end of Time; which is true of the "profane duration," of History, but not of the liturgical time inaugurated by the Incarnation. The Christological *illud tempus* will not be done away with at the end of History.

These few cursory observations have shown us in what sense Christianity is prolonging a "mythical" conduct of life into the modern world. If we take account of the true nature and function of the myth, Christianity does not appear to have surpassed the mode of being of archaic man; but then it could not. **Homo naturaliter Christianus**. It remains, however, to enquire what has taken the place of the myth among those of the moderns who have preserved nothing of Christianity but the dead letter.

* * *

It seems unlikely that any society could completely dispense with myths, for, of what is essential in mythical behaviour—the exemplary pattern, the repetition, the break with profane duration and integration into primordial time—the first two at least are consubstantial with every human condition. Thus, it is not so difficult to recognise, in all that modern people call instruction, education and **didactic** culture, the function that is fulfilled by the myth in archaic societies. This is so not only because myths represent both the sum of ancestral traditions and the norms it is important not to transgress, and because their transmission— generally secret, initiatory—is equivalent to the more or less official "education" of a modern society. The **homology** of the respective functions of the myth and of our public instruction is verified above all when we consider the origins of the exemplary models upheld by European education. In antiquity there was no **hiatus** between mythology and history: historical personages endeavoured to imitate their archetypes, the gods and mythical heroes.

And the lives and deeds of those personages, in their turn, became paradigms for posterity. [...] The moral and civic virtues of these illustrious personages continued to provide the supreme criteria for European pedagogy, especially after the Renaissance. Right to the end of the nineteenth century European education for citizenship was still following the archetypes of classical antiquity, those models which had been made manifest *in illo tempore*, in that privileged interval of time which educated Europeans regarded as the highest point of the Greco-Latin culture.

But they did not think of assimilating the functions of mythology to the process of instruction, because they overlooked one of the chief characteristics of the myth, which is the creation of exemplary models for a whole society. In this, moreover, we recognise a very general human tendency; namely, to hold up one life-history as a paradigm and turn a historical personage into an archetype. This tendency survives even among the most eminent representatives of the modern mentality. As **Gide** has rightly observed, **Goethe** was highly conscious of a mission to lead a life that would be exemplary for the rest of humanity. In all that he did he was trying to *create an example*. In his own life he, in his turn, was imitating, if not the lives of the gods and mythical heroes, at least their behaviour. As **Paul Valery** wrote in 1932: "He represents for us, *gentlemen of the human race*, one of our best attempts to render ourselves like gods."

But this imitation of model lives is promoted not only by means of school education. Concurrently with official pedagogy, and long after this has ceased to exert its authority, modern man is subjected to the influence of a potent if diffuse mythology that offers him a number of patterns for imitation. Heroes, real and imaginary, play an important part in the formation of European adolescents: the characters in tales of adventure, heroes of war, screen favourites, etc. This mythology is continually enriched with the growing years; we meet, one after another, the exemplary figures thrown up by changes of fashion, and we try to become like them. Critical writers have often pointed out modern versions of, for example, **Don Juan**, the political or the military hero, the hapless lover; of the cynic, the nihilist, the melancholy poet, and so forth: all these models are carrying on mythological traditions which their topical forms reveal in mythical behaviour. The copying of these archetypes betrays a certain discontent with one's own personal history; an obscure striving to transcend one's own local, provincial history and to recover some "Great Time" or other—though it be only the mythic Time of the first **surrealist** or **existentialist** manifesto.

Connections 8b: Eliade, Myth, and the "Buddy" Genre

One variation of the standard "monomyth" is today informally known as the "buddy" narrative, in which the hero has a companion who is nearly his equal. Even in the well-known heroic epic *Star Wars: A New Hope* (1977), the monomythic hero Luke Skywalker has his loyal friend companion Han Solo. The model for this format dates back at least 4,000 years to the Near Eastern *Epic of Gilgamesh*. Discovered in the mid-1800s and translated by the end of the century, the epic tells of an ancient King Gilgamesh who, though part god, is not well liked by his subjects. At one point, Gilgamesh is challenged by Enkidu, a child of nature created by the gods to defeat him, but the two become friends and embark on various adventures. When Enkidu dies, Gilgamesh is distraught, and unsuccessfully seeks the secret to immortality. He returns to his kingdom a changed man; finally loved by his subjects, he gains immortality through the ritual celebration of his adventures.

This model can be found throughout Western literature. Robin Hood has his trusted companion Little John; the Lone Ranger has his Tonto. Sometimes the "buddy" complicates the narrative: Jesus's closest Apostle Judas may be a model here, but a similar betrayal can be seen in Shakespeare's Iago from *Othello*. In any case, the "buddy" is distinct from the hero in ways that suggest that the two are opposite sides of the same coin—two aspects of one personality. Enkidu is of nature born and lacks the sophistication (and arrogance) of the worldly (and part-divine) Gilgamesh.

In modern works, the "buddy" often is not only psychologically and temperamentally distinct but also (occasionally) culturally different in some way; the Lone Ranger is European American; Tonto is Native American. In the American context, this has been represented most often by pairing African American "sidekicks" with European American protagonists—often in "action" films like those in the *Lethal Weapon* franchise (film and television). Some critics have decried this construction as relegating the African American to secondary or subservient status and maintaining past racialized power dynamics. Others have suggested that it plays on the stereotype of the "magical Negro," a figure "othered" not only by race but by a mystical power to solve problems in ways that transcend nature.

Increasingly, reflecting changing cultural dynamics in the United States (and the global viewing audience), European Americans have been paired with Asians or Asian Americans; less commonly, African Americans have been paired with Asians or Asian Americans. An increasingly common version of the genre is the female "buddy" film, a subgenre given a profound boost by the film *Thelma and Louise* (1991), but one which has been the subject of some controversy among those who don't consider it an example of feminist equality but rather akin to a male "buddy" narrative in drag.

But an adequate analysis of the diffuse mythologies of the modern world would run into volumes: for myths and mythological images are to be found everywhere, laicised, degraded or disguised; one only needs to be able to recognise them. We have referred to the mythological basis of New Year celebrations, and of the festivities that mark any "new beginning"; in which we can discern anew the nostalgia for a *renewal*, the yearning for the world to be renovated; that one might enter upon a new History, in a world reborn; that is, *created afresh*. It would be easy to multiply instances. The myth of the lost paradise still survives in the images of a paradisiac island or a land of innocence; a privileged land where laws are abolished and Time stands still. For it is important to underline this fact—that it is, above all, *by analysing the attitude of the modern man towards Time that we can penetrate the disguises of his mythological behaviour*. We must never forget that one of the essential functions of the myth is its provision of an opening into the Great Time, a periodic re-entry into Time primordial. This is shown by a tendency to a neglect of the present time, of what is called the "historic moment."

[...] But thus to embark on a present adventure as the reiteration of a mythic saga is as much as to put the present time out of mind. Such disinclination to face historic time, together with an obscure desire to share in some glorious, primordial, total Time, is betrayed, in the case of modern people, by a sometimes desperate effort to break through the homogeneity of time, to "get beyond" duration and re-enter a time qualitatively different from that which creates, in its course, their own history. It is with this in mind that we can render the best account of what has become of myths in the world of today. For modern man, too, by means that are multiple, but **homologous**, is endeavouring to liberate himself from his "history" and to live in a qualitatively different temporal rhythm. And in so doing he is returning, without being aware of it, to the mythical style of life.

One can understand this better if one looks more closely at the two principal ways of "escape" in use by modern people—visual entertainment and reading. We need not go into all the mythical precedents for our public spectacles; it is enough to recall the ritual origins of bull-fighting, racing and athletic contests; they all have this point in common, that they take place in a "concentrated time," time of a heightened intensity; a residuum of, or substitute for, magico-religious time. This "concentrated time" is also the specific dimension of the theatre and the cinema. Even if we take no account of the ritual origins and mythological structure of the drama or the film, there is still the important fact that these are two kinds of spectacle that make us live in time of a quality quite other than that of "secular duration," in a temporal rhythm, at once concentrated and articulated, which, apart from all æsthetic implications, evokes a profound echo in the spectator.

* * *

When we turn to reading, the question is of greater subtlety. It is concerned, on the one hand, with the forms and the mythical origins of literature and, on the other, with the mythological function that reading performs in the mind that feeds upon it. The successive stages of myth, legend, epic and modern literature have often been pointed out and need not detain us here. Let us merely recall the fact that the mythical archetypes survive to some degree in the great modern novels. The difficulties and trials that the novelist's hero has to pass through are prefigured in the adventures of the mythic Heroes. It has been possible also to show how the mythic themes of the primordial waters, of the isles of Paradise, of the quest of the Holy Grail, of heroic and mystical initiation, etc., still dominate modern European literature. Quite recently we have seen, in surrealism, a prodigious outburst of mythical themes and primordial symbols. As for the literature of the bookstalls, its mythological character is obvious. Every popular novel has to present the exemplary struggle between Good and Evil, the hero and the villain (modern incarnation of the Demon), and repeat one of those universal motives of folklore, the persecuted young woman, salvation by love, the unknown protector, etc. Even detective novels, as **Roger Caillois** has so well demonstrated, are full of mythological themes.

Need we recall how much lyric poetry renews and continues the myths? All poetry is an effort to *re-create* the language; in other words, to abolish current language, that of every day, and to invent a new, private and personal speech, in the last analysis *secret*. But poetic creation, like linguistic creation, implies the abolition of time—of the history concentrated in language—and tends towards the recovery of the paradisiac, primordial situation; of the days when one could *create spontaneously*, when the past did not exist because there was no consciousness of time, no memory of temporal duration. It is said, moreover, in our own days, that for a great poet the past does not exist: the poet discovers the world as though he were present at the **cosmogonic** moment, contemporaneous with the first day of the Creation. From a certain point of view, we may say that every great poet is *re-making* the world, for he is trying to see it as if there were no Time, no History. In this his attitude is strangely like that of the "primitive," of the man in traditional society.

But we are interested chiefly in the mythological function of reading in itself; for here we are dealing with a specific phenomenon of the modern world, unknown in earlier civilisations.

Reading replaces not only the oral folk traditions, such as still survive in rural communities of Europe, but also the recital of the myths in the archaic societies. Now, reading, perhaps even more than visual entertainment, gives one a break in duration, and at the same time an "escape from time." Whether we are "killing time" with a detective story, or entering into another temporal universe as we do in reading any kind of novel, we are taken out of our own duration to move in other rhythms, to live in a different history. In this sense reading offers us an "easy way," it provides a modification of experience at little cost: for the modern man it is the supreme "distraction," yielding him the illusion of a *mastery of Time* which, we may well suspect, gratifies a secret desire to withdraw from the implacable becoming that leads toward death.

The defence against Time which is revealed to us in every kind of mythological attitude, but which is, in fact, inseparable from the human condition, reappears variously disguised in the modern world, but above all in its *distractions*, its amusements. It is here that one sees what a radical difference there is between modern cultures and other civilisations. In all traditional societies, every responsible action reproduced its mythical, transhuman model, and consequently took place in sacred time. Labour, handicrafts, war and love were all sacraments. The re-living of that which the Gods and Heroes had lived *in illo tempore* imparted a sacramental aspect to human existence, which was complemented by the sacramental nature ascribed to life and to the Cosmos. By thus opening out into the Great Time, this sacramental existence, poor as it might often be, was nevertheless rich in significance; at all events it was not under the tyranny of Time. The true "fall into Time" begins with the secularisation of work. It is only in modern societies that man feels himself to be the prisoner of his daily work, in which he can never escape from Time. And since he can no longer "kill" time during his working hours—that is, while he is expressing his real social identity—he strives to get away from Time in his hours of leisure: hence the bewildering number of distractions invented by modern civilisation. In other terms, it is just as though the order of things were reversed from what it is in traditional societies, for there, "distractions" hardly exist; every responsible occupation is itself an "escape from Time." It is for this reason that, as we have just seen, in the great majority of individuals who do not participate in any authentic religious experience, the mythical attitude can be discerned in their distractions, as well as in their unconscious psychic activity (dreams, fantasies, nostalgias, etc.). And this means that the "fall into Time" becomes confused with the secularisation of work and the consequent mechanisation of existence—that it brings about a scarcely disguisable loss of freedom; and the only escape that remains possible upon the collective plane is distraction.

Glossary

CAILLOIS, Roger (1913–78): French sociologist, game theorist, writer.
COSMOGONIC: referring or related to the origin of the universe.
DIDACTIC: instructional, so as to teach, often in a patronizing way.
ELEVENTH OF NOVEMBER: Armistice Day (in the United States, also known as Veterans Day), it is the holiday commemorating the day in 1918 on which hostilities between warring parties in the First World War ceased.
EXISTENTIALIST: related to existence, or to the reality of the existence of something.

GIDE, André (1869–1951): French writer, winner of the Nobel Prize in Literature in 1947.

GNOSIS: knowledge, as of spiritual or mystic matters.

GOETHE, Johann Wolfgang von (1749–1832): German poet, writer.

HIATUS: a pause, rest, or break in actions or processes.

HIC ET NUNC: "here and now" (Latin).

HOMO NATURALITER CHRISTIANUS: "Naturally Christian man" (Latin).

HOMOGENEOUS: alike, or of one kind, style, manner, or pattern.

HOMOLOGY/HOMOLOGOUS: of, or having, the same position, role, or structure.

IN ILLO TEMPORE/ILLUD TEMPUS: "in that time" (Latin), of a time of origin or significance.

JUAN, Don: fictional character; hero, lover

KIERKEGAARD, Søren (1813–55): Danish philosopher, Protestant theologian.

LAICISATION/LAICISED: of, or being returned to, the lay congregant or parishioner.

LITURGICAL: related to the ritual and pattern of public worship.

PSYCHE: the human soul, mind, or spirit.

SUI GENERIS: unique; arising from no other source.

SURREALIST: beyond real; drawing from the sub- or unconscious mind or imagination.

VALERY, Paul (1871–1945): French poet and writer.

Questions for Conversation

Eliade's understanding of myth was primarily developed as a way to compare and analyze "archaic" societies, who lived under relatively simpler economic and social conditions supported by oral traditions and face-to-face relationships. How does he argue for the relevance of this view of myth for modern societies beset by secularization and laicization?

How do the dreams, fantasies, longings, unconscious and half-conscious activities of individuals relate to myth? (Compare especially, to the excerpt from Freud).

How does Christianity represent the survival of the "mythical conduct of life" in the modern world?

According to Eliade, how does myth function in education? What roles do heroes and exemplars play in sustaining mythic modes of thinking?

How might we find mythic themes in modern "visual entertainments" like film and TV? Do you think that newer forms of heroes and visual entertainments, invented since Eliade wrote his essay, sustain these mythic themes? Consider, for example, computer games and Marvel superhero films.

How might we find mythic themes in modern reading habits, especially novels and stories? Are some genres of literature more "mythic" than others?

Time and history are crucial categories for Eliade's theories. How does myth alter the sense of time and history experienced in "secularized" everyday life? Put another way, how does myth make time "sacred" over and against time that is "profane"? Hint: Consider Eliade's notions *in illo tempore*, primordial time, nostalgia, and "concentrated time."

Although not much covered in this excerpt, Eliade's theories address mythic notions of space in addition to time. How might popular culture support notions of spaces that are sacred and provide a sense of renewal and revitalization, supporting myth?

Eliade argues that many in the modern era long to "escape" from the lives they live, in spite of the many advantages to modern societies. Why is this the existential condition of modern peoples? What drives the modern longing for a mythic "mode of being"?

Suggestions for Additional Reading

The following is a list of supplemental readings that provide additional information about, apply, or respond critically to the ideas presented in this chapter.

Allen, Douglas. *Myth and Religion in Mircea Eliade*. New York: Routledge, 1998.

Caillois, Roger. *The Mystery Novel*, trans. Roberto Yahni and A.W. Sadler. New York: Laughing Buddha Press, 1984.

Campbell, Joseph. *The Hero with a Thousand Faces*. New York: Pantheon Books, 1949.

Campbell, Joseph. *The Power of Myth*, with Bill Moyers. New York: Doubleday, 1988.

Christ, Carol P. "Mircea Eliade and the Feminist Paradigm Shift," *Journal of Feminist Studies in Religion* 7, no. 2 (1991): 75–94.

Derry, Ken, and John C. Lyden, eds. *The Myth Awakens: Canon, Conservatism, and Fan Reception of Star Wars*. Eugene, OR: Cascade Books, 2018.

Eliade, Mircea. *The Myth of the Eternal Return: Cosmos and History*, trans. Willard R. Trask. Princeton, NJ: Princeton University Press, 1954.

Eliade, Mircea. *Patterns in Comparative Religion*, trans. Rosemary Sheed. London: Sheed and Ward, 1957.

Eliade, Mircea. *The Sacred and the Profane: The Nature of Religion*, trans. Willard Trask. New York: Harcourt, Inc. 1959.

Eliade, Mircea. *Myths, Dreams and Mysteries: The Encounter between Contemporary Faiths and Archaic Realities*, trans. Philip Mairet. New York: Harper and Brothers Publishers, 1960.

Ellwood, Robert. "Mircea Eliade and Nostalgia for the Sacred," in *The Politics of Myth: A Study of C.G. Jung, Mircea Eliade, and Joseph Campbell*, 79–126. Albany: State University of New York Press, 1999.

The Epic of Gilgamesh. New York: Penguin Books, 2003 (This version was translated by N.K. [Nancy Katharine] Sandars in 1960).

Glenn, Cerise L., and Landra J. Cunningham. "The Power of Black Magic: The Magical Negro and White Salvation in Film," *Journal of Black Studies* 40, no. 2 (2009): 135–52.

Henderson, Mary S. *Star Wars: The Magic of Myth*. New York: Bantam Books, 1997.

Hughey, Matthew W. "Cinethetic Racism: White Redemption and Black Stereotypes in "Magical Negro" Films," *Social Problems* 56, no. 3 (2009): 543–77.

Iaccino, James. *Jungian Reflections within the Cinema: A Psychological Analysis of Sci-Fi and Fantasy Archetypes*. Westport, CT: Praeger Publishers, 1998.

Idinopulos, Thomas A., and Edward A. Yonan, eds. *Religion and Reductionism: Essays on Eliade, Segal, and the Challenge of the Social Sciences for the Study of Religion*. Leiden: E. J. Brill, 1994.

Jewett, Robert, and John Shelton Lawrence. *The American Monomyth*. Garden City, NY: Anchor Press, 1977; 2nd edn. Lanham, MD: University Press of America, 1988.

Jung, Carl. *The Archetypes and the Collective Unconscious*, trans. R. F. C. Hull. Princeton, NJ: Bollingen Foundation/Princeton University Press, 1969.

Keller, Mary L. "Indigenous Studies and 'the Sacred,'" *American Indian Quarterly* 38 (2014): 82–109.

Kotsopoulos, Aspasia. "Gendering Expectations: Genre and Allegory in Readings of Thelma and Louise," *Left History* 8, no. 2 (2003): 10–38.

Lawrence, John Shelton, and Robert Jewett. *Myth of the American Superhero*. Grand Rapids, MI: W.B. Eerdmans, 2002.

Locke, Brian. *Racial Stigma on the Hollywood Screen from World War II to the Present: The Orientalist Buddy Film*. New York: Palgrave Macmillan, 2009.

Saiving, Valerie. "Androcentrism in Religious Studies," *Journal of Religion* 56 (1976): 177–97.

Strenski, Ivan. "Eliade's Theory of Myth and the 'History of Religions,'" in *Four Theories of Myth in Twentieth-Century History: Cassirer, Eliade, Levi Strauss, and Malinowski*, 104–28. Iowa City: University of Iowa Press, 1987.

9 Peter Berger

Peter L. Berger (1929–2017) earned his PhD at the New School for Social Research (New York) and taught there, at Rutgers University, and at Boston College before joining the faculty at Boston University. The author of works that address a specifically Christian audience, such as *The Noise of Solemn Assemblies* (1961), he was considered by many scholars to be an author with great appeal across various subdisciplines in the study of religion.

Berger, who as a young man entertained thoughts of becoming a Lutheran minister, retained an interest in Christianity throughout his career, and despite what some might consider a somewhat "heretical" approach, he continued to identify as a Christian. Methodologically he attributed the greatest influence of his to have come from the work of Max Weber, and like most sociologists of his era, he was initially an ardent advocate of what has come to be known as the "secularization thesis"—an argument with its roots in the middle of the nineteenth century and used by social scientists until the later decades of the twentieth century to understand the changing role of religion in society. However, over time it became clear to Berger and others that a rise in modernity did not necessarily lead to an increase in secularism. As a result, Berger came to see the secularization thesis (in its original formulation) as rather limited. Rather than leading to secularization, Berger argued, modernity leads more directly to pluralism, which he defined as "the coexistence in the society of different worldviews and value systems under conditions of civic peace and under conditions where people interact with each other." Able to reconcile the possibility of people being religious with also living in a modern (or even postmodern) society, the introduction of the notion of pluralism permits for the multiplicity of options; some are traditionally religious, some are not traditionally religious, and some are not religious at all. The difference, argued Berger, was not that people were less religious, but rather they were religious in different ways; in societies where its members experience a high level of cultural pluralism—in whatever form—assertions of certainty in one expression of that form is harder to maintain.

Although Berger identified the 1970s and 1980s as the period when his own thinking about the secularization thesis began to evolve, in hindsight one can still see the seeds of such notions as pluralism in his 1967 work *The Sacred Canopy* (excerpted here). Published one year after *The Social Construction of Reality* (his highly influential collaboration with Thomas Luckmann), *The Sacred Canopy* became a profoundly influential work in the sociological study of religion and, for many religion scholars using a sociological approach, the study of religion and popular culture.

The reading excerpted here is from *The Sacred Canopy*'s first chapter, in which Berger provides a map to understand the social construction of reality—that humans are, by design, social creatures that require a social setting to survive, and that this social setting is the product of a process that inhabitants shape even as they are shaped by it. Using language as an example, Berger reminds us that, while humans (among other living creatures) are designed for the ability to make sounds, languages are very human constructions (even if we cannot name the specific people who created them). It is constantly evolving—every year we celebrate the addition of "new words" to great dictionaries—and yet, the rules by which these languages are spoken are considered inviolate; much is communicated by (and much is learned about) those who violate the rules, who use it "incorrectly." The social construction of the entirety of the human world gives each human the tools to function socially, to feel a part of the social structure even as they are shaped by it. Things make sense because they are constantly reaffirmed by the "conversation" of all of the individuals participating in it. It is when the unexpected or tragic occurs—that which threatens the conversation among the inhabitants—that society is in its gravest danger. A religious worldview, which can serve as a higher, overarching "conversation," however, has the power to protect the stability of the socially constructed world and provides a "sacred canopy" over all of society by giving meaning to the radically meaningless.

While Berger did not intend for nontraditional ways of being in the world to supplant the more recognizably religious ways, his approach has provided a foundation for scholars of religion and popular culture in their search to understand how some can construct worldviews from the popular—as opposed to the religious—materials around them.

"Religion and World Construction" (1967)[1]

Society is a **dialectic** phenomenon in that it is a human product, and nothing but a human product, that yet continuously acts back upon its producer. Society is a product of man. It has no other being except that which is bestowed upon it by human activity and consciousness. There can be no social reality apart from man. Yet it may also be stated that man is a product of society. Every individual biography is an episode within the history of society, which both precedes and survives it. Society was there before the individual was born and it will be there after he has died. What is more, it is within society, and as a result of social processes, that the individual becomes a person, that he attains and holds onto an identity, and that he carries out the various projects that constitute his life. Man cannot exist apart from society. The two statements, that society is the product of man and that man is the product of society, are not contradictory. They rather reflect the inherently dialectic character of the societal phenomenon. Only if this character is recognized will society be understood in terms that are adequate to its empirical reality.

The fundamental dialectic process of society consists of three moments, or steps. These are **externalization**, **objectivation**, and **internalization**. [...]

Externalization is an anthropological necessity. Man, as we know him empirically, cannot be conceived of apart from the continuous outpouring of himself into the world in which

---

[1]Peter Berger, excerpt from "Religion and World Construction," in *The Sacred Canopy: Elements of a Sociological Theory of Religion* (New York: Anchor Books, 1967), 3–28.

he finds himself. Human being cannot be understood as somehow resting within itself, in some closed sphere of **interiority**, and *then* setting out to express itself in the surrounding world. Human being is externalizing in its essence and from the beginning. [...] There is no man-world in the above sense. Man's world is imperfectly programmed by his own constitution. It is an open world. That is, it is a world that must be fashioned by man's own activity.

Compared with the other higher mammals, man thus has a double relationship to the world. Like the other mammals, man is *in* a world that antedates his appearance. But unlike the other mammals, this world is not simply given, prefabricated for him. Man *must* make a world for himself. The world-building activity of man, therefore, is not a biologically extraneous phenomenon, but the direct consequence of man's biological constitution.

[...] Only in such a world produced by himself can he locate himself and realize his life. But the same process that builds his world also "finishes" his own being. In other words, man not only produces a world, but he also produces himself. More precisely, he produces himself in a world.

[...] Biologically deprived of a man-world, he constructs a human world. This world, of course, is culture. Its fundamental purpose is to provide the firm structures for human life that are lacking biologically. It follows that these humanly produced structures can never have the stability that marks the structures of the animal world. Culture, although it becomes for man a "second nature," remains something quite different from nature precisely because it is the product of man's own activity. Culture must be continuously produced and reproduced by man. Its structures are, therefore, inherently precarious and predestined to change. [...]

[...] [W]hile society appears as but an aspect of culture, it occupies a privileged position among man's cultural formations. This is due to yet another basic anthropological fact, namely the essential sociality of man. *Homo sapiens* is the social animal. This means very much more than the surface fact that man always lives in collectivities and, indeed, loses his humanity when he is thrust into isolation from other men. Much more importantly, the world-building activity of man is always and inevitably a collective enterprise. [...] Society, therefore, is not only an outcome of culture, but a necessary condition of the latter. Society structures, distributes, and co-ordinates the world-building activities of men. And only in society can the products of those activities persist over time.

The understanding of society as rooted in man's externalization, that is, as a product of human activity, is particularly important in view of the fact that society appears to common sense as something quite different, as independent of human activity and as sharing in the inert givenness of nature. [...]

Society, then, is a product of man, rooted in the phenomenon of externalization, which in turn is grounded in the very biological constitution of man. As soon as one speaks of externalized products, however, one is implying that the latter attain a degree of distinctiveness as against their producer. This transformation of man's products into a world that not only derives from man, but that comes to confront him as a **facticity** outside of himself, is intended in the concept of objectivation. The humanly produced world becomes something "out there." It consists of objects, both material and non-material, that are capable of resisting the desires of their producer.

Once produced, this world cannot simply be wished way. Although all culture originates and is rooted in the subjective consciousness of human beings, once formed it cannot be reabsorbed into consciousness at will. It stands outside the subjectivity of the individual as, indeed, a world. In other words, the humanly produced world attains the character of objective reality.

This acquired objectivity of man's cultural products pertains both to the material and the non-material ones. [...]

If culture is credited with the status of objectivity, there is a double meaning to this appellation. Culture is objective in that it confronts man as an assemblage of objects in the real world existing outside his own consciousness. Culture is *there*. But culture is also objective in that it may be experienced and apprehended, as it were, in company. Culture is *there for everybody*. This means that the objects of culture (again, both the material and non-material ones) may be shared with others. This distinguishes them sharply from any constructions of the subjective consciousness of the solitary individual. This is obvious when one compares a tool that belongs to the technology of a particular culture with some utensil, however interesting, that forms part of a dream. The objectivity of culture as shared facticity, though, is even more important to understand with reference to its non-material constituents. The individual may dream up any number of, say, institutional arrangements that might well be more interesting, perhaps even more functional, than the institutions actually recognized in his culture. As long as these sociological dreams, so to speak, are confined to the individual's own consciousness and are not recognized by others as at least empirical possibilities, they will exist only as shadowlike **phantasmata**. By contrast, the institutions of the individual's society, however much he may dislike them, will be *real*. In other words, the cultural world is not only collectively produced, but it remains real by virtue of collective rerecognition. To be in culture means to share in a particular world of objectivities with others.

The same conditions, of course, apply to that segment of cultures we call society. It is not enough, therefore, to say that society is rooted in human activity. One must also say that society is *objectivated* human activity, that is, society is a product of human activity that has attained the status of objective reality. The social formations are experienced by man as elements of an objective world. Society confronts man as external, subjectively opaque and coercive facticity. Indeed, society is commonly apprehended by man as virtually equivalent to the physical universe in its objective presence—a "second nature," indeed. Society is experienced as given "out there," extraneous to subjective consciousness and not controllable by the latter. [...] Since society is encountered by the individual as a reality external to himself, it may often happen that its workings remain opaque to his understanding. He cannot discover the meaning of a social phenomenon by introspection. He must, for this purpose, go outside himself and engage in the basically same kind of empirical inquiry that is necessary if he is to understand anything located outside his own mind. Above all, society manifests itself by its coercive power. The final test of its objective reality is its capacity to impose itself upon the reluctance of individuals. Society directs, sanctions, controls, and punishes individual conduct. In its most powerful **apotheosis** (not a loosely chosen term, as we shall see later), society may even destroy the individual.

The coercive objectivity of society can, of course, be seen most readily in its procedures of social control, that is, in those procedures that are specifically designed to "bring back into line" recalcitrant individuals or groups. Political and legal institutions may serve as obvious illustrations of this. It is important to understand, however, that the same coercive objectivity characterizes society *as a whole* and is present in *all* social institutions, including those institutions that were founded on consensus. This (most emphatically) does *not* mean that all societies are variations of tyranny. It *does* mean that no human construction can be accurately called a social phenomenon unless it has achieved that measure of objectivity that compels the individual to recognize it as real. In other words, the fundamental coerciveness of society lies not in its machineries of social control, but in its power to constitute and to impose itself as reality. [...]

Connections 9a: Berger And McDonald's as Sacrament of Modernity

Berger enjoyed a long productive scholarly career subsequent to his seminal works of the 1960s. In later works he notably reversed his views on the inevitability of seculari-zation and recognized that modernity sustained, and even cultivated, new and vibrant forms of religiosity. One area of particular interest was how various societies around the world responded to globalization, especially as the consumption of various products, like fast food, became cultural markers of modernity. He muses on whether this held meaning akin to the rituals of traditional religions.

By far the most visible manifestation of the emerging global culture is in the vehicle of popular culture. It is propagated by business enterprises of all sorts (such as Adidas, McDonald's, Disney, MTV, and so on). Although control of these enter-prises is exercised by elites, popular culture penetrates broad masses of peo-ple all over the world. . . . Much of the consumption of this popular culture is arguably superficial, in the sense that it does not have a deep effect on people's beliefs, values, or behavior. In principle, an individual could wear jeans and running shoes, eat hamburgers, even watch a Disney cartoon, and remain fully embed-ded in this or that traditional culture. . . . I would suggest a differentiation between "sacramental" and "nonsacramental" consumption. Anglican theology defines a sacrament as the visible sign of an invisible grace; *mutatis mutandis*, the defini-tion applies here as well. Some consumption of the globalizing popular culture is quite "nonsacramental." To paraphrase Freud, sometimes a hamburger is just a hamburger. But in other cases, the consumption of a hamburger, especially when it takes place under the golden icon of a McDonald's restaurant, is a visible sign of the real or imagined participation in global modernity. The research on McDonald's restaurants in East Asia . . . suggests that there is a switch from "sac-ramental" to "nonsacramental" consumption as this type of fast food becomes commonplace over time. In Beijing, as in other places, when McDonald's was a newcomer, people went there not just to eat hamburgers but to participate vicari-ously in American-style modernity. In Tokyo or Taipei, where McDonald's had been around for a long time, going there was just one consumer option among many: the hamburger was just a hamburger. Needless to say, there is no way of deciding a priori which type of consumption prevails. It will always be a matter of empirical inquiry. (Berger and Huntington 2003: 6–7)

The objectivity of society extends to all its constituent elements. Institutions, roles, and identities exist as objectively real phenomena in the social world, though they and this world are at the same time nothing but human productions. [...] Thus, in the final resort, the objectivation of human activity means that man becomes capable of objectivating a part of himself within his own consciousness, confronting himself within himself in figures that are generally available as objective elements of the social world. For example, the individual *qua* "real self" can carry on an internal conversation with himself *qua* archbishop. Actually, it is only by means of such internal dialogue with the objectivations of oneself that socialization is possible in the first place. The world of social objectivations, produced by externalizing consciousness, confronts consciousness as an external facticity. It is apprehended as such. This apprehension, however, cannot as yet be described as internalization, any more than can the apprehension of the world of nature. Internalization is rather the reabsorption into consciousness of the objectivated world in such a way that the structures of this world come to determine the subjective structures of consciousness itself. That is, society now functions as the formative agency for individual consciousness. Insofar as internalization has taken place, the individual now apprehends various elements of the objectivated world as phenomena internal to his consciousness at the same time as he apprehends them as phenomena of external reality.

Every society that continues in time faces the problem of transmitting its objectivated meanings from one generation to the next. This problem is attacked by means of the processes of socialization, that is, the processes by which a new generation is taught to live in accordance with the institutional programs of the society. Socialization can, of course, be described psychologically as a learning process. The new generation is initiated into the meanings of the culture, learns to participate in its established tasks and to accept the roles as well as the identities that make up its social structure. Socialization, however, has a crucial dimension that is not adequately grasped by speaking of a learning process. The individual not only learns the objectivated meanings but identifies with and is shaped by them. He draws them into himself and makes them *his* meanings. He becomes not only one who possesses these meanings, but one who represents and expresses them.

The success of socialization depends upon the establishment of symmetry between the objective world of society and the subjective world of the individual. If one imagines a totally socialized individual, each meaning objectively available in the social world would have its analogous meaning given subjectively within his own consciousness. Such total socialization is empirically non-existent and theoretically impossible, if only by reason of the biological variability of individuals. However, there are degrees of success in socialization. [...]

Man's world-building activity is always a collective enterprise. Man's internal appropriation of a world must also take place in a collectivity. It has by now become a social-scientific platitude to say that it is impossible to become or to be human, in any empirically recognizable form that goes beyond biological observations, except in society. This becomes less of a platitude if one adds that the internalization of a world is dependent on society in the same way, because one is thereby saying that man is incapable of conceiving of his experience in a comprehensively meaningful way unless such a conception is transmitted to him by means of social processes. The processes that internalize the socially objectivated world are *the same* processes that internalize the socially assigned identities. The individual is socialized *to be* a designated person and to *inhabit* a designated world. Subjective identity and subjective reality are produced in the same dialectic (here, in the etymologically literal sense) between the individual and those significant others who are in charge of his socialization. It is possible to sum up the dialectic formation of identity by saying that the individual becomes that which he is addressed as by others. One may add that the individual appropriates the world in conversation with others and, furthermore, that both identity and world remain real to himself only as long as he can continue the conversation.

The last point is very important, for it implies that socialization can never be completed, that it must be an ongoing process throughout the lifetime of the individual. This is the subjective side of the already remarked-upon precariousness of all humanly constructed worlds. The difficulty of keeping a world going expresses itself psychologically in the difficulty of keeping this world subjectively plausible. The world is built up in the consciousness of the individual by conversation with significant others (such as parents, teachers, "peers"). The world is maintained as subjective reality by the same sort of conversation, be it with the same or with new significant others (such as spouses, friends, or other associates). If such conversation is disrupted (the spouse dies, the friends disappear, or one comes to leave one's original social milieu), the world begins to totter, to lose its subjective plausibility. In other words, the subjective reality of the world hangs on the thin thread of conversation. The reason why most of us are unaware of this precariousness most of the time is grounded in the continuity of our conversation with significant others. The maintenance of such continuity is one of the most important imperatives of social order.

[…]

It may now be understandable if the proposition is made that the socially constructed world is, above all, an ordering of experience. A meaningful order, or **nomos**, is imposed upon the discrete experiences and meanings of individuals. To say that society is a world-building enterprise is to say that it is ordering, or **nomizing**, activity. The presupposition for this is given, as has been indicated before, in the biological constitution of *homo sapiens*. Man, biologically denied the ordering mechanisms with which the other animals are endowed, is compelled to impose his own order upon experience. Man's sociality presupposes the collective character of this ordering activity. The ordering of experience is endemic to any kind of social interaction. Every social action implies that individual meaning is directed toward others and ongoing social interaction implies that the several meanings of the actors are integrated into an order of common meaning. It would be wrong to assume that this **nomizing** consequence of social interaction must, from the beginning, produce a nomos that embraces *all* the discrete experiences and meanings of the participant individuals. If one can imagine a society in its first origins (something, of course, that is empirically unavailable), one may assume that the range of the common nomos expands as social interaction comes to include ever broader areas of common meaning. It makes no sense to imagine that this nomos will ever include the totality of individual meanings. Just as there can be no totally socialized individual, so there will always be individual meanings that remain outside of or marginal to the common nomos. Indeed, as will be seen a little later, the marginal experiences of the individual are of considerable importance for an understanding of social existence. All the same, there is an inherent logic that impels every nomos to expand into wider areas of meaning. If the ordering activity of society never attains to totality, it may yet be described as totalizing.

Connections 9b: Berger and Monsters of Chaos

Paradoxically, Berger's connection of nomos and societal order often finds popular expression in its opposite, "nomic disruption" or the threat of chaos. For example, tales of "chaos monsters" that threaten to destroy human communities are among the oldest and most widely circulated mythologies. Ancient Near Eastern creation stories, for example, feature heroic figures who create the possibility of ordered social life by fighting and destroying monsters. In turn these stories infiltrate the biblical tradition in places like the book of Job and Revelation. As they menace and threaten "civilization," the drama often centers on organized efforts to contain the chaos by destroying or subduing the monster and reestablishing nomos. In contemporary popular culture, monsters abound in film, computer gaming, television and other media, many taken from folktales and classic literature. Whether it is Mary Shelley's monster created by Dr. Frankenstein, or its possible narrative source the golem—a mythical clay being of Jewish folklore that was supposedly given life by the same mystical powers that operate in the Divine words of scripture—these beings are created to protect their masters or expand their knowledge or power, but often end up being feared or pursued by others and then demonized for the destruction they cause. Often these monsters are metaphors for current or long-standing conflicts within human society, or conflicts over the very definition of what it means to be human. Can Dr. Frankenstein create life from death? Should humans be developing and testing nuclear weaponry? For religion scholar Timothy Beal, monsters like Godzilla represent "eco-horror," fears rooted in "deep anxieties about the effects of modern science and technology on complex ecological systems that we do not understand." The message of these monsters is moral and "impossible to miss . . . pull back into your proper place, let God be God and creature be creature, or you will pay for your hubris" (2002: 161).

The objective nomos is internalized in the course of socialization. It is thus appropriated by the individual to become his own subjective ordering of experience. It is by virtue of this appropriation that the individual can come to "make sense" of his own biography. The discrepant elements of his past life are ordered in terms of what he "knows objectively" about his own and others' condition. His ongoing experience is integrated into the same order, though the latter may have to be modified to allow for this integration. The future attains a meaningful shape by virtue of the same order being projected into it. In other words, to live in the social world is to live an ordered and meaningful life. Society is the guardian of order and meaning not only objectively, in its institutional structures, but subjectively as well, in its structuring of individual consciousness.

It is for this reason that radical separation from the social world, or **anomy**, constitutes such a powerful threat to the individual. It is not only that the individual loses emotionally satisfying ties in such cases. He loses his orientation in experience. In extreme cases, he loses his sense of reality and identity. He becomes **anomic** in the sense of becoming world-less. Just as an individual's nomos is constructed and sustained in conversation with significant others, so is the individual plunged toward anomy when such conversation is radically interrupted. The circumstances of such nomic disruption may, of course, vary. They might involve large collective forces, such as the loss of status of the entire social group to which the individual belongs. They might be more narrowly biographical, such as the loss of significant others by death, divorce, or physical separation. It is thus possible to speak of collective as well as of individual states of anomy. In both cases, the fundamental order in terms of which the individual can "make sense" of his life and recognize his own identity will be in process of disintegration. Not only will the individual then begin to lose his moral bearings, with disastrous psychological consequences, but he will become uncertain about his cognitive bearings as well. The world begins to shake in the very instant that its sustaining conversation begins to falter.

The socially established nomos may thus be understood, perhaps in its most important aspect, as a shield against terror. Put differently, the most important function of society is nomization. The anthropological presupposition for this is a human craving for meaning that appears to have the force of instinct. Men are **congenitally** compelled to impose a meaningful order upon reality. This order, however, presupposes the social enterprise of ordering world-construction. To be separated from society exposes the individual to a multiplicity of dangers with which he is unable to cope by himself, in the extreme case to the danger of imminent extinction. Separation from society also inflicts unbearable psychological tensions upon the individual, tensions that are grounded in the root anthropological fact of sociality. The ultimate danger of such separation, however, is the danger of meaninglessness. This danger is the nightmare *par excellence*, in which the individual is submerged in a world of disorder, senselessness and madness. Reality and identity are malignantly transformed into meaningless figures of horror. To be in society is to be "sane" precisely in the sense of being shielded from the ultimate "insanity" of such anomic terror. Anomy is unbearable to the point where the individual may seek death in preference to it. Conversely, existence within a nomic world may be sought at the cost of all sorts of sacrifice and suffering—and even at the cost of life itself, if the individual believes that this ultimate sacrifice has nomic significance.

[…]

In other words, the marginal situations of human existence reveal the innate precariousness of all social worlds. Every socially defined reality remains threatened by lurking "irrealities." Every socially constructed nomos must face the constant possibility of its collapse into anomy. Seen in the perspective of society, every nomos is an area of meaning carved out of a vast mass of meaninglessness, a small clearing of lucidity in a formless, dark, always ominous jungle. Seen in the perspective of the individual, every nomos represents the bright "dayside" of life, tenuously held onto against the sinister shadows of the "night." In both perspectives, every nomos is an edifice erected in the face of the potent and alien forces of chaos. This chaos must be kept at bay at all cost. To ensure this, every society develops procedures that assist its members to remain "reality-oriented" (that is, to remain within the reality as "officially" defined) and to "return to reality" (that is, to return from the marginal spheres of "irreality" to the socially established nomos). These procedures will have to be looked at more closely a little later. For the moment, suffice it to say that the individual is provided by society with various methods to stave off the nightmare world of anomy and to stay within the safe boundaries of the established nomos.

[...]

Whenever the socially established nomos attains the quality of being taken for granted, there occurs a merging of its meanings with what are considered to be the fundamental meanings inherent in the universe. Nomos and cosmos appear to be co-extensive. In archaic societies, nomos appears as a microcosmic reflection, the world of men as expressing meanings inherent in the universe as such. In contemporary society, this archaic cosmization of the social world is likely to take the form of "scientific" propositions about the nature of men rather than the nature of the universe. Whatever the historical variations, the tendency is for the meanings of the humanly constructed order to be projected into the universe as such. It may readily be seen how this projection tends to stabilize the tenuous nomic constructions, though the mode of this stabilization will have to be investigated further. In any case, when the nomos is taken for granted as appertaining to the "nature of things," understood **cosmologically** or anthropologically, it is endowed with a stability deriving from more powerful sources than the historical efforts of human beings. It is at this point that religion enters significantly into our argument.

Religion is the human enterprise by which a sacred cosmos is established. Put differently, religion is cosmization in a sacred mode. By sacred is meant here a quality of mysterious and awesome power, other than man and yet related to him, which is believed to reside in certain objects of experience. [...]

[...] The historical manifestations of the sacred vary widely, though there are certain uniformities to be observed cross-culturally (no matter here whether these are to be interpreted as resulting from cultural diffusion or from an inner logic of man's religious imagination). The sacred is apprehended as "sticking out" from the normal routines of everyday life, as something extraordinary and potentially dangerous, though its dangers can be domesticated and its potency harnessed to the needs of everyday life. Although the sacred is apprehended as other than man, yet it refers to man, relating to him in a way in which other non-human phenomena (specifically, the phenomena of non-sacred nature) do not. The cosmos posited by religion thus both transcends and includes man. The sacred cosmos is confronted by man as an immensely powerful reality other than himself. Yet this reality addresses itself to him and locates his life in an ultimately meaningful order.

On one level, the antonym to the sacred is the profane, to be defined simply as the absence of sacred status. [...]

On a deeper level, however, the sacred has another opposed category, that of chaos. The sacred cosmos emerges out of chaos and continues to confront the latter as its terrible contrary. This opposition of cosmos and chaos is frequently expressed in a variety of **cosmogonic myths**. The sacred cosmos, which transcends and includes man in its ordering of reality, thus provides man's ultimate shield against the terror of anomy. To be in a "right" relationship with the sacred cosmos is to be protected against the nightmare threats of chaos. To fall out of such a "right" relationship is to be abandoned on the edge of the abyss of meaninglessness. [...] But behind this danger is the other, much more horrible one, namely that one may lose all connection with the sacred and be swallowed up by chaos. All the nomic constructions, as we have seen, are designed to keep this terror at bay. In the sacred cosmos, however, these constructions achieve their ultimate culmination—literally, their apotheosis.

Human existence is essentially and inevitably externalizing activity. In the course of externalization men pour out meaning into reality. Every human society is an edifice of externalized and objectivated meanings, always intending a meaningful totality. Every society is engaged in the never completed enterprise of building a humanly meaningful world. Cosmization implies the identification of this humanly meaningful world with the world as such, the former now being grounded in the latter, reflecting it or being derived from it in its fundamental structures. Such a cosmos, as the ultimate ground and validation of human **nomoi** need not necessarily be sacred. [...]

It can thus be said that religion has played a strategic part in the human enterprise of world-building. Religion implies the farthest reach of man's self-externalization, of his infusion of reality with his own meanings. Religion implies that human order is projected into the totality of being. Put differently, religion is the audacious attempt to conceive of the entire universe as being humanly significant.

Glossary

ANOMY, **ANOMIC**: a state of chaos, isolation, or lack of structure/order.
APOTHEOSIS: the culmination or climax of development; glorification to a divine level.
CONGENITALLY: present from birth, either inherited or developmental.
COSMOGONIC MYTHS: myths about the origin of the universe.
COSMOLOGICALLY: referring to the origins of the physical or religious universe.
DIALECTIC: confrontation or comparison of related opposites.
EXTERNALIZATION: the perception or projection of ideas or self on to the world beyond the self; compare to **INTERNALIZATION**.
FACTICITY: the quality of being a fact or truth.
INTERIORITY: the quality of being interior.
INTERNALIZATION: the incorporation of the external into the self; compare to **EXTERNALIZATION**.
NOMOS, **NOMOI**, **NOMIZING**: law, structure, or order.
OBJECTIVATION: the process of making an object or process from an abstraction.
PHANTASMATA: representation of fantasy or the fantastical.

Questions for Conversation

Does Berger's assertion of the social construction of reality suggest that "anything goes"? Can we build any kind of society or any kind of reality we like?

Berger sees society as a dialectical process. What does he mean by this?

What is externalization and how does it work? How is it related to human biology?

In his discussion of objectivation Berger argues that both the "material and non-material" aspects of culture "exist" and are "real." This might be easy to demonstrate in terms of material objects like buildings and products, but how do ideas about spirits and Gods (often thought to be invisible and immaterial) achieve "objective" status?

What needs to happen to an individual for internalization to take place? Is internalization ever a complete process?

Berger notes that "[s]ociety directs, sanctions, controls, and punishes individual conduct . . . [and] may even destroy the individual." Where does it get this power?

What are nomos and nomizing activity for Berger and why are they so important for social life?

What is anomy how does it contrast with nomos?

What is cosmos (or cosmological understanding) and why is it so closely associated with nomos?

How does Berger's definition of religion, "the human enterprise by which a sacred cosmos is established," build upon his general theories of social dialectical processes?

How does Berger define the sacred? See especially his use of contrasting terms, profane, and chaos.

For Berger, how is religion a "projection" of human activity? How is it "audacious"?

Suggestions for Additional Reading

The following is a list of supplemental readings that provide additional information about, apply, or respond critically to the ideas presented in this chapter.

Barzilai, Maya. *Golem: Modern Wars and Their Monsters*. New York: New York University Press, 2016.

Beale, Timothy K. *Religion and Its Monsters*. New York: Routledge, 2002.

Berger, Peter L. *The Heretical Imperative: Contemporary Possibilities of Religious Affirmation*. Garden City, NY: Anchor Press, 1979.

Berger, Peter. *The Sacred Canopy: Elements of a Sociological Theory of Religion*. Garden City, NY: Doubleday, 1967.

Berger, Peter L. *The Noise of Solemn Assemblies: Christian Commitment and the Religious Establishment in America*. Garden City, NY: Doubleday, 1961.

Berger, Peter L., and Samuel P. Huntington, eds. *Many Globalizations: Cultural Diversity in the Contemporary World*. New York: Oxford University Press, 2003.

Bickel, Robert. *Peter Berger on Modernization and Modernity: An Unvarnished Overview*. New York: Routledge, 2017.

Gilmore, David. *Monsters: Evil Beings, Mythical Beasts, and All Manner of Imaginary Terrors*. Philadelphia: University of Pennsylvania Press, 2009.

Hammond, Phillip E. "Peter Berger's Sociology of Religion: An Appraisal," *Soundings* 52, no. 4 (Winter 1969): 415–24.

Harvey, Van A. "Some Problematical Aspects of Peter Berger's Theory of Religion," *Journal of the American Academy of Religion* 41, no. 1 (1973): 75–93.

Hjelm, Titus. "Rethinking the Theoretical Base of Peter L. Berger's Sociology of Religion: Social Construction, Power, and Discourse," *Critical Research on Religion* 7 (2019): 223–36.

Luckmann, Thomas, and Peter Berger. *The Social Construction of Reality: A Treatise in the Sociology of Knowledge*. Garden City, NY: Doubleday, 1966.

Martín, Eloísa. "Peter Berger's Theory of Secularization in Latin America: Two Sacred Canopies," *Journal of the American Academy of Religion* 85 (2017): 1137–46.

Mathewes, Charles T. "An Interview with Peter Berger," *The Hedgehog Review* 8, no. 1/2 (2006): 152–61.

Mikles, Natasha L., and Joseph P. Laycock. *Religion, Culture, and the Monstrous: Of Gods and Monsters*. Lanham, MD: Lexington Books, 2021.

Poole, W. Scott. *Monsters in America: Our Historical Obsession with the Hideous and the Haunting*. Waco, TX: Baylor University Press, 2011.

Ritzer, George. *The McDonaldization of Society: Into the Digital Age*, 9th ed. Thousand Oaks, CA: Sage Publishing, 2018.

Thomas, Pradip. "Selling God/Saving Souls: Religious Commodities, Spiritual Markets and the Media," *Global Media and Communication* 5, no. 1 (2009): 57–76.

Ukah, Asonzeh, and Tammy Wilks. "Peter Berger, *The Sacred Canopy*, and Theorizing the African Religious Context," *Journal of the American Academy of Religion* 85 (2017): 1147–54.

Woodhead, Linda, et al., eds. *Peter Berger and the Study of Religion*. New York: Routledge, 2001.

Wuthnow, Robert, James Davison Hunter, Albert Bergeson, and Edith Kurzweil. "The Phenomenology of Peter Berger," in *Cultural Analysis: The Work of Peter L. Berger, Mary Douglas, Michel Foucault, and Jürgen Habermas*, 21–76. New York: Routledge, 2010.

10   Clifford Geertz

Clifford Geertz (1926–2006) was a wide-ranging and influential cultural anthropologist whose major theoretical works charted strategies for the symbolic interpretation of cultures. Much of his work built upon his own ethnographic studies of various societies in Indonesia and North Africa, as well as theoretical influences from sociology, philosophy, and other academic disciplines.

After service in the Navy during the Second World War, Geertz studied at Harvard under Talcott Parsons, known for his general social theories (much indebted to Max Weber), and Clyde Kluckhohn, known for his detailed studies of Native American societies and theories of culture. Geertz's own career in anthropology began with ethnographic work done in Java and later other parts of the Indonesian archipelago, notably Bali, and North Africa. Over his career, he would hold positions at the University of Chicago and the Institute for Advanced Study at Princeton, in addition to earning numerous honorary degrees. Early in his career, he published numerous essays and books based on his ethnographic work, included *Religion of Java* (1960), *Agricultural Involution* (1963), *Peddlers and Princes* (1963), and *Islam Observed* (1968). Later he turned to more theoretical works, the most influential being a collection of essays, *The Interpretation of Cultures* (1973). This text included his celebrated essay "Notes on a Balinese Cock Fight" as well as his "Religion as a Cultural System" in which he developed a novel and highly influential definition of religion, excerpted here.

Readers have long praised Geertz's careful attention to detail in this definition, especially his painstaking efforts to elaborate each element with explanation and examples. Through Parsons, Geertz absorbs much of pioneering sociologist Max Weber's insistence that the study of human societies attend to meanings, especially how human beings create webs of meanings to understand and navigate their social structures (family, clan, class, and nation) and the material productions necessary to sustain these structures. Systems of symbols, especially religious symbols, help different societies orient themselves to basic values, emotional states, and societal ideals (ethos and worldview), as well as give them conceptual resources to wrestle with larger existential dilemmas like suffering and loss (the "problem of meaning"). In methodological elaborations found elsewhere in his writings, Geertz encouraged scholars of religion to both delve into the descriptive detail of an event, like a ritual, and to try to understand the participants' human intentions and emotional dispositions—a combination he called "thick description." The analysis of culture, he insists in a famous turn of phrase, is "not an experimental science in search of a law, but an interpretive one in search of meaning." To that end, he devoted much of his written corpus to "passionate particularism"—detailed, almost novelistic, accounts of small communities and the key events that animated them.

Critics have argued that Geertz's attention to meanings and emotional states led him to neglect some of the other salient issues surrounding religious events. Notably, that they are often shaped by social and political powers who demand the acceptance of certain "truths," moral codes, and bodily disciplines. Thus where Geertz seems to accept to givenness of a culture's symbolic content and tries to decode it, a more critical anthropology might look to how symbols come to be constructed and then accepted as authoritative and "natural" (Asad 1983). Others noted that in spite of his considerable skills as a writer on particular anthropological phenomena, his theoretical emphasis on cultural interpretation, symbol, and meaning shifted anthropology away from its long-standing goal of developing a broader science of human behavior and social development. Nonetheless, Geertz's general orientation to exploring how systems of symbols generate and sustain meaning remain influential, perhaps because they can be applied not only to the analysis of religion in traditional societies but also to less codified forms of cultural expression, like film and television, which also generate symbols and meanings for their audiences.

"Religion as a Cultural System" (1973)[1]

As we are to deal with meaning, let us begin with a paradigm: viz., that sacred symbols function to synthesize a people's **ethos**—the tone, character, and quality of their life, its moral and aesthetic style and mood—and their world view—the picture they have of the way things in sheer actuality are, their most comprehensive ideas of order. In religious belief and practice a group's ethos is rendered intellectually reasonable by being shown to represent a way of life ideally adapted to the actual state of affairs the world view describes, while the world view is rendered emotionally convincing by being presented as an image of an actual state of affairs peculiarly well-arranged to accommodate such a way of life. This confrontation and mutual confirmation has two fundamental effects. On the one hand, it objectivizes moral and aesthetic preferences by depicting them as the imposed conditions of life implicit in a world with a particular structure, as mere common sense given the unalterable shape of reality. On the other, it supports these received beliefs about the world's body by invoking deeply felt moral and aesthetic sentiments as experiential evidence for their truth. Religious symbols formulate a basic congruence between a particular style of life and a specific (if, most often, implicit) metaphysic, and in so doing sustain each with the borrowed authority of the other.

[…][A] *religion* is:

(1) a system of symbols which acts to (2) establish powerful, pervasive, and long-lasting moods and motivations in men by (3) formulating conceptions of a general order of existence and (4) clothing these conceptions with such an aura of factuality that (5) the moods and motivations seem uniquely realistic.
   a system of symbols which acts to …

Such a tremendous weight is being put on the term "symbol" here that our first move must be to decide with some precision what we are going to mean by it. This is no easy task,

---

[1]Clifford Geertz, excerpt from "Religion as a Cultural System," in *The Interpretation of Cultures: Selected Essays* (New York: Basic Books, 1973), 87–125.

for, rather like "culture," "symbol" has been used to refer to a great variety of things, often a number of them at the same time.

In some hands it is used for anything which signifies something else to someone: dark clouds are the symbolic precursors of an on-coming rain. In others it is used only for explicitly conventional signs of one sort or another: a red flag is a symbol of danger, a white of surrender. In others it is confined to something which expresses in an oblique and figurative manner that which cannot be stated in a direct and literal one, so that there are symbols in poetry but not in science, and symbolic logic is misnamed. In yet others, however, it is used for any object, act, event, quality, or relation which serves as a vehicle for a conception—the conception is the symbol's "meaning"—and that is the approach I shall follow here. The number 6, written, imagined, laid out as a row of stones, or even punched into the program tapes of a computer, is a symbol. But so also is the Cross, talked about, visualized, shaped worriedly in air or fondly fingered at the neck, the expanse of painted canvas called "**Guernica**" or the bit of painted stone called a **churinga**, the word "reality," or even the morpheme "-ing." They are all symbols, or at least symbolic elements, because they are tangible formulations of notions, abstractions from experience fixed in perceptible forms, concrete embodiments of ideas, attitudes, judgments, longings, or beliefs. To undertake the study of cultural activity—activity in which symbolism forms the positive content—is thus not to abandon social analysis for a **Platonic** cave of shadows, to enter into a mentalistic world of introspective psychology or, worse, speculative philosophy, and wander there forever in a haze of "Cognitions," "Affections," "Conations," and other elusive entities. Cultural acts, the construction, apprehension, and utilization of symbolic forms, are social events like any other; they are as public as marriage and as observable as agriculture.

[…]

So far as culture patterns, that is, systems or complexes of symbols, are concerned, the generic trait which is of first importance for us here is that they are extrinsic sources of information. By "extrinsic," I mean only that—unlike genes, for example—they lie outside the boundaries of the individual organism as such in that intersubjective world of common understandings into which all human individuals are born, in which they pursue their separate careers, and which they leave persisting behind them after they die. By "sources of information," I mean only that—like genes—they provide a blueprint or template in terms of which processes external to themselves can be given a definite form. As the order of bases in a strand of DNA forms a coded program, a set of instructions, or a recipe, for the synthesis of the structurally complex proteins which shape organic functioning, so culture patterns provide such programs for the institution of the social and psychological processes which shape public behavior. […]

[…] [C]ultural patterns are "models," [in] that they are sets of symbols whose relations to one another "model" relations among entities, processes or what-have-you in physical, organic, social, or psychological systems by "paralleling," "imitating," or "simulating" them. The term "model" has, however, two senses—an "of" sense and a "for" sense—and though these are but aspects of the same basic concept they are very much worth distinguishing for analytic purposes. In the first, what is stressed is the manipulation of symbol structures so as to bring them, more or less closely, into parallel with the pre-established nonsymbolic system, as when we grasp how dams work by developing a theory of hydraulics or constructing a flow chart. The theory or chart models physical relationships in such a way—that is, by expressing their structure in **synoptic** form—as to render them apprehensible; it is a model *of* "reality." In the second, what is stressed is the manipulation of the nonsymbolic systems in terms of the relationships expressed in the symbolic, as when we construct a dam according to the specifications implied in an hydraulic theory or the conclusions drawn from a flow chart. Here, the theory is a model under whose guidance physical relationships are organized: it is a model *for* "reality." For psychological and social systems, and for cultural models that we would not ordinarily refer to as "theories," but rather as "doctrines," "melodies," or "rites," the case is in no way different. Unlike genes, and other nonsymbolic information sources, which are only models *for*, not models *of*, culture patterns have an intrinsic double aspect: they give meaning, that is, objective conceptual form, to social and psychological reality both by shaping themselves to it and by shaping it to themselves.

It is, in fact, this double aspect which sets true symbols off from other sorts of significative forms. Models *for* are found, as the gene example suggests, through the whole order of nature; for wherever there is a communication of pattern, such programs are, in simple logic, required. [...] But models *of*—linguistic, graphic, mechanical, natural, etc., processes which function not to provide sources of information in terms of which other processes can be patterned, but to represent those patterned processes as such, to express their structure in an alternative medium—are much rarer and may perhaps be confined, among living animals, to man. The perception of the structural congruence between one set of processes, activities, relations, entities, and so on, and another set for which it acts as a program, so that the program can be taken as a representation, or conception—a symbol—of the programmed, is the essence of human thought. The intertransposability of models *for* and models *of* which symbolic formulation makes possible is the distinctive characteristic of our mentality.

... to establish powerful, pervasive, and long-lasting moods and motivations in men by
...

So far as religious symbols and symbol systems are concerned this intertransposability is clear. The endurance, courage, independence, perseverance, and passionate willfulness in which the vision quest practices the Plains Indian are the same flamboyant virtues by which he attempts to live: while achieving a sense of revelation he stabilizes a sense of direction. [...] Whether one sees the conception of a personal guardian spirit, a family tutelary, or an immanent God as synoptic formulations of the character of reality or as templates for producing reality with such a character seems largely arbitrary, a matter of which aspect, the model *of* or model *for*, one wants for the moment to bring into focus. The concrete symbols involved—one or another mythological figure materializing in the wilderness, the skull of the deceased household head hanging censoriously in the rafters, or a disembodied "voice in the stillness" soundlessly chanting enigmatic classical poetry—point in either direction. They both express the world's climate and shape it.

They shape it by inducing in the worshipper a certain distinctive set of dispositions (tendencies, capacities, propensities, skills, habits, liabilities, pronenesses) which lend a chronic character to the flow of his activity and the quality of his experience. A disposition describes not an activity or an occurrence but a probability of an activity being performed or an occurrence occurring in certain circumstances: [...] [T]o be pious is not to be performing something we would call an act of piety, but to be liable to perform such acts. [...]

[...]

So far as religious activities are concerned (and learning a myth by heart is as much a religious activity as detaching one's finger at the knuckle), two somewhat different sorts of disposition are induced by them: moods and motivations.

Connections 10a: Geertz at the Movies

One element of Clifford Geertz's approach to studying religion lends itself particularly well to the study of the religious aspects of film. Religions, according to Geertz, are particularly powerful in the way that they function as "models of" and "models for" reality. They also motivate thought and action when "models of" do not seem to match up with "models for," when the world or situations in which we find ourselves conflict with our sense of the way things ought to be. In Geertz's terms, this is a conflict between "ethos" and "worldview." Symbols, texts, and stories drawn from what are typically described as religious traditions serve to provide critical leverage through which to evaluate the harmony between ethos and worldview. But aspects of popular culture can also serve this function.

John Lyden's approach to studying film as religion through this aspect of Geertz's perspective has been influential. In Lyden's view, movies can create alternate realities that operate like myths, providing a view of how the world is as well as how it ought to be. In his book *Film as Religion: Myths, Morals, and Rituals*, Lyden engages closely with Geertz's theory, critically questioning some of Geertz's own hesitation to consider that cultural phenomena like sports or movies might function religiously, and providing readers with much to consider about religion, film, popular culture, and the work of meaning-making more generally.

Another influential scholar of religion and film S. Brent Plate has expanded on this aspect of film, exploring the religious nature of film through the lens of "worldmaking." Movies are worlds, and filmmaking is the making of worlds, according to Plate, and therefore entail methods and elements similar to religion. Moreover, audiences are just as critical to the making and remaking of these worlds as artists, directors, and producers.

For both Lyden and Plate, films are not simply venues for escape or pleasure. They are also critical arenas for imagining—and experiencing—alternative realities, for asking "what if?"

A motivation is a persisting tendency, a chronic inclination to perform certain sorts of acts and experience certain sorts of feeling in certain sorts of situations, [...] As a motive, "flamboyant courage" consists in such enduring propensities as to fast in the wilderness, to conduct solitary raids on enemy camps, and to thrill to the thought of counting coup. "Moral circumspection" consists in such ingrained tendencies as to honor onerous promises, to confess secret sins in the face of severe public disapproval, and to feel guilty when vague and generalized accusations are made at seances. And "dispassionate tranquility" consists in such persistent inclinations as to maintain one's poise come hell or high water, to experience distaste in the presence of even moderate emotional displays, and to indulge in contentless contemplations of featureless objects. Motives are thus neither acts (that is, intentional behaviors) nor feelings, but liabilities to perform particular classes of act or have particular classes of feeling. And when we say that a man is religious, that is, motivated by religion, this is at least pan—though only part—of what we mean.

Another part of what we mean is that he has, when properly stimulated, a susceptibility to fall into certain moods, moods we sometimes lump together under such covering terms as "reverential," "solemn," or "worshipful." Such generalized rubrics actually conceal, however, the enormous empirical variousness of the dispositions involved, and, in fact, tend to assimilate them to the unusually grave tone of most of our own religious life. The moods that sacred symbols induce, at different times and in different places, range from exultation to melancholy, from self-confidence to self-pity, from an incorrigible playfulness to a bland listlessness—to say nothing of the erogenous power of so many of the world's myths and rituals. No more than there is a single sort of motivation one can call piety is there a single sort of mood one can call worshipful.

The major difference between moods and motivations is that where the latter are, so to speak, vectorial qualities, the former are merely scalar. Motives have a directional cast, they describe a certain overall course, gravitate toward certain, usually temporary, consummations. But moods vary only as to intensity: they go nowhere. They spring from certain circumstances but they are responsive to no ends. Like fogs, they just settle and lift; like scents, suffuse and evaporate. When present they are totalistic: if one is sad everything and everybody seems dreary; if one is gay, everything and everybody seems splendid. Thus, though a man can be vain, brave, willful, and independent at the same time, he can't very well be playful and listless, or exultant and melancholy, at the same time. Further, where motives persist for more or less extended periods of time, moods merely recur with greater or lesser frequency, coming and going for what are often quite unfathomable reasons. But perhaps the most important difference, so far as we are concerned, between moods and motivations is that motivations are "made meaningful" with reference to the ends toward which they are conceived to conduce, whereas moods are "made meaningful" with reference to the conditions from which they are conceived to spring. We interpret motives in terms of their consummations, but we interpret moods in terms of their sources. We say that a person is industrious because he wishes to succeed; we say that a person is worried because he is conscious of the hanging threat of nuclear holocaust. And this is no less the case when the interpretations are ultimate. Charity becomes Christian charity when it is enclosed in a conception of God's purposes; optimism is Christian optimism when it is grounded in a particular conception of God's nature. The assiduity of the Navaho finds its rationale in a belief that, since "reality" operates mechanically, it is coercible; their chronic fearfulness finds its rationale in a conviction that, however "reality" operates, it is both enormously powerful and terribly dangerous.

… by formulating conceptions of a general order of existence and …

That the symbols or symbol systems which induce and define dispositions we set off as religious and those which place those dispositions in a cosmic framework are the same symbols ought to occasion no surprise. For what else do we mean by saying that a particular mood of awe is religious and not secular, except that it springs from entertaining a conception of all-pervading vitality like **mana** and not from a visit to the Grand Canyon?

Or that a particular case of **asceticism** is an example of a religious motivation, except that it is directed toward the achievement of an unconditioned end like **nirvana** and not a conditioned one like weight-reduction? If sacred symbols did not at one and the same time induce dispositions in human beings and formulate, however obliquely, inarticulately, or unsystematically, general ideas of order, then the empirical differentia of religious activity or religious experience would not exist. A man can indeed be said to be "religious" about golf, but not merely if he pursues it with passion and plays it on Sundays: he must also see it as symbolic of some transcendent truths. [...] What any particular religion affirms about the fundamental nature of reality may be obscure, shallow, or, all too often, perverse; but it must, if it is not to consist of the mere collection of received practices and conventional sentiments we usually refer to as moralism, affirm something. [...]

[... W]e believe, as **James** remarked, all that we can and would believe everything if we only could. The thing we seem least able to tolerate is a threat to our powers of conception, a suggestion that our ability to create, grasp, and use symbols may fail us, for were this to happen, we would be more helpless, as I have already pointed out, than the beavers. The extreme generality, diffuseness, and variability of man's innate (that is, genetically programmed) response capacities means that without the assistance of cultural patterns he would be functionally incomplete, not merely a talented ape who had, like some underprivileged child, unfortunately been prevented from realizing his full potentialities, but a kind of formless monster with neither sense of direction nor power of self-control, a chaos of spasmodic impulses and vague emotions. Man depends upon symbols and symbol systems with a dependence so great as to be decisive for his creatural viability and, as a result, his sensitivity to even the remotest indication that they may prove unable to cope with one or another aspect of experience raises within him the gravest sort of anxiety: [...]

[...] There are at least three points where chaos—a tumult of events which lack not just interpretations but *interpretability*—threatens to break in upon man: at the limits of his analytic capacities, at the limits of his powers of endurance, and at the limits of his moral insight. Bafflement, suffering, and a sense of intractable ethical paradox are all, if they become intense enough or are sustained long enough, radical challenges to the proposition that life is comprehensible and that we can, by taking thought, orient ourselves effectively within it—challenges with which any religion, however "primitive," which hopes to persist must attempt somehow to cope.

[...] As a religious problem, the problem of suffering is, paradoxically, not how to avoid suffering but how to suffer, how to make of physical pain, personal loss, worldly defeat, or the helpless contemplation of others' agony something bearable, supportable—something, as we say, sufferable. [...] Where the more intellective aspects of what **Weber** called the Problem of Meaning are a matter affirming the ultimate explicability of experience, the more affective aspects are a matter of affirming its ultimate sufferableness. As religion on one side anchors the power of our symbolic resources for formulating analytic ideas in an authoritative conception of the overall shape of reality, so on another side it anchors the power of our, also symbolic, resources for expressing emotions—moods, sentiments, passions, affections, feelings—in a similar conception of its pervasive tenor, its inherent tone and temper. For those able to embrace them, and for so long as they are able to embrace them, religious symbols provide a cosmic guarantee not only for their ability to comprehend the world, but also, comprehending it, to give a precision to their feeling, a definition to their emotions which enables them, morosely or joyfully, grimly or cavalierly, to endure it.

[...]

The Problem of Meaning in each of its intergrading aspects (how these aspects in fact intergrade in each particular case, what sort of interplay there is between the sense of analytic, emotional, and moral impotence, seems to me one of the outstanding, and except for Weber untouched, problems for comparative research in this whole field) it [sic] a matter of affirming, or at least recognizing, the inescapability of ignorance, pain, and injustice on the human plane while simultaneously denying that these irrationalities are characteristic of the world as a whole. And it is in terms of religious symbolism, a symbolism relating man's sphere of existence to a wider sphere within which it is conceived to rest, that both the affirmation and the denial are made.

... and clothing those conceptions with such an aura of factuality that ...

There arises here, however, a more profound question: how is it that this denial comes to be believed? How is it that the religious man moves from a troubled perception of experienced disorder to a more or less settled conviction of fundamental order? Just what does "belief" mean in a religious context? [...]

Connections 10b: Geertz and the American Flag as a Sacred Symbol

Sacred symbols, Clifford Geertz wrote, "at one and the same time induce dispositions in human beings and formulate, however obliquely, inarticulately, or unsystematically, general ideas of order" (1973: 98). In American popular culture, the American flag is a central and powerful sacred symbol.

Consider the reverence that Americans pay to their flag. There are proper protocols for its treatment, enshrined in US federal law as the "United States Flag Code," Title 4 of the United States Code. Protocols include proper modes of display of the flag ("The flag should never touch anything beneath it"; "the flag should never be carried flat or horizontally"), forbidden uses ("The flag should never be used for advertising purposes in any manner whatsoever"; "the flag should never be used as wearing apparel, bedding, or drapery"), and proper dignified disposal of a torn or worn flag ("preferably by burning").

More impressively, consider the reactions that Americans have to the perceived mistreatment of the flag. For instance, American citizens, in a number of circumstances since the 1960s, have protested American governmental policies by burning the American flag. Both the act of setting the flag ablaze and the visceral reaction to this act by those who oppose it reveal that the flag is far more than simply a piece of cloth. As a sacred symbol in Geertz's terms, the flag functions "to synthesize a people's ethos—the tone, character, and quality of their life, its moral and aesthetic style and mood—and their world view—the picture they have of the way things in sheer actuality are, their most comprehensive ideas of order" (1973: 89). To destroy or disrespect the flag is to trouble the very order of reality.

For some Americans, the "general ideas of order" connect American identity and purpose with divine, often Christian, power and providence. Images of the American flag combined with Christian symbols like the cross, the Bible, or Jesus circulate through social media across the World Wide Web. A popular image, reproduced in a variety of media after the terrorist attack on September 11, 2001, presented an American flag flying beside a cross of steel beams found among the debris at the World Trade Center (popularly known as "the Ground Zero Cross"), connecting these two sacred symbols and inviting viewers to read them in reference to each other as part of one system of symbolic meaning.

Yet, as the example of the Ground Zero Cross and flag burning protests suggests, the American flag does not necessarily always function to unite, or even to express shared values and identity. Like any sacred symbol, it can also be heavily contested, a site of tension and opposition, as the rifts within a community or society each lay claim to its meaning. In Geertz's terms, this might result from a contradiction between a community's ethos and its worldview. From other perspectives, such as Stuart Hall's and Charles H. Long's, it suggests that the unity of identity and values presented by the dominant fraction of society is an ideological construction, not accurately reflecting the reality and masking internal difference. David Chidester has called this contradiction "the political economy of the sacred."

It seems to me that it is best to begin any approach to this issue with frank recognition that religious belief involves not a **Baconian induction** from everyday experience—for then we should all be **agnostics**—but rather a prior acceptance of authority which transforms that experience. The existence of bafflement, pain, and moral paradox—of The Problem of Meaning—is one of the things that drives men toward belief in gods, devils, spirits, totemic principles, or the spiritual efficacy of cannibalism (an enfolding sense of beauty or a dazzling perception of power are others), but it is not the basis upon which those beliefs rest, but rather their most important field of application: [...]

[...] The basic axiom underlying what we may perhaps call "the religious perspective" is everywhere the same: he who would know must first believe.

[I]t is in ritual—that is, consecrated behavior—that this conviction that religious conceptions are **veridical** and that religious directives are sound is somehow generated. It is in some sort of ceremonial form—even if that form be hardly more than the recitation of a myth, the consultation of an oracle, or the decoration of a grave—that the moods and motivations which sacred symbols induce in men and the general conceptions of the order of existence which they formulate for men meet and reinforce one another. In a ritual, the world as lived and the world as imagined, fused under the agency of a single set of symbolic forms, turn out to be the same world, producing thus that idiosyncratic transformation in one's sense of reality [...] Whatever role divine intervention may or may not play in the creation of faith—and it is not the business of the scientist to pronounce upon such matters one way or the other—it is, primarily at least, out of the context of concrete acts of religious observance that religious conviction emerges on the human plane [...]

[...I]t is mainly certain more elaborate and usually more public ones, ones in which a broad range of moods and motivations on the one hand and of metaphysical conceptions on the other are caught up, which shape the spiritual consciousness of a people. [...W]e may call these full-blown ceremonies "cultural performances" and note that they represent not only the point at which the dispositional and conceptual aspects of religious life converge for the believer, but also the point at which the interaction between them can be most readily examined by the detached observer: [...]

Of course, all cultural performances are not religious performances, and the line between those that are and artistic, or even political, ones is often not so easy to draw in practice, for, like social forms, symbolic forms can serve multiple purposes. [...] Where for "visitors" religious performances can, in the nature of the case, only be presentations of a particular religious perspective, and thus aesthetically appreciated or scientifically dissected, for participants they are in addition enactments, materializations, realizations of it—not only models of what they believe, but also models for the believing of it. In these plastic dramas men attain their faith as they portray it.

> *... that the moods and motivations seem uniquely realistic.*

But no one, not even a saint, lives in the world religious symbols formulate all of the time, and the majority of men live in it only at moments. The everyday world of common-sense objects and practical acts is [...] the paramount reality in human experience—paramount in the sense that it is the world in which we are most solidly rooted, whose inherent actuality we can hardly question (however much we may question certain portions of it), and from whose pressures and requirements we can least escape. A man, even large groups of men, may be aesthetically insensitive, religiously unconcerned, and unequipped to pursue formal scientific analysis, but he cannot be completely lacking in common sense and survive. The dispositions which religious rituals induce thus have their most important impact—from a human point of view—outside the boundaries of the ritual itself as they reflect back to color the individual's conception of the established world of bare fact. [...] Religion is sociologically interesting not because, as vulgar positivism would have it, it describes the social order (which, in so far as it does, it does not only very obliquely but very incompletely), but because, like environment, political power, wealth, jural obligation, personal affection, and a sense of beauty, it shapes it.

The movement back and forth between the religious perspective and the common-sense perspective is actually one of the more obvious empirical occurrences on the social scene, though, again, one of the most neglected by social anthropologists, virtually all of whom have seen it happen countless times. Religious belief has usually been presented as a homogeneous characteristic of an individual, like his place of residence, his occupational role, his kinship position, and so on. But religious belief in the midst of ritual, where it engulfs the total person, transporting him, so far as he is concerned, into another mode of existence, and religious belief as the pale, remembered reflection of that experience in the midst of everyday life are not precisely the same thing, [...]

[...] Having ritually "lept" (the image is perhaps a bit too athletic for the actual facts—"slipped" might be more accurate) into the framework of meaning which religious conceptions define, and the ritual ended, returned again to the common-sense world, a man is—unless, as sometimes happens, the experience fails to register—changed. And as he is changed, so also is the common-sense world, for it is now seen as but the partial form of a wider reality which corrects and completes it.

But this correction and completion is not, as some students of "comparative religion" would have it, everywhere the same in content. The nature of the bias religion gives to ordinary life varies with the religion involved, with the particular dispositions induced in the believer by the specific conceptions of cosmic order he has come to accept. [...] What men believe is as various as what they are—a proposition that holds with equal force when it is inverted.

[…]

For an anthropologist, the importance of religion lies in its capacity to serve, for an individual or for a group, as a source of general, yet distinctive, conceptions of the world, the self, and the relations between them, on the one hand—its model *of* aspect—and of rooted, no less distinctive "mental" dispositions—its model *for* aspect—on the other. From these cultural functions flow, in turn, its social and psychological ones.

Religious concepts spread beyond their specifically metaphysical contexts to provide a framework of general ideas in terms of which a wide range of experience—intellectual, emotional, moral—can be given meaningful form. […] A synopsis of cosmic order, a set of religious beliefs, is also a gloss upon the mundane world of social relationships and psychological events. It renders them graspable.

But more than gloss, such beliefs are also a template. They do not merely interpret social and psychological processes in cosmic terms—in which case they would be philosophical, not religious—but they shape them. In the doctrine of original sin is embedded also a recommended attitude toward life, a recurring mood, and a persisting set of motivations. […]

The tracing of the social and psychological role of religion is thus not so much a matter of finding correlations between specific ritual acts and specific secular social ties—though these correlations do, of course, exist and are very worth continued investigation, especially if we can contrive something novel to say about them. More, it is a matter of understanding how it is that men's notions, however implicit, of the "really real" and the dispositions these notions induce in them, color their sense of the reasonable, the practical, the humane, and the moral. How far they do so (for in many societies religion's effects seem quite circumscribed, in others completely pervasive), how deeply they do so (for some men, and groups of men, seem to wear their religion lightly so far as the secular world goes, while others seem to apply their faith to each occasion, no matter how trivial), and how effectively they do so (for the width of the gap between what religion recommends and what people actually do is most variable cross-culturally)—all these are crucial issues in the comparative sociology and psychology of religion. […]

Glossary

AGNOSTICS: Skeptics or doubters, particularly (but not exclusively) with regard to knowledge of the nature or existence of the Divine.

ASCETICISM: A discipline of self-denial or renunciation, particularly of material goods.

BACONIAN: A reference to Sir Francis Bacon (1561–1626), British attorney, politician, author, and philosopher of science and the scientific method.

CHURINGA: a sacred object, made of wood or stone.

GUERNICA: painting by Pablo Picasso, inspired by the bombing of the city of the same name during the Spanish Civil War, 1937.

JAMES, William (1842–1910): American philosopher and psychologist, and author of *The Varieties of Religious Experience* (1902).

MANA: pervasive supernatural power or spirit in the material world.

NAVAHO: one of the Native American communities of New Mexico and Arizona.

NIRVANA: from Hinduism and Buddhism; ultimate state of spiritual perfection.
PLATONIC: reference to the Greek philosopher Plato (ca. 428–348 BCE); in this case, a reference to a dialogue from Republic, in which prisoners chained to a wall inside a cave understand reality only by the shadows cast onto the blank wall they face.
SYNOPTIC: shared or common.
VERIDICAL: true.
WEBER, Max (1864–1920): German sociologist, author of *The Protestant Ethic and the Spirit of Capitalism* (1904).

Questions for Conversation

According to Geertz, what are "ethos" and "world view," and how does their synthesis constitute religion?

According to Geertz, what is a symbol, and what kinds of symbols are generated by religions?

Why might Geertz emphasize the public and extrinsic character of religious symbols?

According to Geertz, how do systems of symbols serve as both models *of* and model *for* reality?

How are the terms "moods" and "motivations" used in Geertz's definition, and how are they distinguished from each other?

How do systems of symbols help societies wrestle with the problem of meaning, especially the ways that chaos, confusion, and suffering tend to "break in" upon human life and consciousness?

What is the role of ritual in Geertz's thought, and how does ritual relate to his other concepts, like symbols, models of and for reality, moods and motivations, order and chaos, etc.?

For Geertz, how does religion contrast with, but also interact with, everyday life and human awareness called "common sense"?

In what sense does Geertz's definition allow us to study and appreciate the varieties of religious traditions found around the world?

How might Geertz's ideas be applied to the study of religion in popular culture?

Suggestions for Additional Reading

The following is a list of supplemental readings that provide additional information about, apply, or respond critically to the ideas presented in this chapter.

Asad, Talal. "Anthropological Conceptions of Religion: Reflections on Geertz," *Man*, new series 18, no. 2 (1983): 237–59.

Chidester, David. *Authentic Fakes: Religion and American Popular Culture*. Berkeley: University of California Press, 2005.

"Flag and Seal, Seat of Government, and the States." 4 U.S.C. 1 (2011). Available online: https://www.govinfo.gov/content/pkg/USCODE-2011-title4/html/USCODE-2011-title4-chap1.htm (accessed January 19, 2021).

Geertz, Clifford. *The Interpretation of Cultures: Selected Essays*. New York: Basic Books, 1973.

Goldstein, Robert Justin. *Burning the Flag: The Great 1989–1990 American Flag Desecration Controversy*. Kent, OH: Kent State University Press, 1996.

Long, Charles H. "Interpretations of Black Religion in America," in *Significations: Signs, Symbols, and Images in the Interpretation of Religion*, 145–70. Aurora, CO: The Davies Group, 1999.

Lyden, John. *Film as Religion: Myths, Morals, and Rituals*. New York: New York University Press, 2003.

Marvin, Carolyn, and David W. Ingle. *Blood Sacrifice and the Nation: Totem Rituals and the American Flag*. Cambridge: Cambridge University Press, 1999.

Morgan, John. "Religion and Culture as Meaning Systems: A Dialogue between Geertz and Tillich," *Journal of Religion* 57, no. 4 (1977): 363–75.

Munson, Henry, Jr. "Geertz on Religion: The Theory and the Practice," *Religion* 16 (1986): 19–32.

Neumann, Iver B. "Pop Goes Religion: Harry Potter Meets Clifford Geertz," *European Journal of Cultural Studies* 9, no. 1 (2006): 81–100.

Ortner, Sherry. *The Fate of Culture: Geertz and Beyond*. Berkeley: University of California Press, 1999.

Plate, S. Brent. *Religion and Film: Cinema and the Re-Creation of the World*, 2nd ed. New York: Columbia University Press, 2017.

Schilbrack, Kevin. "Religion, Models of, and Reality: Are We Through with Geertz?" *Journal of the American Academy of Religion* 73, no. 2 (2005): 429–52.

11 Edward W. Said

Edward Said (1935–2003) was born in British Mandate Palestine in 1935, spent his youth in Cairo, and from the age of sixteen was educated in the United States, attending a private high school and Princeton University before earning a PhD in English literature at Harvard University and a position at Columbia University in the early 1960s. His most powerful contribution is likely his critique of the production of knowledge to express dominance and maintain power relations, particularly as it reflected Euro-American (primarily British and French, but also American) colonialism and interaction with the Arab Middle East. His 1978 work *Orientalism* (the introduction of which is excerpted here) is often cited as the foundation for the field of postcolonial studies. Putting a label to a critique from those (primarily Arab) peoples living in European outposts who struggled for independence since the Second World War, Said's theory provided a foundation that examined not only political influences but also the cultural and intellectual production of the colonizers as mechanisms supporting the status quo.

Drawing inspiration in part from the Frankfurt School but more directly from the knowledge-power nexus explored by Michele Foucault (1926–84), Said sought to understand what he called the "imaginative geography" that seemed clearly and powerfully to separate the "Occident" (in this case, Western Europe and the United States) from the "Orient" (for Said, the Arab Middle East). Seeing this separation as less a "fact of nature" than a "fact of human production," Said argued that the nature of these constructs created a fiction—the "Orient"—that, particularly with regard to Arab peoples, came to represent danger, lack of education and sophistication, and an "Other" that was both foreign and unable to be assimilated into the dominant culture. Said argued that this construction permeated the centers of intellectual and cultural production—including Western universities—rendering those who studied "the Orient" part of the machinery producing the fiction. He concluded that the resulting fictions—"Occident" and "Orient"—"must be studied as integral components of the social, and not the divine or natural, world." For Said, this required not only an examination of the "object" to be studied but also of the "subject"—or, more precisely, the subjectivity—of the one doing the studying. As he put it in "Orientalism Reconsidered," a follow-up to the piece excerpted here, "there could be no Orientalism without, on the one hand, the Orientalists, and on the other, the Orientals." Because it challenged the premise upon which Western cultural power was defined, Orientalist analysis became popular in the study of any social dynamic in which "un- or mis-represented human groups" sought the right "to speak and represent themselves in domains defined, politically and intellectually, as normally excluding them": women's studies, race and ethnic studies, and (as noted earlier) postcolonial studies.

Critics of the theory have expressed concern that it is inappropriately polarizing. Those identified as "Orientalist" are seen as complicit with the West's domination of non-Western peoples: Eurocentric, imperialist, and racist. Others have expressed concern that it encourages oversimplification and the creation of political and cultural binaries while discouraging reflection, leading its advocates uncritically to accept the narratives of the colonized while rejecting the narratives of the colonizing.

To his critics, Said seemed unconcerned about any lack of critical reflection; there is little doubt that he saw his role as an intellectual as a partisan in the struggle. He was certainly not beyond controversy. A staunch defender of the Palestinian people, Said was accused of falsifying elements of his biography to make his early years seem more tragic than they might actually have been. His writing on the Israeli-Palestinian conflict was condemned by politically conservative intellectuals, both Jewish and not. In 2000 he was photographed throwing stones across the Lebanese border at an Israeli military outpost, claiming initially that he was engaged in a throwing contest with his son. And not surprisingly, he was the subject of intense criticism from scholars who saw themselves as defenders of the impartial study of the Arab Middle East.

Religion scholar Richard King (2005) points out that since the very term "religion" is a "product of the cultural and political history of the West," the application of the Orientalist critique strikes at the very foundation of the comparative study of religion. Nonetheless, scholars of religion and popular culture have with great success used Orientalism in their analyses of depictions of Arabs, as well as Asians and other formerly colonized peoples.

"Introduction" (from *Orientalism*, 1978)[1]

I

On a visit to Beirut during the terrible civil war of 1975-1976 a French journalist wrote regretfully of the gutted downtown area that "it had once seemed to belong to … the **Orient of Chateaubriand** and **Nerval**." He was right about the place, of course, especially so far as a European was concerned. The Orient was almost a European invention, and had been since antiquity a place of romance, exotic beings, haunting memories and landscapes, remarkable experiences. Now it was disappearing; in a sense it had happened, its time was over. Perhaps it seemed irrelevant that Orientals themselves had something at stake in the process, that even in the time of Chateaubriand and Nerval Orientals had lived there, and that now it was they who were suffering; the main thing for the European visitor was a European representation of the Orient and its contemporary fate, both of which had a privileged communal significance for the journalist and his French readers.

Americans will not feel quite the same about the Orient, which for them is much more likely to be associated very differently with the Far East (China and Japan, mainly). Unlike the Americans, the French and the British—less so the Germans, Russians, Spanish, Portuguese, Italians, and Swiss—have had a long tradition of what I shall be calling *Orientalism*, a way of coming to terms with the Orient that is based on the Orient's special

---

[1]Edward Said, excerpt from "Introduction," in *Orientalism* (London: Routledge and Kegan Paul, 1978), 1–26.

place in European Western experience. The Orient is not only adjacent to Europe; it is also the place of Europe's greatest and richest and oldest colonies, the source of its civilizations and languages, its cultural contestant, and one of its deepest and most recurring images of the other. In addition, the Orient has helped to define Europe (or the West) as its contrasting image, idea, personality, experience. Yet none of this Orient is merely imaginative. The Orient is an integral part of European *material* civilization and culture. Orientalism expresses and represents that part culturally and even ideologically as a mode of discourse with supporting institutions, vocabulary, scholarship, imagery, doctrines, even colonial bureaucracies and colonial styles. In contrast, the American understanding of the Orient will seem considerably less dense, although our recent Japanese, Korean, and **Indochinese** adventures ought now to be creating a more sober, more realistic "Oriental" awareness. Moreover, the vastly expanded American political and economic role in the Near East (the Middle East) makes great claims on our understanding of that Orient.

It will be clear to the reader (and will become clearer still throughout the many pages that follow) that by Orientalism I mean several things, all of them, in my opinion, interdependent. The most readily accepted designation for Orientalism is an academic one, and indeed the label still serves in a number of academic institutions. Anyone who teaches, writes about, or researches the Orient and this applies whether the person is an anthropologist, sociologist, historian, or philologist either in its specific or its general aspects, is an Orientalist, and what he or she does is Orientalism. [...]

Related to this academic tradition, whose fortunes, transmigrations, specializations, and transmissions are in part the subject of this study, is a more general meaning for Orientalism. Orientalism is a style of thought based upon an **ontological** and **epistemological** distinction made between "the Orient" and (most of the time) "the **Occident**." [...]

The interchange between the academic and the more or less imaginative meaning of Orientalism is a constant one, and since the late eighteenth century there has been a considerable, quite disciplined perhaps even regulated traffic between the two. Here I come to the third meaning of Orientalism, which is something more historically and materially defined than either of the other two. Taking the late eighteenth century as a very roughly defined starting point Orientalism can be discussed and analyzed as the **corporate** institution for dealing with the Orient—dealing with it by making statements about it, authorizing views of it, describing it, by teaching it, settling it, ruling over it: in short, Orientalism as a Western style for dominating, restructuring, and having authority over the Orient. [...] In brief, because of Orientalism the Orient was not (and is not) a free subject of thought or action. This is not to say that Orientalism unilaterally determines what can be said about the Orient, but that it is the whole network of interests inevitably brought to bear on (and therefore always involved) any occasion when that peculiar entity "the Orient" is in question. [...]

[...] My point is that Orientalism derives from a particular closeness experienced between Britain and France and the Orient, which until the early nineteenth century had really meant only India and the Bible lands. From the beginning of the nineteenth century until the end of World War II France and Britain dominated the Orient and Orientalism; since World War II America has dominated the Orient, and approaches it as France and Britain once did. [...]

II

I have begun with the assumption that the Orient is not an inert fact of nature. It is not merely *there*, just as the Occident itself is not just *there* either: We must take seriously **Vico**'s great observation that men make their own history, that what they can know is what they have made, and extend it to geography: as both geographical and cultural entities—to say nothing of historical entities—such locales, regions geographical sectors as "Orient" and "Occident" are manmade. Therefore as much as the West itself, the Orient is an idea that has a history and a tradition of thought, imagery, and vocabulary that have given it reality and presence in and for the West. The two geographical entities thus support and to an extent reflect each other.

Having said that, one must go on to state a number of reasonable qualifications. In the first place, it would be wrong to conclude that the Orient was *essentially* an idea, or a creation with no corresponding reality. When **Disraeli** said in his novel *Tancred* that the East was a career, he meant that to be interested in the East was something bright young Westerners would find to be an all-consuming passion; he should not be interpreted as saying that the East was *only* a career for Westerners. There were—and are—cultures and nations whose location is in the East, and their lives, histories, and customs have a brute reality obviously greater than anything that could be said about them in the West. About that fact this study of Orientalism has very little to contribute, except to acknowledge it tacitly. But the phenomenon of Orientalism as I study it here deals principally, not with a correspondence between Orientalism and Orient, but with the internal consistency of Orientalism and its ideas about the Orient (the East as career) despite or beyond any correspondence, or lack thereof, with a "real" Orient. My point is that Disraeli's statement about the East refers mainly to that created consistency, that regular constellation of ideas as the pre-eminent thing about the Orient, and not to its mere being, as **Wallace Stevens**'s phrase has it.

A second qualification is that ideas, cultures, and histories cannot seriously be understood or studied without their force, or more precisely their configurations of power, also being studied. To believe that the Orient was created—or, as I call it, "Orientalized"—and to believe that such things happen simply as a necessity of the imagination, is to be disingenuous. The relationship between Occident and Orient is a relationship of power, of domination, of varying degrees of a complex **hegemony**, and is quite accurately indicated in the title of **K. M. Panikkar**'s classic *Asia and Western Dominance*. The Orient was Orientalized not only because it was discovered to be "Oriental" in all those ways considered commonplace by an average nineteenth-century European, but also because it *could be*—that is, submitted to being—*made* Oriental. There is very little consent to be found, for example, in the fact that **Flaubert**'s encounter with an Egyptian courtesan produced a widely influential model of the Oriental woman; she never spoke for herself, she never represented her emotions, presence, or history. *He* spoke for her and represented her. He was foreign, comparatively wealthy, male, and these were historical facts of domination that allowed him not only to possess Kuchuk Hanem physically but to speak for her and tell his readers in what way she was "typically Oriental." My argument is that Flaubert's situation of strength in relation to Kuchuk Hanem was not an isolated instance. It fairly stands for the pattern of relative strength between East and West, and the discourse about the Orient that it enabled.

This brings us to a third qualification. One ought never to assume that the structure of Orientalism is nothing more than a structure of lies or of myths which were the truth about them to be told, would simply blow away. I myself believe that Orientalism is more particularly valuable as a sign of European-Atlantic power over the Orient than it is as a **veridic** discourse about the Orient (which is what, in its academic or scholarly form, it claims to be). Nevertheless, what we must respect and try to grasp is the sheer knitted together strength of Orientalist discourse, its very close ties to the enabling socioeconomic and political institutions, and its redoubtable durability. After all, any system of ideas that can remain unchanged as teachable wisdom (in academies, books, congresses, universities, foreign-service institutes) from the period of **Ernest Renan** in the late 1840s until the present in the United States must be something more formidable than a mere collection of lies. Orientalism, therefore, is not an airy European fantasy about the Orient but a created body of theory and practice in which, for many rations, there has been a considerable material investment. Continued investment made Orientalism, as a system of knowledge about the Orient, an accepted grid for filtering through the Orient into Western consciousness, just as that same investment multiplied—indeed, made truly productive—the statements proliferating out from Orientalism into the general culture.

Connections 11a: Said, Race, and Religion

In October 2008, at a Republican town hall event in Minnesota, an older woman stood up and declared her inability to trust Sen. Barack Obama, Sen. John McCain's Democratic opponent. "He's an Arab," she exclaimed as her justification. Sen. McCain retrieved the microphone and responded: "No, ma'am. He's a decent family man . . . citizen, that I just happen to have disagreements with on fundamental issues."

This exchange points to two important issues underlying the discussion of Orientalism. First, the woman seemed to be confusing a specific ethnicity (Arab) with the religion of Islam. Many people confuse the two, or consider them synonymous, not realizing that (as of 2010) the world's largest populations of Muslims could be found in five non-Arab countries: Indonesia, India, Pakistan, Bangladesh, and Nigeria. The first Arab country to make the list was Egypt (#6 overall), and #7 was Iran—whose citizens proudly distinguish themselves as Persian and not as Arab. Fewer than 20 percent of the global Muslim population live in the Arab Middle East and North Africa; over 60 percent live in the "Asia-Pacific" region. Clearly not every Muslim is an Arab and not every Arab is a Muslim; Edward Said, who devoted so much of his adult life to the Palestinian people—was a life-long Episcopalian who was married to a Quaker.

The second issue raised by the exchange was McCain's seeming refusal to refute the woman's underlying concern. It seems unlikely that the woman meant to identify Obama as an Arab—his father was Kenyan, his mother was born in Kansas to parents who were of British, Welsh, Scottish, Irish, German, and Swiss lineage—but instead as a Muslim, as was falsely rumored throughout the campaign. Rather, it is more likely that McCain understood the woman to be accusing Obama of being a Muslim. Nonetheless, he didn't reply that the rumors were false or that even were his opponent a Muslim he would still have every right to run for President. Instead, he countered that Obama was "a decent family man" and a "citizen"—suggesting that, rather than being either a Muslim or an Arab, his opponent was instead "a decent person," and thus fit to be president. "If I didn't' think I'd be a heck of lot better President I wouldn't be running," McCain concluded.

One of the many contributions of Said's discussion of orientalism is the attention it brought to discussions of ethnicity/race; one of the continuing applications of orientalism is the expansion of it to discussions of religion as well, particularly in an increasingly global society where products marketed popularly cross these often-fluid boundaries.

Gramsci has made the useful analytic distinction between civil and political society in which the former is made up of voluntary (or at least rational and noncoercive) affiliations like schools, families, and unions, the latter of state institutions (the army, the police, the central bureaucracy) whose role in the polity is direct domination. Culture, of course, is to be found operating within civil society, where the influence of ideas, of institutions, and of other persons works not through domination but by what Gramsci calls consent. In any society not **totalitarian**, then, certain cultural forms predominate over others, just as certain ideas are more influential than others; the form of this cultural leadership is what Gramsci has identified as *hegemony*, an indispensable concept for any understanding of cultural life in the industrial West. It is hegemony, or rather the result of cultural hegemony at work, that gives Orientalism the durability and the strength I have been speaking about so far. Orientalism is never far from what **Denys Hay** has called the idea of Europe, a collective notion identifying "us" Europeans as against all "those" non-Europeans, and indeed it can be argued that the major component in European culture is precisely what made that culture hegemonic both in and outside Europe: the idea of European identity as a superior one in comparison with all the non-European peoples and cultures. There is in addition the hegemony of European ideas about the Orient, themselves reiterating European superiority over Oriental backwardness usually overriding the possibility that a more independent, or more skeptical, thinker might have had different views on the matter.

In a quite constant way, Orientalism depends for its strategy on this flexible *positional* superiority, which puts the Westerner in a whole series of possible relationships with the Orient without ever losing him the relative upper hand. And why should it have been otherwise, especially during the period of extraordinary European ascendancy from the late **Renaissance** to the present? The scientist, the scholar, the missionary, the trader, or the soldier was in, or thought about, the Orient because he *could be there*, or could think about it, with very little resistance on the Orient's part. Under the general heading of knowledge of the Orient, and within the umbrella of Western hegemony over the Orient during the period from the end of the eighteenth century, there emerged a complex Orient suitable for study in the academy, for display in the museum, for reconstruction in the colonial office, for theoretical illustration in anthropological, biological, linguistic, racial, and historical theses about mankind and the universe, for instances of economic and sociological theories of development, revolution, cultural personality, national or religious character. Additionally, the imaginative examination of things Oriental was based more or less exclusively upon a sovereign Western consciousness out of whose unchallenged centrality an Oriental world emerged, first according to general ideas about who or what was an Oriental, then according to a detailed logic governed not simply by empirical reality but by a battery of desires, regressions, investments, and projections. If we can point to great Orientalist works of genuine scholarship like **Silvestre de Sacy**'s *Chrestomathie arabe* or **Edward William Lane**'s *Account of the Manners and Customs of the Modern Egyptians*, we need also to note that Renan's and **Gobineau**'s racial ideas came out of the same impulse, as did a great many Victorian pornographic novels (see the analysis by **Steven Marcus** of "**The Lustful Turk**").

[…] What I am interested in doing now is suggesting how the general liberal consensus that "true" knowledge is fundamentally nonpolitical (and conversely, that overtly political knowledge is not "true" knowledge) obscures the highly if obscurely organized political circumstances obtaining when knowledge is produced. No one is helped in understanding this today when the adjective "political" is used as a label to discredit any work for daring to violate the protocol of pretended suprapolitical objectivity. We may say, first, that civil society recognizes a gradation of political importance in the various fields of knowledge. To some extent the political importance given a field comes from the possibility of its direct translation into economic terms; but to a greater extent political importance comes from the closeness of a field to ascertainable sources of power in political society. Thus an economic study of long-term **Soviet** energy potential and its effect on military capability is likely to be commissioned by the Defense Department, and thereafter to acquire a kind of political status impossible for a study of **Tolstoi**'s early fiction financed in part by a foundation. Yet both works belong in what civil society acknowledges to be a similar field, Russian studies, even though one work may be done by a very conservative economist, the other by a radical literary historian. My point here is that "Russia" as a general subject matter has political priority over nicer distinctions such as "economics" and "literary history," because political society in Gramsci's sense reaches into such realms of civil society as the academy and saturates them with significance of direct concern to it.

[…] I doubt that it is controversial, for example, to say that an Englishman in India or Egypt in the later nineteenth century took an interest in those countries that was never far from their status in his mind as British colonies. To say this may seem quite different from saying that all academic knowledge about India and Egypt is somehow tinged and impressed with, violated by, the gross political fact—and yet *that is what I am saying* in this study of Orientalism. For if it is true that no production of knowledge in the human sciences can ever ignore or disclaim its author's involvement as a human subject in his own circumstances, then it must also be true that for a European or American studying the Orient there can be no disclaiming the main circumstances of *his* actuality: that he comes up against the Orient as a European or American first, as an individual second. And to be a European or an American in such a situation is by no means an inert fact. It meant and means being aware, however dimly, that one belongs to a power with definite interests in the Orient, and more important, that one belongs to a part of the earth with a definite history of involvement in the Orient almost since the time of Homer.

Put in this way, these political actualities are still too undefined and general to be really interesting. Anyone would agree to them without necessarily agreeing also that they mattered very much, for instance, to Flaubert as he wrote *Salammbô*, or to **H.A.R. Gibb** as he wrote *Modern Trends in Islam*. The trouble is that there is too great a distance between the big dominating fact, as I have described it, and the details of everyday life that govern the minute discipline of a novel or a scholarly text as each is being written. Yet if we eliminate from the start any notion that "big" facts like imperial domination can be applied mechanically and deterministically to such complex matters as culture and ideas, then we will begin to approach an interesting kind of study. My idea is that European and then American interest in the Orient was political according to some of the obvious historical accounts of it that I have given here, but that it was the culture that created that interest, that acted dynamically along with brute political, economic, and military rationales to make the Orient the varied and complicated place that it obviously was in the field I call Orientalism.

Therefore, Orientalism is not a mere political subject matter or field that is reflected passively by culture, scholarship, or institutions; nor is it a large and diffuse collection of texts about the Orient; nor is it representative and expressive of some nefarious "Western" imperialist plot to hold down the "Oriental" world. It is rather a *distribution* of geopolitical awareness into aesthetic, scholarly, economic, sociological, historical, and philological texts; it is an *elaboration* not only of a basic geographical distinction (the world is made up of two unequal halves, Orient and Occident) but also of a whole series of "interests" which, by such means as scholarly discovery, philological reconstruction, psychological analysis, landscape and sociological description, it not only creates but also maintains; it is, rather than expresses, a certain *will* or *intention* to understand, in some cases to control, manipulate, even to incorporate, what is a manifestly different (or alternative and novel) world; it is, above all, a discourse that is by no means in direct, corresponding relationship with political power in the raw, but rather is produced and exists in an uneven exchange with various kinds of power, shaped to a degree by the exchange with power political (as with a colonial or imperial establishment), power intellectual (as with reigning sciences like comparative linguistics or anatomy, or any of the modern policy sciences), power cultural (as with orthodoxies and canons of taste, texts, values), power moral (as with ideas about what "we" do and what "they" cannot do or understand as "we" do). Indeed, my real argument is that Orientalism is—and does not simply represent—a considerable dimension of modern political-intellectual culture, and as such has less to do with the Orient than it does with "our" world.

[...]

Connections 11b: Said's Orientalism, Religion, and Popular Culture

There is an old story that, in order to prepare for his role as Kwai Chang Caine in the 1970s television series *Kung Fu*, David Carradine studied the figure he considered to be the consummate model of the Buddhist monk: Mr. Spock, the Vulcan from the original television series *Star Trek*. There's another about nuclear physicist J. Robert Oppenheimer thinking (upon seeing the mushroom cloud of the first atomic bomb test blast in New Mexico): "I am become death, destroyer of worlds"—a quote from the Hindu Bhagavad Gita. And a comedian, joking about the very notion of an Olympic boxer from India, mimicked an imagined nonviolent athlete, fists raised, taking blow after blow to the head and body while repeating in a stereotypical accent "Oh, thank you very much." From the exotic Hindu to the contemplative Buddhist, Western popular culture is overflowing with "essentialized" images of adherents of religions founded not only around the Mediterranean but beyond it as well.

While Edward Said's articulation of "Orientalism" transformed conversations in the academic world, be they in (or about) the classroom, in academic presentations, or in print. Of central importance to the study of religion and popular culture has been the way these conversations have expanded considerations of non-Western individuals, images, and traditions, as well as the ways in which these considerations have presented those topics; that is to say, not only have scholars expanded conversations beyond biblical parallels and "Christ figures," for example, but they have also expanded investigations to what presentations of such figures (and others) may represent in terms of power dynamics of the various people represented or signified thereby. While often not considered in such a context, the fact that this conversation (in the American context) came on the heels of the various late 1960s ethno-religious and gender empowerment movements provided a language and justification to the exploration of non-White, non-Euro-American people, traditions, and ideas while also providing for a corrective redress of previous analyses of those same (and other) cultural phenomena.

The kind of political questions raised by Orientalism, then, are as follows: What other sorts of intellectual, aesthetic, scholarly, and cultural energies went into the making of an imperialist tradition like the Orientalist one? How did **philology**, **lexicography**, history, biology, political and economic theory, novel-writing, and lyric poetry come to the service of Orientalism's broadly imperialist view of the world? What changes, modulations, refinements, even revolutions take place within Orientalism? What is the meaning of originality, of continuity, of individuality, in this context? How does Orientalism transmit or reproduce itself from one epoch to another? In fine, how can we treat the cultural, historical phenomenon of Orientalism as a kind of *willed human work*—not of mere, unconditioned **ratiocination**—in all its historical complexity, detail, and worth without at the same time losing sight of the alliance between cultural work, political tendencies, the state, and the specific realities of domination? Governed by such concerns a humanistic study can responsibly address itself to politics *and* culture. But this is not to say that such a study establishes a hard-and-fast rule about the relationship between knowledge and politics. My argument is that each humanistic investigation must formulate the nature of that connection in the specific context of the study, the subject utter, and its historical circumstances.

[...]

It is clear, I hope, that my concern with authority does not entail analysis of what lies hidden in the Orientalist text, but analysis rather of the text's surface, its exteriority to what it describes. I do not think that this idea can be overemphasized. Orientalism is premised upon exteriority, that is, on the fact that the Orientalist, poet or scholar, makes the Orient speak, describes the Orient renders its mysteries plain for and to the West. He is never concerned with the Orient except as the first cause of what he says. What he says and writes, by virtue of the fact that it is said or written, is meant to indicate that the Orientalist is outside the Orient, both as an existential and as a moral fact. The principal product of this exteriority is of course representation: as early as **Aeschylus**'s play *The Persians* the Orient is transformed from a very far distant and often threatening Otherness into figures that are relatively familiar (in Aeschylus's case, grieving Asiatic women). The dramatic immediacy of representation in *The Persians* obscures the fact that the audience is watching a highly artificial enactment of what a non-Oriental has made into a symbol for the whole Orient. My analysis of the Orientalist text therefore places emphasis on the evidence, which is by no means invisible, for such representations *as representations*, not as "natural" depictions of the Orient. This evidence is found just as prominently in the so-called truthful text (histories, philological analyses, political treatises) as in the avowedly artistic (i.e., openly imaginative) text. The things to look at are style, figures of speech, setting, narrative devices, historical and social circumstances, *not* the correctness of the representation nor its fidelity to some great original. The exteriorly of the representation is always governed by some version of the truism that if the Orient could represent itself, it would; since it cannot, the representation does the job, for the West, and **faute de mieux**, for the poor Orient. [...]

Another reason for insisting upon exteriority is that I believe it needs to be made clear about cultural discourse and exchange within a culture that what is commonly circulated by it is not "truth" but representations. It hardly needs to be demonstrated again that language itself is a highly organized and encoded system, which employs many devices to express, indicate, exchange messages and information, represent, and so forth. In any instance of at least written language, there is no such thing as a delivered presence, but a *re-presence*, or a representation. The value, efficacy, strength, apparent veracity of a written statement about the Orient therefore relies very little, and cannot instrumentally depend, on the Orient as such. On the contrary, the written statement is a presence to the reader by virtue of its having excluded, displaced made **supererogatory** any such *real thing* as "the Orient." Thus all of Orientalism stands forth and away from the Orient: that Orientalism makes sense at all depends more on the West than on the Orient, and this sense is directly indebted to various Western techniques of representation that make the Orient visible, clear, "there" in discourse about it. And these representations rely upon institutions, traditions, conventions, agreed-upon codes of understanding for their effects, not upon a distant and amorphous Orient.

The difference between representations of the Orient before the last third of the eighteenth century and those after it (that is, those belonging to what I call modern Orientalism) is that the range of representation expanded enormously in the later period. It is true that after **William Jones** and **Anquetil-Duperron**, and after Napoleon's **Egyptian expedition**, Europe came to know the Orient more scientifically, to live in it with greater authority and discipline than ever before. But what mattered to Europe was the expanded scope and the much greater refinement given its techniques for receiving the Orient. When around the turn of the eighteenth century the Orient definitively revealed the age of its languages—thus outdating Hebrew's divine pedigree—it was a group of Europeans who made the discovery, passed it on to other scholars, and preserved the discovery in the new science of Indo-Europeans philology. A new powerful science for viewing the linguistic Orient was born, and with it, as **Foucault** has shown in *The Order of Things*, a whole web of related scientific interests. Similarly **William Beckford**, **Byron**, **Goethe**, and **Hugo** restructured the Orient by their art and made its colors, lights, and people visible through their images, rhythms, and motifs. At most, the "real" Orient provoked a writer to his vision; it very rarely guided it.

Orientalism responded more to the culture that produced it than to its putative object, which was also produced by the West. Thus the history of Orientalism has both an internal consistency and a highly articulated set of relationships to the dominant culture surrounding it. My analyses consequently try to show the field's shape and internal organization, its pioneers, patriarchal authorities, canonical texts, **doxological** ideas, exemplary figures, its followers, elaborators, and new authorities; I try also to explain how Orientalism borrowed and was frequently informed by "strong" ideas, doctrines, and trends ruling the culture. Thus there was (and is) a linguistic Orient, a **Freudian** Orient, a **Spenglerian** Orient, a **Darwinian** Orient, a racist Orient and so on. Yet never has there been such a thing as a pure, or unconditional, Orient; similarly, never has there been a nonmaterial form of Orientalism, much less something so innocent as an "idea" of the Orient. In this underlying conviction and in its ensuing methodological consequences do I differ from scholars who study the history of ideas. For the emphases and the executive form, above all the material effectiveness, of statements made by Orientalist discourse are possible in ways that any **hermetic** history of ideas tends completely to scant. Without those emphases and that material effectiveness Orientalism would be just another idea, whereas it is and was much more than that. Therefore I set out to examine not only scholarly works but also works of literature, political tracts, journalistic texts, travel books, religious and philological studies. In other words, my hybrid perspective is broadly historical and "anthropological," given that I believe all texts to be worldly and circumstantial in (of course) ways that vary from genre to genre, and from historical period to historical period.

[…]

One aspect of the electronic, **postmodern** world is that there has been a reinforcement of the stereotypes by which the Orient is viewed. Television, the films, and all the media's resources have forced information into more and more standardized molds. So far as the Orient is concerned, standardization and cultural stereotyping have intensified the hold of the nineteenth-century academic and imaginative demonology of "the mysterious Orient." This is nowhere more true than in the ways by which the Near East is grasped. […]

Glossary

AESCHYLUS (ca. 525–455 BCE): Greek playwright, often called the "father of tragedy."

ANQUETIL-DUPERRON, Abraham Hyacinthe (1731–1805): one of the first scholars of India.

BECKFORD, William (1760–1844): British novelist.

BYRON, Lord George Gordon (1788–1824): British poet and author.

CHATEAUBRIAND, François René (1768–1848): French diplomat and author, considered one of the early writers of the Romantic period.

CORPORATE: often used to refer to a large group or social institution.

DARWINIAN: referring to Charles Darwin (1809–82), British naturalist, author of *On the Origin of Species* (1859).

DISRAELI, Benjamin (1804–81): British novelist, politician, and two-time prime minister.

DOXOLOGICAL: (from doxology: traditionally, a hymn of praise for God); often used to suggest standard or common beliefs and dogmas, secular or religious.

EGYPTIAN EXPEDITION: the invasion and attempted occupation of Egypt by French forces between 1798 and 1800.

EPISTEMOLOGICAL: of or having to do with a theory of knowledge, and the distinction between reasonable belief and opinion.

FAUTE DE MIEUX: "for want of an alternative" (French).

FLAUBERT, Gustave (1821–80): French novelist.

FOUCAULT, Michel (1926–84): French philosopher and historian.

FREUDIAN: referring to Sigmund Freud (1856–1939), Austrian psychologist (see separate entry in this volume).

GIBB, H.A.R. (Hamilton Alexander Rosskeen Gibb, 1895–1971): Scottish scholar and historian of Islam and the Middle East.

GOBINEAU, Arthur de (1816–82): French diplomat and writer on theories of race.

GOETHE, Johann Wolfgang von (1749–1832): German novelist and poet of the early Romantic period.

GRAMSCI, Antonio (1891–1937): Italian political philosopher, founder of the Italian communist party.

HAY, Denys (1915–94): British historian, author of *Europe: The Emergence of an Idea* (1968).

HEGEMONY: cultural, social, or political dominance.

HERMETIC: separated, contained, sealed off.

HUGO, Victor (1802–85): French poet and novelist of the Romantic period.

INDOCHINESE: referring to mainland Southeast Asia and the area encompassed by the modern countries of Myanmar, Thailand, Cambodia, Laos, Vietnam, and mainland Malaysia.

JONES, William (1746–94): British attorney, linguist, and scholar of Hinduism, India, and Iran.

LANE, Edward William (1801–76): British linguist and scholar of Egypt and Islam.

LEXICOGRAPHY: the study and/or organization of definitions and semantics of words.

"The LUSTFUL TURK": an erotic novel (subtitled "Lascivious Scenes from a Harem") by John Benjamin Brookes, first published anonymously in 1828.

MARCUS, Steven (1928–2018): American literary critic and scholar of Victorian era literature.

NERVAL, Gérard de (1808–55): pen name of Gérard Labrunie, French poet and travel writer.

"OCCIDENT": term often used to identify Western Europe and America.

ONTOLOGICAL: knowledge of or related to the nature of being.

"ORIENT": term often used to identify Asia (South Asia, East Asia, etc. — but not Australia or New Zealand), Persia, and as well as the Arab countries and cultures on the eastern edge of the Mediterranean Sea.

PANIKKAR, Kavalam Madhava "K. M." (1895–1963): Indian historian and diplomat, author of *Asia and Western Dominance* (1959).

PHILOLOGY: the study of the history, nature, and structure of language.

POSTMODERN: term used to describe recent culture in which the "modern" (nation-state defined, industrialist, largely "Western" cultural attitude that has supported a dominant or singular historical narrative) has been challenged by a more global, non-industrialist culture with greater sensitivity to diverse (and traditionally marginal) historical and social perspectives.

RATIOCINATION: the process of exact thinking.

RENAISSANCE: period of European intellectual and political history (1300s–1600s) marked by a "rediscovery" of Greek and Roman literature, philosophy, and intellectual materials.

RENAN, Joseph Ernest (1823–92): French historian, linguist, and scholar of Semitic and Near Eastern religions.

SILVESTRE de SACY, Antoine Isaac (1758–1838): French linguist and scholar of Middle Eastern languages.

SOVIET: referring to the Soviet Union, the successor state of tsarist Russia, which collapsed into constituent states in the late 1980s.

SPENGLERIAN: referring to Oswald Spengler (1880–1936), German historian, philosopher of history, and author of *The Decline of the West* (1918).

STEVENS, Wallace (1879–1955): American poet.

SUPEREROGATORY: more than is wanted or required.

TOLSTOI, Leo (1828–1910): Russian author, novelist.

TOTALITARIAN: related to dictatorial authority and complete subservience.

VERIDIC: relating to beliefs that seem to be confirmed later.

VICO, Giovanni Battista "Giambattista" (1668–1744): Italian philosopher of history and law.

Questions for Conversation

Said defines Orientalism as many things: an academic activity, an imaginative "style of thought," and a "corporate institution" for dealing with the Orient. How are these related?

According to Said, in what way is power essential for understanding the development and continued existence of Orientalism?

Why does Said think that Orientalism is not simply "lies and myths" that knowledge of the truth would be able to dispel? What makes it strong and durable?

How does Said use the concepts of civil society, political society, and hegemony?

Why, according to Said, has Orientalism never been far from the concept of the "European"?

How does Said challenge the liberal notion that "true" knowledge is non-political? Why is knowledge seeking and knowledge production politicized?

How deep does Orientalism go? Why does Said believe that both scientific studies and artistic works are pervasively shaped by Orientalism?

Why does Said look to "exteriorities" in texts about the Orient and "Western techniques of representation" to find evidences of Orientalism?

How do modern media and popular culture—especially film, television, and news reporting—reflect the deeper influence of earlier academic Orientalism?

Ultimately, what does Orientalism tell us about "the Orient"? What does it tell us about the "Orientalizers"?

Suggestions for Additional Reading

The following is a list of supplemental readings that provide additional information about, apply, or respond critically to the ideas presented in this chapter.

Classen, Chris. "Becoming the 'Noble Savage': Nature Religion and the 'Other' in *Avatar*," in *Avatar and Nature Spirituality*, ed. Bron Taylor, 143–60. Waterloo, ON: Wilfrid Laurier University Press, 2013.

Dimitrova, Diana. "Hinduism and Its Others in Bollywood Film of the 2000s," *Journal of Religion & Film* 20 (2016): Article 10. Available online: http://digitalcommons.unomaha.edu/jrf/vol 20/iss1/10

Halliday, Fred. "'Orientalism' and Its Critics," *British Journal of Middle Eastern Studies* 20, no. 2 (1993): 145–63.

Iwamura, Jane Naomi. "The Oriental Monk in American Popular Culture," in *Religion and American Popular Culture*, ed. Bruce David Forbes and Jeffrey H. Mahan, rev. ed., 25–43. Berkeley: University of California Press, 2005.

Iwamura, Jane Naomi. *Virtual Orientalism: Asian Religions and American Popular Culture*. New York: Oxford University Press, 2011.

Jones, Catherine, and Atsushi Tajima. "The Caucasionization of Jesus: Hollywood Transforming Christianity into a Racially Hierarchical Discourse," *Journal of Religion and Popular Culture* 27 (2015): 202–19.

Kalman, Julie. *Orientalizing the Jew: Religion, Culture, and Imperialism in Nineteenth-Century France*. Bloomington: Indiana University Press, 2017.

King, Richard. *Orientalism and Religion: Post-Colonial Theory, India, and the "Mystical East."* New York: Routledge, 1999.

King, Richard. "Orientalism and the Study of Religions," in *Routledge Companion to the Study of Religion*, ed. John R. Hinnells, 275–90. New York: Routledge, 2005.

Lee, Robert G. *Orientals: Asian Americans in Popular Culture*. Philadelphia, PA: Temple University Press, 1999.

Lewis, Bernard. "The Question of Orientalism," *New York Review of Books* 29, no. 11 (June 24, 1982): 49–56.

Mullen, Eve. "Orientalist Commercializations: Tibetan Buddhism in American Popular Film," *Journal of Religion & Film* 2 (2015): Article 5. Available online: http://digitalcommons.unomaha.edu/jrf/vol2/iss2/5

Muravchik, Joshua. "Enough Said: The False Scholarship of Edward Said," *World Affairs* 175, 6 (2013): 9–21.

Nichols, Michael. "Returning the Demon's Gaze: Analyzing the Buddhist Figure of Mara in Popular Culture," *Journal of Religion and Popular Culture* 29 (2017): 44–54.

Said, Edward W. *Orientalism*. New York: Pantheon Books, 1978.

Said, Edward W., Oleg Grabar, and Bernard Lewis. "Orientalism: An Exchange," *New York Review of Books* 29, no. 13 (August 12, 1982): 46–8.

Said, Edward W. "Orientalism Reconsidered," *Cultural Critique* 1 (1985): 89–107.

Schroeder, Caroline T. "Ancient Egyptian Religion on the Silver Screen: Modern Anxieties about Race, Ethnicity, and Religion," *Journal of Religion & Film* 7 (2016): Article 1. Available online: http://digitalcommons.unomaha.edu/jrf/vol7/iss2/1

Shaheen, Jack G. *The TV Arab*. Bowling Green, OH: Bowling Green State University Popular Press, 1984.

Shaheen, Jack G. "Reel Bad Arabs: How Hollywood Vilifies a People," *Annals of the American Society of Political Science* 588 (2003): 171–93.

Strömberg, Fredrik. "'Yo, rag-head!': Arab and Muslim Superheroes in American Comic Books after 9/11," *Amerikastudien/American Studies* 56 (2011): 573–601.

Turner, Bryan S. *Orientalism, Postmodernism and Globalism*. New York: Routledge, 2002.

Turner, Bryan S. "Edward W. Said: Overcoming Orientalism," *Theory, Culture & Society* 21, no. 1 (2004): 173–7.

Zebra, Kate. "The Redeployment of Orientalist Themes in Contemporary Islamophobia," *Studies in Contemporary Islam* 10 (2008): 4–44.

12 Stuart Hall

When Stuart Hall (1932–2014) moved from his native Jamaica to London for graduate school to study English, he soon became more interested in politics than in his studies. He left Oxford University to teach in adult education, then to work as the founding editor for the political journal *The New Left Review* in 1960. He joined the Centre for Contemporary Cultural Studies at the University of Birmingham after writing an influential study of film, *The Popular Arts*, and became its director in 1968, a position he served until 1979 when he was appointed professor at the Open University.

Hall is considered a founding figure of what has come to be known as the Birmingham School of Cultural Studies. Other important figures associated with the Birmingham School include Richard Hogart, Paul Gilroy, Angela McRobbie, Larry Grossberg, Richard Johnson, Paul Willis, and Dick Hebdige. The Birmingham School was influenced by but criticized Frankfurt School's critical theory, saying that the Frankfurt School put too much emphasis on producers, while Birmingham School, still interested in power, emphasized the consumer/audience/reception side of cultural dynamics. Hall's theory of "encoding/decoding" explored the distinction between the ideological messages "encoded" in cultural products by their producers (which was the primary interest of scholars like Horkheimer and Adorno) and the "decoding" of those messages by audiences. Against the Frankfort School's depiction of audiences as swallowing dominant ideologies whole, Hall argued that audiences had a more active and dynamic role in interpreting those messages. They might, for instance, reject the ideology "encoded" by media producers or "negotiate" their reading of cultural products by accepting part, rejecting part, or otherwise interpreting them in ways not fully in line with dominant ideologies.

As a middle-class Jamaican in Britain, Hall was especially attuned to the ways that the media and cultural producers represented race, class, and ethnicity, and the ways that such representations were bound up with issues of power, politics, and identity. Likewise, as the excerpt here shows, Hall was concerned with the way that social, economic, and political power was maintained through culture, especially by presenting some cultural practices and products as "high" or legitimate and others as "low" or illegitimate. By taking "popular culture" seriously, Hall was not only valorizing the cultural work of "the people" but also analyzing how distinctions between high and low, or elite and popular culture are politically and ideologically charged and produced.

Like Horkheimer and Adorno, Stuart Hall wrote little on religion himself. One exception is his discussion of Rastafarianism as a "cultural revolution" of Black colonial identity, in a 1995 essay in *The New Left Review*. Nevertheless, his perspective has had a profound influence on the study of popular culture, and his analyses of identity and power are deeply relevant to thinking about religion.

"Notes on Deconstructing 'The Popular'" (1981)[1]

Throughout the long transition into agrarian capitalism and then in the formation and development of industrial capitalism, there is a more or less continuous struggle over the culture of working people, the labouring **classes** and the poor. This fact must be the starting point for any study, both on the basis for, and of the transformations of, popular culture. The changing balance and relations of social forces throughout that history reveal themselves, time and again, in struggles over the forms of the culture, traditions and ways of life of the popular classes. **Capital** had a stake in the culture of the popular classes because the constitution of a whole new social order around capital required a more or less continuous, if intermittent, process of re-education, in the broadest sense. And one of the principle sites of **resistance** to the forms through which this "reformation" of the people was pursued lay in popular tradition. That is why popular culture is linked, for so long, to questions of tradition, of traditional forms of life and why its "traditionalism" has been so often misinterpreted as a product of a merely conservative impulse, backward-looking and anachronistic. Struggle and resistance—but also, of course, appropriation and *ex*-propriation. Time and again, what we are really looking at is the active destruction of particular ways of life, and their transformation into something new. "Cultural change" is a polite euphemism for the process by which some cultural forms and practices are driven out of the centre of popular life, actively marginalized. Rather than simply "falling into disuse" through the **Long March** of modernization, things are actively pushed aside, so that something else can take their place. The magistrate and the **evangelical** police have, or ought to have, a more "honoured" place in the history of popular culture than they have usually been accorded. Even more important than ban and proscription is that subtle and slippery customer—"reform" (with all the positive and unambiguous overtones it carries today). One way or another, "the people" are frequently the object of "reform": often, for their own good, of course—"in their best interests". We understand struggle and resistance, nowadays, rather better than we do reform and transformation. Yet "transformations" are at the heart of the study of popular culture. I mean the active work on existing traditions and activities, their active reworking, so that they come out a different way: they appear to "persist"—yet, from one period to another, they come to stand in a different relation to the ways working people live and the ways they define their relations to each other, to "the others" and to their conditions of life. Transformation is the key to the long and protracted process of the "moralisation" of the labouring classes, and the "demoralisation" of the poor, and the "re-education" of the people. Popular culture is neither, in a "pure" sense, the popular traditions of resistance to these processes; nor is it the forms which are superimposed on and over them. It is the ground on which the transformations are worked.

---

[1] Stuart Hall, excerpt from "Notes on Deconstructing 'the Popular,'" in *People's History and Socialist Theory*, ed. Raphael Samuel (London: Routledge and Kegan Paul, 1981), 227–40.

In the study of popular culture, we should always start here: with the double stake in popular culture, the double movement of **containment** and resistance, which is always inevitably inside it.

The study of popular culture has tended to oscillate wildly between the two alternative poles of that **dialectic**—containment/resistance. We have had some striking and marvelous reversals. Think of the really major revolution in historical understanding which has followed as the history of "polite society" and the **Whig** aristocracy in eighteenth-century England has been upturned by the addition of the history of the turbulent and ungovernable people. The popular traditions of the eighteenth-century labouring poor, the popular classes and the "loose and disorderly sort" often, now, appear as virtually independent formations: tolerated in a state of permanently unstable equilibrium in relatively peaceful and prosperous times; subject to arbitrary excursions and expeditions in times of panic and crisis. Yet though formally these were the cultures of the people "outside the walls", beyond political society and the triangle of power, they were never, in fact, outside of the larger field of social forces and cultural relations. They not only constantly pressed on "society"; they were linked and connected with it, by a multitude of traditions and practices. Lines of "alliance" as well as lines of cleavage. From these cultural bases, often far removed from the dispositions of law, power and authority, "the people" threatened constantly to erupt; and, when they did so, they broke on to the stage of patronage and power with a threatening din and clamour—with fife and drum, **cockade** and effigy, proclamation and ritual—and, often, with a striking, popular, ritual discipline. Yet never quite overturning the delicate strands of paternalism, deference and terror within which they were constantly if insecurely constrained. In the following century, when the "labouring" and the "dangerous" classes lived without benefit of that fine distinction the reformers were so anxious to draw (this was a *cultural* distinction as well as a moral and economic one: and a great deal of legislation and regulation was devised to operate directly on it), some areas preserved for long periods a virtually impenetrable enclave character. It took virtually the whole length of the century before the representatives of "law and order"—the new police—could acquire anything like a regular and customary foothold within them. Yet, at the same time, the penetration of the cultures of the labouring masses and the urban poor was deeper, more continuous—and more continuously 'educative' and reformatory—in that period than at any time since.

[...] There is no separate, autonomous, "authentic" layer of working-class culture to be found. Much of the most immediate forms of popular recreation, for example, are saturated by popular imperialism. Could we expect otherwise? How could we explain, and what would we *do* with the idea of, the culture of a dominated class which, despite its complex interior formations and differentiations, stood in a very particular relation to a major restructuring of capital; which itself stood in a peculiar relation to the rest of the world; a people bound by the most complex ties to a changing set of material relations and conditions; who managed somehow to construct "a culture" which remained untouched by the most powerful dominant ideology—popular imperialism? Especially when that ideology—belying its name—was directed as much at them as it was at Britain's changing position in a world capitalism expansion?

Think, in relation to the question of popular imperialism, of the history and relations between the people and one of the major means of cultural expression: the press. To go back to displacement and superimposition—we can see clearly how the liberal middle-class press of the mid-nineteenth century was constructed on the back of the active destruction and marginalisation of the indigenous radical and working-class press. But, on top of that process, something qualitatively new occurs towards the end of the nineteenth century and the beginning of the twentieth century in this area: the active, mass insertion of a developed and mature working-class audience into a new kind of *popular*, commercial press. This has had profound cultural consequences: though it isn't in any narrow sense exclusively a "cultural" question at all. It required the whole reorganisation of the capital basis and structure of the cultural industry; a harnessing of new forms of technology and of labour processes; the establishment of new types of distribution operating through the new cultural mass markets. But one of its effects was indeed a reconstituting of the cultural and political relations between the dominant and the dominated classes: a change intimately connected with that containment of popular democracy on which "our democratic way of life" today appears to be so securely based. Its results are all too palpably with us still, today: a popular press, the more strident and virulent as it gradually shrinks; organised by capital "for" the working classes; with, nevertheless, deep and influential roots in the culture and language of the "underdog," of "Us": with the power to represent the class to itself in its most traditionalist form. This is a slice of the history of "popular culture" well worth unravelling.

Of course, one could not begin to do so without talking about many things which don't usually figure in the discussion of "culture" at all. They have to do with the reconstruction of capital and the rise of the collectivism and the formation of a new kind of "educative" state as much as with recreation, dance and popular song. As an area of serious historical work, the study of popular culture is like the study of labour history and its institutions. To declare an interest in it is to correct a major imbalance, to mark a significant oversight. But, in the end, it yields most when it is seen in relation to a more general, a wider history.

[...]

Connections 12a: Hall, Race, Identity, and Popular Music

In Stuart Hall's view, religion, like all cultural forms, is always bound up with other social, material, and ideological forces; it doesn't have an intrinsic, atemporal truth or meaning. But it is not random; it has long, enduring historical connections to a society and is a basic cultural language and system of expression through which members of a society articulate self, community, power, and orientation. One of Hall's interests was in the use of biblical language and symbols among Rastafarians, particularly in the musical form associated with the religion, reggae, which began in Hall's birthplace of Jamaica but soon became popular in England, the United States, and worldwide. Hall viewed the resignification of biblical text, a cultural form introduced to displaced people of African origins by their enslavers and a dominant European culture, as a religiously based form of cultural work that produced a new orientation and sense of self in a new situation:

> In the case of the Rastafarians in Jamaica: Rasta was a funny language, borrowed from a text—the Bible—that did not belong to them; they had to turn the text upside-down, to get a meaning which fit their experience. But in turning the text

upside-down they remade themselves; they positioned themselves differently as new political subjects; they reconstructed themselves as blacks in the new world: they became what they are. And, positioning themselves in that way, they learned to speak a new language. And they spoke it with a vengeance. They learned to speak and sing. And in so doing, they did not assume that their only cultural resources lay in the past. They did not go back and try to recover some absolutely pure "folk culture", untouched by history, as if that would be the only way they could learn to speak. No, they made use of the modern media to broadcast their message. "Don't tell us about tom-toms in the forest. We want to use the new means of articulation and production to make a new music, with a new message." This is a cultural transformation. It is not something totally new. It is not something which has a straight, unbroken line of continuity from the past. It is transformation through a reorganization of the elements of a cultural practice, elements which do not in themselves have any necessary political connotations. It is not the individual elements of a discourse that have political or ideological connotations, it is the ways those elements are organized together in a new discursive formation. (Hall 1996: 143)

Reggae was not the only new form of religious music that expressed a community identity and orientation in the African diaspora. In the United States, theologian James Cone earlier explored the spirituals and the blues as popular culture, spiritual orientation, and cultural resources in his book *The Spirituals and the Blues* (1972).

The development of Hip Hop culture and rap music was heavily influenced by another religious tradition that operated to produce an oppositional race-based identity to American Christianity, the Five Percent Nation (also known as the Nation of Gods and Earths), an offshoot of the Nation of Islam. Like Hall, scholars such as Michael Muhammed Knight (2013) and Felicia Miyakawa (2005) have interpreted the formations of this musical genre in the material and historical context of a marginalized people resisting dominant cultural frameworks of identity and power.

[...] To write a history of the culture of the popular classes exclusively from inside those classes, without understanding the ways in which they are constantly held in relation with the institutions of dominant cultureal production, is not to live in the twentieth century. The point is clear about the twentieth century. I believe it holds good for the nineteenth and eighteenth centuries as well.

[...]

Next, I want to say something about "popular." The term can have a number of different meanings: not all of them useful. Take the most common-sense meaning: the things which are said to be "popular" because masses of people listen to them, buy them, read them, consume them, and seem to enjoy them to the full. This is the "market" or commercial definition of the term: the one which brings socialists out in spots. It is quite rightly associated with the manipulation and debasement of the culture of the people. In one sense, it is the direct opposite of the way I have been using the word earlier. I have, though, two reservations about entirely dispensing with this meaning, unsatisfactory as it is.

First, if it is true that, in the twentieth century, vast number of people *do* consume and even indeed enjoy the cultural products of our modern culture industry, then it follows that very substantial numbers of working people must be included within the audiences for such products. Now, if the forms and relationships on which participation in this sort of commercially provided "culture" depend are purely manipulative and debased, then the people who consume and enjoy them must either be themselves debased by these activities or else living in a permanent state of "false consciousness." They must be "cultural dopes" who can't tell that what they are being fed is an updated form of the opium of the people. That judgment may make us feel right, decent and self-satisfied about our denunciations of the agents of mass manipulation and deception—the capitalist cultural industries: but I don't know that it is a view which can survive for long as an adequate account of cultural relationships; and even less as a socialist perspective on the culture and nature of the working class. Ultimately, the notion of the people as a purely *passive*, outline force is a deeply unsocialist perspective.

Second, then: can we get around this problem without dropping the inevitable and necessary attention to the manipulative aspect of a great deal of commercial popular culture? There are a number of strategies for doing so, adopted by radical critics and theorists of popular culture, which, I think, are highly dubious. One is to counterpose to it another, whole, "alternative" culture—the authentic "popular culture"; and to suggest that the "real" working class (whatever that is) isn't taken in by the commercial substitutes. This is a heroic alternative; but not a very convincing one. Basically what is wrong with it is that it neglects the absolutely essential relations of cultural power—of domination and subordination— which is an intrinsic feature of cultural relation. I want to assert on the contrary that there is no whole, authentic, autonomous "popular culture" which lies outside the field of force of the relations of cultural power and domination. Second, it greatly underestimates the power of cultural implantation. This is a tricky point to make, for as soon as it *is* made, one opens oneself to the charge that one is subscribing to the thesis of cultural incorporation. The study of popular culture keeps shifting between these two, quite unacceptable, poles: pure "autonomy" or total incapsulation [*sic*].

Actually, I don't think it is necessary or right to subscribe to either. Since ordinary people are not cultural dopes, they are perfectly capable of recognizing the way the realities of working-class life are organized, reconstructed and reshaped by the way they are represented (i.e. re-presented) in, say, **Coronation Street**. The cultural industries do have the power constantly to rework and reshape what they represent; and, by repetition and selection, to impose and implant such definitions of ourselves as fit more easily the descriptions of the dominant or preferred culture. That is what the concentration of cultural power—the means of culture-making in the heads of the few—actually means. These definitions don't have the power to occupy our minds; they don't function on us as if we are blank screens. But they do occupy and rework the interior contradictions of feeling and perception in the dominated classes; they *do* find or clear a space of recognition in those who respond to them. Cultural domination has real effects—even if these are neither all-powerful nor all-inclusive. If we were to argue that these imposed forms have no influence, it would be tantamount to arguing that the culture of the people can exist as a separate enclave, outside the distribution of cultural power and the relations of cultural force. I do not believe that.

Rather, I think there is a continuous and necessarily uneven and unequal struggle, by the dominant culture, constantly to disorganise and reorganize popular culture; to enclose and confine its definitions and forms within a more inclusive range of dominant forms. There are points of resistance; there are also moments of supersession. This is the dialectic of cultural struggle. In our times, it goes on continuously, in the complex lines of resistance and acceptance, refusal and capitulation, which make the field of culture a sort of constant battlefield. A battlefield where no once-for-all victories are obtained but where there are always strategic positions to be won and lost.

This first definition, then, is not a useful one for our purposes; but it might force us to think more deeply about the complexity of cultural relations, about the reality of cultural power and about the nature of cultural implantation. If the forms of provided commercial popular culture are not purely manipulative, then it is because, alongside the false appeals, the foreshortenings, the trivialisation and short circuits, there are also elements of recognition and identification, something approaching a re-creation of recognizable experiences and attitudes, to which people are responding. The danger arises because we tend to think of cultural forms as whole and coherent: either wholly corrupt or wholly authentic. Whereas they are deeply contradictory; they play on contradictions, especially when they function in the domain of the "popular." The language of the **Daily Mirror** is neither a pure construction of **Fleet Street** "**newspeak**" nor is it the language which its working-class readers actually speak. It is a highly complex species of linguistic *ventriloquism* in which the debased brutalism of popular journalism is skillfully combined and intricate with some elements of the directness and vivid particularity of working-class language. It cannot get by without preserving some element of its roots in a real vernacular—in "the popular." It wouldn't get very far unless it were capable of reshaping popular elements into a species of canned and neutralized demotic populism.

The second definition of "popular" is easier to live with. This is the descriptive one. Popular culture is all those things that "the people" do or have done. This is close to an "anthropological" definition of the term: the culture, mores, customs and folkways of "the people." What defines their "distinctive way of life." I have two difficulties with this definition, too.

First, I am suspicious of it precisely because it is too descriptive. This is putting it mildly. Actually, it is based on an infinitely expanding inventory. Virtually *anything* which "the people" have ever done can fall into the list. Pigeon-fancying and stamp collecting, flying ducks on the wall and garden gnomes. The problem is how to distinguish this infinite list, in any but a descriptive way, from what popular culture is *not*.

But the second difficulty is more important—and relates to a point made earlier. We can't simply collect into one category all the things which "the people" do, without observing that the real analytic distinction arises, not from the list itself—an inert category of things and activities—but from the key opposition: the people/not of the people. That is to say, the structuring principle of 'the popular' in this sense is the tensions and oppositions between what belongs to the central domain of elite or dominant culture, and the culture of the "periphery." It is this opposition which constantly structures the domain of culture into the "popular" and the "non-popular." But you cannot construct these oppositions in a purely descriptive way. For, from period to period, the *contents* of each category change. Popular forms become enhanced in cultural value, go up the cultural escalator—and find themselves on the opposite side. Others [*sic*] things cease to have high cultural value, and are appropriated into the popular, becoming transformed in the process. The structuring principle does not consist of the contents of each category—which, I insist, will alter from one period to another. Rather, it consists of the forces and relations which sustain the distinction, the difference: roughly, between what, at any time, counts as an elite cultural activity of form, and what does not. These categories remain, though the inventories change. What is more, a whole set of institutions and institutional processes are required to sustain each—and to continually mark the difference between them. The school and the education system is one such institution—distinguishing the valued part of the culture, the cultural heritage, the history to be transmitted, from the "valueless" part. The literary and scholarly apparatus is another—marking off certain kinds of valued knowledge from others. The important fact, then, is not a mere descriptive inventory—which may have the negative effect of freezing popular culture into some timeless descriptive mould—but the relations of power which are constantly punctuating and dividing the domain of culture into its preferred and its residual categories.

Connections 12b: Hall, Dominance, and Resistance through Popular Culture

If Clifford Geertz was interested in how symbols and cultural acts shared common meanings within a culture; and Roland Barthes revealed how cultural phenomena like fashion and professional sports act as myths that naturalize dominant structures of power; and Max Horkheimer and Theodor Adorno maintained that the culture industry turned audiences into passive consumers of market interests and capitalist ideology, then Stuart Hall's work took a radical turn away from this emphasis on *sameness* and shared meaning by paying particular attention to the uses that audiences and consumers made of texts and media productions. To Hall, authors and producers were only one element of the "circuit of culture." Cultural products were, to Hall, sites of negotiation where the meanings intended by their producers could be subverted or resignified by consumers and audiences. Popular (and religious) culture was therefore a resource for producing and expressing alternative, resistant, and oppositional values, identities, and forms of community to those of the dominant ideology.

Some examples of scholarship building from Hall's approach include Lynn Schofield Clark's study of American teenage audiences of supernaturally themed television shows, *From Angels to Aliens* (2003). Contrary to either blind acceptance or rejection of representations of supernatural beings and forces as portrayed in these shows, Clark found a variety of "different ways in which young people approach and incorporate what they learn from the media into their beliefs and practices related to religion and spirituality" (19). These perspectives ranged from outright rejection of popular media as an authority on spiritual and religious knowledge to an experimental exploration of the possibilities of pop cultural assertions of supernatural beings.

In a more politically charged context, Purnima Mankekar's *Screening Culture, Viewing Politics* examined female audiences of Doordarshan, state-run nationalist television programs in India, many based on mythological or epic texts such as the Ramayana and the Mahabharata. She found, following Hall, that audience were not simply compliant to the nationalist values presented by the programs, but neither were they necessarily resistant. Instead, the women she studied naturalized, appropriated, or subverted dominant discourses depending upon the inequalities and differences related to the positions they occupied on various axes of power. Doordarshan, Mankekar argued, "played a crucial role in the discursive slippages between 'national culture' and 'Hindu culture,' and in the exclusion of experiences, memories, and modes of living not authorized by upper-caste, upper-class Hindu elites" (1999: 8).

Romance texts, from novels to television shows to movies, have been of particular interest to some feminist scholars of religion and popular culture, illuminating both the strong persistence of male-dominated heteronormative gender roles that are often legitimized by appeals to religious values, on the one hand, and resistant and oppositional readings by consumers who find ways to negotiate alternatives to those assumptions. Lynn S. Neal's *Romancing God* (2005), for example, showed evangelical Christian women interpreting gender expectations in surprising ways. Likewise, feminist Mormon theologian Margaret M. Toscano presented Mormon author Stephanie Meyer's *Twilight* vampire novels as a resistant, oppositional treatment of LDS teachings about relationships, sexuality, marriage, and morality, reflecting yet subverting Mormon expectations. Toscano showed how a popular culture text that might appear to uphold socially conservative gender roles of dominant American society, when read in a Mormon context, unfolds a host of more challenging interpretations.

Stuart Hall's important refocusing of attention on the active, dynamic, productive labor of consumers and audiences has been a critical influence on cultural studies, and on studies of religion that emphasize how religion is "lived" and practiced in everyday life by religious individuals and communities. Top-down perspectives that assume a seamlessly shared community of belief, practice, and identity that reflects the perspectives and intentions of religious leaders appear too static and simplistic.

So I settle for a third definition of "popular," though it is a rather uneasy one. This looks, in any particular period, at those forms and activities which have their roots in the social and material conditions of particular classes; which have been embodied in popular traditions and practices. In this sense, it retains what is valuable in the descriptive definition. But it goes on to insist that what is essential to the definition of popular culture is the relations which define "popular culture" in a continuing tension (relationship, influence and antagonism) to the dominant culture. It is a conception of culture which is polarized around this cultural dialectic. It treats the domain of cultural forms and activities as a constantly changing field. Then it looks at the relations which constantly structure this field into dominant and subordinate formations. It looks at the process by which these relations of dominance and subordination are articulated. It treats them as a process: the process by means of which some things are actively preferred so that others can be dethroned. It has at its centre the changing and uneven relations of force which define the field of culture—that is, the question of cultural struggle and its many forms. Its main focus of attention is the relation between culture and questions of hegemony.

What we have to be concerned with, in this definition, is not the question of the "authenticity" of organic wholeness of popular culture. Actually, it recognizes that almost *all* cultural forms will be contradictory in this sense, composed of antagonistic and unstable elements. The meaning of a cultural form and its place or position in the cultural field is *not* inscribed inside its form. Nor is its position fixed once and for ever. This year's radical symbol or slogan will be neutralized into next year's fashion; the year after, it will be the object of a profound cultural nostalgia. Today's rebel folksinger ends up, tomorrow, on the cover of the **Observer** color magazine. The meaning of a cultural symbol is given in part by the social field into which it is incorporated, the practices with which it articulates and is made to resonate. What matters is *not* the intrinsic or historically fixed objects of culture, but the state of play in cultural relations: to put it bluntly and in an oversimplified form—what counts is the class struggle in and over culture.

Almost every fixed inventory will betray us. Is the novel a "**bourgeois**" form? The answer can only be historically provisional: When? Which novels? For whom? Under what conditions?

[...]

Cultural struggle, of course, takes many forms: incorporation, distortion, resistance, negotiation, recuperation. Raymond Williams has done us a great deal of service by outlining some of the processes, with his distinction between emergent, residual and incorporated moments. We need to expand and develop this rudimentary schema. The important thing is to look at it dynamically: as an historical process. Emergent forces reappear in ancient historical disguise; emergent forces, pointing to the future, lose their anticipatory power, and become merely backward-looking; today's cultural breaks can be recuperated as a support to tomorrow's dominant system of values and meanings. The struggle continues: but it is almost never in the same place, over the same meaning or value. It seems to me that the cultural process—cultural power—in our society depends, in the first instance, on this drawing of the line, always in each period in a different place, as to what is to be incorporated into "the great tradition" and what is not. Educational and cultural institutions, along with the many positive things they do, also help to discipline and police this boundary.

This should make us think again about that tricky term in popular culture, "tradition." Tradition is a vital element in culture; but it has little to do with the mere persistence of old forms. It has much more to do with the way elements have been linked together or articulated. These arrangements in a national-popular culture have no fixed or inscribed position, and certainly no meaning which is carried along, so to speak, in the stream of historical tradition, unchanged. Not only can the elements of "tradition" be rearranged, so that they articulate with different practices and positions, and take on a new meaning and relevance. It is also often the case that cultural struggle arises in its sharpest form just at the point where different, opposed traditions meet, intersect. They seek to detach a cultural form from its implantation in one tradition, and to give it a new cultural resonance or accent. Traditions are not fixed forever: certainly not in any universal position in relation to a single class. Cultures, concieved not as separate "ways of life," but as "ways of struggle," constantly intersect: the pertinent cultural struggles arise at the points of intersection. [...]

This provides us with a warning against those self-enclosed approaches to popular culture which, valuing "tradition" for its own sake, and treating it in an ahistorical manner, analyse popular cultural forms as if they contained within themselves, from their moment of origin, some fixed and unchanging meaning or value. The relationship between historical position and aesthetic value is an important and difficult question in popular culture. But the attempt to develop some universal popular aesthetic, founded on the moment of origin of cultural forms and practices, is almost certainly profoundly mistaken. [...]

[...]

The term "popular" has very complex relations to the term "class." We know this, but are often at pains to forget it. We speak of particular forms of working-class culture; but we use the more inclusive term "popular culture" to refer to the general field of enquiry. It's perfectly clear that what I've been saying would make little sense without reference to a class perspective and to class struggle. But it is also clear that there is no one-to-one relationship between a class and a particular cultural form or practice. The terms "class" and "popular" are deeply related, but they are not absolutely interchangeable. The reason for that is obvious. There are no wholly separate "cultures" paradigmatically attached, in a relation of historical fixity, to specific "whole" classes—although there are clearly distinct and variable class-cultural formations. Class cultures tend to intersect and overlap in the same field of struggle. The term "popular" indicates this somewhat displaced relationship of culture to classes. More accurately, it refers to that alliance of classes and forces which constitute the "popular classes." The culture of the oppressed, the excluded classes: this is the area to which the term "popular" refers us. And the opposite side to that—the side with the cultural power to decide what belongs and what does not—is, by definition, not another "whole" class, but that other alliance of classes, strata and social forces which constitute what is not "the people" and not the "popular classes": the culture of the power bloc.

The people versus the power bloc: this, rather than "class-against-class," is the central line of contradiction around which the terrain of culture is polarised. Popular culture, especially, is organised around the contradiction: the popular forces versus the power bloc. This gives to the terrain of cultural struggle its own kind of specificity. But the term "popular," and even more, the collective subject to which it must refer—"the people"—is highly problematic. It is made problematic by, say, the ability of Mrs. **Thatcher** to pronounce a sentence like "We have to limit the power of the trade unions because that is what the people want." That suggests to me that, just as there is no fixed content to the category of "popular culture," so there is no fixed subject to attach to it—"the people." "The people" are not always back there, where they have always been, their culture untouched, their liberties and their instincts intact, still struggling on against the **Norman** yoke or whatever: as if, if only we can "discover" them and bring them back on stage, they will always stand up in the right, appointed place and be counted. The capacity to *constitute* classes and individuals as a popular force—that is the nature of political and cultural struggle: to *make* the divided classes and the separate peoples—divided and separatred by culture as much as by other factors—into a popular-democratic cultural force.

We can be certain that other forces also have a stake in defining "the people" as something else: "the people" who need to be disciplined more, ruled better, more effectively policed, whose way of life needs to be protected from "alien cultures," and so on. There is some part of both those alternatives inside each of us. Sometimes we can be constituted as a force against the power bloc: that is the historical opening in which it is possible to construct a culture which is genuinely popular. But, in our society, if we are not constituted like that, we will be constituted into its opposite: an effective populist force, saying "Yes" to power. Popular culture is one of the sites where this struggle for and against a culture of the powerful is engaged: it is also the stake to be won or lost in that struggle. It is the arena of consent and resistance. It is partly where **hegemony** arises, and where it is secured. It is not a sphere where **socialism**, a socialist culture—already fully formed—might be simply "expressed." But it is one of the places where socialism might be constituted. That is why "popular culture" matters. Otherwise, to tell you the truth, I don't give a damn about it.

Glossary

BOURGEOIS: of, or relating to, the "middle class," often implying a preference for materialism and traditional values.

CAPITAL: wealth used to acquire more wealth; it can also refer to the people and institutions in positions of power who benefit most from a capitalist system of economics.

CLASSES: Socioeconomic positions within a capitalist economy; in social theory, class is an important factor in analyzing relationships of social power.

COCKADE: a cluster of ribbons, usually shaped as a flower and worn as a badge or in a hat.

CONTAINMENT: The processes by which the powerful restrict, limit, and control the actions and political abilities of the less powerful.

CORONATION STREET: British soap opera (ITV, 1960–present).

DAILY MIRROR: a British newspaper.

DIALECTIC: A dynamic process consisting of ongoing movement between two contradictory positions and their resolution, usually taking the form of a statement or position ("thesis") giving rise to an opposing or contradicting reaction ("antithesis"), resulting in a resolution ("synthesis") of the contradiction into a new thesis.

EVANGELICAL: in this case, one who is overly enthusiastic or forceful.

FLEET STREET: a reference to the British press, particularly the print media.

HEGEMONY: domination or control, as in one country or culture over another.

LONG MARCH: series of retreats by Chinese Communists from Chinese Nationalists in 1934–5.

NEWSPEAK: from George Orwell's novel *Nineteen Eighty-Four* (1949), the language of the ruling elites that is an abbreviated vocabulary based on the combination of English words.

NORMAN: the Norse people who settled in the northwestern French area of Normandy and, after the Battle of Hastings (1066), replaced the Anglo-Saxons as the British ruling elite.

OBSERVER: British weekly newspaper, published on Sundays; known for its more liberal social positions.

RESISTANCE: Practices of opposing, contesting, and combating a dominant power, or its cultural, political, and social regime, by those with less power.

SOCIALISM: a social system in which the people share ownership of, and control over, the economic institutions and its products.

THATCHER, Margaret (1925–2013): British Prime Minister, 1979–90.

WHIG: the dominant power in eighteenth-century England, who gained economic and political power through the rise of capitalism and the decline in power of the monarchy.

WILLIAMS, Raymond (1921–88): Welsh Marxist literary and cultural critic; influential in the formation of the field of cultural studies.

Questions for Conversation

What does Hall insist that the study of popular culture start from an awareness of the "double-state" of containment and resistance?

Hall, like the Frankfort School and other theorists, recognizes the power of modern societies to shape and manipulate popular culture. But he also recognizes that working people "are not dupes." Why?

What are the three major meanings of the term "popular" discussed by Hall? Which does he prefer and why?

Why should popular culture be studied in relationship to economic development, especially the growth of capital?

What, according to Hall, is complicated about the relationship between popular culture, class, and tradition?

Hall is clearly an advocate of the political left—a socialist. What forms of popular culture do you think are most supportive of the left? Conversely, what forms of popular culture are more favorable to the political right?

Hall says little explicitly about religion in his essay. Can you make connections between other theorists' perspectives on religion and popular culture and Hall's views on class, economics, and the popular?

Suggestions for Further Readings

The following is a list of supplemental readings that provide additional information about, apply, or respond critically to the ideas presented in this chapter.

Baraka, Amiri. *Blues People: Negro Music in White America*. New York: William Morrow, 1963.

Braunlein, Peter J. "Who Defines 'the Popular'?: Post-Colonial Discourses on National Identity and Popular Christianity in the Philippines," in *Religion, Tradition and the Popular: Transcultural Views from Asia and Europe*, ed. Judith Schlehe and Evamaria Sandkuhler, 75–113. Bielefeld: transcript Verlag, 2014.

Clark, Lynn Schofield. *From Angels to Aliens: Teenagers, the Media, and the Supernatural*. New York: Oxford University Press, 2003.

Cone, James H. *The Spirituals and the Blues: An Interpretation*. New York: Orbis Books, 1972.

Engstrom, Erika, and Joseph M. Valenzano, III. *Television, Religion, and Supernatural: Hunting Monsters, Finding Gods*. Lanham, MD: Lexington Books, 2014.

Fessenden, Tracy. *Religion Around Billie Holiday*. University Park, PA: Penn State University Press, 2018.

Galal, Ehab. "Reimagining Religious Identities in Children's Programs on Arabic Satellite-TV: Intentions and Values," *New Media in the Middle East: Centre for Contemporary Middle East Studies, University of Southern Denmark Working Paper Series* 7 (2006): 105–19.

Gilroy, Paul. *The Black Atlantic: Modernity and Double-Consciousness*. Cambridge, MA: Harvard University Press, 1995.

Hall, Stuart. "Culture, Community, Nation," *Cultural Studies* 7 (1993): 349–63.

Hall, Stuart. "Notes on Deconstructing 'the Popular,'" in *People's History and Socialist Theory*, ed. Raphael Samuel, 227–40. London: Routledge and Kegan Paul, 1981.

Hall, Stuart. "On Postmodernism and Articulation: An Interview with Stuart Hall," edited by Lawrence Grossberg, in *Stuart Hall: Critical Dialogues in Cultural Studies*, ed. David Morley and Kuan-Hsing Chen, 131–50. London: Routledge, 1996.

Hall, Stuart. "Response to Saba Mahmood," *Cultural Studies* 10 (1996): 12–15.

Knight, Michael Muhammed. *The Five Percenters: Islam, Hip-Hop, and the Gods of New York*. London: Oneworld Publications, 2013.

Lyden, John C. "Film," in *Routledge Companion to Religion and Popular Culture*, ed. John C. Lyden and Eric Michael Mazur, 80–99. New York: Routledge, 2015.

Mahmood, Saba. "A Brief Response to Stuart Hall's Comments on My Essay 'Cultural Studies and Ethic Absolutism'," *Cultural Studies* 10 (1996): 506–7.

Mahmood, Saba. "Cultural Studies and Ethnic Absolutism: Comments on Stuart Hall's 'Culture, Community, Nation'," *Cultural Studies* 10 (1996): 1–11.

Mankekar, Purnima. *Screening Culture, Viewing Politics*. Durham, NC: Duke University Press, 1999.

Martino, Luis Mauro Sa. "Mediatization of Religion and Cultural Studies: A Reading of Stuart Hall," *Matrizes* 10 (2016): 143–56.

McRobbie, Angela, Lawrence Grossberg, and Paul Gilroy. *Without Guarantees: In Honour of Stuart Hall*. London: Verso, 2000.

Miller, Monica R. *Religion and Hip Hop*. New York: Routledge, 2013.

Miller, Monica R., Anthony B. Pinn, and Bernard. "Bun B," Freeman, eds. *Religion in Hip Hop*. New York: Bloomsbury, 2015.

Miyakawa, Felicia. *Five Percenter Rap: God Hop's Music, Message, and Black Muslim Mission*. Bloomington: Indiana University Press, 2005.

Neal, Lynn S. *Romancing God: Evangelical Women and Inspirational Fiction*. Chapel Hill: University of North Carolina Press, 2005.

Pinn, Anthony B. *Noise and Spirit: The Religious and Spiritual Sensibilities of Rap Music*. New York: New York University Press, 2003.

Scott, David W. "Mormon 'Family Values' Versus Television: An Analysis of the Discourse of Mormon Couples Regarding Television and Popular Culture," *Critical Studies in Media Communication* 20 (2003): 313–33.

Taira, Teemu. "Reading Bond Films through the Lens of 'Religion': Discourses of 'the West and the Rest,'" *Journal for Religion, Media, and Film* 5, no. 2 (2019): 119–39.

Toscano, Margaret M. "Mormon Morality and Immorality in Stephanie Meyer's *Twilight* Series," in *Bitten by* Twilight*: Youth Culture, Media, and the Vampire Franchise*, ed. Melissa A. Click, Jennifer Stevens Aubrey, and Elizabeth Behm-Morawitz, 21–36. New York: Peter Lang, 2010.

13 Elaine Showalter

"Until very recently," wrote Elaine Showalter (b. 1941) in 1981, who retired from the Princeton University English faculty in 2003, "feminist criticism has not had a theoretical basis; it has been an empirical orphan in the theoretical storm." Like Said's Orientalism, it was originally seen more as a matter of perspective—inquiry, really—into how something had come to be the way it was. Rather than the Orient/Occident dialectic, however, feminism originally concerned itself with the male/female dialectic, wherein patriarchal (male-dominated) social institutions not only maintained women in subservient, inferior, or marginal status but had created societies wherein that status seemed both normal and reasonable.

Feminism as the struggle of women for rights comparable to men is ageless; as an organized political and intellectual movement, however, it has its roots in the European Enlightenment, most specifically in the realization that the aims of democratic responses to European monarchies were themselves undemocratic if they did not include women. In the nineteenth and early twentieth century, women (and men)—later identified as "first-wave" feminists—sought to expand women's legal rights (e.g., in voting, business, property ownership). "Second-wave" feminism emerged as a product of the post-Second World War return of men from deployment, which displaced women who had taken positions in traditionally male-dominated occupations on the home front. The 1949 publication of Simone de Beauvoir's *The Second Sex* ("One is not born, but rather becomes, woman")— translated from the French and published in the United States in 1953—followed in 1963 by the publication of Betty Friedan's *The Feminine Mystique* (exploring "[t]he problem that has no name": pervasive unhappiness among middle-class housewives), gave feminists a strong vocabulary to critique the representation, status, and roles of women. Much of the energy of the movement focused on identifying (and addressing) less formal social forms of gender discrimination, including husband/wife dynamics in marriage and divorce, equal opportunities for women in education and in the workforce, protection of women in abusive situations, and childcare opportunities for women seeking careers. "Third-wave" feminism emerged in the early 1990s from the growing concern that feminism as it had been expressed previously was concerned primarily with middle-class Euro-American issues and did not adequately represent issues central to women of color. Advocates of "Womanism" (a term offered by author Alice Walker) argued that issues of race—as much as (if not more than) gender— were central to understanding the plight of women, while advocates of "Intersectionality" argued that consideration of all of the factors of race, gender, and economics was vital in explaining experiences of oppression; economically marginal African American women had a different experience of the world than did economically marginal African American men, but also than economically marginal European-American women.

One of Showalter's contributions to this subfield has been in chronicling the transformation of its theoretical foundations and, in the larger piece from which the following excerpt has been taken, charting the various ways in which feminist theory has moved across different disciplines in the humanities and social sciences. But of greater importance may be her coining of the word "gynocritics," by which she means not the analysis of writings about women but rather the study of (as she puts in here) "the history, styles, themes, genres, and structures of writing by women; the psychodynamics of female creativity; the trajectory of the individual or collective female career; and the evolution and laws of a female literary tradition." While she has written on aspects of popular culture, religion—long the subject of criticism as the institutional embodiment of patriarchal oppression—is not part of Showalter's critique presented here. Working primarily in the academic tradition of literary criticism, her critique nonetheless illuminates the problems inherent in investigating both the role women play in religion and popular culture, and the role (perspective; bias) of women (and men) as writers about religion and popular culture. This shift in perspective has been as powerful a corrective as those presented by critics writing on colonialism and class.

"Feminist Criticism in the Wilderness" (1981)[1]

There are two distinct modes of feminist criticism, and to conflate them (as most commentators do) is to remain permanently bemused by their theoretical potentialities. The first mode is ideological; it is concerned with the feminist as *reader*, and it offers feminist readings of texts which consider the images and stereotypes of women in literature, the omissions and misconceptions about women in criticism, and woman-as-sign in semiotic systems. [...]

This invigorating encounter with literature, which I will call *feminist reading* or the *feminist critique*, is in essence a mode of interpretation, one of many which any complex text will accommodate and permit. It is very difficult to propose theoretical coherence in an activity which by its nature is so eclectic and wide-ranging, although as a critical practice feminist reading has certainly been very influential. [...]

[...]

＊ ＊ ＊

[...] Feminist criticism has gradually shifted its center from revisionary readings to a sustained investigation of literature by women. The second mode of feminist criticism engendered by this process is the study of women *as writers*, and its subjects are the history, styles, themes, genres, and structures of writing by women; the psychodynamics of female creativity; the trajectory of the individual or collective female career; and the evolution and laws of a female literary tradition. No English term exists for such a specialized critical **discourse**, and so I have invented the term "gynocritics." Unlike the feminist critique, gynocritics offers many theoretical opportunities. To see women's writing as our primary subject forces us to make

[1] Elaine Showalter, excerpt from "Feminist Criticism in the Wilderness," *Critical Inquiry* 8, no. 2 (Winter 1981): 179–205.

the leap to a new conceptual vantage point and to redefine the nature of the theoretical problem before us. It is no longer the ideological dilemma of reconciling revisionary pluralisms but the essential question of difference. [...]

[...]

Theories of women's writing presently make use of four models of difference: biological, linguistic, psychoanalytic, and cultural. Each is an effort to define and differentiate the qualities of the woman writer and the woman's text; each model also represents a school of gynocentric feminist criticism with its own favorite texts, styles, and methods. They overlap but are roughly sequential in that each incorporates the one before. [...]

* * *

[...]

Organic or biological criticism is the most extreme statement of gender difference, of a text indelibly marked by the body: anatomy is textuality. Biological criticism is also one of the most **sibylline** and perplexing theoretical formulations of feminist criticism. Simply to invoke anatomy risks a return to the crude essentialism, the phallic and ovarian theories of art, that oppressed women in the past. [...]

While feminist criticism rejects the attribution of literal biological inferiority, some theorists seem to have accepted the *metaphorical* implications of female biological difference in writing. [...]

Some radical feminist critics, primarily in France but also in United States, insist that we must read these metaphors as more playful; that we must seriously rethink and redefine biological differentiation and its relation to women's unity. They argue that "women's writing proceeds from the body, that our sexual differentiation is also our source." [...]

Feminist criticism written in the biological perspective generally stresses the importance of the body as a source of imagery. [...]

Feminist criticism which itself tries to be biological, to write from the critic's body, has been intimate, confessional, often innovative in style and form. [...] Such criticism makes itself defiantly vulnerable, virtually bares its throat to the knife, since our professional taboos against self-revelation are so strong. When it succeeds, however, it achieves the power and the dignity of art. Its existence is an implicit rebuke to women critics who continue to write, according to **Rich**, "from somewhere outside their female bodies." [...]

[...] The study of biological imagery in women's writing is useful and important as long as we understand that factors other than anatomy are involved in it. Ideas about the body are fundamental to understanding how women conceptualize their situation in society; but there can be no expression of the body which is unmediated by linguistic, social, and literary structures. The difference of woman's literary practice, therefore, must be sought (in **Miller**'s words) in "the body of her writing and not the writing of her body."

* * *

[...]

Linguistic and textual theories of women's writing ask whether men and women use language differently; whether sex differences in language use can be theorized in terms of biology, socialization, or culture; whether women can create new languages of their own; and whether speaking, reading, and writing are all gender marked. American, French, and British feminist critics have all drawn attention to the philosophical, linguistic, and practical problems of women's use of language, and the debate over language is one of the most exciting areas in gynocritics. Poets and writers have led the attack on what Rich calls "the oppressor's language," a language sometimes criticized as sexist, sometimes as abstract. But the problem goes well beyond reformist efforts to purge language of its sexist aspects. [...]

[...]

But scholars who want a women's language that is intellectual and theoretical, that works *inside* the academy, are faced with what seems like an impossible paradox, as **Xavière Gauthier** has lamented: "As long as women remain silent, they will be outside the historical process. But, if they begin to speak and write *as men do*, they will enter history subdued and alienated; it is a history that, logically speaking, their speech should disrupt." What we need, **Mary Jacobus** has proposed, is a women's writing that works within "male" discourse but works "ceaselessly to deconstruct it: to write what cannot be written," and according to **Shoshana Felman**, "the challenge facing the woman today is nothing less than to 'reinvent' language, ... to speak not only against, but outside of the specular **phallogocentric** structure, to establish a discourse the status of which would no longer be defined by the **phallacy** of masculine meaning.'"

Beyond rhetoric, what can linguistic, historical, and anthropological research tell us about the prospects for a women's language? First of all, the concept of a women's language is not original with feminist criticism; it is very ancient and appears frequently in folklore and myth. In such myths, the essence of women's language is its secrecy; what is really being described is the male fantasy of the enigmatic nature of the feminine.

[...]

The advocacy of a women's language is thus a political gesture that also carries tremendous emotional force. But despite its unifying appeal, the concept of a women's language is riddled with difficulties. Unlike Welsh, Breton, Swahili, or Amharic, that is, languages of minority or colonized groups, there is no mother tongue, no **genderlect** spoken by the female population in a society, which differs significantly from the dominant language. English and American linguists agree that "there is absolutely no evidence that would suggest the sexes are pre-programmed to develop structurally different linguistic systems." Furthermore, the many specific differences in male and female speech, intonation, and language use that have been identified cannot be explained in terms of "two separate sex-specific languages" but need to be considered instead in terms of styles, strategies, and contexts of linguistic performance. Efforts at quantitative analysis of language in texts by men or women [...] can easily be attacked for treating words apart from their meanings and purposes. At a higher level, analyses which look for "feminine style" in the repetition of stylistic devices, image patterns, and syntax in women's writing tend to confuse innate forms with the overdetermined results of literary choice. Language and style are never raw and instinctual but are always the products of innumerable factors, of genre, tradition, memory, and context.

The appropriate task for feminist criticism, I believe, is to concentrate on women's access to language, on the available lexical range from which words can be selected, on the ideological and cultural determinants of expression. The problem is not that language is insufficient to express women's consciousness but that women have been denied the full resources of language and have been forced into silence, euphemism, or circumlocution. [...]

"All that we have ought to be expressed-mind and body." Rather than wishing to limit women's linguistic range, we must fight to open and extend it. The holes in discourse, the blanks and gaps and silences, are not the spaces where female consciousness reveals itself but the blinds of a "prison-house of language." Women's literature is still haunted by the ghosts of repressed language, and until we have exorcised those ghosts, it ought not to be in language that we base our theory of difference.

* * *

Connections 13a: Showalter and the Long Arc of Joan

A fascinating example of how feminist analysis can enrich our understanding of religion and popular culture is the long-standing and very complicated fame of Joan of Arc. Her story was improbable and compelling. Born into a peasant family in northern France in the early fifteenth century, as a teenager she reported having religious visions that compelled her to actively support the French forces trying to defeat the English in Hundred Years War. This led to her participation in various successful sieges and military campaigns, as she donned soldier's garb, participated in battles, advised military leaders, and helped rally troops and popular support. These actions brought her fame and notoriety, particularly as victories were seen as divine favor for the French cause. Later captured by an oppositional faction, she was imprisoned, tried for heresy and sorcery, and executed by burning at the stake in 1431—all before her twentieth birthday. From there her story and image take many twists and turns. Declared innocent by a different Roman Catholic court in 1456, she was named as a martyr and eventually beatified and canonized in the twentieth century. For France, she helped rally nationalistic sentiment as the nation-state took shape in the early modern period, culminating in being recognized as a national symbol by Napoleon in 1803. As historian Robin Blaetz has documented, "the Maid" has a long history in popular culture, in France and elsewhere, "envisioned in thousands of novels, poems, plays, songs, operas, and biographies, and in media ranging from women's magazines to . . . dramas." Further, her image "has been invoked by advertisers and politicians to sell everything from cigars to beans to political agendas" (2001: xi). Blaetz focused on how Joan of Arc is represented in the United States, especially in biographical films like the 1948 version starring Ingrid Bergman. She also explored films that use "Joan-like" characters and static images in material culture like posters, toys, prayer cards, jewelry, medallions, and other personal objects. Her approach to the films assumed that while the plots follow the life of the historical Joan, their content reflects more the cultural anxieties and aspirations of the time of their production. During wartime, for example, films on the warrior-saint Joan explored women's roles in relation to armed conflict. Using a combination of feminist and other forms of film analysis, Blaetz gave careful readings of these films and the responses to them, finding prominent themes of "androgyny, virginity, and sacrificial violence." She found that Joan's story could be inflected in very different ways. In general terms, the story of peasant woman under religious inspiration rising to prominence in a very hierarchical and male dominated society is intrinsically feminist. However, Blaetz argued, films about

Joan often stress her conformity to conventional piety, her loyalty to the feudal system, and her chastity, suggesting a desire by filmmakers (mostly male) to domesticate the message.

Psychoanalytically oriented feminist criticism locates the difference of women's writing in the author's **psyche** and in the relation of gender to the creative process. It incorporates the biological and linguistic models of gender difference in a theory of the female psyche or self, shaped by the body, by the development of language, and by sex-role socialization. Here too there are many difficulties to overcome; the Freudian model requires constant revision to make it gynocentric. [...] **Penis envy**, the **castration complex**, and the **Oedipal** phase have become the Freudian coordinates defining women's relationship to language, fantasy, and culture. Currently the French psychoanalytic school dominated by **Lacan** has extended castration into a total metaphor for female literary and linguistic disadvantage. Lacan theorizes that the acquisition of language and the entry into its symbolic order occurs at the Oedipal phase in which the child accepts his or her gender identity. This stage requires an acceptance of the phallus as a privileged signification and a consequent female displacement [...].

In psychoanalytic terms, "lack" has traditionally been associated with the feminine, although Lac(k)anian critics can now make their statements linguistically. Many feminists believe that psychoanalysis could become a powerful tool for literary criticism, and recently there has been a renewed interest in Freudian theory. But feminist criticism based in Freudian or post-Freudian psychoanalysis must continually struggle with the problem of feminine disadvantage and lack. [...]

[...] Women's novels which are centrally concerned with fantasies of romantic love belong to the category disdained by **George Eliot** and other serious women writers as "silly novels"; the smaller number of women's novels which inscribe a fantasy of power imagine a world for women outside of love, a world, however, made impossible by social boundaries. There has also been some interesting feminist literary criticism based on alternatives to Freudian psychoanalytic theory: [...] And for the past few years, critics have been thinking about the possibilities of a new feminist psychoanalysis that does not revise **Freud** but instead emphasizes the development and construction of gender identities.

The most dramatic and promising new work in feminist psychoanalysis looks at the pre-Oedipal phase and at the process of psychosexual differentiation. [...] Women's difficulties with feminine identity come after the Oedipal phase, in which male power and cultural hegemony give sex differences a transformed value. [...]

But what is the significance of feminist psychoanalysis for literary criticism? One thematic carry-over has been a critical interest in the mother-daughter configuration as a source of female creativity. Elizabeth Abel's bold investigation of female friendship in contemporary women's novels uses **Chodorow**'s theory to show how not only the relationships of women characters but also the relationship of women writers to each other are determined by the psychodynamics of female bonding. Abel too confronts **Bloom**'s paradigm of literary history, but unlike **Gilbert** and **Gubar** she sees a "triadic female pattern" in which the Oedipal relation to the male tradition is balanced by the woman writer's pre-Oedipal relation to the female tradition. "As the dynamics of female friendship differ from those of male,"

Abel concludes, "the dynamics of female literary influence also diverge and deserve a theory of influence attuned to female psychology and to women's dual position in literary history."

[...] Although psychoanalytically based models of feminist criticism can now offer us remarkable and persuasive readings of individual texts and can highlight extraordinary similarities between women writing in a variety of cultural circumstances, they cannot explain historical change, ethnic difference, or the shaping force of generic and economic factors. To consider these issues, we must go beyond psychoanalysis to a more flexible and comprehensive model of women's writing which places it in the maximum context of culture.

* * *

[...]

A theory based on a model of women's culture can provide, I believe, a more complete and satisfying way to talk about the specificity and difference of women's writing than theories based in biology, linguistics, or psychoanalysis. Indeed, a theory of culture incorporates ideas about woman's body, language, and psyche but interprets them in relation to the social contexts in which they occur. The ways in which women conceptualize their bodies and their sexual and reproductive functions are intricately linked to their cultural environments. The female psyche can be studied as the product or construction of cultural forces. Language, too, comes back into the picture, as we consider the social dimensions and determinants of language use, the shaping of linguistic behavior by cultural ideals. A cultural theory acknowledges that there are important differences between women as writers: class, race, nationality, and history are literary determinants as significant as gender. Nonetheless, women's culture forms a collective experience within the cultural whole, an experience that binds women writers to each other over time and space. It is in the emphasis on the binding force of women's culture that this approach differs from Marxist theories of cultural hegemony.

Hypotheses of women's culture have been developed over the last decade primarily by anthropologists, sociologists, and social historians in order to get away from masculine systems, hierarchies, and values and to get at the primary and self-defined nature of female cultural experience. In the field of women's history, the concept of women's culture is still controversial, although there is agreement on its significance as a theoretical formulation. [...]

In defining female culture, historians distinguish between the activities, tastes, and behaviors prescribed and considered appropriate for women and those activities, behaviors, and functions actually generated out of women's lives. In the late-eighteenth and nineteenth centuries, the term "woman's sphere" expressed the **Victorian** and **Jacksonian** vision of separate roles for men and women, with little or no overlap and with women subordinate. If we were to diagram it, the Victorian model would look like this:

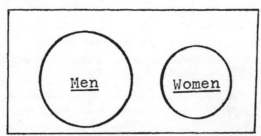

[...]

Some feminist historians have accepted the model of separate spheres and have seen the movement from woman's sphere to women's culture to women's-rights activism as the consecutive stages of an evolutionary political process. Others see a more complex and perpetual negotiation taking place between women's culture and the general culture. [...]

Lerner's views are similar to those of some cultural anthropologists. A particularly stimulating analysis of female culture has been carried out by two Oxford anthropologists, **Shirley and Edwin Ardener**. The Ardeners have tried to outline a model of women's culture which is not historically limited and to provide a terminology for its characteristics. Two essays by Edwin Ardener, "Belief and the Problem of Women" (1972) and "The 'Problem' Revisited" (1975), suggest that women constitute a *muted group*, the boundaries of whose culture and reality over-lap, but are not wholly contained by, the *dominant (male) group*. A model of the cultural situation of women is crucial to understanding both how they are perceived by the dominant group and how they perceive themselves and others. Both historians and anthropologists emphasize the incompleteness of **androcentric** models of history and culture and the inadequacy of such models for the analysis of female experience. In the past, female experience which could not be accommodated by androcentric models was treated as deviant or simply ignored. Observation from an exterior point of view could never be the same as comprehension from within. Ardener's model also has many connections to and implications for current feminist literary theory, since the concepts perception, silence, and silencing are so central to discussions of women's participation in literary culture.

By the term "muted," Ardener suggests problems both of language and of power. Both muted and dominant groups generate beliefs ordering ideas of social reality at the unconscious level, but dominant groups control the forms or structures in which consciousness can be articulated. Thus muted groups must mediate their beliefs through allowable forms of dominant structures. Another way of putting this would be to say that all language is the language of the dominant order, and women, if they speak at all, must speak through it. How then, Ardener asks, "does the symbolic weight of that other mass of persons express itself?" In his view, women's beliefs find expression through ritual and art, expressions which can be deciphered by the ethnographer, either female or male, who is willing to make the effort to perceive beyond the screens of the dominant structure.

Let us now look at Ardener's diagram of the relationship of dominant and the muted group:

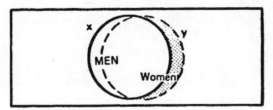

Unlike the Victorian model of complementary spheres, Ardener's groups are represented by intersecting circles. Much of muted circle Y falls within the boundaries of dominant circle X; there is also a crescent of Y which is outside the dominant boundary and therefore (in Ardener's terminology) "wild." We can think of the "wild zone" of women's culture spatially, experientially, or metaphysically. Spatially it stands for an area which is literally no-man's-land, a place forbidden to men, which corresponds to the zone in X which is off limits to women. Experientially it stands for the aspects of the female life-style which are outside of and unlike those of men; again, there is a corresponding zone of male experience alien to women. But if we think of the wild zone metaphysically, or in terms of consciousness, it has no corresponding male space since all of male consciousness is within the circle of the dominant structure and thus accessible to or structured by language. In this sense, the "wild" is always imaginary; from the male point of view, it may simply be the projection of the unconscious. In terms of cultural anthropology, women know what the male crescent is like, even if they have never seen it, because it becomes the subject of legend (like the wilderness). But men do not know what is in the wild.

Connections 13b: Showalter and the Varieties of Gender Experience

One of the critiques of feminism—and by extension, many of the other orienting and reorienting perspectives that sought to conserve or reconceptualize single factors such as "sex," race, and ethnicity—was that it sought to replace Euro-centric male preoccupation with Euro-centric female preoccupation. One response was the emergence of "womanism," which sought to include the experiences and perspectives of African American women (and other women of color). Others followed, including gender theory (which differentiated between sex and gender), performance theory (which differentiated between an inherent self and the acted-out self), and queer theory (which differentiated more diversely among sex, gender, and performance in the construction of assignment, self-identification, orientation, and attraction).

All of these areas of study have been rich in their contribution to critical studies of culture generally, and to the study of religion more specifically. In many ways, Mary Daly's 1973 work *Beyond God the Father* not only expanded Western theological conversations to include women (and the societal limitations placed upon them); it also provided space for a greater understanding of women-centered religious practice. Within six years of its publication, Daly's work had been followed by Starhawk's *The Spiral Dance* and Margot Adler's *Drawing Down the Moon*, both published in 1979 and both providing popular insight into contemporary goddess religions. Other works would follow, examining not only female perspectives on religious ideas and the roles women have played in the lives of religious institutions but also the communication and maintenance of power in male-dominated, tradition-bound religious dynamics.

A different kind of critique emerged from those who argued that isolating one aspect of a person's identity was (at best) misleading and (at worst) a biased form of essentialism that said more about the person reducing to one characteristic than the person so reduced. Intersectionality argued that such identities required examination at their intersection, and that all of the aspects demand attention. Kimberlé Crenshaw, one of the early leading proponents of intersectionality, argued that (for example) African American women suffered at the hands of societal power structures because of the combination of her race and her gender, and in ways that were not shared by European-American women or African American men.

All of these perspectives have broadened the study of religion and popular culture, not only by reinforcing the study of women's roles in cultural phenomenon but also by problematizing the very nature of sexuality, gender, and the performance of identity, and the academic inclination to study a topic by isolating a characteristic rather than observing it in conjunction with others.

For some feminist critics, the wild zone, or "female space," must be the address of a genuinely women-centered criticism, theory, and art, whose shared project is to bring into being the symbolic weight of female consciousness, to make the invisible visible, to make the silent speak. French feminist critics would like to make the wild zone the theoretical base of women's difference. In their texts, the wild zone becomes the place for the revolutionary women's language, the language of everything that is repressed, and for the revolutionary women's writing in "white ink." It is the **Dark Continent** in which **Cixous**' laughing **Medusa** and **Wittig**'s *guérillères* reside. Through voluntary entry into the wild zone, other feminist critics tell us, a woman can write her way out of the "cramped confines of patriarchal space." The images of this journey are now familiar in feminist quest fictions and in essays about them. The writer/heroine, often guided by another woman, travels to the "mother country" of liberated desire and female authenticity; crossing to the other side of the mirror, like Alice in Wonderland, is often a symbol of the passage.

Many forms of American radical feminism also romantically assert that women are closer to nature, to the environment, to a matriarchal principle at once biological and ecological. **Mary Daly**'s *Gyn/Ecology* and **Margaret Atwood**'s novel *Surfacing* are texts which create this feminist mythology. In English and American literature, women writers have often imagined Amazon Utopias, cities or countries situated in the wild zone or on its border: [...]

These fantasies of an idyllic enclave represent a phenomenon which feminist criticism must recognize in the history of women's writing. But we must also understand that there can be no writing or criticism totally outside of the dominant structure; no publication is fully independent from the economic and political pressures of the male-dominated society. The concept of a woman's text in the wild zone is a playful abstraction: in the reality to which we must address ourselves as critics, women's writing is a "double-voiced discourse" that always embodies the social, literary, and cultural heritages of both the muted and the dominant.

[...]

Women writing are not, then, *inside* and *outside* of the male tradition; they are inside two traditions simultaneously, "undercurrents," in **Ellen Moers**' metaphor, of the mainstream. To mix metaphors again, the literary estate of women, as **Myra Jehlen** says, "suggests ... a more fluid imagery of interacting juxtapositions, the point of which would be to represent not so much the territory, as its defining borders. Indeed, the female territory might well be envisioned as one long border, and independence for women, not as a separate country, but as open access to the sea." As Jehlen goes on to explain, an aggressive feminist criticism must poise itself on this border and must see women's writing in its changing historical and cultural relation to that other body of texts identified by feminist criticism not simply as literature but as "men's writing."

The difference of women's writing, then, can only be understood in terms of this complex and historically grounded cultural relation. An important aspect of Ardener's model is that there are muted groups other than women; a dominant structure may determine many muted structures. A black American woman poet, for example, would have her literary identity formed by the dominant (white male) tradition, by a muted women's culture, and by a muted black culture. She would be affected by both sexual and racial politics in a combination unique to her case; [...] Thus the first task of a gynocentric criticism must be to plot the precise cultural locus of female literary identity and to describe the forces that intersect an individual woman writer's cultural field. A gynocentric criticism would also situate women writers with respect to the variables of literary culture, such as modes of production and distribution, relations of author and audience, relations of high to popular art, and hierarchies of genre.

Insofar as our concepts of literary periodization are based on men's writing, women's writing must be forcibly assimilated to an irrelevant grid; we discuss a **Renaissance** which is not a **renaissance** for women, a **Romantic** period in which women played very little part, a modernism with which women conflict. At the same time, the ongoing history of women's writing has been suppressed, leaving large and mysterious gaps in accounts of the development of genre. [...]

Our current theories of literary influence also need to be tested in terms of women's writing. If a man's text, as Bloom and **Edward Said** have maintained, is fathered, then a woman's text is not only mothered but parented; it confronts both paternal and maternal precursors and must deal with the problems and advantages of both lines of inheritance. **Woolf** says in *A Room of One's Own* that "a woman writing thinks back through her mothers." But a woman writing unavoidably thinks back through her fathers as well; only male writers can forget or mute half of their parentage. The dominant culture need not consider the muted, except to rail against "the woman's part" in itself. Thus we need more subtle and supple accounts of influence, not just to explain women's writing but also to understand how men's writing has resisted the acknowledgment of female precursors.

We must first go beyond the assumption that women writers either imitate their male predecessors or revise them and that this simple dualism is adequate to describe the influences on the woman's text. [...] One of the great advantages of the women's-culture model is that it shows how the female tradition can be a positive source of strength and solidarity as well as a negative source of powerlessness; it can generate its own experiences and symbols which are not simply the obverse of the male tradition.

How can a cultural model of women's writing help us to read a woman's text? One implication of this model is that women's fiction can be read as a double-voiced discourse, containing a "dominant" and a "muted" story, what Gilbert and Gubar call a "**palimpsest**." I have described it elsewhere as an object/field problem in which we must keep two alternative oscillating texts simultaneously in view: [...]

Another interpretive strategy for feminist criticism might be the contextual analysis that the cultural anthropologist **Clifford Geertz** calls "thick description." Geertz calls for descriptions that seek to understand the meaning of cultural phenomena and products by "sorting out the structures of signification ... and determining their social ground and import." A genuinely "thick" description of women's writing would insist upon gender and upon a female literary tradition among the multiple strata that make up the force of meaning in a text. No description, we must concede, could ever be thick enough to account for all the factors that go into the work of art. But we could work toward completeness, even as an unattainable ideal.

In suggesting that a cultural model of women's writing has considerable usefulness for the enterprise of feminist criticism, I don't mean to replace psychoanalysis with cultural anthropology as the answer to all our theoretical problems or to enthrone Ardener and Geertz as the new white fathers in place of Freud, Lacan, and Bloom. No theory, however suggestive, can be a substitute for the close and extensive knowledge of women's texts which constitutes our essential subject. Cultural anthropology and social history can perhaps offer us a terminology and a diagram of women's cultural situation. But feminist critics must use this concept in relation to what women actually write, not in relation to a theoretical, political, metaphoric, or visionary ideal of what women ought to write.

I began by recalling that a few years ago feminist critics thought we were on a pilgrimage to the promised land in which gender would lose its power, in which all texts would be sexless and equal, like angels. But the more precisely we understand the specificity of women's writing not as a transient by-product of sexism but as a fundamental and continually determining reality, the more clearly we realize that we have misperceived our destination. We may never reach the promised land at all; for when feminist critics see our task as the study of women's writing, we realize that the land promised to us is not the serenely undifferentiated universality of texts but the tumultuous and intriguing wilderness of difference itself.

Glossary

ABEL, Elizabeth (b. 1945): literary critic, author of "(E)Merging Identities" (1981).

ANDROCENTRIC: focused on, advantageous to, or privileging the perspective of men; compare **PHALLOGOCENTRIC, GYNOCENTRIC**.

ARDENER, Shirley and Edwin (1927–87): British social anthropologists; respectively, editor of and contributor to *Perceiving Women* (1975).

ATWOOD, Margaret (b. 1939): Canadian author; author of *Surfacing* (1972).

BLOOM, Harold (b. 1930): American literary critic.

CASTRATION COMPLEX: theoretical stage of a child's psychological development, as presented by Sigmund Freud: among young boys it presents as the fear the father figure will remove the child's penis as a response to that child's attraction to the mother (see **Oedipal**); among young girls it presents as the desire to show that they have a symbolic equivalent to the penis, and the blaming of the mother for the penis's actual absence.

CHODOROW, Nancy (b. 1944): American sociologist, psychoanalyst, feminist theorist.

CIXOUS, Hélèle (b. 1937): French philosopher, essayist, feminist theorist; author of "Le Rire de la Méduse" ("The Laugh of the Medusa," 1975).

DALY, Mary (1928-2010): American theologian, philosopher; author of *Gyn/Ecology: The Metaethics of Radical Feminism* (1978).

DARK CONTINENT: Nineteenth-century Euro-American reference to sub-Saharan Africa; also used to suggest an undiscovered land.

DISCOURSE: communication, conversation, or debate, often related to a particular topic, and often presented as authoritative.

ELIOT, George: pen name of British author Mary Anne Evans (1819–80).

FELMAN, Shoshana (b. 1942): American literary critic, feminist theorist.

FREUD, Sigmund (1856–1939): Austrian psychologist (see separate entry in this volume).

GAUTHIER, Xavière (b. 1942): French journalist, literary critic; author of *Surréalisme et sexualité* (1971).

GEERTZ, Clifford (1926–2006): American anthropologist (see separate entry in this volume).

GENDERLECT: type or style of speech or communication used by a specific gender.

GILBERT, Sandra (b. 1936) and **GUBAR, Susan** (b. 1944): American literary critics; coauthored *The Madwoman in the Attic: The Woman Writer and the Nineteenth Century Literary Imagination* (1979).

GUÉRILLÈRES: female combatants; see Wittig, Monique.

GYNOCENTRIC: focused on, advantageous to, or privileging the perspective of women; compare **ANDROCENTRIC**.

JACKSONIAN: a reference to the political and social influence of the American movement named for Andrew Jackson (1767–1845), seventh president of the United States, that privileged greater democracy for the "common man."

JACOBUS, Mary (b. 1944): British literary critic, feminist theorist.

JEHLEN, Myra (b. 1940): American literary critic.

LACAN, Jacques (1901–81): French psychoanalyst.

LERNER, Gerda (1920–2013): Austrian-born American historian, poet, screenplay writer; credited with founding the field of women's history.

MEDUSA: a monster of Greek mythology; female with snakes for hair, who would turn to stone those who looked at her.

MILLER, Nancy (b. 1941): American literary critic, writer, feminist theorist.

MOERS, Ellen (1928–79): American literary scholar; pioneered the study of the "female Gothic" nineteenth-century genre.

OEDIPAL: reference to the "Oedipal complex," an early stage of psychological development in which the child desires only the opposite-sex parent; derived by psychoanalyst Sigmund Freud from the Greek dramatic series *Oedipus Rex* by Sophocles.

PALIMPSEST: a piece of writing on which the original has been removed and replaced by other writing, but on which traces of the original remain.

PENIS ENVY: Theoretical stage of female psychological development in which young girls experience anxiety about not being male (having a penis); introduced by psychoanalyist Sigmund Freud.

PHALLACY: patriarchal assertion (play on the word "fallacy"), drawn here from a 1975 book review by Shoshana Felman.

PHALLOGOCENTRIC: privileging the masculine perspective in the construction of meaning; compare **ANDROCENTRIC**.

PSYCHE: the totality of the human mind or spirit (as opposed to the physical "brain").

RENAISSANCE: period of European intellectual and political history (1300s–1600s) marked by a "rediscovery" of Greek and Roman literature, philosophy, and intellectual materials; also used to imply a rebirth or renewal.

RICH, Adrienne (1929–2012): American poet, essayist, feminist theorist.

ROMANTIC: of or related to romanticism, a broad intellectual movement of the late eighteenth and early nineteenth centuries, influential in the arts, philosophy, religion, music, and other fields, that emphasized individualism, emotion, spontaneity, intuition, and the inspirational character of "Nature" (as opposed to "nature"). Also used to describe the expression of love or one who expresses love for another.

SAID, Edward (1935–2003): literary critic (see separate entry in this volume).

SIBYLLINE: prophetic or oracular; derived from the term for ancient Greek prophetesses.
VICTORIAN: reference to British culture during the reign of Queen Victoria (1837–1901).
WITTIG, Monique (1935–2003): French author, feminist theorist; author of *Les Guérillères* (1969).
WOOLF, Virginia (1882–1941): British author and essayist, including the 1929 essay "A Room of One's Own."

Questions for Conversation

Showalter states that feminist criticism was still "in the wilderness" in the 1980s and cites other feminist scholars who saw feminism more as a set of "interchangeable strategies [with] varied methodologies and ideologies" than a single coherent theoretical statement. Was this "wilderness" status necessarily a problem? Does scholarship, especially critical scholarship, need consistent theory?

Showalter's focus as a scholar is the study of literature, which usually includes novels, short stories, poetry, and essays. How might her ideas be applied to the study of religion and popular culture?

How does Showalter distinguish between feminist reading and the study of women writers, or "gynocriticism"?

What are the four "models of difference" that Showalter outlines as sources of feminist theory? What are the basic characteristics of each?

Showalter sees particular promise in the "cultural" approach to feminist scholarship. Why? How might a cultural approach be applied to the study of religion and popular culture?

Showalter builds upon theorists we have explored earlier, notably Freudian psychoanalysis and the "thick description" of Geertz. How does she refit these ideas and methods for feminist analysis?

Suggestions for Additional Reading

The following is a list of supplemental readings that provide additional information about, apply, or respond critically to the ideas presented in this chapter.

Adler, Margot. *Drawing Down the Moon: Witches, Druids, Goddess-Worshippers, and Other Pagans in America Today*. New York: Viking Press, 1979.
Ahmed, Sara. *Living a Feminist Life*. Durham, NC: Duke University Press, 2017.
Beauvoir, Simone de. *The Second Sex*, trans. H. M. Parshley. New York: Knopf, 1952.
Blaetz, Robin. *Visions of the Maid: Joan of Arc in American Film and Culture*. Charlottesville: University of Virginia Press, 2001.
Butler, Judith. "Sex and Gender in Simone de Beauvoir's *Second Sex*," *Yale French Studies* 72 (1986): 35–49.
Butler, Judith. "Performative Acts and Gender Constitution: An Essay in Phenomenology and Feminist Theory," *Theatre Journal* 40, no. 4 (1988): 519–31.

Butler, Judith. *Gender Trouble: Feminism and the Subversion of Identity*. New York: Routledge, 1990.

Castelli, Elizabeth A., and Rosamond C. Rodman, eds. *Women, Gender, Religion: A Reader*. New York Palgrave, 2001.

Christ, Carol P. "Feminist Studies in Religion and Literature: A Methodological Reflection," *Journal of the American Academy of Religion* 44, no. 2 (1976): 317–25.

Crenshaw, Kimberlé. "Demarginalizing the Intersection of Race and Sex: A Black Feminist Critique or Antidiscrimination Doctrine, Feminist Theory and Antiracist Politics," *University of Chicago Legal Forum* 1 (1989): 139–67.

Crenshaw, Kimberlé. "Intersectionality, Identity Politics, and Violence Against Women of Color," *Stanford Law Review* 43, no. 6 (1991): 1241–99.

Daly, Mary. *Beyond God the Father: Toward a Philosophy of Women's Liberation*. Boston, MA: Beacon Press, 1973.

Friedan, Betty. *The Feminine Mystique*. New York: W.W. Norton & Company, 1963.

Gillis, Stacy, Gillian Howie, and Rebecca Munford, eds. *Third Wave Feminism: A Critical Exploration*. New York: Palgrave Macmillan, 2004.

Greenebaum, Jessica. "Placing Jewish Women into the Intersectionality of Race, Class and Gender," *Race, Gender & Class* 6, no. 4 (1999): 41–60.

Hill Collins, Patricia. *Black Feminist Thought: Knowledge, Consciousness and the Politics of Empowerment*. Boston, MA: Unwin Hyman, 1990.

Hill Collins, Patricia. "What's in a Name? Womanism, Black Feminism, and Beyond," *The Black Scholar* 26, no. 1 (1996): 9–17.

hooks, bell. *Ain't I a Woman? Black Women and Feminism*. Boston, MA: South End Press, 1981.

Kolodny, Annette. "Letting Go Our Grand Obsessions: Notes Toward a New Literary History of the American Frontiers," *American Literature* 64, no. 1 (1992): 1–18.

Loughlin, Gerard. *Queer Theology: Rethinking the Western Body*. Malden, MA: Blackwell Publishers, 2007.

Maddox, Peggy. "Retiring the Maid: The Last Joan of Arc Movie," *Journal of Religion and Popular Culture* 3, no. 1 (Spring 2003). Limited access available online: http://www.usask.ca/relst/jrpc/art-joanofarc-print.html

Marinucci, Mimi. *Feminism Is Queer: The Intimate Connection between Queer and Feminist Theory*, 2nd ed. London: Zed Books, 2016.

Moraga, Cherríe, and Gloria E. Anzaldúa, eds. *This Bridge Called My Back: Writings by Radical Women of Color*. Watertown, MA: Persephone Press, 1981.

Paglia, Camille. *Sexual Personae: Art and Decadence from Nefertiti to Emily Dickenson*. New Haven, CT: Yale University Press, 1990.

Paglia, Camille. "The Joy of Presbyterian Sex," *New Republic* 205, no. 23 (1991): 24–7.

Radway, Janice A. "Women Read the Romance: The Interaction of Text and Context," *Feminist Studies* 9, no. 1 (Spring 1983): 53–78.

Ruether, Rosemary Radford. "The Feminist Critique in Religious Studies," *Soundings* 64, no. 4 (1981): 388–402.

Schippert, Claudia. "Implications of Queer Theory for the Study of Religion and Gender: Entering the Third Decade," *Religion and Gender* 1, no. 1 (2011): 66–84.

Showalter, Elaine. "Feminist Criticism in the Wilderness," *Critical Inquiry* 8, no. 2 (1981): 179–205.

Showalter, Elaine. "Women's Time, Women's Space: Writing the History of Feminist Criticism," *Tulsa Studies in Women's Literature* 3, no. 1/2 (1984): 29–43.

Showalter, Elaine. *Inventing Herself: Claiming a Feminist Intellectual Heritage*. New York: Simon and Schuster, 2001.

Smith, Barbara. "Toward a Black Feminist Criticism," *The Radical Teacher* 7 (1978): 20–7.

Starhawk. *The Spiral Dance: A Rebirth of the Ancient Religion of the Goddess*. San Francisco, CA: Harper and Row, 1979.

Suzack, Cheryl, and Shari M. Huhndorf. *Indigenous Women and Feminism: Politics, Activism, and Culture*. Vancouver: UBC Press, 2010.

Vollmer, Ulrike. *Seeing Film and Reading Feminist Theology: A Dialogue*. New York: Palgrave Macmillan, 2007.

Walker, Alice. *In Search of Our Mothers' Gardens: Womanist Prose*. New York: Harcourt, 1983.

Wilcox, Melissa M. *Queer Nuns: Religion, Activism, and Serious Parody*. New York: New York University Press, 2018.

14 Catherine Bell

Catherine Bell (1953–2008) was born in New York City and attended Manhattanville College where she studied philosophy and religion. She completed her graduate work at the Chicago Divinity School where she focused on the history of religions, ritual studies, and Chinese religions. After teaching positions and fellowships in Japan, Taiwan, and Berkeley, California, she spent the balance of her academic career at Santa Clara University where she specialized in Chinese religions and the general study of ritual, before multiple sclerosis forced her into early retirement. Her major academic work, *Ritual Theory, Ritual Practice* (1992), was immediately recognized as a significant contribution to the discipline, as it both synthesized the ideas of earlier scholars and framed the analysis of ritual in ways that have proven generative for other scholars.

In it, Bell made two basic arguments. First, she argues that previous studies of ritual tended to be somewhat circular, as scholars tended to define their object of study in ways that corresponded to their preferred methods of inquiry. In line with scholars like Jonathan Z. Smith, she insisted that scholars be far more self-reflexive about the framing of their inquiries. Second, she sets forth the possibility of new directions in ritual studies, to focus less on "ritual as set of special practices in favor of a focus on some of the more common strategies of 'ritualization' . . . defined as a way of acting that differentiates some acts from others" (1992: xv). To do so would refocus scholars on many of the "practical" matters of ritual, as well as bring attention to the "origins, purposes, and efficacy" of ritualized actions. In short, scholars of ritual, by examining ritual as a process, could ask new questions about who created rituals, what motivated them, and the reasons for their success over time.

Although Bell modestly (although probably inaccurately) claimed not to set forth any new theory of ritual in her wide-ranging work, her careful attention to the nuances of other theorists, evocative case studies, and clear prose have helped generations of students better understand the role of ritual in both religious and popular culture. In addition to *Ritual Theory*, she also produced a more "holistic and pragmatic" text for undergraduates, *Ritual: Perspectives and Dimensions* (1997, excerpted here). In it, Bell analyzes typical dimensions of ritual process that can be observed in a range of human activities, religious and otherwise. In drawing these examples together, she reveals the broad scope of ritualization, shaping human lives in diverse ways and serving a variety of human interests. Thus, ritualization can be found as readily in the pomp and pageantry of popular culture as in the formal ceremonial activities of popes and monarchs.

"Characteristics of Ritual-Like Activities" (1997)[1]

In modern Western society, we tend to think of ritual as a matter of special activities inherently different from daily routine action and closely linked to the sacralities of tradition and organized religion. Such connections encourage us to regard ritual as somewhat antiquated and, consequently, as somewhat at odds with modernity. Hence, ritual often seems to have more to do with other times and places than with daily life as we know it in postindustrial Europe and America. This view is borne out to a great extent by the examples … [of] those rituals that most people would tend to agree are good examples of what ritual is about [such as processions of religious leaders and shamanic dances]. With the examples that follow, however, the perspective is different. It will focus on a variety of common activities that are "ritualized" to greater or lesser degrees. Instead of ritual as a separate category or an essentially different type of activity, the examples described here illustrate general processes of ritualization as flexible and strategic ways of acting.

As in the preceding section, the examples discussed here can be loosely organized into six general categories, each focusing on a major attribute of "ritual-like" action, such as formalism, the varying degrees to which activities may be formalized and thereby deemed akin to ritual. The categories of formalism, traditionalism, disciplined invariance, rule-governance, sacral symbolism, and performance are, of course, neither exclusive nor definitive. Many ritual-like activities evoke more than one of these features, and such activities span various continuums of action from the religious to the secular, the public to the private, the routine to the improvised, the formal to the casual, and the periodic to the irregular [...]

In particular, these examples of ritual-like behavior demonstrate the importance of the body and its way of moving in space and time. The body acts within an environment that appears to require it to respond in certain ways, but this environment is actually created and organized precisely by means of how people move around it. The complex reciprocal interaction of the body and its environment is harder to see in those classic examples of ritual where the emphasis on tradition and the enactment of codified or standardized actions lead us to take so much for granted about the way people actually do things when they are acting ritually. If examples of ritual-like activity can throw light on what goes into the activities of ritualizing, they may also clarify the significance of the distinctions people draw between various types of activities, including ritual and non-ritual actions. However ritual-like heavyweight boxing may appear to be at times, for most people it is not the same thing as Sunday church service, and the differences are far from unimportant to them. In contrast to those in the previous section, the examples explored here will tend to be somewhat less established as public events, less codified by tradition, and less likely to appeal to divine beings. Yet they have all been deemed ritual or ritual-like on occasion, and their proximity to more conventional examples of ritual effectively informs our general cultural understanding of what ritual basically means to us.

---

[1]Catherine Bell, excerpt from "Characteristics of Ritual-Like Activities," in *Ritual: Perspectives and Dimensions* (New York: Oxford University Press, 1997), 138–64.

Formalism

Formality is one of the most frequently cited characteristics of ritual, even though it is certainly not restricted to ritual per se. In fact, as a quality, formality is routinely understood in terms of contrast and degree. That is, formal activities set up an explicit contrast with informal or casual ones; and activities can be formalized to different extents. In general, the more formal a series of movements and activities, the more ritual-like they are apt to seem to us. When analyzed, formality appears to be, at least in part, the use of a more limited and rigidly organized set of expressions and gestures, a "restricted code" of communication or behavior in contrast to a more open or "elaborated code." Formal speech, for example, tends to be more conventional and less idiosyncratic or personally expressive. Likewise, formal gestures are fewer in number than informal ones and are more prescribed, restrained, and impersonal. By limiting or curbing *how* something can be expressed, restricted codes of behavior simultaneously influence *what* can be expressed as well. The injunction to speak politely at formal events means that people tend to avoid frank discussions of topics about which they personally care a great deal; they tend to stick to more standard opinions on more impersonal subjects. And if personal political positions should become the topic on such an occasion, one is less likely to hear emotional or abusive characterizations of opposing positions, although sarcasm and wit can have the same effect without violating the formality of the situation. For the most part, high degrees of formality force people to state or affirm very generalized and rather impersonal sentiments about relatively abstract concerns.

Formalization, it has been argued, is very effective in promoting a loose social **acquiescence** to what is going on. While people might challenge the expression of specific or concrete ideas, they tend not to challenge the routine expression of formulas or clichés. [Many traditional societies] adopt a mode of formalized oratory that differs from everyday speech in numerous ways, notably loudness, intonation, syntactic forms, limited vocabulary, and the fixity of the order and style. [Anthropologists have] found that what can be said in this formalized way is quite limited, and as a mode of communication that is stylistically very determined, oratory can appear to be all style and no content. Yet in that quality may lie its effectiveness: if people do not bother to challenge the style, they are effectively accepting the content. In other words, formalized speech appears to induce acceptance, compliance, or at least forbearance with regard to any overt challenge [...]

Generally, formalization forces the speaker and the audience into roles that are more difficult to disrupt. For this reason, [...] highly formalized ways of speaking and communicating tend to be closely connected with traditional forms of social hierarchy and authority, effectively maintaining the implicit assumptions on which such authority is based. In other words, formality most often reinforces the larger social **status quo**. It may be for this reason that many types of social, political, and artistic challenges to the content of the status quo have felt it necessary to challenge simultaneously the conventions of polite speech and conduct, no matter how minor such challenges might seem. Indeed, those making such challenges are apt to be dismissed as extremists or quacks because they challenge style as much as content, and such dismissals further insulate the community from taking such challenges seriously. [...]

Formality, therefore, is not necessarily empty or trivial. As a restricted code of behavior, formalized activities can be **aesthetically** as well as politically compelling, invoking what [sociologist **Basil Bernstein**] describes as "a metaphoric range of considerable power, a simplicity and directness, a vitality and rhythm." The restriction of gestures and phrases to a small number that are practiced, perfected, and soon quite evocatively familiar can endow these formalized activities with great beauty and grace. Indeed, mechanical or routinized action is not what we usually mean by formality because they lack just this aesthetic dimension. In addition, it appears that formalized activities can communicate complex sociocultural messages very economically, particularly messages about social classification, hierarchical relationships, and the negotiation of identity and position in the social nexus. [...]

[...]

Traditionalism

The attempt to make a set of activities appear to be identical to or thoroughly consistent with older cultural precedents can be called "traditionalization." As a powerful tool of legitimation, traditionalization may be a matter of near-perfect repetition of activities from an earlier period, the adaptation of such activities in a new setting, or even the creation of practices that simply evoke links with the past. The more obvious forms of traditionalization include the use of ancient costumes, the repetition of older social customs, and the preservation of archaic linguistic forms. For example, the **Amish** communities in Pennsylvania retain the dress, customs, and speech patterns of the late 17th and early 18th century, when **Jacob Amman** led them to break with the less conservative **Mennonites** in Europe. Likewise, the **Hasidic** communities concentrated in and near New York City and Jerusalem maintain the basic dress of Eastern European Jews from more than a century ago, often with the same fine-tuned distinctions in dress that marked important differences in social and religious status. These methods of traditionalization tend to privilege an older historical model and make assimilation into the modern world both difficult and highly suspect. Such dramatically traditionalized patterns of dress establish a high-profile identity for those closely following the older ways, thereby helping to maintain the boundaries as well as the authority of the traditional community.

Connections 14a: Bell, Religion, and Nationalism

Few forces in the modern world have been as potent as nationalism, and most modern nations cultivate reverence, emotional connection, a sense of duty and other personal and social attitudes through rituals. National anthems, careful treatment of the nation's flag, exuberant celebrations of national holidays, pilgrimages to shrines for founders, and memorials to soldiers lost in battle are but of a few of the ways that nationalism shapes the hearts and minds of a nation's citizens.

Is this then a form of religion? Bell's categories of ritualization suggest many family resemblances, most especially formalism, traditionalism, and sacred symbolism. But this begs another question, just what is a nation? Where do they come from? And how are they able to make such stringent demands, up to and including martyrdom and sacrificial death, of their members?

These questions have animated historians of national traditions, especially those who saw the passionate devotion to national identity as fueling the devastating world wars and other social conflicts over twentieth century. As they explored the topic of nationalism, however, they found a number of conundrums. Most especially, many of the things thought to be "traditional" and rooted in the mists of time were in fact quite modern, often assembled during the eighteenth or nineteenth centuries as nation-states industrialized and adopted modern political systems. This era saw a nearly universal trend toward nationalism around the globe, but paradoxically what really seemed to give each national tradition power and potency were localized particularities and unique characteristics. So in a sense, everyone got "nationalistic" but did so in their own distinctive way, be that Greek, British, Brazilian, Japanese, etc. Finally, for all its power to motivate and inspire, nationalism often seems philosophically "thin." Most national traditions themselves are a mish-mash of ideas and practices, often inconsistent and mutable, making it very challenging to establish a clear definition that can be used across the board (another area of kinship with "religion").

Given these problems, there have been various efforts to unpack the history of nationalism, provide some basic definitions, and sort out the relationship between nationalisms and religions. British historian E. J. Hobsbawm and other scholars have argued that nationalisms are best understood as "invented traditions"—"set[s] of practices, normally governed by overtly or tacitly accepted rules and of a ritual or symbolic nature, which seek to inculcate certain values and norms of behavior by repetition, which automatically implies continuity with the past" (Hobsbawm 1983). Through various case studies, like the traditions of Scottish highlanders and the rituals of the British monarchy, Hobsbawm and his colleagues show how invented traditions attempt "to structure at least some parts of social life . . . as unchanging and invariant" in spite of the dynamic changes that roil modern societies.

Building upon this basic insight, historian Benedict Anderson defines a nation as "an imagined political community" where persons who may or may not know one another nonetheless think of themselves as essentially connected. Furthermore, the nation has a sense of limitations, and it excludes persons from other nations and sets boundaries, even if these are permeable and elastic at times. The nation also establishes sovereignty, bestowing legitimacy and authority to its laws and traditions. Andersen does not go so far as to equate nationalism with a religion, but he asserts their close connections, both historically and as things that can motivate thought and action (Anderson 1983).

More recent scholarship on religion and nationalism finds considerable diversity. For example, J. Christopher Soper and Joel Fetzer's global survey finds a range of relationships, from "deep contestation between religious and national allegiances to a fusion of them" (Soper and Fetzer 2018: 1). They argue for three basic models. In the first, religious nationalism is found where a nation's identity is closely associated with a particular religious tradition and the powers of the state directly support the religion of the majority. In contrast, secular nationalism occurs in places where a modern state directly challenges the authority of religion, or in some cases mounts a "friendly takeover" of its functions. Finally, civil religious nationalism occurs where a state broadly affirms connections to the transcendent, but allows for considerable religious pluralism, stressing the "spiritual connections" between different religious groups and their broader acceptance in the fabric of the "blessed" nation (Soper and Fetzer 2018: 8–9).

Returning to Bell's basic arguments, regardless of model, nations do ritualizing work as part of their ongoing efforts to build solidarity. In some cases, a nation can draw upon a religious tradition in framing these rituals, but even highly secular and religiously plural nations can "invent traditions" that create national identity, inspire their citizens, and reinforce their core values. These rituals are, by definition, meant to reach the masses and thus are central to the popular culture in any nation.

Most rituals appeal to tradition or custom in some way, and many are concerned to repeat historical precedents very closely. A ritual that evokes no connection with any tradition is apt to be found anomalous, inauthentic, or unsatisfying by most people. Thus, traditionalism is an important dimension of what we tend to mean and identify as ritual, while activities that are not explicitly called "rituals" may seem ritual-like if they invoke forms of traditionalism. Often formalism and traditionalism go together and underscore the **nonutilitarian** nature of activities, further heightening their ritual-like nature. Yet traditionalism can also be invoked without much concern for formality. For example, a Thanksgiving dinner may not be particularly formal if there is the usual chaos of cooking and company, but it makes a clear appeal both to a supposed historical precedent when the early **Puritans** and their friendly Indian neighbors shared a plentiful meal of turkeys and corn and to the particular domestic customs of the family itself. Such customs may be as simple as always using great grandmother's lace tablecloth, having rhubarb pie instead of the more common pumpkin or apple pie, or always delegating a particular person to say grace and carve the turkey. Indeed, most families are more likely to observe their own little traditions than simply to formalize the meal. Although Thanksgiving Day's "myth of origins" is far from solid historical fact, a clear national tradition of Thanksgiving has been institutionalized in American public life. Yet it is clearly an event that is traditionalized primarily in domestic ways.

[…]

Various theories argue that the power of traditionalism is rooted in the dominance of certain social classes, the symbolic power of cultural ideals, or even the need in modern life for the means to render contradictory experiences coherent. As such, traditionalism presupposes authoritative ideals embodied in an earlier time — even when such ideals, and even the image itself of an earlier time, are something of an innovation. This is aptly described as "the invention of tradition." Traditions can be invented [according to historian **Eric Hobsbawn**] by a "process of formalization and ritualization, characterized by reference to the past, if only by imposing repetition." Indeed, many so-called traditions of contemporary life are quite recent in origin. The British monarchy, for example, is probably enveloped in more elaborate ceremonial than any other European institution with the possible exception of the Catholic **papacy** in Rome. And most educated people, especially journalists, routinely describe these ceremonies as a "thousand year-old tradition," as having "gone on for hundreds of years," or as following "centuries of precedent." In truth, however, most of the royal ceremonial that attends the **House of Windsor** goes no further back than the very end of the 19th century and the beginning of the 20th, when a number of clumsy, older rites were extensively revised and elaborated, while many more new ceremonies were completely invented. This period of great creativity in British royal ritual coincided with a dramatic loss in real power for the monarchy; the elaborate ceremonial aggrandizement became a new way to exercise royal influence. With the crowning of **Queen Victoria** as empress of India in 1877 and especially the celebration of her diamond jubilee in 1897, the scale and grandeur of royal events took on not only unprecedented pageantry but also frequent and quite unfounded appeals to "immemorial tradition." Some historians have argued that the unprecedented industrial and social changes of the period, as well as the effects of a burgeoning popular press, made it both "necessary and possible" to package the monarchy in a new way—as a ritualistic "symbol of consensus and continuity to which all might defer." […]

[…]

Invariance

One of the most common characteristics of ritual-like behavior is the quality of invariance, usually seen in a disciplined set of actions marked by precise repetition and physical control. For some theorists, this feature is the prime characteristic of ritual behavior. The emphasis may be on the careful choreography of actions, the self-control required by the actor, or the rhythm of repetition in which the orchestrated activity is the most recent in an exact series that unites past and future. While traditionalism involves an appeal to the authority of the past that subordinates the present, invariance seems to be more concerned with ignoring the passage of time in general. It appears to suppress the significance of the personal and particular moment in favor of the timeless authority of the group, its doctrines, or its practices. The component of discipline certainly suggests that one effect of invariance is generally understood to be the molding or shaping of persons according to enduring guidelines and conditions.

Much human activity can be sufficiently repetitious to afford ready if trivial comparisons to ritual. A famous spoof on the elaborate daily routines of Americans obsessed with rigid codes of hygiene, grooming, and beauty describes them as the "body rites" of an exotic people called the "**Nacirema**." But it is not repetition alone that makes these acts ritualistic; more important is the punctiliousness with which the "natives" attend to the mouth, skin, and hair while standing in front of an altar-like box set into the wall above an ablution basis [sic] in the one or more shrine rooms found in every house. This is also true of Freud's characterization, examined earlier, of obsessive-compulsive disorders as ritual-like: repetition is part of this attribution, but the repetition is inseparable from a fixation on non-utilitarian thoroughness and exactitude. In a somewhat different example, the well-known format of the weekly meetings of Alcoholics Anonymous, often deemed ritual-like because of the unvarying program, suggests that in some contexts punctilious concern with repetition may have great utility.

[…]

Rule Governance

The novelist **Joyce Carol Oates** once introduced an essay on boxing and the career of **Mohammed Ali** with the following observation: "Though highly ritualized, and as rigidly bound by rules, traditions, and taboos as any religious ceremony, [boxing] survives as the most primitive and terrifying of contests ... [it] is a stylized mimicry of a fight to the death ... a **Dionysian** rite of cruelty, sacrifice and redemption ... [a] romance of (expendable) maleness—in which The Fight is honored, and even great champions come, and go." Aside from the appeals to repetition and traditionalism, these observations reflect another major characteristic accorded ritual-like activity, rule-governance. Rule-governed activity is often compared to ritual, particularly rule-governed contests in which violent chaos is barely held in check by complex codes of orchestration. This tendency has led some analysts to talk about driving a car as ritualistic, although others find such a comparison absurd. There is greater consensus around rule-governed activities that engage the rapt attention of an audience, as in the "ritualized combat" readily identified in sports, martial arts, traditional duels, feuds, or such cultural specialties as the bullfight. Yet both the scholar and the unschooled observer are apt to appreciate something ritual-like in many other games and forms of play, such as stylized displays of sexual sadomasochism, the controlled suicide of hara-kiri, or the chess-like lineup of traditional armies on both sides of a battlefield. Examples of controlled engagements of violence and disorder also include the highly coded forms of dress, speech, and gestures that identify rival teams, gangs, political parties, or armies. Should sheer brute force or the chaos of personal self-interest override the rules of controlled engagement, then the ritual-like nature of the event would certainly evaporate.

Much interest and conjecture attend the question of how sports may have originally emerged from religious ritual or been closely linked to it, as in the **Mayan-Aztec ball court game** or the Greek Olympic games. Whether or not any such lineage is relevant to understanding modern sports, some observers are fascinated by the way in which sports attract various taboos, pollution beliefs, and "magical" practices. They point to the enormous number of patently non-utilitarian gestures used, such as pitchers who tug their caps in a particular way before each throw or the team taboo against crossing bats. Such miniature rituals, defined as prescribed behavior that is scrupulously observed in order to affect an outcome, may not be part of the game in itself but on close examination seem nearly inseparable from real participation in sports. For others, like Joyce Carol Oates, the ritualism of sports derives from the importance of the more encompassing sets of rules that define and regulate the activity. These rules constrain the contenders and force them to follow very controlled patterns of interaction. In the tension between the brute human energy being expended and the highly coded means of engagement, the sports event seems to evoke in highly symbolic ways a fundamental conflict or experience at the core of social life. While this perception about sports overlaps features discussed in the next sections, there is a real stress on how the rules create the event and hence its meaning and dramatic spectacle.

[...]

Connections 14b: Bell and Parades

Parades are among the most universal of ritual forms, used by all sorts of societies and organizations, religious and secular. Structured around ordered progression through space, the more elaborate parades engage multiple senses, often employing music, costumes, banners, dancing, trained performers, flowers and other scented plants, as well as specialized vehicles and floats to convey special persons or things that are being celebrated. All these elements require considerable planning and artistic input. They are also major social events, in some cases requiring thousands of participants and drawing millions of viewers. Durkheim's theories of the "totemic" have often been used to interpret the social dimensions of key symbols used in parades. To these we can add Bell's ideas about ritualization—formalism, traditionalism, disciplined invariance, rule-governance, sacral symbolism, and performance—which provide a framework for understanding *how and why* parades are staged.

Archaeological evidence attests to parades in ancient societies, and they have been used more or less continuously right down to the present day (Latham 2016). Of course parades come in many flavors with distinctive contents and purposes according to their particular social and historical contexts. Because they are so ancient and seemingly so simple, parades are sometimes dismissed as "primitive" forms of popular culture. Sympathetic scholars, however, have found them interesting ways to understand social dynamics and cultural change, most especially those parades that intermingle the sacred and the secular (Payne 2017).

Most religious groups include parades or processions in their repertoires of ritual activities, often focusing these events on religious leaders, images, statues, or other symbolic representations of the sacred. In Christianity, processions started early, modeled on pagan traditions and accounts from the Bible. Accompanied by hymns, prayers, incense, and music, processions are often done with sacred spaces, like churches, as part of standard liturgical life. However, they can be brought into the streets, for anyone and everyone to view. Saints' feasts, high holidays like Easter, and celebrations of the Virgin Mary often feature large parades. Because of their scale and requirements for public venues, larger parades disrupt everyday life in ways that normal religious rituals do not. Normal rules and processes of secular life, most especially for traffic, commerce, and communications, must be temporarily restructured.

Parades are widely used by secular entities too. Nation states, political parties, and civil authorities stage some of the most elaborate parades, often as an expression of civil religion. Usually staged on national holidays, these parades extol the nation's heroic achievements, sacrifices, and core values. Other secular parades are staged by military groups, organizations aiming to foster civic pride, in support of sporting events, or corporations looking to boost sales and secure public goodwill. In the United States, for example, two of the most popular are the Thanksgiving parade staged by the Macy's department store chain in New York City, and the Rose Parade put on by the Pasadena, CA Tournament of Roses Association on or about New Year's Day. Both are renowned for their elaborate floats, marching bands, celebrity guests, and for Macy's, gigantic balloons.

Parades embody celebration, but they can be sites of political and social tensions, if not outright conflict. In many contexts, a parade staged by a particular ethnic group or political entity can be used to assert one type of identity over and against others (Newman 1997). Ireland, for example, has long been the site of rival parading traditions, reflecting political and religious divisions between Catholics and Protestants (Fraser 2000). The conspicuous display of rank is a common motif in parades as leaders march in special costumes or ride in impressive vehicles, a visual reinforcement of their right to rule. Conversely, parades can aim to increase public visibility for minority groups, often in tandem with calls for greater social acceptance or political rights. In the United States, Irish Roman Catholic groups, in part to respond to anti-Catholic attitudes, built St. Patrick's Day parades into a national phenomenon, eventually embraced by non-Catholics as well (Moss 1995). "Pride" parades, now a global phenomenon, originated in the 1970s as part of a larger movement to secure rights for gay and lesbian persons. Like any parading traditions, religious or otherwise, the creators of Pride had to self-consciously ritualize their vision by establishing common symbols and themes, building content from existing performance traditions, inventing new forms of expression, securing community support, and developing local variations (Bruce 2016).

Sacred Symbolism

Activities that explicitly appeal to supernatural beings are readily considered to be examples of ritual, even if the appeal is a bit indirect, as when the president of the United States takes the oath of office by placing his left hand on the Bible and swearing to uphold the duties and responsibilities of the presidency. Although it is not part of the institutional life of a specific religious group, the oath of office clearly derives from Christian ritual and represents the Christian values in American civic religion. Many other activities are not so overt in their appeal to a supernatural reality. More subtly, they simply assume and variously express a fundamental difference between sacred things on the one hand and profane things on the other. In doing so, these activities express generalized belief in the existence of a type of sacrality that demands a special human response. Aside from religious examples, such as the symbols of the Christian cross and the star of David, there are secular examples as well. National flags and monuments are routinely regarded as more than mere signs representing a country or an idea; they are symbols that embody values, feelings, and histories of national ideals and loyalty. In the many public arguments over how the flag of the United States should be treated, no one argues that the flag itself is holy. Yet, many people seem to feel that this piece of cloth, when deliberately crafted as a flag, should be handled in very specific and respectful ways. It is thought to stand for something as large and diffuse as "the American way" and as specific as ideas about freedom, democracy, free enterprise, hard work, and national superiority. According to the anthropologist **Sherry Ortner**, the flag "does not encourage reflection on the logical relations among these ideas, nor on the logical consequences of them as they are played out in social actuality, over time and history. On the contrary, the flag encourages a sort of all-or-nothing allegiance to the whole package, best summed … [by] 'Our flag, love it or leave.'" Symbols like the flag, which Ortner calls "summarizing" symbols, effectively merge many ideas and emotions under one image. This type of totalization generates a loose but encompassing set of ideas and emotions that readily evoke a collective sense of "we"—as in "our" flag.

The complicated nature of such symbols becomes apparent when people attempt to define what it is that makes a piece of cloth into the flag as a sacral symbol: is it the specific red-white-and-blue arrangement of stars and stripes, the cloth itself, or would a paper flag merit as much respect? If so, what about a flag drawn in crayon on a white linen sheet?

In other words, when is a flag "the" flag? In religious traditions, such questions have been answered through rituals of consecration: the Hindu statue of the god **Siva** is just a bit of clay until it is consecrated; then it must be treated with the respect one would have for the deity himself. The same is true in the Roman Catholic and Greek Orthodox traditions, where the ritual of consecration is thought to transform bread and wine into the body and blood of Jesus Christ himself. Such forms of consecration are not explicitly invoked in the secular or civic arena, although people tend to carry the concept over in various ways. Associations like the Boy Scouts and the armed forces teach "official" techniques for how to fold the flag, salute it, raise it each morning on a flagpole, and bring it down each evening. These rule-governed procedures underscore the ethos that a flag should never be treated as just another piece of colored cloth. Yet Supreme Court decisions that burning the flag is a protected form of First Amendment free speech are widely interpreted as retreating from the religious language of a sacred flag and all the legal complexities that would develop on how to define it.

Activities that generate and express the sacral significance of key symbols like the flag are often considered to be ritual-like. While ritual-like action is thought to be that type of action that best *responds* to the sacred nature of things, in actuality, ritual-like action effectively *creates* the sacred by explicitly differentiating such a realm from a profane one. If we were to try to pin down the exact nature of the sacrality evoked in such symbols, however, we would find a type of circularity by which sacredness, when not explicitly a religious claim to divinity, is a quality of specialness, not the same as other things, standing for something important and possessing an extra meaningfulness and the ability to evoke emotion-filled images and experiences. In other words, with regard to objects as sacred symbols, their sacrality is the way in which the object is more than the mere sum of its parts and points to something beyond itself, thereby evoking and expressing values and attitudes associated with larger, more abstract, and relatively transcendent ideas. This quality of sacrality is attributed not only to objects, of course, but also to places, buildings, and even people.

[...]

Performance

In recent years, much attention has focused on what ritual has in common with theatrical performances, dramatic spectacles, and public events. Most of these comparisons rest on a recognition that the performative dimension per se—that is, the deliberate, self-conscious "doing" of highly symbolic actions in public—is key to what makes ritual, theater, and spectacle what they are. While a performative dimension often coexists with other characteristics of ritual-like behavior, especially in rule-governed sports contests or responses to sacral symbols, in many instances performance is clearly the more dominant or essential element. For example, a number of studies address the ritual-like aspects of clowns and clowning. They point out how clowns follow certain rules, usually rules of inversion, by which they upset and mock the status quo. By extension, clowns themselves function as powerful symbols of cultural inversion, **ludic** freedom, and social innocence. However, what is most essential to what clowning is all about is the elaborately dramatic "acting out" that it involves.

The qualities of performance can be analyzed in terms of several overlapping features. First of all, performances communicate on multiple sensory levels, usually involving highly visual imagery, dramatic sounds, and sometimes even tactile, olfactory, and gustatory stimulation. By marching with a crowd, crying over a tragic drama, or applauding an unconvincing politician, even the less enthusiastic participants of the audience are cognitively and emotionally pulled into a complex sensory experience that can also communicate a variety of messages. Hence, the power of performance lies in great part in the effect of the heightened multisensory experience it affords: one is not being told or shown something so much as one is led to experience something. [...]

Another feature of performance lies in the dynamics of framing. As noted with regard to sacral symbols, distinctions between sacred and profane, the special and the routine, transcendent ideals and concrete realities can all be evoked by how some activities, places, or people are set off from others. Intrinsic to performance is the communication of a type of frame that says, "This is different, deliberate, and significant—pay attention!" By virtue of this framing, performance is understood to be something other than routine reality; it is a specific type of demonstration. It can also confer on the performance the ability to signify or denote larger truths under the guise of make-believe situations. Hence, since the person talking is framed by all the conventions of a theater production—stage, curtains, tickets, audience, familiar script—we know that he is not really Hamlet, Prince of Denmark. Although his overt identity is make-believe, by virtue of the way in which the theatrical framework sets his words and deeds off from day-to-day reality, the performance is credited with the ability to convey universal truths by means of an experience not readily accessible elsewhere.

Such frames not only distinguish performance as such, they also create a complete and condensed, if somewhat artificial world—like sacral symbols, a type of microcosmic portrayal of the macrocosm. Since the real world is rarely experienced as a coherently ordered totality, the microcosm constructed on stage purports to provide the experience of a mock-totality, an interpretive appropriation of some greater if elusive totality. [...]

[...]

Conclusion

The spectrum of rituals and ritual-like activities in the preceding sections reveal basic ways in which people ritualize, that is, create, deploy, and reproduce rites. The most clear-cut examples of ritual, those depicting various genres of ritual, tend to be a matter of communal ceremonies closely connected to formally institutionalized religions or clearly invoking divine beings. However, the examples of ritual-like activity suggest that what goes on in ritual is not unique to religious institutions or traditions. There are many ways to act ritually and many situations in which people have recourse to these ways, and degrees, of ritualizing. The survey of genres and ways of acting demonstrates that there is no intrinsic or universal understandings [sic] of what constitutes ritual. Indeed, few cultures have a single word that means exactly what is meant by the English word "ritual"—and [...] even the English term has meant a number of things. For historical and social reasons, many cultures do not make the same distinctions that lie behind the English term. For example, although European and American societies are apt to describe table etiquette, sports, theater productions, and political rallies as ritual-like, there is still a general consensus that they are not the best examples of what we usually mean by ritual. No matter how ritual-like sports and theater might appear to be at times, we are not apt to consider them the same thing as a church wedding ceremony. We have found it appropriate to see some basic distinctions among these ways of acting even if we occasionally note how blurred those distinctions can become. Other cultures also draw and blur various distinctions. What a culture distinguishes and with what degree of clarity can reveal interesting aspects of the ways in which people in that culture are likely to experience and interpret the world.

Glossary

ACQUIESCENCE: To defer or accept without protest or dissent.

AESTHETICALLY: Relating to beauty or the study of artistic excellence.

ALI, Mohammed (1942–2016): American gold medal winning Olympic and three-time champion professional heavy weight boxer.

AMISH: Protestant religious communities in the United States noted for strict doctrine and simple lifestyles that reject many forms of modern technology.

AMMAN, Jacob (also Jakob Ammann;1644–1712?): Founder of the Amish branch of Protestant Christianity.

BERNSTEIN, Basil (1924–2000): British sociologist of education and sociolinguistics.

DIONYSIAN: From the Greek deity Dionysus, pertaining to the sensual, emotional, and spontaneous aspects of human nature.

HASIDIC: Of or having to do with one of the most tradition-based forms of Judaism.

HOBSBAWM, Eric (1917–2012): British historian known for major works on Europe during the nineteenth and twentieth centuries.

WINDSOR, House of: Descendent of Queen Victoria, the current ruling family of the UK.

LUDIC: Playful or having to do with play.

MAYAN-AZTEC BALL COURT GAME: Ancient competitive sport played in long courts by pre-Columbian Mesoamericans.

MENNONITES: Originally followers of Anabaptist Menno Simons (1496–1561), Protestant communities known for simplicity and mission work, now a global denomination.

NACIREMA: "American" spelled backwards, it was a term first used by anthropologist Horace Miner in a 1956 article critiquing those who on "exotic" peoples to study ritual.

NONUTILITARIAN: Activity pursued without expectation of material gain or direct pleasure.

OATES, Joyce Carol (b. 1938): Prolific American writer of novels, short stories, plays, poetry, essays, reviews, and nonfiction.

ORTNER, Sherry (b. 1941): Anthropologist and author of various books on Sherpa culture, gender, and anthropological theory.

PAPACY: Pertaining to the office or authority of the Roman Catholic pope.

PURITANS: Protestant movement within England and later the American colonies advocating Calvinist reforms.

SIVA (also Shiva): A major Hindu deity.

STATUS QUO: Latin phrase for the existing state of affairs, especially in reference to social structures or political power.

VICTORIA, Queen (1819–1901): Queen of the UK (1837–1901), Empress of India (1876–1901), and longest reigning monarch of the UK to that point.

Questions for Conversation

How is ritualization a "flexible and strategic" way of acting in the world?

What is formalism and how does it shape ritualization?

Does formalism express power? Why is it "difficult to disrupt" according to Bell?

Is formalism beautiful? How?

Why do many ritual processes invoke traditionalism? What do traditionalists stand to gain by invoking the past, seemingly at the expense of the present?

Why do some forms of ritualization "invent" tradition? Consider especially the rituals of the British monarchy.

Many rituals insist on detailed and exacting actions that do not vary. Why? Is this invariance irrational, or a form of obsessive neurosis?

How are rule-governed activities like sports akin to religious rituals? How are they different?

How does ritualization make an ordinary thing, like bread or a piece of cloth, into a sacred symbol like the Eucharist or a national flag?

How are rituals like performances? Consider especially, effects on the senses and the ways that framing can evoke larger truths.

Overall, what does ritualization say about social priorities? In your response, consider some rituals you personally experience on a regular basis – holidays, daily habits, etc.

Suggestions for Additional Reading

The following is a list of supplemental readings that provide additional information about, apply, or respond critically to the ideas presented in this chapter.

Anderson, Benedict. *Imagined Communities: Reflections on the Origin and Spread of Nationalism*. New York: Verso, 1983.

Bell, Catherine M. *Ritual Theory, Ritual Practice*. New York: Oxford University Press, 1992.

Bell, Catherine M. *Ritual: Perspectives and Dimensions*. New York: Oxford University Press, 1997.

Bell, Catherine, ed. *Teaching Ritual*. New York: Oxford University Press, 2007.

Berry, Jan. "Whose Threshold? Women's Strategies of Ritualization," *Feminist Theology* 14, no. 3 (2006): 273–88.

Bruce, Katherine McFarland. *Pride Parades: How a Parade Changed the World*. New York: New York University Press, 2016.

Couldry, Nick. *Media Rituals: A Critical Approach*. New York: Routledge, 2003.

Faber, Alyda. "Saint Orlan: Ritual as Violent Spectacle and Cultural Criticism," *TDR/The Drama Review* 46, no. 1 (2002): 85–92.

Fraser, T. G., ed. *The Irish Parading Tradition: Following the Drum*. New York: St. Martin's Press, 2000.

Godlove, Jr., Terry F. *Religion, Interpretation, and Diversity of Belief: The Framework Model from Kant to Durkheim to Davidson*. New York: Cambridge University Press, 1989.

Gonzalez, George. "The Ritualization of Consumer Capitalism: Catherine Bell's *Ritual Theory, Ritual Practice* in the Age of Starbucks," *Implicit Religion* 18, no. 1 (2015): 3–44.

Hobsbawm, Eric. "Introduction: Inventing Traditions," in *The Invention of Tradition*, ed. Eric Hobsbawm and Terence Ranger, 1–14. Cambridge: Cambridge University Press, 1983.

Hogue, D. A. "Catching the Dog's Own Tail: An Essay in Honor of Catherine Bell," *Religious Studies Review* 36, no. 3 (2010): 175–81.

Klassen, Pamela E., and John W. Marshall. "Saint as Cipher: Paul, Badiou, and the Politics of Ritual Repudiation," *History of Religions* 51, no. 4 (2012): 344–63.

Latham, Jacob A. *Performance, Memory and Processions in Ancient Rome*. Cambridge: Cambridge University Press, 2016.

Moss, Kenneth. "St. Patrick's Day Celebrations and the Formation of Irish-American Identity, 1845–1875," *Journal of Social History* 29, no. 1 (1995): 125–48.

Newman, Simon P. *Parades and the Politics of the Street: Festive Culture in the Early American Republic*. Philadelphia: University of Pennsylvania Press, 1997.

O'Neill, Kevin Lewis. "Pastor Harold Caballeros Believes in Demons: Belief and Believing in the Study of Religion," *History of Religions* 51, no. 4 (2012): 299–316.

Pantti, Mervi, and Johanna Sumiala. "Till Death Do Us Join: Media, Mourning Rituals and the Sacred Centre of the Society," *Media, Culture, & Society* 31, no. 1 (2009): 119–35.

Patton, Laurie L. "The Enjoyment of Cows: Self-Consciousness and Ritual Action in the Early Indian Grhya Sutras," *History of Religions* 51, no. 4 (2012): 364–81.

Payne, Rodger. "Religious Parades and Processions in America," in *Oxford Research Encyclopedia of Religion*. New York: Oxford University Press, 2017. Available online: https://oxfordre.com/religion/view/10.1093/acrefore/9780199340378.001.0001/acrefore-9780199340378-e-543 (accessed January 28, 2020).

Schilbrack, Kevin. "Ritual Metaphysics," *Journal of Ritual Studies* 18, no. 2 (2004): 77–90.

Soper, Christopher, and Joel Fetzer. *Religion and Nationalism in Global Perspective*. New York: Cambridge University Press, 2018.

Unit III Durable Forms in the Study of Religion and Popular Culture

Introduction to Unit III

There is, in the study of religion, a long-raging debate over the act of comparison. Max Müller, often considered one of the founders of the academic study of religion, argued famously that, in terms of religious traditions or practices, "he who knows one, knows none"; in other words, that comparison was the basis for understanding. This became one of the models for the field—hence departments of comparative religion (or religions) at such US institutions as Drew University (New Jersey), Miami University (Ohio), and Western Michigan University, among others.

But according to its critics, the dangers of comparison were ever-present. In the early 1960s, as state-supported colleges and universities were taking a cue from the US Supreme Court's decision affirming the constitutionality of teaching about religion and broadening beyond theology and Christianity in their course offerings, Rabbi Samuel Sandmel—professor of biblical literature and past president of the Society of Biblical Literature and Exegesis—was warning fellow scholars against "parallelomania." In an article on early Christian texts, Sandmel applied the term he traced back to an unidentified French text from the 1830s to scholars in his own field and defined it as "that extravagance among scholars which first overdoes the supposed similarity in passages and then proceeds to describe source and derivation as if implying literary connection flowing in an inevitable or predetermined direction" (1962: 1). Sandmel admitted that he was "not seeking to discourage the study of these parallels, but . . . to encourage them." Nonetheless, he felt it necessary to advise "caution about exaggerations" as they related to "parallels," as well as their "source and derivation," and he admonished his colleagues to "recognize parallelomania for the disease that it is" (1962: 13).

Twenty years later, history of religions scholar Jonathan Z. Smith argued in an essay titled "In Comparison a Magic Dwells" that one who engages in comparison is actually being "more impressionistic than methodical." Although a scholar may be drawn to a topic "by a sense of its uniqueness," he argued, nonetheless "at some point along the way, as if unbidden, as a sort of déjà vu, the scholar remembers that he has seen 'it' or 'something like it' before," and that the similarity "must then be accorded significance and provided with an explanation." Smith asks: "is comparison an enterprise of magic or science?" and concludes that it "appears to be more a matter of memory than a project for inquiry" (1982: 22). It is, therefore, entirely suspect.

The fear is that, through overzealous comparison, scholars might endorse a position articulated as the title of a work by British poet and artist William Blake: *All Religions Are One* (1795). Better known as "perennialism" (from Aldous Huxley's 1945 work *The Perennial Philosophy*), this approach suggested that, while different in the details, all religions were basically the same at some deeper level. Described by analogy in the words of one of the presumed champions of this approach, philosopher of religion Huston Smith, "It is possible to climb life's mountain from any side, but when the top is reached trails converge" (1991: 73).

For a variety of reasons—including the willingness either to define "religion" broadly or to abandon any willingness to define it at all—the problem seems only amplified in the study of religion and popular culture. In their 2000 work *Religion and Popular Culture in America*, Bruce David Forbes and Jeffrey H. Mahan suggest that one way of understanding the intersection of religion and popular culture is where participants in some aspect of popular culture act as if that aspect was a religion. This is a common enough approach in the study of the topic; one of the more important early models examined *Star Trek* fandom as a religious phenomenon (Jindra 1994). The danger, though, is not that the author will argue that all religions are the same, but rather that anything (or everything) can be considered a religion. Sean McCloud, describing the relatively new subfield of "fandom as religion," diagnoses these investigators as afflicted by "the approaches of scholars who connect the facile similarities between popular culture fandoms and religious movements so thoroughly that they see them as being the same thing" (2003: 191).

But while Huston Smith may have been a perennialist, the line quoted above—about all religious "paths converging at the top" of the mountain—was part of Smith's description of an "idea that comes out more clearly" in Hinduism than "through the other great religions; namely, her [i.e., the Hindu tradition's] conviction that the various major religions are alternate paths to the same goal" (1991: 72–3). In this part of Huston Smith's discussion of Hinduism, he is drawing primarily from the nineteenth-century mystic Ramakrishna, who sought to experience the divine in a wide variety of religious traditions, and whose most famous student (Swami Vivekananda) is often credited with introducing Hinduism to the English-speaking world. We cannot confirm from this quote whether or not Huston Smith was a perennialist; there is strong evidence that he was, but this isn't it. What we can confirm is only that he understood (rightly or wrongly) that Hinduism took this view.

The lesson here might be that, like most arguments, reality (or practice) probably lies somewhere in between the two positions. In his own article, McCloud concludes that "several studies do show some persuasive parallels between popular culture fandoms and religious movements" (2003: 198). Comparison is an important aspect of the path to understanding. If something is unique and beyond comparison, then there is no way it can be contextualized, and is therefore beyond comprehension; but if it is just one more example of "more of the same," then is there no real point in seeking to understand it, since there is no particular lesson to be learned.

Comparison may even be a necessary element in the study of human cultural activity. Anthropologist Clifford Geertz reminds us that the study of culture is "not an experimental science in search of laws but an interpretive one in search of meaning." Citing sociologist Max Weber's concept that "man is an animal suspended in webs of significance he himself has spun," Geertz identifies culture as "those webs" so spun by humanity, and that it is "explanation" he seeks, answers to the riddles of why people do what they do (1973: 5). By comparing, we begin the process of evaluating impressions, and finding explanations — probably not *the* explanation, but at the very least, *an* explanation — for the social phenomena we encounter in our world.

But there is no doubt that, as important as comparison might be, it should be done with a great deal of caution, and with full recognition that contrary facts must be accounted for and not bulldozed under the romance of symmetry.

Durable Forms

Which brings us to Unit III.

Much of popular culture is distinctively modern and makes robust use of the media and mass replication technologies that have emerged in recent centuries — print, radio, television, film, the Internet, etc. Many of the theories we explored in Units I and II necessarily focus on the modern period and concepts like the "culture industry" that address distinctively modern modes of power and communication. And yet some aspects of popular culture are not particularly new. Various modes of storytelling, collective rituals, and mythical motifs that are widely disseminated today (and in fact seem to thrive in the contemporary media environment) have been around for a very long time and seem to have been employed by many different societies. Thus in this section we turn to durable forms of popular culture, which have endured beyond the particularities of historical eras and thrive across different cultural traditions. We find them in societies around the globe, ancient, medieval, and modern. Although not an exhaustive list, we emphasize five general areas for the study of durable forms that serve as a useful introduction to a historical appreciation of the study of religion and popular culture:

- "Who We Are" begins our journey through self-examination and explores our use of heroes and monsters in describing ourselves;
- "Where We Are" examines our desire to construct meaning-filled space, and what that can communicate about our sense of place;
- "What We Know" considers the way myths function as the mechanism used to transfer basic knowledge of the world in which we live, and in ways that may not always be obvious;
- "Where We Go" explores the ways that seekers find meaning in pilgrimages to sacred places, whether physical or imagined; and
- "What We Do" focuses on the things we do and the ways we can be in the world, through carnivals and festivals.

While these particular forms seem to transcend time and locale, we note here at the outset the importance of cultural difference, as articulated by many of the theorists in Unit II. There are certainly enough points of obvious similarity to make comparison compelling and interesting, much as we have seen in the academic study of comparative religion. For example, monsters in Japan, Europe, and among indigenous peoples share some family resemblances — they are horrific, disruptive, ravenous, superhuman, etc. And yet, as more detailed scholarship has emerged, we have come to understand that monsters have distinctive roles to play in the popular lore of their host societies. They respond to distinctive political orders, social changes, national traumas, and other unique motivations, not the least of which is the underlying religious culture. Even monsters that, thanks to modern media, are now globally recognized—like King Kong and Godzilla—can hold very different meanings for different audiences.

So what to prioritize in our exploration of durable forms? We suggest two general lines of questioning that will be helpful to any case study or comparative inquiry (be that comparison historical or cross-cultural). The first examines power and function: How does the durable form function in its particular context in terms of social, political, and economic power? Does it serve the powerful in ways that are explicit? For example, parades and processions often have as their basic purpose a clear demonstration of who is in charge. To look upon the king, a statue of a divine figure, the high priest, the elected president, or a military brigade is to submit, consciously or unconsciously, to their right to rule. On the other hand, some durable forms seem to undermine authority. A recurring figure in many European-derived carnival traditions is the "Lord of Misrule" who temporarily "governs" events given over to excess, inversions of social hierarchies, rule breaking, and other forms of social chaos. This "lord" suggests that power is slippery in these events and can be quickly challenged and reversed.

The second line of inquiry explores the wellsprings of cultural creativity: How do the durable forms serve as foundations for the kinds of novel cultural combinations and blendings that we associate with creativity? In this we can see these forms in ways analogous to, on the one hand, artistic creativity, and on the other, the work of entrepreneurs who create new products and services. Take, for example, fairy tales, many of which are of ancient origin and have long been recognized by folklorists as a core feature of local cultures who use them for entertainment and moral instruction. Traditionally exchanged between parents and children as part of an oral culture, fairy tales became "literary" in the nineteenth century thanks to collectors like the Brothers Grimm who committed them to print. With the emergence of film and television in the twentieth century, fairy tales became blockbusters, meticulously animated and carefully wrought by elaborate teams of artisans under the managerial hand of Walt Disney and other big media companies. With each transition, there were creative decisions to be made—what to include and exclude, how to render particular characters, what kind of language to use (verbal and visual), etc. We might even ask if the persistence of these durable forms can be explained not by their essential stability but by their ability to get reinvented over time in new cultural contexts and in new media. While we might recognize some connections between the latest Disney princesses and their forbearers in medieval European storytelling, we also need to see them in the light of present-day changes in the status of women, modern psychological views on childhood development, and the ambitions of a big media conglomerate aiming to expand its "brand." Likewise, circling back to the issue of power, we can ask: How do durable forms foster creative cultural responses, especially to social, economic, and political changes?

Like religion in a more general sense, these durable forms provide a framework for communities as they adapt to new conditions and strive to creatively express their inner longings and anxieties. Because of their symbolic density and wide scope—they are all "popular" in both the sense of accessibility and in the numbers of participants—they become particularly rich resources for exploring how the study of religion in popular culture speaks to a wide range of topics. Thus we find that scholars' analyses draw upon the full range of theoretical perspectives, from social and psychological dynamics, political and economic power, creative artistry, theological reflection, and often combinations of these vital themes.

What's Here

The format of each of the chapters in this unit may seem rather informal; they are intended to be more conversational than assertive. Our hope is that each chapter provides an example of how we might approach the study of the broader topic of the unit (with some discussion of related issues, of course), to reveal not only the basic structures of the investigations but the basic formation of some of the questions that go into such a study. With some notions for starting points of these topics, we expect that readers will explore more thoroughly (maybe via the Internet) the examples we have selected to illuminate the durable forms; that they will seek to identify their own examples; or that they will seek to use other theorists to make some kind of sense of it all. Carnivals and sacred spaces, monsters and pilgrimage sites—there is a world of information available to you; we hope merely to get you started.

Works Cited

Blake, William. *All Religions Are One*. Paris: Trianon Press, 1795/1970.

Geertz, Clifford. "Thick Description: Toward an Interpretive Theory of Culture," in *The Interpretation of Cultures: Selected Essays by Clifford Geertz*, ed. Clifford Geertz, 87–125. New York: Basic Books, 1973.

Huxley, Aldous. *The Perennial Philosophy*. New York: Harper & Brothers, 1945.

Jindra, Michael. "Star Trek Fandom as a Religious Phenomenon," *Sociology of Religion* 55, no. 1 (1994): 27–51.

McCloud, Sean. "Popular Culture Fandoms, the Boundaries of Religious Studies, and the Project of the Self," *Culture and Religion* 4, no. 2 (2003): 187–206.

Sandmel, Samuel. "Parallelomania," *Journal of Biblical Literature* 81, no. 1 (1962): 1–13.

Smith, Huston. *The World's Religions: Our Great Wisdom Traditions*. New York: HarperCollins, 1991. [Originally published in 1958 as *The Religions of Man*.]

Smith, Jonathan Z. "In Comparison a Magic Dwells," in *Imagining Religion: From Babylon to Jonestown*, ed. Jonathan Z. Smith, 19–35. Chicago: The University of Chicago Press, 1982.

15   Who We Are

Saints, Heroes, and Monsters

All over the world, mass-mediated popular culture does "religious work" to use David Chidester's term. Rather than turning to the texts, teachings, and rituals of the world's institutionalized religions—or in addition to these sources—people turn to movies, television shows, novels, and comic books for representations of good and evil and for familiar narratives that help them to contextualize and interpret events and experiences. Some of the most powerful religious work of popular culture comes in the form of characterizations of heroes and monsters. Godzilla. The Creature from the Black Lagoon. Zombies. Vampires. Werewolves. Cannibals. War heroes. Superheroes. Sports heroes. Monsters and heroes are some of the more obvious examples of religion in popular culture and of popular culture producing religious characters, expressing moral values, and representing images of good and evil. And they do not stay stuck to the screen (or the page), either: in our celebrity culture public personas are often typecast as one or another manifestation of these classifications as gossip and media portrayal become allegories of morality. These characters do a great deal of religious work in contemporary American popular culture, as they have throughout history as enduring religious forms.

Taking each of these figures in turn, the scholar of religion might illuminate their significance as ideal types that derive from particular religious histories and vocabularies but have expanded to serve as models *of* and *for* moral character, at the same time that they both reflect and potentially criticize prevailing social values.

Heroes

The classical form of the hero in the West can be found in Greek and Roman mythology and epic literature. The word "hero" is derived from the Greek *heros*, "protector" or "defender." Figures like Heracles, Theseus, Perseus, and Odysseus were ideals of manhood, strong and brave and proven in overcoming great challenges. As heroes their stories were familiar, told and retold as foundational to the culture that produced them. These heroes were human, but also something more than human. They performed tasks that were generally considered beyond human capacity, and sometimes, as in the case of Theseus and Heracles and others, had both human and divine parents. Still today, children in the United States are familiar with these stories of bravery through versions of Greek and Roman myths that they read at home or at school, and through refigurings and retellings in popular publications like Rick Riordan's *Percy Jackson and the Olympians* book and film franchise.

While classical Greek and Roman heroes have long been treated as aspects of Western cultural literacy, and therefore are familiar to most Europeans and Americans, they of course do not exhaust the catalog of ancient heroes. From Mesopotamia's Gilgamesh to Old English Beowulf, to India's Rama, the heroic warrior/leader who overcomes great odds to uphold the community and its prevailing conceptions of virtue and truth has been considered by some comparative scholars of religion to be universal.

The study of the formulaic nature of the hero narrative historically has been an important subfield of comparative mythology, literature, and folklore studies. One of the most influential studies was Vladimir Propp's *The Morphology of the Folktale* (1968 [1928]), which was not strictly a study of hero narratives, but rather of Slavic *maerchen*, or fairy tales. These tales, according to Propp's analysis of their form, always have a hero who leaves home and faces a challenge where he (and it is usually he) must overcome a villain or some sort of lack. Propp identified thirty-one "functions," or units, of analysis from which such tales are composed. He defined a function as "an act of a character, defined from the point of view of its significance for the course of the action" (21). While all Slavic fairy tales are not the same, Propp argued that they are all made up of the same building blocks and present variations on a similar structure.

Taking Propp's analysis further and adding a psychological perspective to it, Joseph Campbell later popularized what he called "the hero's journey" into a universal form that he claimed could be found in hero tales throughout the world. The hero's journey was a "monomyth," a term Campbell borrowed from James Joyce's *Finnegans Wake* to signify the singularity of form of all mythic narratives. Behind this conception of a human universal was psychotherapist Carl Jung's theory of a shared collective unconscious of all humanity, made up of shared archetypes. The hero's tale was archetypal, according to Campbell, and independent of any particular social, cultural, or historical setting. In Campbell's formulation, the narrative had a basic three-part structure of *departure*, *initiation*, and *return*, each of which was made up of five or six subparts. In part one the hero sets out on a journey, often reluctantly, and may meet a mentor or guide. In part two, the hero leaves the ordinary world, encountering obstacles and ordeals, to gain a reward before returning to the ordinary world. Finally, in part three, the hero returns, transformed and wise, to the ordinary world. For Campbell these stories, as essentially psychological in nature, were allegories of psychological growth and spiritual transformation and were culturally important because they presented models for growth and wisdom. His monomyth model has been influential in popular culture not only as a theory of myth, psychology, and hero narratives but as a model for storytelling. In a particularly telling example, George Lucas consciously modeled *Star Wars* on Campbell's format.

Closely tied to Campbell's view of heroes and heroic journeys as archetypes, similar across traditions, is historian of religion Mircea Eliade's notion of heroes as "mythicized" historical personalities (1971). Both men emphasized the power of the archetypal narrative. However, if Campbell was interested in heroes as psychological models, Eliade was rather concerned with how historical actors became ahistorical mythical heroes, disconnected from the social and historical particularities of their actual existence to become "timeless." This was, to Eliade, a common feature of "archaic man" or *homo religiosus*. In this view, heroes, like all religious archetypes, were "beyond" history, functioning as a stable reality outside of the transformations of time and space. They were, in that sense, "Real," and the foundation of orientation in the world. Heroes tended to be founders of religions and nations, and great warriors, and—typically—men. They were those who founded the grounding structures of reality or kept chaos at bay. As their stories were told, they fitted closer and closer to what was expected in the hero story, losing particulars and gaining mythical characteristics.

A sociologist like Emile Durkheim might approach heroic figures as collective representations of social identity, a sort of totem embodying the ideals of a society and mirroring them back to the society itself. This was the perspective of Durkheimian historian Henri Hubert, who saw heroes also as links between the sacred and the profane (2009). Neither fully gods nor fully humans, heroes operate as a kind of superhuman, an ideal, that has its place and meanings in both traditionally religious and secular contexts. As heroes, the actions of particular people are idealized and given significance, while simultaneously social ideals are made personal and familiar in the context of narratives about individuals' actions.

In the United States, the range of figures who are characterized as heroes is broad. From founding fathers and Revolutionary War heroes like George Washington and Paul Revere to mythical heroic settlers of the imagined wild west like Daniel Boone and Davey Crockett; from liberators like Harriette Tubman and Dr. Martin Luther King, Jr. to industrious workers like Joe Magarac and John Henry; to everyday heroes like firefighters, police officers, health-care workers, and individuals who put others before themselves. One might say that the term "hero" has become diluted. On the other hand, this variety is an illustration of the diversity of settings in which heroism might be signified. A critical question for scholars of religion and popular culture to ask is *for whom* is a particular figure a hero, and *on what terms*? Because societies are complex and diverse, what is valued and ideal to one group or community within a given society may be oppressive to another. Heroes, therefore, say something about their social setting, and their study should take this into account. Historian of religion Charles H. Long noted that concepts like American Civil Religion— and the symbols and images of that idea, including its heroes—imagine a united national population of shared values where in fact there have been historically great disparities of power and inclusion within that population (1974). Recent movements to remove statues of Confederate leaders, white supremacists, and others in American public spaces have highlighted the contested nature of heroic representation and are a ripe area for the study of popular claims and conflicts over heroes and their signification.

What Eliade called "mythicization," Marxist historian Eric Hobsbawm, coming from a field outside of the study of religion, would label "the invention of tradition" (1983). Like Eliade, Hobsbawm was concerned with the ways that the "traditions" that people believed were ancient, even timeless, were formed. Whereas Eliade tied this process to the "archaic" project of myth-making through the repetition of remembering and telling heroic stories, a basic ontology of orientation, Hobsbawm emphasized that such myth-making was a political act related to constructing and maintaining power. Most of the heroes that interested Eliade were kings, warriors, and founders of nations or religions. Hobsbawm, however, was more interested in the subversive figures who were characterized as criminals by those in power but as heroes by peasants in agricultural societies. "Social bandits," he called these figures, were considered heroes by the oppressed and marginalized (1959, 1969). They stood up to the powers of the ruling class and worked against them in the name of the powerless. The classic example of the social bandit is Robin Hood, who stole from the rich to give to the poor. In the folklore and popular culture of the American West, examples include Jesse James, Pretty Boy Floyd, and Belle Starr. In Mexico, Pancho Villa and Subcomandante Marcos represent folk heroes who would not be recognized in a national pantheon of heroes but whose deeds have been heroic for a particular stratum of society. In the twenty-first century, with increased awareness of the diversity within nations and societies, there are growing calls for an equally diverse representation of heroes—or for attentiveness to the fact that the heroes often memorialized and honored in public space and popular culture are not necessarily representative of the values and ideals of the public as a whole. Popular culture forms such as films, television, comics, novels, and music have helped to spread this awareness, at the same time that popular culture itself is being called to pay attention to its own history of narrow representations of diverse cultures and audiences.

Superheroes

Representation has been a particular concern with American superheroes, the more-than-human characters who have dedicated themselves to fighting evil and protecting the good. Superheroes emerged in the late 1930s in the context of comic strips and pulp fiction magazines. The first was Superman, created by Jerry Siegel and Joe Shuster in 1938, followed a year later by Bob Kane and Bill Finger's Batman. The superhero field grew quickly; by the early 1940s there were over twenty comic book companies selling tens of millions of copies each month. Marvel and DC dominated and continue to be the largest comic book companies in the United States. The biggest superhero names were created during this time, too: The Flash, Green Lantern, Aquaman, Daredevil, Captain Marvel, Captain America, and others. Superheroes soon jumped from the page to the radio, and then to the screen, appearing in multiple serial films in the 1940s as well. By the 1950s, they migrated to television. *Adventures of Superman* ran from 1952 to 1958; *Batman* from 1966 to 1968; *Wonder Woman* from 1975 to 1979. By the 1970s, following wider trends in American culture, superheroes started diversifying: Luke Cage was the first Black superhero to be the title character of a comic book, and he was followed quickly by Black Panther, Black Lightning, and others. Asian superheroes also appeared in American markets, usually as martial arts experts (see Iwamura [2011] for an excellent analysis of the *Kung Fu* television series). The late twentieth century saw a resurgence of interest and production of superhero films that has only grown in the first decades of the 2000s.

Now a huge franchise with a life of its own, bridging television, film comic books, toys, food, and more, the superhero genre raises a host of issues for scholars of religion and popular culture. From the start, these larger-than-human representatives of moral ideals were wrapped in the flag of nationalism and patriotism (Superman's catch phrase was "truth, justice, and the American way"). How have superheroes embodied, or challenged, dominant American values or conceptions of the meaning of the nation? How have the particular concerns of different eras shape superhero storylines and images? Theodor Adorno and Max Horkheimer would push scholars to examine how the culture industry—the commercial marketplace in which these figures exist—has shaped their stories, images, production, distribution, and messages. In turn, how have those interests then informed audience ideas about national and personal identity and values? There have been female superheroes since the early days of the genre, but they have rarely been the superstars and have been far outnumbered by men. How are ideologies of gender and sexuality produced and reproduced through these figures and their storylines? Are these related in any way to messages presented by religious cultures? Do they challenge these messages? How have representations of gender and sexuality changed, if at all, over time? How have the physical characteristics of masculinity and femininity been signified and idealized by superheroes? (Cocca 2016) If superheroes in some sense represent American values, then Edward Said would have us carefully examine the way that the enemies against whom they fight are represented; are the enemies in the superhero world drawn from Orientalist imaginations about non-American others? How does the history of Orientalism shape American ideas about both American-ness and non-American-ness? In the twenty-first century in particular, the predominantly white, male pantheon of superheroes has been diversifying. Have the issues, plots, and themes of superhero films and comics changed along with this new representation? These are all important questions that can help scholars to analyze our contemporary popular cultural heroes to learn more about ourselves.

Saints

In a sense, saints are Christian heroes. The origins of the concept of the *saint* lie in the history of Christianity. Deriving from the Latin *sanctus*, for "holy," the past participle of *sancire*, "to consecrate," the Old French word *seint* entered the Catholic world in the twelfth century to designate individuals who were canonized by the Roman Catholic Church for their exceptional holiness. In that tradition, saints are human beings whose character and behavior showed them to be closer to God than other human beings. According to Catholic tradition, saints have superhuman powers that enable them to perform miracles. Protestant Christians rejected the veneration of Catholic saints as idolatry and widened the term to include, potentially, all Christians. In the comparative study of religion, the term was expanded further to become a universal signifier of people considered to be exceptionally holy or connected to the divine. From there it was a short jump to secularized usage of the term to designate people considered to be especially moral or exhibiting remarkable character, especially in difficult circumstances. For instance, Saint Theresa of Calcutta, the Roman Catholic nun who received the Nobel Peace Prize in 1979 for her work with the Missionaries of Charity, was canonized by the Catholic Church in 2016—a process that involved the identification of her performance of two miracles. She is officially recognized as a saint by that institution. More widely, though, even in a secular context Mother Theresa has been described as a "saint" not because she performed miracles but due to her purported selfless giving and moral character. She has become a symbol of selfless behavior.

Like heroes, public representations of morality and character are always entangled with issues of power and are therefore open to contestation. Popular atheist author and political commentator Christopher Hitchens' critical stance on the religious and secular veneration of Mother Theresa serves as an example. In his book *The Missionary Position: Mother Theresa in Theory and Practice* (1995) he castigated the nun for gaining prestige on the suffering of others and her hypocritical (in Hitchens's view) refusal to oppose church doctrines that might help to alleviate poverty (such as those relating to contraception and abortion). Rather than recognizing her as pure, moral, and godly, Hitchens instead saw her as an example of the church's misguided and self-interested refusal to support more systemic economic and behavioral changes.

Also, like heroes, communities often recognize saints that are not necessarily "officially" recognized by religious institutions (like the Roman Catholic Church). For instance, for complex reasons relating to their colonial history some Mexican Catholic communities venerate local "folk" saints that are not canonized by the church. Juan Soldado, for example, was a private in the Mexican army who was executed in 1938 for the rape and murder of a child from Tijuana. Many in that area maintained that he was innocent, framed by a superior who had actually committed the crime. They reported supernatural occurrences at his gravesite, such as seeping blood and disembodied voices, and began attributing miracles to Soldado—often related to crossing the Mexican/American border. Today there are shrines to him throughout the region. Migrants seek Juan Soldado's support before attempting to cross into the United States.

Folk saints become figures in stories, novels, and films. They are the subjects of songs and murals. In popular usage, saints ("official" or "folk") become centerpieces of alters for devotional practice or marking sites of death or powerful events. They signify identity and community belonging and ritualize physical, symbolic, and emotional border crossings. And saints (or their images) can also become commodified, sold as T-shirts, posters, and illustrations on coffee mugs. Votive candles, traditionally lit as a ritual element of praying to or thanking a saint in some forms of Christian practice, are an interesting example. One style of votive candle, highly recognizable as a ritual object, is a tall, wax-filled cylindrical glass jar that has an image of a particular saint printed on its side. Today, these are used not only by Catholics but by others in nonreligious (or nontraditionally-religious) ways as ethnic or cultural décor. More recently, this style of candle can be purchased with images of decidedly secular "saints" such as Supreme Court Justice Ruth Bader Ginsberg, scientist Albert Einstein, and musician David Bowie. What might Theodor Adorno and Max Horkheimer make of this? Are these simply ironic or playful, or do they represent a shifting locus of veneration?

Monsters

In heroic narratives, the hero often becomes a hero by slaying a monster. Therefore, perhaps a society's monsters are even more significant and revealing than its heroes. The word "monster" comes from the Latin *monstrum*, from *moneo*, "to warn, to foretell." The appearance of a monster, classically, was a sign of warning or of divine displeasure. Threatening to undo order and creation, producing chaos, they must be defeated by a hero to maintain the order of the cosmos. So heroes signify order, the way things ought to be, while monsters are the threatened undoing of our taken-for-granted reality. To study monsters is to study what threatens a society or community, what signals the limits of belonging or acceptance (Beale 2002).

According to historian Scott Poole, "the narrative of American history can be read as a tale of monsters slain and monsters loved" (2011: 4). The monsters of American history "emerge out of the central anxieties and obsessions that have been a part of the United States from colonial times to the present and from the structures and processes where those obsessions found historical expression" (2011: 4). Therefore, monsters change with time and context; they are, as Stuart Hall has called race, "floating signifiers," which "gain their meanings not because of what they contain in their essence, but in the shifting relations of difference which they establish with other concepts and ideas in a signifying field" (1997). Comparing monsters to the concept of race is intentional, for race has often been a factor in defining monsters in American history and popular culture. Race and sexuality are common aspects of what has made up the monstrous in the United States, as monsters call attention to the *body* as a site of religious, political, and cultural contestation. Monsters have been on the scene since the first arrival of colonizing Europeans to the land they called the "New World," shape-shifting along with the changes of history. From Puritan concerns with demonic beings and forces to representations of indigenous peoples as cannibals and savages, to the imagination of Africans as superhuman, oversexualized, and unpredictable, Americans have cast their fears and anxieties into monstrous figures—drawing social distinctions and cultural boundaries all along.

While the dominant white Christian culture has tended to signify its "others" as monstrous (from people of color to those whose sexuality does not align with binary heteronormative expectations, to people or communities who transgress dominant values or are perceived as threats to them), those "others" have also used the rhetoric and image of monstrosity to critique and resist the powers that be as well. For instance, folklorist Gladys-Marie Fry's *Night Riders in Black Folk History* (1975) details the ways that slaveholders in the United States used fear of supernatural beings and powers to control the Black population by masquerading as ghosts and spreading rumors of evil spirits. But she also described how this history, which carried through to the Tuskegee Study of the 1930s and beyond and included rumors of "night doctors" who stole and sold cadavers and kidnapped and experimented on Black people, became a source of rumors, beliefs, and legends about the dangers of being Black in a white supremacist society where, in fact, great evil did lurk in the streets. These stories of monstrous whites were in part created by whites to control people of color but were also in part warnings and revelations about very real oppressive and violent structures of life.

Likewise, the *windigo* (also spelled wendigo) is a cannibalistic monster whose roots lie in Algonquian-speaking Native communities in the United States and Canada and the subject of many filmic and comic depictions (as well as historical and psychological theories about cannibalism and deprivation) that have usually been produced without input from Algonquian perspectives. Religious studies scholar Brady DeSanti, himself an enrolled member of the Lac Courte Oreilles Ojibwe tribe, has examined these representations of the windigo, concluding that "the windigo of popular culture has been wrenched from its Ojibwe setting to present thematically familiar horror stories in which innocent people are trapped, stalked, and dispatched in gruesome ways" (2015: 198). The Ojibway meaning of *windigo* refers to gluttony and selfishness, and one becomes a windigo by exhibiting selfish behavior. With this in mind, Jack D. Forbes, one of the founders of modern American Indian Studies, has described colonialism and capitalism as manifestations of the windigo disease (2008). American religious historian Kenneth Morrison has further elaborated how Jesuit priests became part of windigo traditional stories as they played a mediating role between greedy fur traders and eastern Algonquian communities in the seventeenth century, "healing" windigo illness by helping mitigate the negative effects of European colonial intrusion and support traditional indigenous social values of reciprocity (1979).

The windigo calls attention to the way that definitions of human and monster are not only formal, biological, or mythical but about relationship. As some humans cross the boundary to become monsters, the similarities and differences between the two become problematic, and also more intensified. Two monsters of this type have had an especially powerful presence in American popular culture over time: vampires and zombies.

Vampires

Blood- and life-sucking creatures like vampires seem to exist in many, if not most, cultures in the world. The greatest influence on American popular culture has come from a European tradition that really only came into its modern form in 1897 with the publication of Bram Stoker's novel *Dracula*. By 1931 it was made into a still-popular film starring Bela Legosi. Initially, vampire stories, as represented by Dracula, were heavily embedded within the twin forces of Christianity (specifically Roman Catholicism) and sexual desire. From Stoker through the popular television series *True Blood* (2008–14), vampires' biting and sucking and transformation of people into eternally living, night-dwelling, ravenous creatures have evoked eroticism and sexuality, even as they have simultaneously been allegories of capitalism, consumption, colonialism, class warfare, exploitation, disease, and more. Tracing a history of the various representations and storylines of vampire films, novels, comics, and other popular cultural productions reveals the depth of the character as a resource for exploring the tensions of danger and desire, and the tenuous line between life and death, production and destruction, morality and immortality. In one provocative study, sociologist of religion Titus Hjelm suggested that the portrayal of vampires in popular movies paralleled changing functions of religion and science in the wider culture (2009). While classic 1960s and 1970s vampire films represented an "old paradigm," in which vampires had demonic origins, malevolent motives, and were defeated by faith and mysticism (particularly the Catholic Church—think crucifixes, holy water, and prayer), a "new paradigm" was evident by the turn of the century (represented by the *Blade* trilogy, and the *Underworld* films). Now, the origin or "cause" of vampirism was genetic (a virus or a gene), their motives were survival and a quest for power, and their nemesis (or "cure") was science and technology. Hjelm concludes that vampire movies illustrate a popular movement away from religious authority. Still, he writes, they exhibit a "lingering fascination with questions of ultimate meaning—the answers are just found in science and technology, not in religion" (2009: 107). Thus, "religion," in an Eliadean sense, has not disappeared; it has changed venues.

More recent vampire films show a further movement into imagining the boundaries of humanity and its others, and the possibilities of living with monsters. The *Twilight* series of novels by Stephanie Meyer, and the film franchise based on them, concern the ability of vampires to integrate into mainstream human life. Can vampires control their appetites? Are authentic vampire-human relationships possible? At base in these portrayals are questions about desire and self-control, and the relevance of biological versus social bases of community and difference. While some have found *Twilight* to present conservative gender roles and views about romance (including female submission to violent male partners), others have argued, in the context of Meyer's Mormon perspective, that the novels and films portray women with the agency to explore and experience danger and taboo subjects, to use their free will to develop their own sense of morality (Tascano 2010).

In a very different setting and style, the HBO *True Blood* series also places vampires in the context of living with and among humans. In this case, the development and availability of a synthetic blood beverage (Tru Blood) allow vampires to live without consuming human blood, opening the possibility for peaceful coexistence. Among other issues, the series follows the struggles of the vampire community for equal rights as they integrate with human society—and the rise of anti-vampire forces (depicted, in one instance, as a fundamentalist Christian organization) who want to see them wiped out. The show has obvious analogies to larger American social issues of the early twenty-first century, most specifically related to the movement for LGBTQ+ equality. But beyond the obvious social concerns, Folklorist Leonard Primiano has suggested that the show also says something more about religion in the United States. The show's powerful title sequence, which juxtaposes and mixes images of violence, nature, decay, and (particularly Southern Pentecostal) religion, provides a context for understanding the show. "The credits of *True Blood* can be seen to showcase, exploit, adore, and simultaneously stand suspicious of that American religious hybrid" that blends European traditions with diverse American experiences, Primiano wrote. "Framing the plot lines of the show, these credits highlight Americans' fascination with occult or secret knowledge, their attraction to the supernatural, and their devotion to personal, experiential religion, even while often denying affiliation with institutional religions" (2011: 55).

Of course, one central aspect of vampire stories is blood—a key religious symbol and substance and a fundamental element of life. Scholarship on vampires might focus on the significance and portrayals of blood in various settings and representations, including its spiritual, biological, medical, technological, contexts, its commodification and circulation and regulation, its rhetorical and political and reproductive functions, and its gendered and sexualized formations.

Zombies

Equally ubiquitous as vampires in American popular culture, zombies also inhabit and blur the boundary between life and death. Perhaps never more popular than today, zombies, like vampires, are both horror movie standbys and metaphors for a host of social, cultural, and economic phenomena, including zombie banks, zombie economies, zombie computer processes, and zombie students. Zombies' roots are in Haitian religious culture, where the *zonbi* was spiritual reflection of the slave colonialism that formed the culture. In Haitian practice, there were two forms of *zonbi*: the astral zonbi, which is a spirit ritually captured from the recent dead and put to work for its "owner"; and the *zonbi kó kadav*, or "walking corpse," which is a body without a spirit that is at the command of its owner. In both cases, the labor and property processes of slavery are spiritualized and given a central religious significance. "Under slavery, Afro-Caribbeans were rendered nonhuman by being legally transposed into commodities," says religion scholar Elizabeth McAlister. "Now, the enslaved hold a *respected place* within the religion," where "the slave is often considered the most efficacious spiritual actor" (2012: 465).

The Haitian zonbi became the American zombie in the early twentieth century, when Hollywood represented the Caribbean as a mysterious, superstitious, and dangerously primitive place in films like *White Zombie* (1932) and *I Walked with a Zombie* (1943). In the background of these film productions was the occupation of Haiti by the US Marines between 1915 and 1934, shaping and underlying such perceptions. But the current-day American idea of the zombie, situated squarely in middle-class America, was invented in 1968 with the release of George Romero's film *Night of the Living Dead*. "That which was religious about the spirit zonbi in Haiti . . . was turned inside out, like the Haitian corpse zonbi. The film zombie is a former human with a body, but no soul, spirit, consciousness, interiority, or identity" (McAlister 2012: 473). Romero created the blueprint for all future American zombie films and images. Purely automatons, the zombies of American pop culture are empty shells that do nothing but seek to consume humans. The metaphorical potential is powerful: runaway, out of control processes consuming what they encounter without any motive or meaning, simply the process of consumption itself, zombies can be seen as critical commentaries on capitalism, consumerism, impersonal forces, unconscious drives, powerful but unguided technologies, and more.

The first decades of the twenty-first century have seen such widespread fascination and dissemination of zombie images and representations in popular culture. While the reasons for this are many, the underlying obsessions with apocalypticism at the turn of the century were certainly a part of it. Indeed, much of the popular discourse was not just about zombies in general but about the impending "zombie apocalypse" in particular. Because zombies in Romero's films and beyond are not singular characters, they come in growing hordes, threatening all in their path, and bringing about the end of the world. The entrance into a new century during a time of rising neoliberalism and globalization, quickly emerging transformations of communication and information technologies, concerns about terrorism, and global climate change certainly awakened apocalyptic energies. According to historian of religion Kelly Baker, the zombie apocalypse echoes deep, long-standing threads of end-time theories and scenarios in American religious culture (2013). And the new preoccupation with zombies was not limited to literature, film, or television: it spilled into the streets in the form of "zombie walks," gatherings of crowds of people dressed as zombies and walking through cities in lurching, zombie-like fashion; it shaped news stories, as in 2012 when a series of violent, seemingly cannibalistic attacks in various places around the country generated fear and questions about the possible reality of zombies; it even influenced the US Centers for Disease Control and Prevention, who in 2011 created a campaign for emergency preparedness that used as its case study a potential zombie apocalypse ("Zombie Preparedness" 2020). The Department of Homeland Security and the Federal Emergency Management Agency also modeled exercises and campaigns on the zombie scenario. Moreover, zombies are popular with survivalist groups whose lives are structured around preparation for impending end-of-society disaster (Baker 2013: 55–71). Zombies merge with conspiracy theories and (given the reverberations of their origins in Haitian religion) reverberate with troubling racist stereotypes and ideologies in their representations.

The human-but-not-human aspect of both vampires and zombies places them squarely in the realm of what Sigmund Freud called the "uncanny," calling attention to the tentative nature of our understandings of reality. The uncanny highlights the strange in the familiar, and the familiar in the strange, leaving us unsure about what is really real, and how we know. In some sense, it evokes some of Mircea Eliade's ideas and edges toward experiences of the sacred in unexpected places. As this chapter has suggested, the force of that sense of the uncanny, the sense that there is something unseen, hidden, lurking below the surface of our taken-for-granted reality, is fueled by what a community or society chooses *not* to acknowledge or see. To use another Freudian concept, the uncanny signals the "return of the repressed," though in this case repression is less psychological than social, in the form of silencing, marginalization, criminalization, and dehumanization. What is repressed, in this sense, does not go disappear; it is pushed out of sight, only to return with vengeance. Monsters, therefore, are always powered by social and cultural anxieties that are, in the American case, shaped by the nation's complex histories of race, violence, and domination interwoven with doctrines of freedom, progress, and innocence. There is a lot to unpack here, for the religious aspects of the United States are as wrapped up in the country's monsters as they are in the institutions, texts, and practices more commonly identified as "religion."

Conclusion: Dialectics of Heroes, Saints, and Monsters

All communities have their heroes and their monsters, and in many cases, as exemplified here by Greek myths and Christian saints, heroes are considered more than human, yet human enough to represent ideals to strive for. In a Durkheimian sense, heroes represent a community's values to itself. But what are the parameters of that sense of community? To what degree are the heroes and saints that a society publicly esteems representative of all members of that society? To what degree do they function to conceal difference and opposition while creating the appearance of unified values? To ask these questions is to recognize that the sorts of theories of religion presented by canonical scholars like Mircea Eliade, Clifford Geertz, Emile Durkheim, Peter Berger, Paul Tillich, and others tend to imagine communities along the lines of unity and consensus, represented in shared religious ideals and meanings. As such, their theoretical projects might be understood as functioning to obscure conflict and difference—fitting for a universalizing model of humanity that tended, as these scholars did, to imagine a movement toward shared global knowledge and values. Increasingly, such theoretical perspectives are being challenged by scholars whose perspectives were shaped by their experiences as members of communities that were not represented in that unity. Stuart Hall, Charles H. Long, Edward Said, Elaine Showalter, and others have noted, they did not see their experiences portrayed in the influential theories that shaped the study of religion and culture for most of the twentieth century. Likewise, the heroes honored by national histories and public monuments, and the events and values those heroes idealized, were not necessarily heroes of all. Frederick Douglass famously asked, "What, to the slave, is the Fourth of July?" One might well ask, who, to the Native American, is Christopher Columbus? Or Andrew Jackson? Who, to the African American, is Thomas Jefferson? Or Robert E. Lee? In some, if not many, cases, heroes turn out not to be monster slayers but in fact to be the monsters themselves. The relationship between heroes, saints, and monsters is one of a dialectic of concealment and revelation, of repression and haunting, and of the policing of social boundaries that are created through representations in popular culture.

So how would a scholar of religion approach the study of heroes, saints, and monsters as enduring forms in contemporary popular culture? This chapter has suggested several issues that such study might attend to, beginning with the relationship of heroes and monsters to social, political, and economic power. How do the particular portrayals function to maintain or subvert existing structures of power? How are ideas about gender, race, sexuality, and class represented in those portrayals? In what ways do stories about heroes, saints, or monsters reflect the values or cosmologies of particular social positions? How are more "traditional" religious and cultural resources represented to carry out this work?

Second, what is the relationship between tradition and creativity? How do particular stories or images of monsters or heroes serve as a foundation for novel cultural combinations or blendings? How do new media transform older forms, and how do new contexts shape new stories? How might tracing the genealogies and sourcing of various plots, characters, and symbols map continuities and disruptures of social, political, and cultural power and representation?

Third, noting that monsters and heroes exist in relation to one another, a scholar of religion and popular culture should be careful to consider this connection, paying attention to the material and social contexts of the production of monsters, saints, and heroes. Genealogical tracing of change over time can help to reveal the ways that otherwise unnoticed aspects of representation are tied to particular contexts. Likewise, attending to similarities and differences across genres—comparing vampires and zombies in a single cultural moment, for example, or windigo stories to the monsters of other colonial settings—might bring to light critical elements informing the production of both the heroic and the monstrous in particular circumstances.

The study of such enduring forms in popular culture draws attention to the ways that modern human beings continue to address ultimate questions, in Paul Tillich's sense; but it is worth noting that those questions are ultimately grounded in, and shaped by, the relationship of human beings to one another and to the world around them. Heroes and monsters illuminate those relationships, even as they have the power to reinforce or challenge them. Not simply entertainment, these elements of popular culture should be taken seriously for their function in producing a sense of reality, cosmic order, and human community (and its limitations). It would do scholars well to step beyond the theoretical insights and methods of European men to find fresh approaches and perspectives to ask to whom, and for what purpose, someone is seen as a hero, or a saint—and whether that same person is, for somebody else, a monster.

Works Cited

Baker, Kelly J. *The Zombies Are Coming!: The Realities of the Zombie Apocalypse in American Culture*. Colorado Springs, CO: Bondfire Books, 2013.

Beale, Timothy K. *Religion and Its Monsters*. New York: Routledge, 2002.

Cocca, Carolyn. *Superwomen: Gender, Power, and Representation*. New York: Bloomsbury Publishing, 2016.

DeSanti, Brady. "The Cannibal Talking Head: The Portrayal of the Windigo 'Monster' in Popular Culture and Ojibwe Traditions," *Journal of Religion and Popular Culture* 27, no. 3 (2015): 186–201.

Eliade, Mircea. *The Myth of the Eternal Return: Or, Cosmos and History.* Princeton: Princeton University Press, 1971/1954.

Hobsbawm, Eric. "Introduction: Inventing Traditions," in *The Invention of Tradition*, ed. Eric Hobsbawm and Terence Ranger, 1–14. Cambridge: Cambridge University Press, 1983.

Forbes, Jack. *Columbus and Other Cannibals: The Wetiko Disease of Exploitation, Imperialism, and Terrorism*. New York: Seven Stories Press, 2008.

Fry, Gladys-Marie. *Night Riders in Black Folk History*. Knoxville: University of Tennessee Press, 1975.

Hall, Stuart. "Race: The Floating Signifier," Media Education Foundation. Video, 1997.

Hitchens, Cristopher. *The Missionary Position: Mother Theresa in Theory and Practice*. New York: Verso, 1995.

Hjelm, Titus. "Celluloid Vampires, Scientization, and the Decline of Religion," in *The Lure of the Dark Side: Satan and Western Demonology in Popular Culture*, ed. Christopher H. Partridge and Eric S. Christianson, 105–21. New York: Routledge, 2014.

Hobsbawm, Eric J. *Primitive Rebels: Studies in Archaic Forms of Social Movements in the 19th and 20th Centuries*. Manchester: Manchester University Press, 1959.

Hobsbawm, Eric J. *Bandits*. London: Weidenfeld and Nicolson, 1969.

Iwamura, Jane Naomi. *Virtual Orientalism: Asian Religions and American Popular Culture*. New York: Oxford University Press, 2011.

Long, Charles H. "Civil Rights—Civil Religion: Visible People and Invisible Religion," in *American Civil Religion*, ed. Russell E. Richey and Donald G. Jones, 212–21. New York: Harper and Row, 1974.

Hubert, Henri. "Preface to Saint Patrick and the Cult of the Hero," in *Saints, Heroes, Myths, and Rites: Classical Durkheimian Studies of Religion and Society*, ed. and trans. Alexander Riley, Sarah Daynes and Cyril Isnart, 39–87. Boulder: Paradigm Publishers, 2009.

McAlister, Elizabeth. "Slaves, Cannibals, and Infected Hyper-Whites: The Race and Religion of Zombies," *Anthropological Quarterly* 85, no. 2 (2012): 457–86.

Morrison, Kenneth E. "Toward a History of Intimate Encounters: Algonkian Folklore, Jesuit Missionaries, and Kiwakwe, the Cannibal Giant," *American Indian Culture and Research Journal* 3, no. 4 (1979): 51–80.

Poole, W. Scott. *Monsters in America: Our Historical Obsession with the Hideous and the Haunting*. Waco, TX: Baylor University Press, 2011.

Primiano, Leonard Norman. "'I Wanna Do Bad Things With You': Fantasia on Themes of American Religion from the Title Sequence of HBO's *True Blood*," in *God in the Details: American Religion in Popular Culture*, ed. Eric Michael Mazur and Kate McCarthy, 2nd ed., 41–61. New York: Routledge, 2011.

Propp, Vladimir. *Morphology of the Folktale*, 2nd ed., trans. Laurence Scott. Austin: University of Texas Press, 1968/1928.

Toscano, Margaret M. "Mormon Morality and Immorality in Stephanie Meyer's *Twilight* Series," in *Bitten by Twilight: Youth Culture, Media, and the Vampire Franchise*, ed. Melissa A. Click, Jennifer Stevens Aubrey, and Elizabeth Behm-Morawitz, 21–36. New York: Peter Lang, 2010.

"Zombie Preparedness," *Centers for Disease Control and Prevention*. Washington, DC, 2020. Available online: https://www.cdc.gov/cpr/zombie/index.htm (accessed January 10, 2021).

16   Where We Are

Sacred Space

It is not uncommon to walk into a space and feel that it is in some way different from other spaces. Maybe it's the lighting (or lack of lighting); maybe it's the sounds (or lack of sounds). Maybe it is what other people are doing (or not doing) in that space. Traditionally, the space has been connected to religion—cathedrals are famous for eliciting these kinds of feelings, as are other large houses of worship and shrines—but in the modern world, sometimes it's not. Maybe the space is related to temporal power, like legislative or judicial buildings, or patriotic memorials, or locations connected to cultural heroes, like sports and media celebrities. Maybe the space is outdoors and connected to a sense of natural power. Whatever the type of space, it is quite common for those who experience it as indescribably different to designate it as "sacred," by which (at the very least) they mean that they want to separate it from other, seemingly less important places. At the very most, those who designate a space as "sacred" are communicating something about the space as "space beyond space," or space that, by virtue of something extraordinary having happened there (often involving contact with powers beyond human), has been reconceived from being space that is useful (i.e., "full of uses") to space that is meaningful (i.e., "full of meaning"). Its "meaning" is now not only greater than other, more "use-filled" spaces, but it is world orienting, at least for those who experience it as sacred.

Central to the notion of sacred space is its difference from profane (mundane, or what we might consider ordinary) space; boundaries between the profane (ordinary) and the sacred—and the thresholds people cross over to get from one to the other—are often the focus of scholarly analysis. Often these boundaries are easiest to identify by our experiences of them when we have crossed from one state into the other. To put it in visual terms, in *The Wizard of Oz* (1939), viewers know that the beginning of the story is filmed in black and white but may only realize how stark are the differences between Dorothy's life in Kansas and her adventures in Munchkinland when she opens the door, and everything is in color. Often it is only after we have entered into a different kind of space that we notice the difference; the contrast with what we just left brings it to our attention. That's why we often don't consider where we live—the actual place of our habitation, wherever we are already—to be sacred space; we live there, so we rarely cross a profane/sacred threshold. Even Dorothy must venture all the way to Oz just to find out that "there's no place like home." We may readily admit that there are people who live in sacred spaces, but we usually are quick to point out that they are often religious folks themselves: Ethiopian monks, for example, who live on the roof of the Church of the Holy Sepulchre in Jerusalem, one of the more sacred Christian shrines in Jerusalem. But most of us are not monks, and so while most of us may visit sacred places, we don't live in them. Or so we tell ourselves.

Maybe this is why identifying as sacred the places that we visit—what we might call "non-residential" spaces—is easier than identifying as sacred the places in which we ("normal" folks, not monks) live, and thus a "durable form" in the study of religion and popular culture. We can go to locations in the natural world—Niagara Falls, for example—and be so overwhelmed by their grandeur and beauty that it seems obvious why some might consider them sacred (see Sears 1989). We can visit religious sites—even ones that are sacred to religions that are not our own, like the Mahabodhi Temple, in Bodh Gaya (India), where the Buddha is said to have achieved enlightenment—and be so awed by the piety of others there that we can feel why it is sacred. We can travel to secular sites—maybe the National September 11 Memorial and Museum in New York City—and sense the power of a modern shrine. We can go on a journey to a sacred city in a distant land—Bodh Gaya, Jerusalem, Mecca, Varanasi (also in India), Vatican City—and appreciate its atmosphere of sacredness. But most of us don't live in these cities, and so "sacred space" seems to remain a category of some place you go to rather than some place where you already are.

There is no doubt that "sacred space" is one of the foundational categories in the academic study of religion, and a quick internet search will reveal that, even in the case of a nontraditional spaces, it is not overwhelmingly difficult to make a case for the sacredness of "shrines" like Elvis's Graceland, or Chicago's Wrigley Field. It would seem that, in the study of religion and popular culture, it is a greater challenge to consider the sacredness of the spaces where we are, to make sense of our own spaces, where the sacred may seem foreign and the mundane might seem overwhelming.

Space as Map

If we were to go to a "sacred" city like Mecca and look around, we would see the people who live there; like any city, it has residents who live there, who work there, who sleep, and eat, and bathe, and engage in other societal and bodily functions there. Because non-Muslims are prohibited from entering Mecca, and this city is the holiest in Islam, they live every day knowing that their city is a sacred city, yet (one imagines) they also worry about buying groceries, paying the rent, being late to work because of traffic, and so on. To some extent, the presence of the profane is part of every sacred space. It would seem reasonable to assert, then, that sacred space—of almost any size—is layered space, and one of the layers is the not-sacred lives folks live as they do or do not function in the sacred layers. The presence of the profane (non-sacred or mundane) does not negate the sacredness of a location; instead, it introduces to us the possibility that the sacred may coexist within nonreligious spaces, even those of more recent, nontradition-based vintage.

One of the more gripping stories retold by Eliade in his 1959 classic *The Sacred and the Profane* is of the Achilpa, a nomadic people who wander according to the seasons and the movement of food supply across the Australian Outback (1959: 32–4). According to Eliade, these people take with them a sacred wooden pole—representative of their community's encounter with the divine, the beyond-human—wherever they go. When they settle for a period of time, they plant the pole as the center of their dwelling space and organize their village according to the cardinal directions around it. If we leave aside any prejudice we might feel toward a culture identified as nomadic—particularly ironic given most Americans' genealogical roots in cultures from other places, as well as our own political history of "westward expansion" and modern mobility—we see that the habit of organizing our living space like the Achilpa is not so unusual. The streets of Manhattan form a directional grid, as do the streets of numerous other American cities and towns. If the Achilpa (and, by extension, planners of cities around the world) are any indication, then sacred space is not only layered space, but it is also "mapped" space—space that is a diagram of how the world (not only profane but sacred as well) should be organized, and orienting us in the whatever cosmos is "layered" on the same (or overlapping) space.

There's another issue to consider. According to Eliade, at some point the Achilpa pole broke, and the members of the community "wandered about aimlessly for a time, and finally lay down on the ground and waited for death to overtake them" (33). The broken connection between the land they occupied and their beyond-human source of meaning meant that the people were both religiously and literally lost, even if (by virtue of being nomads) they were not physically lost. Again, this does not, on its face, seem far-fetched. On one level, we often succumb to the "poetry" of the sacred and romanticize the religious behaviors of others, particularly if (on some level) we admire their "simpler," more devout lifestyle. Eliade's retelling of the Achilpa story is so nearly mystical that we *want* to believe it, to believe that there are still people in the world whose attachment to their religious ideals is so profound that they're willing to do what we all know we should do if we believe something is so important, so central to our way of understanding the cosmos. On another level, we live among people who have—metaphorically, at least, or historically—experienced something similar to the breaking of the Achilpa sacred pole: Native Americans who were forcibly relocated onto lands designated for them by the American government, and Africans forced into slavery in countries across the Middle Passage. Like the Achilpa, these peoples were torn away from their sacred poles—the lands where they were in direct contact with their divine energies—and as a result have experienced geographic dislocation and cosmic disorientation within their world.

Politics of Sacred Space

But sometimes the near-mystical nature of sacred space—and our desire to believe in its reality—blinds us to the reality of the world and how it often works despite the high ideals of the pious. First, at least one person chose not to lie down to await death: the person who related the story to the explorers whom Eliade quotes. Second, why do we assume that the people who lay down to await death actually waited that long? Maybe they waited for what they felt was an appropriate length of time—an hour, maybe two—before getting up and getting another pole, fixing the one they had, or settling for the larger of the two remaining pieces. It is a desire to see space as sacred—and therefore, to treat it in the way that we feel it should be treated—that leads us to believe (naively) that these people would rather die than to believe that, like most of us, they'd actually just deal with the situation and move on.

The disjunction between what we want to believe and what might actually be the case is part of the debate of sacred space generally. One side, most often represented by Eliade, conceptualizes sacred space as *sui generis*, as being of its own existence, inherently sacred; in other words, sacred space is sacred space because it is . . . well, sacred. Some who follow this argument, like Belden Lane (2001), argue that the relationship between a particular space and a particular person (or group of people) is dynamic, and that this dynamism (possibly experienced at some times and not at others) is what makes the space sacred. The other side of the sacred space argument, often traced to Emile Durkheim (1912/1995), might agree (to a point) with scholars like Lane—that the relationship between the space and the person is dynamic—but would certainly disagree that the two elements (person and space) are equal participants in that dynamism. Durkheim—and those whose arguments follow from him, like Jonathan Smith (1987) or David Chidester and Ed Linenthal (1995)— argue that spaces become sacred as a result of social processes which are engaged for very specific purposes: affirmations or contests over power, or meaning, or significance of a space and what it means or reflects about those engaged in the conflicts.

The Durkheim-related argument illustrates what some call the "politics of the sacred." If sacred space is both layered and mapped, it is almost inevitable that there will be conflicts at the edges of the layers, and over the meaning of the maps that are the result of declaring a space sacred. While some might consider a space to be sacred, others might consider it to be just a space like any other; or "Group B" might find a space to be sacred, but for reasons entirely different from those of "Group A"—reasons that might discount, or even refute, the reasons of "Group A." Thus not only is there a level of subjectivity in determining the sacred, but there is also the potential for conflict over that space, either between folks who see a space as sacred and those who do not, or between those who see it as sacred for one reason and those who see it as sacred for another. The very act of identifying a location as sacred is itself an assertion of power over that space; analyses of "sacred" spaces from Jerusalem to Mt. Rushmore bear this out.

But the conflict does not necessarily have to be obvious—or even visible—in public, and the presumption that it must be is a misreading of this argument; the lack of any appearance of conflict does not negate that space's chances of being considered sacred. It is unlikely that one could find a space that was not party to some kind of conflict—tension might be a better word—even if it is only within the minds or psyches of those who consider it sacred. Graceland is a good example; the property was purchased and owned by Elvis Presley, and while there may be some neighbors who wish it did not attract as many visitors as it does, they are hardly noticeable at the location. Rather, the "conflicts" that make this final home and resting place sacred for the thousands of fans who visit it every year are the larger, cultural tensions over what Elvis might have represented, to the fans and to the culture in which both Elvis and those fans functioned. Did Elvis's music sound "too Black" (the reason for which his music was initially banned from "Whites' only" radio stations)? Was he "too sexual" (the reason he was not permitted to be filmed on early television appearances)? Was his music (rock 'n' roll, in the general sense) blasphemous? These were important questions surrounding those who adored him, as well as those who abhorred him; his home is simply the focus of the tensions between them (see Doss 1999).

Durable Form: City as Sacred Space

According to historian Karen Armstrong (2005), Jerusalem was a city nearly 2,000 years before the Common Era (BCE). By the time we encounter it in the Tanakh (Hebrew scripture, roughly comparable to the Old Testament in Christianity), it is a city within—but not controlled by—the Tribe of Benjamin also known as "Jebus" because it was controlled by the Jebusites (see Judg. 19:7-12). David, whose initial capital was Hebron (II Sam. 2:1), takes Jerusalem after he is recognized as the King of Israel and Judah (meaning all of the Tribes; see II Sam. 5:3-9). The city becomes both the political and the religious capital of the kingdom when David's son Solomon is empowered to construct the Holy Temple there (I Chr. 28:3-6). In 586 BCE, that Temple is destroyed and the city is conquered by the Babylonian Empire, which less than a century later is in turn defeated by the Persian Empire, whose king (Cyrus) permits the Hebrews to return to Jerusalem and rebuild the Temple (II Chr. 36:23), which is destroyed by the Roman Empire in the first century of the Common Era. In 637, only five years after the death of the Prophet Muhammad, the Muslim Empire under Caliph Umar takes the city from the remnants of the Roman Empire and holds it until 1099, when Christian Crusaders capture it. It is retaken by the Muslim Empire in the middle of the thirteenth century, with whom it remains (for the most part) until the fall of the Ottoman Empire after the First World War.

The city most familiar to nonresidents today is known familiarly as the "Old City," the area within thick walls constructed in the mid-1500s under the direction of Suleiman the Magnificent. It is, in many ways, a strong example of what we might expect in a "sacred" city. It is subdivided—uneven geometrically, but most precariously balanced politically—into four "quarters": Muslim, Jewish, Christian, and Armenian, with each "quarter" centered on a site of central sacredness to that community. The Muslim and Jewish "quarters" are adjacent to the Temple Mount / Haram al-Sharif' (where stood the Holy Temple, and now stand the al-Aqsa Mosque and the Dome of the Rock [mosque]), and the Christian "quarter" contains the Church of the Holy Sepulchre. It is the center of the liturgical universe for Jews (who pray in the direction of the city and whose prayers still recall a return to Jerusalem; see Psalm 137), the third holiest city in Islam, and a Christian pilgrimage destination since before the Muslim conquest. For some, it is sacred because of its contents: for Jews, it is a city built upon the cornerstone of the world, beneath the remnants of the First and Second Holy Temples; for Muslims, it is built on the location where Muhammad ascended to heaven during his "Night Journey" from Mecca; and for others, it is where Jesus entered the last part of his ministry on Earth, where he was arrested, crucified, entombed, and transcended death. It is an ancient city in the midst of a modern city, the "City of Peace" in the midst of the most difficult of conflicts.

Maybe because Jerusalem has been, for many people, a tradition-based sacred space that they might visit rather than the city in which they live, it became a transferable model—a symbolic, layered map—of sacred space. This is particularly true for Protestants in the New World, who were removed from the city by centuries of Muslim control. Puritans, who saw themselves as the new generation of Hebrews escaping enslavement in Pharaoh's Egypt (England) by crossing the Red Sea (the Atlantic Ocean), understood North America to be the new Promised Land. But while the Puritans (and early colonists) understood this comparison figuratively—as a metaphor for the people occupying the land and their religious mission related to it—others understood it literally. The Book of Mormon, the central scripture of the Church of Jesus Christ of Latter-day Saints, describes a family's journey from Jerusalem to the New World in the sixth century BCE, before the Babylonian destruction of the city and the Holy Temple therein. Transferring the sacred geography of the Middle East onto the New

World, Mormons physically remapped both the beginning and end of all of human history onto Missouri: the Garden of Eden was determined to be located in Spring Hill (see Doctrine & Covenants 116), and the New Jerusalem—the land of Zion, the land promised by God to Abraham and his descendants, wherein the faithful would be gathered and made a great nation—was determined to be located in Independence (see Doctrine and Covenants 57: 1–3). By late summer 1833, Mormon leader and prophet Joseph Smith, Jr. had authorized a plan for the "City of Zion," arranged very much like the Achilpa encampment: oriented to the cardinal directions, square city blocks making square city neighborhoods, all sounding the city's Mormon Temple, which would be its geographic and spiritual center. Smith's lynching in 1844 precipitated the Mormon relocation to the basin of the Great Salt Lake and the remapping of the Promised Land from Missouri to the Utah Territory. Like the Puritans (and their model, the Hebrews), the Mormons settled the land and gave the spaces names with which they were familiar: drawn from important members of the Mormon community (such as Brigham City, Cannonville, and Heber City), figures from the Old Testament (such as Canaan Mountain, Eden, Hebron, Jordan River, and Moab), and figures from the Book of Mormon (such as Bountiful, Kolob Canyon, Lehi, Manti, Moroni, and Nephi). Unlike the Puritans—who in Protestant fashion saw the New Jerusalem not as a location but as a metaphoric reference to God's elect—but very much like the Hebrews, the Mormons established Salt Lake City as their New Jerusalem, both the political and the sacred center of the Mormon cosmos. Streets and plazas, secular and sacred structures would be organized according to a grid pattern aligned to the cardinal directions, with the Mormon Temple at the conceptual center (i.e., the point at which the streets converge) if not the geographic center. Encouraging visitors to the Chicago World's Fair to venture westward, an 1893 pamphlet published by the Denver and Rio Grande Railroad Company made the connection explicit, describing how, as you travel from Denver,

> you behold the silver sheen of Utah Lake, the great body of fresh water which is the sea of Tiberias in the Promised Land. Its outlet is the Jordan River, which empties into the Great Salt Lake and completes the strange parallel which exists between the ancient Canaan and the modern Deseret. (20)

If the words were not enough, the pamphlet included an image comparing the Great Salt Lake and Utah Lake on one side and the Sea of Galilee and Dead Sea on the other, with a caption reading "A Striking Comparison! The Holy Land and Utah" (15).

But as much as Mormons may have intended to emulate Jerusalem, Salt Lake City seems to emulate the capital of the nation with whose powers the Mormons were—for the first century of their existence—in increasing tension. The City of Washington, in the District of Columbia, was officially created out of nothing by Article I, section 8 (clause 17) of the Constitution of the United States. It was envisioned as a perfect square (10 miles by 10 miles), at the near center of the new Republic much like Jerusalem had been at the near center of the land controlled by the Twelve Tribes. Unlike Jerusalem, Washington did not require conquering—there had been a native presence, but it was long pacified by the presence of numerous forts, as well as the villages of Georgetown and Alexandria. By carving the capital city from Maryland and Virginia and making it a federal district rather than a city within a state, the planners hoped to avoid the territorial power issues that David could avoid by placing Jerusalem in a conquered Jebusite city. The city's design was a blend of influences, including Greek, Roman, and French, the latter providing the model for the city's street-level atmosphere. Drawing from the model as old as the Achilpa, the streets of Washington were organized according to the cardinal directions. Numbered streets were to go north-south, lettered streets to go east-west, all of which were focused by a crosshair created by the intersection of North, South, and East Capitol Streets—with what would have been "West Capitol Street" being cultivated into the Mall. All of the numbers and letters increased from the central point, the Capitol Building on Capitol Hill, the American "sacred pole" by which the American people mapped their cosmos. This sacred center—of Washington, DC, and American democracy—reaffirmed the supremacy of the legislative branch (and within it the "People's House," a reference to the House of Representatives who were, originally, the only element of the federal government directly elected by "the people"). The Mall, which today takes one from the base of Capitol Hill to the Potomac, is a celebration of human—but mostly American—accomplishments contained in the various buildings of the Smithsonian Institution, as well as the most profound recognition of American greatness as represented in the monuments and memorials also situated thereon.

Layers, Maps, and Tensions

It is useful to remember the lessons of feminist and orientalist scholars who have brought to our attention the importance of including not only the voices of those who have been marginal (or marginalized) but also the views of them among those who have considered them, or kept them, or made them marginal. Conversations about Jerusalem, Salt Lake City, and Washington, DC, are no different. All three—sacred in their own way, yet profane, ordinary cities in which people live everyday lives—have characteristics drawn from an Eliadean vision of sacred space. Not least of these is the sense that believers—adherents of the Abrahamic faiths, Mormons, and patriotic American citizens, respectively—sense the sacredness of these cities as virtually inherent in their very existence. Yet all three function as temporal power centers, capital cities of Israel, Utah, and the United States. All three retain in their sacred memories the tensions that are understood to be at the core of their being, be it between Jews and non-Jews (or, in the same space, Muslims and non-Muslims, and Christians and non-Christians), Mormons and non-Mormons, or (more complicatedly) between different understandings of who is an authentic "American." Together they are home to millions, yet the "sacred" narratives of each of them rely on one group's ability to overwhelm another. Studies of the sacred nature of Washington, DC, for example, are rich, maybe because they take into account the complex nature of the city's role in American culture. It is not coincidental, for example, that Washington came to more closely resemble an Eliadean sacred space as its role in the American political and cultural power structure expanded. Disaster and war—and the power of the federal government to respond to them—played an important role. Having given the section south of the Potomac back to Virginia before the Civil War, the District was better able to realize many of the original plans for the city after the conclusion of the Civil War—that is, after the federal government exerted its authority over renegade states. Many of the solemn and celebratory edifices on and around the Mall were the result of building projects sponsored by the federal government in response to the Great Depression and the Second World War. Even the highway system that rings the city—reinforcing the intentional space of the District by circling the square—

was not fully realized until after the Second World War. One could argue that the sacredness of the nation's capital increased not only as a direct result of its growing role in national and international affairs but also on the backs of those who were defeated.

If we can do this with Jerusalem, Salt Lake City, and Washington, DC, then we can do it with almost anywhere people live. Eliade argues that one of the powers of the sacred is that it defies geometric limitations: "Whatever the extent of the territory involved, the cosmos that it represents is always perfect" (1959: 42). In other words, the "sacredness" of a space is not diminished by expanding that sacredness into larger spaces. The Kaaba, the structure considered by Muslims to be the center of the cosmos and the cornerstone upon which the foundation of the world was built, is undeniably sacred. But so, too, is the Masjid al-Haram (the Sacred Mosque), the complex of buildings of which the Kaaba is a part. And so, too, is the entire city of Mecca wherein one finds the Masjid al-Haram, and the Kaaba therein. Not only are non-Muslims prohibited from approaching the Kaaba, not only are non-Muslims prohibited from entering the Masjid al-Haram but so, too, are non-Muslims prohibited from entering Mecca. The city is, in a very real way, just as sacred as the smaller areas within it. With each expansion of space there is an equal expansion of the sacred—it is neither diminished nor diluted. This means that, at least according to Eliade, while the shrine, and its building, and its city, are concentric circles of expanding geographic space, each expanding circle is nonetheless equally sacred to the previous one.

Maybe this is the case for Washington, DC, home of many "sacred" shrines and spaces; it must also be the case for other dwelling areas. Among the more obvious targets for such analysis are those cities built specifically to be a nation's capital—"purpose-built" cities, like Brasília (see Tauxe 1996). But so are other "intentional" (if temporary) "cities," like Black Rock City, home of the Burning Man Festival, or "the Land," (in Oceana County, Michigan), the site of the now-defunct Michigan Womyn's Music Festival. However, there is always the danger of overextending the analysis; sometimes spaces are just spaces that may not withstand scrutiny for any level of sacredness. Even meticulous intentional planning does not automatically make a city sacred; in 1958, California City, California, was carefully plotted, and its streets marked out over an area larger than Chicago, but today it is a near ghost town (Budds 2017). All too often—particularly in an attempt to define a novel space as sacred—researchers overlook an important element; while the definition of "sacred" may be subjective, it still helps if it is seen that way by more than just the investigator. In their sacred space analysis of Walt Disney World, Eric Mazur and Tara Koda acknowledge the conference participant who, upon hearing a presentation of their work, noted that she did not consider the place to be sacred, even after numerous trips there (2011: 321 n2). This does not necessarily mean the analysis is flawed; it just proves that sacred or not, spaces large and small are subject to differing interpretations because they are not "obviously" sacred.

Postscript

This chapter was written as governments around the world were responding to the Covid-19 pandemic of 2020. One way that governments responded was by ordering people to "shelter in place," requiring them to become near shut-ins to help lessen the spread of the coronavirus. Most of those who fell under these orders were Christians and Jews who were about to celebrate the holidays of Easter and Pesah, two holy days that require engagement—in church or at home—with fellow adherents. Those who could—students, teachers, and those who worked in information-related industries—reorganized their lives by relocating their work, prayer, and even communal rituals and meals onto online platforms like Zoom and Google. These platforms (and others) facilitated not only the exchange of information and ideas but also the possibility of "real-time" classes, meetings, rituals, and social gatherings that were now prohibited by local, state, and federal authorities in accordance with medical experts who were advocating physical distancing. It seemed that lives that were no longer permitted in physical space were now relocated into the "virtual" world; even religious institutions reconfigured rituals to accommodate the new circumstances.

Studies of whether and how the sacred might exist in cyberspace date back to the early years of the Internet age. The reality of being homebound provided a keen reminder that, regardless of one's knowledge of, or experience with, social media platforms before the rise of the pandemic, with no other alternatives, those who sought the sacred either had to do without, or they had to make their own. The fact that some chose to do so—and could— online and from home reminds us that the category of sacred space is not only mapped, layered, and a location to confront tensions but also transferrable.

Works Cited

Armstrong, Karen. *Jerusalem: One City, Three Faiths*. New York: Ballantine Books, 2005.

Budds, Diana. "This California Ghost City Is a Monument to Bad Planning," *Fast Company* (July 20, 2017). Available online: https://www.fastcompany.com/90133913/this-california-ghost-city -is-a-monument-to-bad-planning (accessed February 11, 2020).

Chidester, David, and Edward T. Linenthal. "Introduction," in *American Sacred Space*, ed. David Chidester and Edward T. Linenthal, 1–42. Bloomington: Indiana University Press, 1995.

Denver and Rio Grande Railroad Co. *The Promised Land: Information for the Visitor of the World's Fair, Chicago, 1893*. Chicago: Rio Grande Western Railway, 1893.

Doss, Erika. *Elvis Culture: Fans, Faith, and Image*. Lawrence: University Press of Kansas, 1999.

Durkheim, Emile. *The Elementary Forms of Religious Life*, trans. Karen E. Fields. New York: The Free Press, 1995 [Originally published as *Formes élèmentaires de la vie religieuse*, 1912].

Eliade, Mircea. *The Sacred and the Profane: The Nature of Religion*, trans. Williard R. Trask. New York: Harcourt, Brace & World, Inc., 1959.

Lane, Belden C. *Landscapes of the Sacred: Geography and Narrative in American Spirituality*, expanded ed. Baltimore, MD: The Johns Hopkins University Press, 2001.

Mazur, Eric Michael, and Tara K. Koda. "The Happiest Place on Earth: Disney's America and the Commodification of Religion," in *God in the Details: American Religion in Popular Culture*, 2nd ed., ed. Eric Michael Mazur and Kate McCarthy, 307–21. New York: Routledge, 2011.

Sears, John F. *Sacred Places: American Tourist Attractions in the Nineteen Century*. New York: Oxford University Press, 1989.

Smith, Jonathan Z. *To Take Place: Toward Theory in Ritual*. Chicago: The University of Chicago Press, 1987.

Tauxe, Caroline. "Mystics, Modernists, and Constructions of Brasilia," *Ecumene* 3, no. 1 (1996): 43–61.

17   What We Know

Myths and Sacred Texts

Today the word "myth" seems to convey a variety of meanings. To many, it suggests something that is not true: "the Tooth Fairy is a myth," one might hear on the playground, or "Slenderman is a myth." The assertion that either of these characters is a myth suggests not only that there may still be those who believe they are real—small children, young teens— and thus in need of refutation (or, possibly, reassurance) but also that the continued belief in them is childish, foolish, or dangerous. Similarly, to others the word "myth" suggests a story from the past, from those ill-defined yet fondly recalled "days of yore" when life was simpler and morality was less ambiguous. As the character "K" says to Det. James Edwards—a New York City cop who has just learned of the presence of extra-terrestrials— in the 1997 film *Men in Black*,

> Fifteen hundred years ago, everybody *knew* that the earth was the center of the universe. Five hundred years ago everybody *knew* that the earth was flat. And fifteen minutes ago, you *knew* that humans were alone on this planet. Imagine what you'll *know* tomorrow.

This connotation suggests a different kind of maturation, a presumption that the people (or peoples) who believed "those" myths were naive and less sophisticated than today's modern citizens, but maybe also blissfully less encumbered by the complications of today's reality. Lastly, and often unconsciously, some people use "myth" as a cultural marker to distinguish their own narratives—that God revealed sacred scripture to a man in Israel—which they know to be true, from the narratives of others—that God revealed sacred scripture to a man in upstate New York—which they know to be untrue. Unless you are a Mormon.

Therein lies the dilemma: if we use the term "myth" to distinguish falsehood in the search for truth, then it is almost always going to be true to those who believe it to be true, and false to those who believe it to be false. In this sense, it is a bit like Schrödinger's cat, both true and false, and yet also neither true nor false. This is why those who work in the academic study of religion (along with other fields who take seriously the category of "myth" in human understanding) prefer to disregard entirely the question of whether or not myths are true and instead think about them as multifaceted reflections of the people who tell them. And retell them. As religion scholar Mircea Eliade points out, "Today . . . the word [myth] is employed both in the sense of 'fiction' or 'illusion' and in that [sense] familiar especially to ethnologists, sociologists, and historians of religions, the sense of 'sacred tradition, primordial revelation, exemplary model'" (Eliade 1963: 1). This may be a bit melodramatic; rather, let us just say that myths are narrative patterns that seek to explain the world or some part of it. If they can do that for the people who tell them (and, just as importantly, for the people who hear them), then we can say that they "work"; if they can't, they don't.

This may be why we think of the narratives of Scandinavia as Norse myths, and also why there are more Lutherans in Sweden and Norway than there are pagans. To most Westerners they represent tales of a bygone age but are also narrative patterns that do not "work" for people like they used to. And yet, these same Norse myths do continue to be of great meaning and significance, both formally for those who believe them to be true—paganism is still a viable spiritual expression (see Pike 2001)—and informally for those who use them as the scaffolding to tell refurbished, similar, or even creatively inventive new narratives. One need only read Neil Gaiman's novel *American Gods* (2001) to see this at work.

In this sense, then, myths are the foundation for all that we know of the world. We are taught (and, with luck, retain) facts and figures, raw data that contribute to our search for explanations for the world or its constituent parts. But it is myths that organize that data into useful and meaning-filled systems by which to make sense of it all. Robert Burton (2019) argues that we tell and retell stories (myths) so that, in a very real sense, we don't go crazy when confronted by situations that call for a learned reaction (such as seeing a lion). Elena Renken (2020) points to brain studies that reveal how we physically and emotionally connect with one another through the very act of telling stories. As we read in Section II of this volume, Peter Berger (1967) identifies these world-explaining narratives as the "sacred canopy" that maintains a culture's stability in times of crisis. French philosopher Georges Bataille (1989: 19) writes that animals live in the world like water in water, meaning that only humans distinguish themselves from their own world. In so doing, we require explanations to make sense of it all. These are the foundations for storytelling; by retelling myths, we have both established and maintained ourselves in the cosmos.

In 1956, anthropologist Horace Miner published an article in which he analyzed the hygiene rituals of a community he identified as the Nacirema. In the article he describes with an anthropologist's eye the various rituals in which these people engage, describing their ablutions and their ritual spaces in great detail. By the end of the article, it is clear that the "Nacirema" he describes are actually just everyday Americans ("Nacirema" spelled backwards). One of Miner's goals was to de-exoticize the study of ritual. By making the exotic seem mundane and by making the mundane seem exotic, Miner was showing his readers that everyone—from the shaman of a small-scale preindustrial society to you and the people next door—engage in ritualized activities. We could find detailed and meaning-filled rituals all around us, if we only removed our biases and took a look around.

By doing the same thing with myth—and maintaining our rejection of a search for "Truth"—we can broaden the focus of myth from "the ancients" to the contemporary. As with the Norse myths, other ancient myths continue to reverberate meaningfully in the way we tell stories. One can read the epic of Gilgamesh—one of the Western world's oldest written narratives—and see the "buddy narrative" at work in the stories of the Lone Ranger and Tonto, Batman and Robin, and maybe even Thelma and Louise. If we describe a narrative in which a being with powers to heal and return the dead to life brings a new knowledge to the innocent is pursued by an evil government who wants to silence him, and ultimately leaves but promises to return, we could be discussing the Jesus narrative as related in the Gospels, or the plot of *E.T. the Extra-Terrestrial* (1982). If we describe a man of simple birth, who is drawn into a cosmic conflict between good and evil, is told of his role in the cosmos, initially rejects it but, in the end, accepts his destiny, again we could be describing the Jesus narrative, or the plot of *Star Wars: Episode IV - A New Hope* (1977). Our goal here is not to belittle the Gospel narrative; as should be clear by now, those who believe it to be true believe it to be universally and unimpeachably true. But as we have discussed earlier in this volume, whether it is the "monomyth," the "American monomyth," or the "buddy narrative"—or one of the other narrative patterns common in our culture (or others)—it is the pattern that is the key. Maybe the two films (and others) adopt the narrative structure they do because they are familiar patterns that facilitate storytelling. But why should we exclude the consideration of a community's sacred scripture just because it is that community's sacred scripture? And why should we exclude today's stories—novels, films, television shows, and more—just because they are not?

Authority

If it is best not to ask whether or not a myth is true—or rather, if we ask but quickly learn that the answer does not really get us anywhere—what can we ask about myth? Robert Segal points out that, when it comes to investigating myths, there are "three main questions": "origin, function, and subject matter" (2004: 2). Because myth is not just the story told but also the pattern replicated in the story, the answers to all three of these questions operate on a variety of levels. In terms of subject, the myth may be about something—a little girl who wears a red riding garment, who while taking goodies to her grandmother encounters a wolf, who then threatens her life (and that of her grandmother) until they are rescued by a noble woodsman—but it may also be about something else: childhood, femininity, masculinity, virginity, sexuality, and more. In terms of origin, a narrative about a global flood may have first been told in the account of Noah starting in the sixth chapter of the book of Genesis, or it may have appeared 1,000 years earlier in the epic of Gilgamesh, or (according to William Ryan and Walter Pitman, 1998) it may even have been spawned from actual events that took place 3,000 or 4,000 years before that: the rapid flooding of the Black Sea by the surging waters of the Mediterranean Sea.

Like the questions of origin and subject matter, "function" also works on two levels and requires us to consider not only how the myth works as a narrative but also for whom it works, and how. This, then, connects us (and myth) to the question that is at the heart of many of the more recent writers we have considered in this collection: the question of authority.

In *Monty Python and the Holy Grail* (1975)—a comic satire of the "quest" myth—King Arthur seeks to obtain some basic information from peasants he encounters who are working in the fields. When they refuse to help him, he demands their respect based upon the fact that (unbeknownst to them) he is their king. One of the peasants asks how he became king, and Arthur responds by recounting his encounter with the Lady of the Lake, the spirit figure who "held aloft Excalibur from the bosom of the water, signifying by divine providence that I, Arthur, was to carry Excalibur. That," he concludes, "is why I am your king." Another peasant ("Dennis") is unconvinced: "Strange women lying in ponds distributing swords is no basis for a system of government." The peasants very clearly reject the authority of the king because they reject the purported source of his authority.

Historian of religion Bruce Lincoln defines authority as "the capacity to make a consequential pronouncement" which commands "not just the attention but the confidence, respect, and trust" of the audience. He distinguishes it from coercion (which implies force) on the one hand, and persuasion (which implies argumentation) on the other, comparing it to the parent who responds to a child's objection to complete a task with "Because I said so" (1994: 3–5). In the legends recounted by Sir Thomas Mallory in his fifteenth-century work *Le Morte D'Arthur*, Arthur's authority as king is accepted because the retelling of his encounter with the Lady in the Lake (and its meaning) is accepted. In the film version, Arthur has no claim of authority over the peasants. At the very idea, Dennis argues that "Supreme executive power derives from a mandate from the masses, not from some farcical aquatic ceremony!" Arthur, realizing that his authority has not been accepted on its face, and that he has not been able to convince the peasant, exercises his only remaining option (coercion) and threatens Dennis.

Much like the subjects of King Arthur—in the legendary version, *not* the Monty Python version—almost by definition members of a religious community accept the authority of their God (or gods) and their sacred writings as truth. For the benefit of members (but also for outsiders looking in), divine authority is often stated directly in the sacred texts of the community, providing a second, more textually grounded source. The Hebrew word *kabbalah*—a term that may be familiar even to non-Jews as a school of Jewish mysticism—comes from the word-root meaning "receiving." This suggests that this form of mysticism establishes its authority in having been received from God. The same is true for all sacred texts. Those who understand Jewish sacred text (Torah) to be authoritative do so not only because they believe it to be so but also because the text declares itself to be so (see *parsha* Yitro, roughly comparable to Exodus 18–20). Likewise, Christian sacred text, in the New Testament (see John 1; 2 Timothy 3). Likewise, Muslim sacred text, in the Qur'an (see Sura 3).[1] Likewise, Mormonism, in the Book of Mormon (see, for example, I Nephi 14:25-26), the Doctrine and Covenants (see, for example, Doctrine and Covenants 20:1-4), and so on. Of course, the Jew does not see Christian text as sacred, and the Christian does not see Muslim text as sacred. While the assertion of authority may make it true for its believers, simply saying it is true is not enough for nonbelievers. The dilemma of seeking "truth" in myth is grounded not only in content, then, but in the authority of that content as well.

Myth also builds and sustains its authority through its provenance, or transmission history. This provides the sacred text's pedigree, proving that what is in front of the community is the genuine text from the original source. For example, the Mishnah (a commentary on Jewish sacred texts) specifically lays out the provenance of Jewish sacred text:

> Moses received the Torah at Sinai and transmitted it to Joshua, Joshua to the elders [who Moses had installed to assist in running the community], and the elders to the prophets, and the prophets to the Men of the Great Assembly. (Pirkei Avot 1:1)

This takes the text from Moses receiving the sacred text from God (Exodus 20) through the remainder of the Tanakh (Hebrew scripture) to the historical moments after the establishment of the rebuilt ("Second") Holy Temple in Jerusalem in the sixth century before the Common Era; in other words, from "myth" to history. Working in a slightly different mode, the followers of Jesus (soon to be called Christians) established apostolic succession—the transference not just of oversight authority for particular geographic areas (bishoprics) but also of religious

---

[1] Thanks to Tom Ellis, Loren Lybarger, and Craig Wansink for their assistance in identifying appropriate texts.

charisma and authority within that area as a representative of the original followers (apostles) of Jesus of Nazareth (see Acts 1:21-26).

As a narrative form, myth also asserts authority by association, often based on the person credited with transmitting it—the "narrator"—not just the most recent person relating the myth but the person in whose "voice" the myth is told. For example, even though the Hebrew scriptures are understood to be (in part or in whole) a revelation from God, there are numerous clues suggesting that it is the product of later narrators. The traditional Jewish notion of Torah—in its entirety, from the first words of Genesis to the last words of Deuteronomy—having been given by God to Moses and the Hebrew people at the base of Mt. Sinai, is challenged by elements within the narrative. Moses—had been prohibited by God from entering the Promised Land (see Num. 20:12; Deut. 1:37; Deut. 34:4)—speaks his last words in the land of Moab "on the other side of the Jordan" (Deut. 1:1) from the person relating the event, where he dies (Deut. 34:5). Moses—who receives the Torah in its entirety—dies before the end of its telling, and the "narrator" notes that "no one knows his burial place to this day" (Deut. 34:6) and that "never again did there arise in Israel a prophet like Moses" (Deut. 34:10). All of this suggests the passage of time between the events described and the telling of them. The fact that the community that considers this text sacred and its various sources authoritative—from God to Moses and from there through the chain of transmission—indicates either that the "narrator" is God (who, as an omniscient Being, would know events to take place after the text's transmission) or is trusted as if he were. It also ensures the authority of those whose job it is to teach and interpret the text.

The acceptance of sages—here understood not only as those who transmit the text as "narrators" but also those who in some substantial way control its use—is yet another source of a text's authority. We believe the text not just because it demands to be believed, and not just because it comes from proper sources, but because we have respect (or devotion) to the figures at the heart of its retelling. "I the Lord am your God who brought you out of the land of Egypt" (Exod. 20:2); "Call me Ishmael" (Melville 1851); "Call me Hi" (*Raising Arizona* 1987); the authority of all narratives relies on those retelling them.

Not surprisingly, most often those in authority—the transmitters or the sages—are men. There are important women in Western scriptures—Deborah comes to mind as the most respected (Judges 4)—but most of time the women function in conjunction with important men (Miriam and Moses, Esther and Mordecai). Many are represented either as non-entities (Noah's wife, who goes unnamed) or as the cause of trouble (Eve, or her predecessor Lilith, the first female of Gen. 1:7, who also goes unnamed in scripture but is labeled in Jewish folklore). In his 1990 work, literary critic Harold Bloom argues that the "Book of J"—one of the "documents" understood by some biblical scholars to be a constituent part of the first six books of the Christian Old Testament—likely had been written by a woman. But for the majority of Western history—from scripture to literature to film—storytelling (and the authority implied or transmitted therein) has been the domain of men.

Women of Authority

The development of feminist theory, Orientalism, and other cultural criticisms of power have shown that there is a strong link between the presence of people from historically marginalized communities with the authority to transmit narratives of meaning on the one hand and their presence in those stories on the other. It stands to reason that, if you're not in the story, you're not behind the story either. Put another way, as Massachusetts Sen. Elizabeth Warren has often said, "If you don't have a seat at the table, you're probably on the menu" (Oh 2014). Historically, members of various historically marginalized communities have not had a seat at the storytelling "table," and therefore have been "on the menu" in the sense that they have been mere commodities to be consumed rather than nuanced, integrated participants in the narrative, but also in the sense that they have been almost entirely without authority, either to be in the story or to tell it.

Graphic artist Alison Bechdel is credited for creating a formula for evaluating the representation of women in film and, by extension, other cultural products (1985). In a strip for *Dykes to Watch Out For*, one of the characters notes that she will only go to see a film if there are two (or more) female characters whose names are known and who have a conversation about something other than men. What Bechdel initially called "The Rule" has since come to be known as the "Bechdel-Wallace Test," in recognition of the contribution of one of Bechdel's friends. Bechdel also has pointed out that something similar to it can be found in author Virginia Woolf's analysis of the work of Jane Austen (Garber 2015; see also Woolf 1935: 124).

The beauty of the "Bechdel-Wallace Test" is its flexibility for measuring the treatment of any number of groups, subcultures, or otherwise marginalized peoples and, whether intended or not, versions of it have been used to test the content for more than the gender equality of characters in narratives. Alaya Johnson created what she calls the "POC!Bechdel Test," a test for how people of color are represented in a narrative: Does it have two named characters who are people of color and who talk to each other about something other than a white person (Johnson 2009)? Members of other traditionally underrepresented groups also have used it to gauge representation of their own members: Are characters portrayed as one-dimensional foils for the more central straight characters? How are Africans or Asians (as well as African Americans or Asian Americans) represented? Are they absent, presented as stereotypes—like the "magical Negro" or the "Oriental Monk," mystical characters who can solve everyone else's problems (see Glenn and Cunningham 2009; Iwamura 2000)—or as complex, nuanced characters who just happen to be visually different from the more traditional white, straight characters? What about characters on the LGBTQ+ spectrum?

Ironically (for a profit-driven mode of myth-telling like modern film), a film's "failure" of the Bechdel-Wallace Test has financial repercussions. An informal study of nearly 2,000 films released between 1970 and 2013 revealed that only half "passed" the Bechdel-Wallace Test: they had "at least one scene in which [two or more named] women talked to each other about something other than a man." Not surprisingly, between 1990 and 2013, films that passed the Bechdel-Wallace Test had smaller budgets than those in which (1) women characters only talked about men, or in which (2) there were fewer than two named women characters. Interestingly, all three of these categories had smaller budgets than films that had named women characters, but those women didn't talk to each other, suggesting that studio financiers were most willing to fund films in which women characters were visually present but silent or dependent on male characters for dialogue—seen but not heard, as it were, or speaking when spoken to—likely because of the overwhelmingly teen male film target audience. And yet, those well-financed films did not provide as high a return on the investment dollar as films in which named female characters only talked about men, which themselves earned even less (per dollar invested) than films that "passed" the Test (Hickey 2014). Put another way, the film industry was more likely to provide more money to those involved in the making of the film but did so with films that provided a better investment for those putting up the money. One wonders if the same is true for films that undergo a cognate of the Bechdel-Wallace Test, for African Americans, for example, or for people of color.

Myths at Work

Of course, myths can also explain authority already established in a past or present situation. For example, the earliest American settlers understood themselves to be reliving the Exodus narrative: they were the ancient Hebrews, escaping their own Pharaoh (the King of England), crossing their own Red Sea (the Atlantic Ocean) to get to a land promised to them by God (North America) (Dow 1890). This explains not only the various sermons to be found during this time but also the history of the organizing myth some historians of religion in America have used to interpret American religious history. In one of the better known early works—Puritan minister Cotton Mather's *Magnalia Christi Americana* ("The Glorious Works of Christ in America"; 1702)—every bountiful harvest or ship's sinking revealed God's hand. Over a century later, the subtitle to Reverend Robert Baird's *Religion in the United States of America* (1844)—"an account of the origin, progress, relations to the state, and present condition of the evangelical churches in the united states, with notices of unevangelical denominations"—made clear the work's emphasis. Even Sydney Ahlstrom's *A Religious History of the American People* (1972) divided American history into Puritan and "Post-Puritan" periods—the latter of which started after the election of John F. Kennedy in 1960, and 850 pages of text, and despite the fact that Catholicism has been the single largest religious denomination in the United States since Baird's time.

Similarly, historians of religion and film have used myth—consciously or not—to interpret the battle over the content of American film. On the one hand, that same myth of the pious Puritan was clearly operating behind the efforts of leaders in the American Catholic community who, fearing for the souls of their own parishioners and the nation, sought to control the product of the American film industry. On the other hand, the myth of the American entrepreneur—the "Protestant work ethic," where anyone can "make it big" with enough hard work—clearly animated the Jews who, evading the monopoly Thomas Edison retained on his film technologies, left the East Coast and established not just the modern studio film industry in California but also "Hollywood" and the images of an America where (in the later words of radio storyteller Garrison Keillor) "all the women are strong, all the men are good looking, and all the children are above average," and where the biggest problems could be solved by having a show in a barn. These two myths come into direct conflict over the "Hollywood Production Code" that established what could and what could not be shown on screen from the decade or so before the Second World War to the decade or so after its conclusion. Interestingly, the government and institutional Protestantism played very little part in the resolution and remained on the sidelines while the two groups struggled with the other to determine how best to be "American."

Most recently, new myths—or unambiguously newer presentations of older myths—have provided meaning for groups of people to make sense of the universe in which they live. Practitioners of what scholars have identified as "fake" (Chidester 2005), "invented" (Cusack 2010), or even "joke" (Simpson 2011) religions have presented a new frontier for the exploration of myth and its authority in the modern world. Jediists (*not* Jedis) derive authority from the myths embedded in the various *Star Wars* films, Matrixists from the *Matrix* films, Dudeists from *The Big Lebowski* (1998). Members of the Church of the Flying Spaghetti Monster (also known as "Pastafarians") have developed ex nihilo a myth system detailing the creation of the universe, the origin of humanity, and the path to salvation. While many observers might minimize the import of these groups (see "Connections: Barth and Religion as Critique" in this volume), all of them (in some way or another) engage in activities that are traditionally reserved for religious communities: some offer ordination for members to perform wedding ceremonies, others have challenged successfully various government allowances granted to religious groups but restricted to nonmembers (wearing a hat in a government identification photo, for example). But all of them identify specific, world-explaining myths at their core, and most exert energy maintaining the authentic and differentiating it from that which is (to use the term of many of them) "non-canonical."

It makes perfect sense that myth would not only animate our past but explain our current world as well, particularly if, as Neal Gabler and others have argued (1998), the lives we live today have become much like the movies we watch, or we expect them to be. We constantly construct our universe in story, and we rely on those stories to both explain and govern our lives. In the modern world of instant story production through popular culture—first in analog then in digital video processes—we should not be surprised to find myths constantly, everywhere, and not only in texts of an ancient (and often, foreign) past.

Works Cited

Ahlstrom, Sydney E. *A Religious History of the American People*. New Haven, CT: Yale University Press, 1972.

Baird, Robert. *Religion in the United States of America: Or, An Account of the Origin, Progress, Relations to the State, and Present Condition of the Evangelical Churches in the United States, with Notices of Unevangelical Denominations*. Glasgow: Blackie and Son, 1844.

Bataille, Georges. *Theory of Religion*, trans. Robert Hurley. New York: Zone Books, 1973/1989.

Bechdel, Alison. "The Rule," *Dykes to Watch Out For*, 1985. Available online: https://www.npr.org/templates/story/story.php?storyId=94202522 (accessed February 8, 2019).

Berger, Peter L. *The Sacred Canopy: Elements of a Sociological Theory of Religion*. Garden City, NY: Doubleday, 1967.

Bloom, Harold. *The Book of J*. New York: Grove Weidenfeld, 1990.

Burton, Robert A. "Our Brains Tell Stories So We Can Live," *Nautilus* 75 (August 8, 2019). Available online: http://nautil.us/issue/75/story/our-brains-tell-stories-so-we-can-live (accessed June 9, 2019).

Chidester, David. *Authentic Fakes: Religion and American Popular Culture*. Berkeley: University of California Press. 2005.

Cusack, Carole M. *Invented Religions: Imagination, Fiction and Faith*. Burlington, VT: Ashgate Publishing, 2010.

Dow, John G. "Hebrew and Puritan," *Jewish Quarterly Review* 3, no. 1 (1890): 52–84.

Eliade, Mircea. *Myth and Reality*, trans. Willard R. Trask. New York: Harper & Row, 1963.

Gabler, Neal. *Life: The Movie: How Entertainment Conquered Reality*. New York: Alfred A. Knopf, Inc, 1998.

Gaiman, Neil. *American Gods: A Novel*. New York: W. Morrow, 2001.

Garber, Megan. "Call It the 'Bechdel-Wallace Test,'" *Atlantic*, August 25, 2015. Available online: https://www.theatlantic.com/entertainment/archive/2015/08/call-it-the-bechdel-wallace-test /402259/ (accessed February 8, 2019).

Glenn, Cerise L., and Landra J. Cunningham. "The Power of Black Magic: The Magical Negro and White Salvation in Film," *Journal of Black Studies* 40, no. 2 (2009): 135–52.

Hickey, Walter. "The Dollar-And-Cents Case Against Hollywood's Exclusion of Women," *FiveThirtyEight*, April 1, 2014. Available online: https://fivethirtyeight.com/features/the-dollar-an d-cents-case-against-hollywoods-exclusion-of-women/ (accessed February 9, 2020).

Iwamura, Jane Naomi. "The Oriental Monk in American Popular Culture," in *Religion and Popular Culture in America*, ed. Bruce David Forbes and Jeffrey H. Mahan, 25–43. Berkeley: University of California Press, 2000.

Johnson, Alaya Dawn. "The Bechdel Test and Race in Popular Fiction," *Angry Black Woman*, September 1, 2009. Available online: http://theangryblackwoman.com/2009/09/01/the-bechd el-test-and-race-in-popular-fiction/ (accessed April 25, 2020).

Lincoln, Bruce. *Authority: Construction and Corrosion*. Chicago: The University of Chicago Press, 1994.

Mather, Cotton. *Magnalia Christi Americana: The Ecclesiastical History of New England from Its First Planting in 1602, Until the Year of Our Lord 1698*. London: Thomas Parkhurst, 1702.

Melville, Herman. *Moby Dick: or, The Whale*. New York: Harper & Brothers, 1851.

Miner, Horace. "Body Ritual among the Nacirema," *American Anthropologist* 58, no. 3 (1956): 503–7.

Oh, Inae. "Elizabeth Warren: Democratic Women Need a Seat at the Governing Table," *Mother Jones*, September 25, 2014. Available online: https://www.motherjones.com/politics/2014/09/ elizabeth-warren-donors-vote-democratic-women/ (accessed December 19, 2020).

Pike, Sarah. *Earthly Bodies, Magical Selves: Contemporary Pagans and the Search for Community*. Berkeley: University of California Press. 2001.

Renken, Elena. "How Stories Connect and Persuade Us: Unleashing the Brain Power of Narrative," *National Public Radio [NPR]*, April 11, 2020. Available online: https://www.npr.org/sections/h ealth-shots/2020/04/11/815573198/how-stories-connect-and-persuade-us-unleashing-the-b rain-power-of-narrative (accessed April 11, 2020).

Ryan, William, and Walter Pitman. *Noah's Flood: The New Scientific Discoveries About the Event that Changed History*. New York: Simon and Schuster, 1998.

Segal, Robert A. *Myth: A Very Short Introduction*. New York: Oxford University Press, 2004.

Simpson, Scott. "Joke Religions: Make-Believe in the Sandbox of the Gods," *Ex Nihilo* 2, no. 6 (2011): 91–118.

Woolf, Virginia. *A Room of One's Own*. London: Hogarth Press, 1935.

18   Where We Go

Pilgrimages

Introduction: Pilgrimage in Religion and Popular Culture

Popular culture often expresses the basic human need to see life as journey with adventures that confer wisdom and power, redefinitions of social status, and distant destinations linked to a larger sense of purpose or salvation. In physical terms, this can inspire *pilgrimages*, trips to places of sacred power and meaning, like temples and shrines, often thought to also have therapeutic and transformative powers. Pilgrimage can also be seen as a literary strategy, giving structure to long and complicated narratives, rendered in poetry, prose, or other media, which involve multiple characters, settings, and storylines. The core themes of pilgrimage stories often involve protagonists performing heroic deeds, facing dilemmas and adversities, battling monstrous evil, or sometimes just meeting new and interesting characters and learning important life lessons. In the general sense, the pilgrimage, physical or literary, holds out the promise of cultural renewal. Along the way listeners learn of healing powers, instructions about ritual, moral teaching, predictions about the future, and other basic ideas that help establish and maintain cultural norms. As cultural forms, pilgrimages are ancient and global phenomena, historically intertwined with the great religious traditions, but not exclusive to them. Among the notable developments of modern popular culture has been the emergence of modern variants, supported across various media and employing contemporary technologies. This chapter will introduce these topics via some particularly illuminating case studies and explore how various theoretical approaches can be applied to their analysis.

Classic Forms of Religious Pilgrimage: Medieval Christianity

Pilgrimage is an important element of all major religions, and in more modest forms, many indigenous religions, new religious movements, and sectarian groups. As an established institution within larger religious groups, it generally involves a location deemed sacred because of events that occurred there and association with key religious figures, for example, birthplaces, sites of great deeds, revelations, or places of martyrdom and sacrificial death. Usually, pilgrimages focus on important religious buildings or other structures, often housing sacred objects for veneration, typically relics of bones or garments. In some cases, natural locations, like sacred mountains, confluences of rivers, or bodies of water are the main destinations. Pilgrims travel to the locations, often over considerable distances and involving some hardship, to see the sacred things and participate in various rituals. Under conditions set down by the tradition, the pilgrim will undergo a strengthening of faith, a sense of religious community, and personal reformation and renewal. Pilgrimages include some of the largest regular gatherings of human beings on the planet. The Hajj in Saudi Arabia regularly hosts over 2 million people and crowd estimates of the Kumbh Mela fairs in India have topped 100 million.

Pilgrimage was a major part of medieval Christianity in Europe and participation was broad and varied. And while built upon ecclesiastically sanctioned activities, pilgrimage was preeminently a popular practice, involving a cross section of believers and seekers from all levels of society. Some of the more ambitious and wealthy pilgrims made long arduous journeys to Jerusalem to visit sites of biblical events, or to Rome to see tombs of the apostles Peter and Paul. Other pilgrims visited relatively local sites, often containing relics of saints, or places made sacred by reports of manifestations of the divine presence. Penance was usually the stated motive for pilgrimage and most pilgrims hoped to strengthen their connection to God. Healing was also a significant motive, and the sick often visited sites with miraculous reputations. Eventually, the medieval map of Europe was peppered with shrines and crisscrossed with pilgrimage routes.

All the varied tensions and disputes over meanings that haunt "the popular" are easily seen in pilgrimages. For example, while elites undertook some of the more elaborate journeys, the typical medieval European pilgrims were often peasants whose lives were defined by repetitive labor, poverty, and piety lived out in rural villages and towns within a few miles of their birthplaces (Sumption 1975). For these, pilgrimage journeys provided a respite from ordinary life—engaging and adventurous experiences wherein participants could meet new people, share stories and ideas, see new things, enjoy fellowship, and hopefully, culminate in an extraordinary experience before the pilgrim had to return home. The fourteenth-century collection *The Canterbury Tales* by Geoffrey Chaucer, for example, recounts various stories from persons of all walks of life, as they travel to a famous shrine in southern England. And while the *Tales* provide many good insights into conventional medieval religious life, many are famously bawdy, recounting illicit affairs, bodily functions, and various vices. Certainly then, the medieval pilgrimage had a mixed character, combining pious journeys with a touch of the carnivalesque.

At the level of theory, many scholars of pilgrimage look to the work of Edith and Victor Turner whose influential *Image and Pilgrimage in Christian Culture* sees pilgrims as partaking in a kind of rite of passage, with stages analogous to the separation, liminality, and reintegration found in more localized ritual processes.

> A pilgrim is an initiand, entering into a new, deeper level of existence than he has known in his accustomed milieu. [Similar to] the ordeals of tribal initiation are the trials, tribulations, and even temptations of the pilgrim's way. And at the end, the pilgrim, like the novice, is exposed to powerful religious sacra (shrines, images, liturgies, curative waters, ritual circumambulations of holy objects, and so on), the beneficial effect of which depends upon the zeal and pertinacity of his quest. (Turner and Turner 2011: 8)

Thus after the separation from home, the pilgrim enters into a series of "liminal" activities, including travel through strange territories to distant locations, immersion into all manner of abnormal activities, and a strong sense of communal bonding to other pilgrims. And while structured according to tradition, particularly as one approaches the main destination, there are opportunities for unique social interactions and choices to be made about how much to engage with the religious dimensions of the pilgrimage.

The durable theoretical debate about the liminal goes to its capacity to spark social change, especially insofar as the liminal activities—inversions, flipped social statuses, humor, subversion, masquerade, etc.—suggest possibilities for new ways of thinking and living. Yet this potential seems, in many societies, to be a fleeting element of ritual process only which overall leads to a reinforcement of social structure. Thus the initiand, while they can play around with identity and behavior during the liminal stage, will ultimately "reintegrate" into society defined by well-established social norms and behaviors. The Turners and others do see some circumstances where the liminal can lead to social challenges, lifestyle experimentation, utopian longing, and other reformist, perhaps even revolutionary, activities in more complex societies. Pilgrims can also bring back new things—knowledge, perspective, confidence, resources—that can help them personally or perhaps enhance their social circles. More recent theorists, while appreciating the work done by the Turners, suggest we reframe our studies of pilgrimages, putting emphasis on what is fundamental to contemporary popular culture: motion, fluidity, and instability (Coleman and Eade 2004).

Recasting the Pilgrimage in Literary Terms: John Bunyan's *The Pilgrim's Progress*

As the medieval European world gave way to the Renaissance and Reformation, the pilgrimage was recast in ways that shifted the emphasis toward other kinds of journeying, sometimes more conceptual than physical. Few popular works in the English-speaking world have the long reach of John Bunyan's novel *A Pilgrim's Progress*. Written by a nonconforming Protestant minister, upon publication in 1678 it was an immediate sensation, destined to become perhaps the most successful English novel of all time. Print editions number in the thousands, including translations into over 200 languages, and the basic story has been adapted into other media like film, cartoons, and video games. A fully animated film version was released as recently as 2019. Bunyan declares in his opening section that his work addresses a "race of saints" who "[f]ell suddenly into an allegory/About their journey, and the way to glory" (Bunyan 1957: 1). The action follows the struggles of "Christian," an adherent of Reformed theology who is seeking a path through life from his current condition in the "City of Destruction" to his version of heaven, the "Celestial City." As Christian travels, he encounters various allegorical characters who variously give him sound advice or inhibit his journey, for example, "Evangelist," "Mr. Worldly Wiseman," "Obstinate," "Timorous," "Superstition," and "Hopeful." He likewise visits places with names corresponding to the moods they evoke or the actions that occur there, for example, the "Slough of Despair," "Vanity Fair," "The Delectable Mountains," "Hill Difficulty," and "House Beautiful." Christian negotiates various dilemmas and difficult straits, and in a gesture back to medieval knightly lore, even battles a monstrous demon, "Apollyon," defeating him with his "Sword of Spirit."

How can we analyze *The Pilgrim's Progress* and its appeal as a religious expression of popular culture? Paul Tillich's ideas about the ability of culture to embody and express "ultimate concerns" in the face of existential doubts and anxieties suggest a basic strategy. Although Tillich never addressed the work in his writings, literature scholar Roger Lundin argues that Tillich's ideas about the interior turn in early modern thought, spurred on by Protestant anxieties about salvation, help explain its popular appeal. Early modern readers, especially those influenced by the Protestant Reformers, held acute fears of "condemnation" (Tillich 1952) and thus "were assailed by dreadful uncertainties about where they stood with God and where they would spend eternity." This in turn drove them "to lofty heights of self-examination and abysmal depths of self-laceration" (Lundin 1994). For his part Bunyan's pilgrimage sought to "map that inner domain and to chart a course out of its mazes." Furthermore, Bunyan's use of allegory, in contrast to medieval Catholic writings that worked from theological system "above" human experience, explored psychologically "subterranean regions." Bunyan's hero, Christian, in a dream, "meets his inner states embodied as a series of temptations, perils, and demons." His "pilgrimage" is thus through his own psychological dispositions, driven by a sense of self-negation and reproach, but also hopeful of some final affirmation, held out as a desirable destination—the "Celestial City." As a novel read in a private setting, the goal of Bunyan's pilgrimage is less a physical place (per medieval Christian tradition) so much as a sense of psychic relief as having survived the rigors of the inner journey.

Other literary scholars of Bunyan's novel, like Philip Edwards, have noted that its fundamental energies are "adventure, keeping to the path, [and] movement forward." These manifest for the Christian reader three key ideas, "the vicissitudes of a Christian's life, arising from external threat and internal disturbance, . . . obeying the strict demands of the true faith, and . . . advancing in the understanding and practice of the Christian life." Here, all those themes are prominent, as well as Edward's insight that "Christian path-keeping . . . means not only keeping to the path, but keeping the whole path. You can only get to the end of the road by traveling the whole road" (Edwards 1980). Tillich might say that this fullness of vision is "ultimate concern" and imparts the faith and courage "to be" by affirming the sense of self in the face of potentially debilitating existential anxiety.

The influence of *Progress* on popular culture in the English-speaking world was both direct and indirect, as the text was circulated and reverently read for centuries. Some families would pass down well-thumbed copies for generations, often in tandem with vernacular versions of the Bible. Indirectly, creative writers adapted Bunyan's notion of a difficult spiritual journey, filled with adversities, told via allegorical methods for their own ends and circumstances, often seeing them as means to comment and update notions of pilgrimage. Colonial era captivity narratives about settlers (especially women) who survived being kidnapped by native peoples, and the escape narratives of ex-slaves that spurred the abolition movement drew freely upon Bunyan's spiritualized landscape of perils and ordeals, punctuated by an escape to freedom. Later, novelists, most famously Mark Twain and Louisa May Alcott, wrote various "new" pilgrim's progresses, often about journeys into the American frontier or trips abroad (Smith 1966).

The Pilgrimage as Modern Multimedia Fantasy: *The Wizard of Oz*

Eventually, these *Progress*-inspired novels departed from Bunyan's explicit Christian theological framework to embrace other ideas, religious and secular, some with spectacular success. Undoubtedly the most influential allegorical pilgrimage in American popular culture has been L.

Frank Baum's fantasy novel *The Wonderful Wizard of Oz* (1900). It, along with the many works it has inspired, including musicals, novels, comics, television series, and most especially, the famous film of 1939 (probably the most watched film of all time), has long served as core point of reference for thinking about American identity and the American dream. The now familiar story recounts the adventures of Dorothy Gale, an orphan girl living on a farm in Kansas which is struck by a cyclone that transports her to a magical land, Oz. There she embarks on a journey to the "Emerald City" to meet the titular wizard who she hopes will help her return to Kansas. Along the way, she meets the famous allegorical characters—the Scarecrow, the Tin Woodsman, and the Cowardly Lion—endures various ordeals, kills two wicked witches, and discovers the true identity of the wizard, before finally realizing her ability to return home. As various scholarly studies have shown, Oz and its spawn have been an enduring part of American popular culture largely because they served as a "secular" and distinctly "American" myth. As the core characters and storylines have been reinvented and reinvigorated for new generations, often in newer forms of media, audiences of very diverse types have responded with distinctive interpretations. These include readings that emphasize political populism, the ideas of the Theosophical movement, queer theory, feminism, positive thinking, as well as those that map the allegory back to Christian ideals (Burger 2012; Nathanson 1991). This diversity suggests that allegorical pilgrimage "travels far" less on the certainty of its destination than on its audiences' delight in its elasticity. Readers can put on the "ruby slippers" (originally silver in the novel) and reinvent themselves in myriad ways.

Contemporary Tourist Pilgrimage: Disney World

If *The Pilgrim's Progress* gave a kind of method for popularizing and adapting the pilgrimage over the transition into the modern period, we should also recognize that physical movement of persons for religious, spiritual, and other purposes actually increased thanks to the expansion of transportation systems. Much of this movement was for economic purposes, but as globalization intensified, so too did exploration, travel, and tourism for their own sake. These can be roughly distinguished from pilgrimage by their motives—the explorer seeks out the unknown for discovery, the traveler has some sense of their destination but is open to finding some new experiences, and the tourist aims to visit sites with well-established venues, often highly commercialized, to cater to their recreational needs and interests. Thus in the modern era, "unnecessary" travel across long distances diversified in terms of its motives, mixing education, adventure, relaxation, and pleasure. But do these constitute a break from traditional pilgrimage motivated by penance, piety, and desire to connect with the sacred? One provocative case study is the popular resort and amusement park, Walt Disney World, in central Florida. Since opening in 1971, the park has become the most popular of its kind in the world, annually serving over fifty million visitors across various hotels, themed venues, rides, waterparks, and other activities. Highlights include meeting actors portraying characters from Disney films, daily parades, and fireworks, various rides and theatrical performances that invoke American history, and sections like EPCOT and Tomorrowland that envision a utopian future.

Art historian Cher Krause Knight argues that while the park is primarily known as a place for family vacations, it embodies all the classical elements of pilgrimage. Echoing the

Turners, she builds a positive comparison based on the experiences of the visitors: "Free from the constraints of home, pilgrims can experience enlightenment and transcendence, but also transgression as inhibitions are loosened." These are driven by a longing to form a new sense of community, however temporary, around intensified activities and "momentary liberation from daily obligations and roles" (Knight 2014: 28). Disney also carefully cultivates forms of cultural memory for its visitors, weaving together highly personal experiences with the various "magical" activities within the park. Many of these are carefully coordinated with the various films and other storytelling platforms created by the Disney studios, as famous characters are embodied by actors, park structures, and thrill rides are modeled on film scenes, etc. One telling Disney ad asserts, "Disney memories! They're magical things that dance in our dreams and live happily ever after in our hearts." Perhaps most revealing is the structural similarity of Disney World to traditional pilgrimage sites like Santiago de Compostela in northern Spain. In comparison, both employ "an arrangement of space that promotes ritual movement and circulation through the site; the use of shrines and symbols that draw upon knowledge gathered prior to visiting the center; and the ability to inspire intense devotion among visitors" (Knight 2014: 29). Testimonials from innumerable visitors, including Knight's own experiences as a child and an adult, reinforce how the Disney World experience has become a contemporary equivalent of a pilgrimage, "touristy" to be sure, but often something more insofar as it reinforces a repeatable series of cathartic emotional responses. Indeed, the Disney media empire relies upon this, recognizing that emotionalism is the "heart and soul of our business" (Knight 2014: 29).

In other parts of the text, Krause adopts a more critical stance, recognizing that the messaging of the Disney parks, in spite of recent efforts at cultural sensitivity and inclusion, was largely formulated as a way to celebrate colonial and imperial assumptions about civilization, hierarchy, and minority groups. In the EPCOT and the Magic Kingdom sections of the park, for example,

> fragmented representations evoke different historical epochs and geographical regions . . . [where] the past is conquered, nature is tamed, other cultures are entertainment, and the future is always promising. . . . [This] depiction of U.S. history privileges white European males while neutralizing racial unrest and gender inequities and rendering social conflicts and temporary setbacks . . . [making] the "other" seem more familiar and the "exotic" palatable to middle American tastes. (Knight 2014: 136)

Likewise, the critical theories of the Frankfort School can also be brought to bear on the ways that a pilgrimage to Disney World is carefully managed and controlled in ways that reinforce cultural uniformity. Recall that Adorno and Horkheimer saw ideologies of capital and economic coercion working through the culture industries via media, advertising, and other forms of popular culture. These reached far into the imaginations and self-formations of all modern peoples exposed to them, especially because the messages were ubiquitous and endlessly repeated. As exemplary outposts of the "culture industry," the "magic" and structured "happy" memories of Disney World are not merely distractions, but actually insidious, subtle, and highly effective modes of propaganda and control. Furthermore, the culture industry was able to exercise this influence because other forms of cultural critique, including dissenting religions and reform movements, had been "neutralized." So while all were "free to dance and enjoy themselves" at places like Disney World, ultimately the "freedom to choose" leisure activities, ideologies, religious activities, etc., "everywhere proves to be freedom to choose what is always the same" (Adorno and Horkheimer 1993/1944).

Conclusion: Pilgrims All?

Brief as this tour of the varieties of pilgrimage has been, we can draw a few tentative conclusions that will be useful to future inquiries. First, pilgrimage has been a very persistent aspect of human societies, and it has been very popular. Generally accessible to people of diverse social backgrounds, pilgrimages have proven appeal and continue to draw large numbers of participants. Thus they are an excellent way to explore religion and popular culture. Most especially, they are rich in symbolism and ritual performances that can be studied to illuminate the social circumstances and psychological motives of pilgrims from different historical eras and diverse religious traditions.

Second, while religious activities and motives are foundational to many forms of pilgrimage, more modern forms have tended to combine other interests, including education, curiosity, tourism, and relaxation. Thus we can speak of secular pilgrimage as an important part of modern popular culture. However, the line between sacred and secular is not always so clear or absolute. Commercial motives often surrounded the pious pilgrimages of religious tradition, including economic benefits in towns along the routes and a brisk trade in religious mementos that pilgrims took home. Arguably, the allegedly "secular" forms of pilgrimage like Disney World are steeped in myth, symbol, and ritual—the very building blocks of religion.

Third, the analysis of pilgrimage as a ritual process provides a basic strategy for comparing the category across cultures and from the past to the present. Medieval pilgrims to Christian shrines and contemporary families enjoying a week at Disney World aim for experiences that lift them out of their ordinary patterns of life into something more intense, symbolically rich, and quite possibly, transformative. Along the way, they cultivate personal stories and memories that hold out the promise of enrichment and meaning and thus make the ordinary tedium of daily life more bearable.

Fourth, as pilgrimage assumed more literary forms under the influence of Protestantism and other strands of modern thinking, they became more explicitly psychological, exploring desires, emotions, and human personalities. Thus "travel" becomes more vicarious via the use of storytelling that emphasizes protagonists whose growth emerges through journeys that involve action, adventure, and allegory. Led by Bunyan's *The Pilgrim's Progress*, the literary pilgrimage would become a staple of popular culture. *The Wizard of Oz* is but one example of how a highly allegorical story, grounded in a journey to a magical world, can sustain popularity over multiple generations and among very diverse audiences. Other prominent examples include the Narnia novels by C. S. Lewis and J. R. R. Tolkien's *Lord of the Rings* cycle.

Finally, the category of pilgrimage builds upon a tension between destination and process. On the one hand, the way of the pilgrim traditionally has been understood as having a clear and meaningful goal associated with a physical place—an extraordinary shrine or object that promises to reveal something of the divine, a presence envisioned as powerful, life-altering, and "real." This can be an "ultimate concern" carefully tended by the authority of a religious tradition, or perhaps, per the Frankfort School, the conformist messaging of consumer capitalism. On the other hand, as we have seen via comparative analysis, pilgrimage is as much about process as it is about place. Pilgrimages, from the road to Compostela to the myriad rides at Disney World, involve movement through lots of places, generating many encounters and stories. These suggest, as Chaucer found among his Canterbury pilgrims and various scholars have found among the rapt audiences of *The Pilgrim's Progress* and *The Wizard of Oz*, that the meaning is as diverse and multivocal as the motion itself.

Works Cited

Adorno, Theodor, and Max Horkheimer. *Dialectic of Enlightenment*. New York: Continuum, 1993/1944.

Bunyan, John. *The Pilgrim's Progress*. New York: Pocket Books, Inc, 1957.

Burger, Alissa. *The Wizard of Oz as American Myth*. Jefferson, NC: McFarland & Company, Inc, 2012.

Coleman, Simon, and John Eade, eds. *Reframing Pilgrimage: Culture in Motion*. London: Routledge, 2004.

Edwards, Philip. "The Journey in The Pilgrim's Progress," in *The Pilgrim's Progress: Critical and Historical Views*, ed. Vincent Newly. Totowa, NJ: Barnes and Noble Books, 1980.

Knight, Cher Krause. *Power and Paradise in Walt Disney's World*. Gainsville: University Press of Florida, 2014.

Lundin, Roger. "Introduction," in *The Pilgrim's Progress*, by John Bunyan. New York: Signet Classics, 1994.

Nathanson, Paul. *Over the Rainbow: The Wizard of Oz as a Secular Myth of America*. Albany: State University of New York Press, 1991.

Smith, David E. *John Bunyan in America*. Bloomington: Indiana University Press, 1966.

Sumption, Jonathan. *Pilgrimage: An Image of Medieval Religion*. Totowa, NJ: Rowan and Littlefield, 1975.

Tillich, Paul. *The Courage to Be*. New Haven: Yale University Press, 1952.

Turner, Edith, and Victor Turner. *Image and Pilgrimage in Christian Culture*. New York: Columbia University Press, 2011.

19 What We Do

Public Ritual, Carnivals, and Festivals

Introduction: Carnival in Rio

The annual celebration of Carnival in Brazil, scheduled just before Lent, is among the world's most colorful and extravagant forms of public ritual. Parades, singing, and dancing in the streets, masquerade balls, and neighborhood parties with feasts and frivolity, all but bring the normal activities in the country to a standstill. In the major cities like Rio de Janeiro, specially designed parade grounds, Sambadromes, host the most elaborate of the parades with massive floats decorated with lights, flowers, and animatronic creatures, all choreographed with bands and dancers in elaborate costumes. Local "samba schools" spend much of the year planning and building their floats and choreographing their processions, which incorporate imagery from the varied ethnic groups and religious traditions that make up Brazil, as well as varied mythological traditions, the natural world, Brazilian history, science fiction, Hollywood films, and whatever else might be of visual interest. The best floats and dancers participate in a nationally televised parade that is viewed by a global audience via internet streaming. Although similar events can be found in other countries, notably the Mardi Gras celebrations found in the United States, Brazil has made carnival a core element of its national tradition and built a substantial tourist industry around it. And while Brazil is still predominantly a Catholic country, it embraces a wider multiculturalism for carnival, reflected in its eclectic use of religious imagery in costumes and themes found in the parades. All the gods come out to dance the samba, it seems, at carnival time.

Carnivals and festivals, briefly defined, are communal events at established times and locations, which involve feasting, music, dancing, costumes, play, and other activities open to public participation. Sometimes quite local, such as family weddings and village feasts for the local saint, major carnivals and festivals can be national, even international, in scope. Work stops for the duration and many events involve the loosening of normal social constraints and the expenditure of surplus resources. Thus they tend to be much loved as opportunities to indulge in transgression, excessive consumption, and expressive performances. They tend to have some basic ritual structure, like scheduled parades, competitions, and theatrical performances. By and large, however, they are defined by their sociability, mixing persons from different social circumstances in events that are open to chance meetings, improvisations, and spontaneous frivolity. Widely practiced in societies of very diverse types, they are generally connected to religious liturgical calendars, secular holidays, or harvest seasons. Historically, carnivals and festivals contrast with times of austerity, fasting, penitence, and strict observance of social proprieties, as typically expected for the high holy days of various religions.

Carnivals and festivals have ancient roots, and aspects of them can survive even when a society converts to a different religion, such as the change from paganism to Christianity in Europe. Thus, like holiday celebrations, they can be analyzed as having multiple layers that build up over their historical development. In terms of religious content, scholars see various elements of carnivals and festivals as rich sources of symbolic meaning ripe for analysis and comparison. For example, historian Peter Burke's broad survey of popular culture in early modern Europe explores the many dimensions of carnivals and festivals in the centuries leading up the Enlightenment. He finds their foundations in general themes of popular culture, especially the widespread interest in magical forces, marvelous events, and supernatural experiences. Likewise, the popular imagination often turned to archetypal characters (see also Chapter 15, "Who We Are")—the hero, the villain, the fool—that served as symbolic role models reflecting and reinforcing the larger value system. The heroes surpassed normal human standards for good behavior with daring, bravery, selflessness, and virtue. The villains terrorized the social system by threatening to disrupt its normal functions. And fools helped reinforce certain norms of behavior by showing, with comic flair, what *not* to do (Burke 1978: 149). Religious figures, especially members of the clergy, could fit into any of these categories, as attested in chap books, popular songs, and other sources of folklore. Thus heroic saints and ascetics, modeled on the example of Jesus and other biblical figures, were celebrated because they fully dedicated their lives to religious devotion, charity, healing the sick, and other religious tasks. In contrast, scheming monks and priests, motivated by greed, lust, and malevolence, were also stock figures in popular culture, especially satirical plays. The "merry friar" who overindulged in drink, song, and other temptations of the flesh often fulfilled the role of the "fool."

Carnivals and festivals in urban settings brought many of these characters into theatrical high relief. According to Burke,

> Carnival may be seen as huge play in which the main streets and squares became stages, the city became a theater without walls and the inhabitants, the actors and spectators, observing the scene from their balconies. . . .The action of this gigantic play was a set of more or less formally structured events . . . [with] less formally structured events . . . spread over the whole town. (Burke 1978: 182)

Costume and masquerades, including fancy outfits with elaborate masks, added to the theatricality of the events. "Men dressed as women, women as men" while others portrayed "fools, wild men and wild animals," or aped religious and other authority figures, "popes, cardinals, monks, devils, courtiers, harlequins, and lawyers all mingled up in one promiscuous crowd." What did these costumed revelers do? The main activities included the eating of meat and other special foods like pancakes and waffles. One source describes an English carnival as including "such boiling and broiling, such roasting and toasting, such stewing and brewing, such baking, frying, mincing, cutting, carving, devouring, and gorbellied gormandizing" that a person could eat enough for two months, or a long voyage (Burke 1978: 183). Participants also drank wines, ales, and other spirits, often well beyond normal levels and leading to public drunkenness. Other excessive practices included, singing and dancing, carried out in both private and public settings, often with bawdy lyrics and other sexual content. Sometimes the actions would flash into violence, including brawling and the slaughter of pigs, chickens, and other animals on their way to becoming parts of the carnival eating binges.

Competitions were also a central feature of festivals, including races on foot or on horses, jousting and quintain, tug of wars, mock battles, and food fights. Presiding over many of the carnival events and often the central figure of processions of feasts was a mock "king," "pope," or "lord," usually a person of low or middling social status, who temporarily ruled over (or rather "misruled") the extravagant events. Typically, this figure was a corpulent man who ate, drank, and celebrated to excess alongside the admiring crowds and also parodied the usual pomp and seriousness of conventional regal ceremonies or religious rituals. All told, Burke asserts themes of food, sex, violence, and mockery animated the early modern carnival, which, of course, can be traced in various lines of descent into contemporary popular culture in venues like rock concerts, stand-up comedy, and eating contests.

The end of carnivals usually was clearly marked and required a reversal of the activities that shaped the revels. In the Catholic calendar, often this meant seasons of austerities and prohibitions, like fasting and other forms of self-denial, typified by the Lenten rules. Often the carnival itself marked this transition symbolically, with an old woman who does "battle" with the carnival "king" (see especially the famous 1559 painting of this by Pieter Breugel), or civic rituals, such as the end of the Mardi Gras in New Orleans where police and street cleaning equipment "sweep" the main thoroughfares and tell everyone to go home.

Given the structural dimensions of European society of that period, hierarchies based on monarchal and aristocratic privileges, supported by an emerging middle class and a vast number of poor peasants and serfs, the carnival seems rather dangerous as a social practice. Often called a "World Turned Upside Down" the carnival seemed to unleash all of the restraints and invert all of the social roles that governed ordinary times. Normal discipline based on the control of appetites, as well as clear deference to authority, was largely suspended for the carnival. Might this suggest a more permanent change in social organization? One might see in the revolutions in the seventeenth and eighteenth centuries, some of which included depositions and even executions of kings and nobles, as making real (in the political sense) the carnivalesque inversions of the old order. On the other hand, scholars see very mixed evidence for carnival leading to real structural change. Therefore many have interpreted the social inversions and mocking as a kind of "safety valve" to blow off pressure built up because of repressions necessary to maintain a social hierarchy. Thus after all the fun, all the excessive eating and drinking, the poor returned to their deprivations and the wealthy to their lavish estates. Burke's view is a bit more nuanced, recognizing that while carnivals and festivals gave cultural unity to early modern Europe, they reflected underlying tensions and social conflicts. Ideologically, they contained a "spectrum of attitudes." These included many "fatalists" who felt the social order could not be changed, "traditionalists" and "moralists" who tended to see the problems of the world as the result of a flawed human nature or the work of wicked villains (thus not the social order), "radicals" energized by the possibilities for social change, and "millenarians" who anticipated some supernatural intervention that would transform the world (Burke 1978: 174).

The transition into the modern world would see many of the elements of carnivals and festivals tamed, and in some places, all but eliminated. In some sense this transition reflects how religious sectarianism and secularism have influenced modern societies. Many of the advocates of the Protestant Reformation, for example, sternly rebuked the carnivals and saints feasts as "Catholic" idolatry, sinful, and inimical to their preferred emphasis on continuous piety, introspection, and self-discipline. Thus where the Protestant traditions took hold, many of the older traditions faded. Likewise, as the modern world became more focused on work, economic dynamism, bureaucratic modes of social organization, and "rationalism" in a general sense, these kinds of events seemed outmoded. And yet carnivals and festivals and their attendant revelries would survive and adapt, often in ways that sustain the ethnic identity of particular groups or as expressions of broader countercultural ideas. A few case studies will illustrate how this occurred.

Adapting the Festival to Modern America: Saint Patrick and the Madonnas

In the United States, Irish immigrants made the feast of St. Patrick a centerpiece of their cultural lives as early as the colonial era and would eventually see this spring festival achieve general popularity. The holiday usually involves parades, speeches, communal meals, and other social events, many of which include carnivalesque elements of excessive consumption, costumes, and boisterous behavior. Historian Kenneth Moss demonstrates that studying the form and significance of these celebrations illustrates how Irish Americans negotiated and adapted their social, religious, and political identities as they made their way in America. Notably, they moved from being a largely "outsider" group, facing sharp discrimination from the American mainstream, to being one of the great American immigrant success stories. St. Patrick was there to both console and celebrate, listening to their laments and toasting their achievements.

Irish immigrants began to arrive in America in large numbers during the 1840s, driven initially by the devastating potato famine. Many were destitute and tended to settle into urban enclaves served by Roman Catholic churches, much disdained by mainstream Protestants. In spite of the hardships, the Irish began a long period of ascendancy in American life, steadily finding their way to social, economic, and political power. As well, the Irish clergy found a prominent role in the American Catholic hierarchy and often presided over a church with diverse ethnic groups. These clergy, along with other Irish leaders, used holiday sermons and orations to encourage serious reflection on Irish identity, especially the meaning of their faith in the face of the many hardships the Irish immigrants had endured. Thus, for example, Archbishop John Hughes, in a sermon given at St. Patrick's Cathedral in 1853, asserts that the suffering of the Irish poor, including the devastating privations and losses due to the potato famine, should be understood as continuous with a deep tradition of Catholic faith sustained in the face of loss. Furthermore, this suffering led to a kind of "purification" which could steady the immigrant in the new world and perhaps even inspire others with its virtue. Thus the holiday was an opportunity to "cherish . . . and propagate" St. Patrick's message of religious conversion and pious discipline (Moss 1995). In time, however, the speakers at St. Patrick's Day events diversified their message, often stressing connections with nationalist movements in Ireland and simultaneously their growing comfort with American culture, especially its democratic values.

Like other carnivals and festivals, St. Patrick's Day has symbolic richness, emotional intensity, and expressive displays that reinforce a sense of community memory and renewal. Parading has long been the most prominent and public aspect of the holiday, and evidence points to small, localized parades in the American colonies before the Revolution. These would steadily grow in number and eventually become major events in cities with large Irish populations, like Boston, Chicago, and New York. Currently, over 100 American cities host St. Patrick's Day parades with the largest drawing thousands of participants and millions of spectators. Retailers' surveys indicate that nearly six billion dollars are spent to celebrate, and 60 percent of the general population will attend a party, visit a bar, watch a parade, or at least wear green ("Retail Holiday" n.d.). Clearly, St. Patrick has "made it" in America, even if some revelers conveniently forget some of the historical figure's commitment to purity, piety, and sobriety.

Other American immigrant communities have looked to feasts honoring the Madonna for a sense of community identity tied to theological meaning. Robert Orsi's much celebrated historical study, *The Madonna of 115th Street: Faith and Community in Italian Harlem, 1880-1950*, recounts how a summer festival served as a kind of anchor for Italian-Americans in New York City as they adapted to modern urban life. Orsi finds that "religion" in this popular series of events held multiple meanings. Many of the events focused on traditional Catholic ideas and practices, including church-based sacramental rituals, earnest prayers seeking grace, and public processions. However, he also details how this festival season is energized by a "Madonna" who steps out of the church, "asked to bless" the streets of Italian Harlem, "a world of parks, stoops, alleyways, hallways, fire escapes, storefronts, traffic, police, courtyards, street crime, and street play" (Orsi 1985: xxi). Orsi finds inner meaning in this festival as a way to reinforce and celebrate *domus*, an enlarged sense of family relations and cultural continuity found among Italian peasants then adapted by immigrants to conditions in the United States. However, close attention to the ideas and sentiments participants associated with the Madonna show how meanings shifted over time. Notably, the "Madonna was not a stationary icon to be worshipped, but the focus of a drama to be acted out . . . the festa provided the context for expressing and experiencing the emotional and moral content underlying the meaning of the symbol" (Orsi 1985: 163). And interpretation was not only the province of official ecclesiastical bodies, as Orsi describes "street theologians" who "proclaimed that suffering and sacrifice were essential links between themselves and the divine . . . [creating] a deep bond of sympathy with the redemptive suffering at the heart of Christianity" (221). Thus Orsi's social history of this religious symbol is valuable both as a particular expression of Italian Catholics and as part of the longer history of Christian worship of feminine expressions of the divine (Pelikan 1998).

Other American Catholics have notable celebrations of the Madonna, including various summer street festivals and parades for Sicilian-derived Madonnas hosted in the North End of Boston and a burgeoning tradition of feasts for Our Lady of Guadalupe among Mexican Americans across the United States in December. In regard to the latter, theologian and sociologist Jeanette Rodriquez finds Our Lady of Guadalupe is a generally unifying "symbol of Mexican consciousness combining elements of Spanish and indigenous roots," of particular "personal or affective" significance to Mexican American women. In interviews focused on the meanings of the various feasts, devotions, pilgrimages, and use of images in public and private spaces, these women affirm interpretations of Our Lady that stress "she is a role model of strength, enduring presence, and new possibilities," and thus not an image of "passive womanhood" (Rodriquez 1994). Orsi finds somewhat more mixed responses to the Madonna of 115th street. On the one hand, she "offered women great support and consolation" and they "draw strength from the identification." However, the image also "reaffirmed those aspects of the culture which oppressed them" notably by focusing stories of the Madonna's redemptive powers on her ability to restore women to the role of mother, at the center of the *domus* (Orsi 1985: 205–8).

Christmas as a "Consumer Rite"

Another way to think about modernization of the carnival is to consider the growth of consumerism in connection with holidays. Leigh Eric Schmidt's *Consumer Rites* traces how commercial interests, retail marketing, advertising, and other economic motives asserted their influence over what once were religious feasts guided by clergy and their faith communities. Thus over the nineteenth and twentieth centuries, celebrations like Christmas and Easter become highly commercialized endeavors, characterized by parades, shopping, and televised holiday entertainment promoted by department stores, corporations, and eventually large media conglomerates. Although these activities drew upon the repertoire of pre- and early modern carnivals and festivals, including emphasis on public displays, excess, and frivolity, a significant cultural shift occurred,

> In many ways, the modern entrepreneurial embrace of the holidays was discontinuous with what had gone before and this was not just a matter of degree or magnitude. Instead the shift suggested a reevaluation of the basic economic and religious convictions that underpinned the advance of industrialization and modernity. (Schmidt 1995: 23)

Work discipline necessary to economic growth required coordination, focus, consistency, and repetition. "Time is money" as the saying goes, and the control of time by industries and employers could be quickly undone by cultures that lived from "feast to feast" and indulged "idleness, dissipation, and immorality" as their ancestors had. The solution, according to Schmidt, was to bring the older patterns "under control" not by eliminating them completely but, rather, by reducing their number and recasting them as events that emphasized "commerce, civic prosperity, and genuine piety" (Schmidt 1995: 23). Likewise, these would be tinged with romantic nostalgia for festivals of the past, recalled as having more freedom, fellowship, and warmer emotions. These tensions, between the drive to create wealth via hard work and the romantic longing for connection, eventually found expression in consumerism, especially the buying and selling of products for holiday gift-giving. Media across the nineteenth century testify to how festivals traditionally oriented toward religious rituals and family events became the preeminent season for merchants and later department stores and web-based retailers to court consumers.

Christmas, for example, went from being "a rich feast of food and song, games and greenery, drinking and revelry" to its modern forms that have an almost complete stranglehold on popular culture, an almost "inexhaustible" season embracing "folklore, religion, festival, art, music, literature, television, food, education, civic ceremony, gender, family, gift exchange, ethnicity, localism, race, class, and commerce" (Schmidt 1995: 106). Perhaps this is best exemplified by the evolution of the meaning and role of Santa Claus, who goes from a localized saint in Europe to a global superstar, ace product promoter, and media darling, signifying gift-giving and abundance. The impersonation of Santa Claus as jolly, rotund, red suited, and knowing is now among the signature trends of the holiday season and was substantially based on popular media depictions and department store practices of the late nineteenth and early twentieth centuries. This begs the question, however, just who is Santa Claus and what shapes his image and meaning? Personas include elements of shamanism, sainthood, salesmen, surveillance, solicitation, and supernaturalism. As the roles Santa played proliferated in popular culture, Schmidt finds a general tendency toward "semiotic confusion" as the "surreal and disorienting juxtaposition . . . of images, and the slippery claims of commercial language . . . tend to drain signifiers of their meaning" (Schmidt 1995: 129).

Contemporary Music and Arts Festivals

The summer musical and arts festival that brings together multiple performers in an outdoor park-like setting for performances over multiple days is now a staple of contemporary popular culture. The famous Monterey Pop and Woodstock festivals of the late 1960s would inspire hundreds of others of various sizes and locales, some which became annual or semiannual events like Bonnaroo in Tennessee, Coachella Valley in California, Lollapallooza in Chicago and Glastonbury in Somerset England. These events have roots in festivals for other musical genres, notably opera, jazz, and folk, as well as the famous "camp meetings" and other Protestant revivals that sprawl across the history and geography of the United States. Although focused on eliciting "born again" experiences via preaching, revivals were energized by music, especially hymns and other religious songs. The recent and contemporary music festivals are less about conversion (at least as an explicit aim), but they often invoke religious and spiritual qualities, hinted at in singer Joni Mitchell's famous song about Woodstock, "We've got to get ourselves back to the garden" (Mitchell 1970).

Religion scholar Christopher Partridge notes that music has distinctive powers, including the capacity "to move, to guide the imagination, [and] to create spaces within which meaning is constructed" (2014: 1). He notes while the connections between music and religions run deep, modern popular forms of music often work on boundaries between the sacred and the profane, influenced by artistic romanticism, a zest for transgression, and yearning for new types of community (Partridge 2014: *passim*). In this light, music festivals set forth expectations that have often been "[i]dealistic, romanticized notions of love, community, spirituality, and a relationship to nature" that set themselves apart from modern urbanized and industrialized society (2014: 127). Another scholar of music festivals, Timothy Miller, asserts those of the 1960s and 1970s "provided the best opportunities for indulgence in the [hippie] sacraments: dope, nudity, sex, rock, community" (quoted in Partridge 2014: 127). Although listening to good music was the primary motivation, many yearned for at least a temporary embodiment of values that were dramatically different from the "square" lifestyles of the mainstream.

How much of the early rock music festivals' countercultural orientation was sustained, especially as these types of festivals proliferated over the next few decades? Some seem to carry on the spirit, notably the Bonnaroo Music and Arts Festival in rural Tennessee. Started in 2002, attendees camp out in fields, listen to diverse musical acts, sample artisanal foods, and explore craft shows. Other large festivals, however, focus on urban settings and thus eschew the "camp" feeling of the rural festivals. Lollapallooza, begun in 1991 as touring show for alternative rock groups, included explicit carnivalesque elements like freak shows and vaudeville-styled side acts. Later it settled in Chicago and established parallel festivals in cities in South America and Europe. Of course many such festivals serve as venues for the commercially driven needs of the music industry and have become ways to aggressively promote new acts and revive interest in older ones.

Burning Man

Another compelling case study of the contemporary carnival spirit comes from "Burning Man" an annual festival of art installations, music, dancing, ritual performance, and temporary countercultural living enacted in a desert in northern Nevada. Started by artists in San Francisco and later moved to the wilderness, Burning Man has grown to a major cultural event where as many as 70,000 people converge to create "Black Rock City, a temporary metropolis dedicated to community, art, self-expression, and self-reliance" ("The Event" n.d.). Participants, known as "Burners," camp for over a week in an arid lakebed and engage in modernized versions of many of the classical themes of carnival—costumes and "cosplay," parodic theatrical performances, ecstatic dancing, and other forms of ritual. Art installations are prominent, including elaborate sculptures and large temporary buildings, often illuminated with colored lights or fire, as are fanciful decorated bicycles and "mutant vehicles," used to transport the large crowds around the events. Some of the classical forms of excess, like meat eating, are less in evidence, but celebrations of "the flesh," nudity, and hedonism of varied types are quite common. Along with participants, scholars of religion have recognized the religious and spiritual character of Burning Man in spite of its anarchic and anti-institutional motivations. With roots in radical art movements, like Dada, Surrealism, and the Situationists, Burning Man has been energized by the general notion of creating something radically different from ordinary life, a "world turned upside down" that can stimulate new types of thinking and experimental lifestyles.

The focal point of Burning Man is an elaborate wooden sculpture of a human being, variable in design and size from year to year but generally decorated with lights. On the last full evening of the event, this figure is burned, with accompanying fireworks, as the crowds dance and cheer. Other rituals and temporary sacred spaces permeate the festival; as detailed by religion scholar Lee Gilmore,

> This ritualizing often involves creative appropriations of cultural and religious motifs from a vast global well of symbolic resources. Crosses, devils, buddhas, goddesses, labyrinths—the list is potentially endless—are here patched together in a heterodox hodgepodge, through which participants explore, comment on, play with, and parody religion and spirituality. . . . Through this process of creatively exploiting a vast array of cultural signs, Burners ritualistically and self-consciously de- and reconstruct ad hoc

frameworks in which to create and perform self-reflexive spiritualties, which can become for many a profound life-changing experience. (Gilmore 2010)

Since 2000, many of the more resonant rituals occur in "the Temple," an installation redesigned each year to be "delicate and beautiful" and to foster a sense of safety and healing. Each year's design echoes sacred buildings from around the world and promoters insist that its meanings are defined by the participants' intentions. Thus the Temple can be "a place of contemplation, a place to rest, a place of reflection, [or] a place of rituals, weddings, reunions, etc." Similar to shrine devotions in established religions, many Temple visitors come to mourn lost loved ones by leaving heartfelt letters, poems, short messages, offerings, or mementos.

Over time, organizational structures and guiding ethical principles have emerged, especially as the event has grown. An elaborate system of permitting and rules governing land use, overseen by the Bureau of Land Management, is now necessary to ensure the event can be done safely. A nonprofit LLC, with a board and full-time staff, help manage the event and promote the "10 principles" that Burners try to embody: "radical inclusion, gifting, decommodification, self-reliance, self-expression, communal effort, civic duty, environmental stewardship, participation, and immediacy" ("10 Principles" n.d.). Between festivals, online networks share media, reflect on the meaning of the festival, and plan for future events.

Conclusion: Theories of Religion and Carnival

How can we interpret all this strange behavior, and what did it mean? Theorizing might begin with Durkheim's notion of "elementary" religious rituals energized by emotional intensity, or what he called "collective effervescence." Such analyses might argue that the focus on key symbolic figures, like the statues and floats in parades or feasts held for particular saints, or the "Burning Man" in Black Rock City, can be understood as "totemic." Thus while participants understand themselves as worshipping a great figure, a supernatural event, or a person who embodies virtue, their deeper motivation is to reinforce the group solidarity necessary for social life. Victor Turner's theories of ritual process, especially his attention to the "liminal" stages that involve inversions, humor, role reversals, and other abnormal activities, have often been used to interpret carnival (even by Turner himself) (Turner 1983). Thus carnivals and festivals are a generalized form of a ritual process that engages an entire society.

A third possible way to analyze carnivals and festivals would employ semiotic analysis and seek to read the inner meaning of the content, especially the rich symbolism of the carnival parade or images of the sacred figures feted. Per Barthes, the carnival is an enactment of mythologies, like the triumph of the hero or the bumbling of the fool, each condensed into a character that signifies something meaningful to a larger social system. This kind of semiotic analysis can be brought to bear on the history of key festival figures, like the Madonnas, who as we have seen, can signify an assertion of Mexican American identity, the power of women in the Italian-American *domus*, or a general affirmation of the right of an immigrant community to dwell and seek prosperity in a new country.

Listening carefully to how women, in particular, tell these stories and interpret their Madonnas shows the influence of feminist analysis as outlined by Showalter. See especially her call for attention to women's culture as a way of making visible the "symbolic weight of female consciousness" and the "multiple layers that make up the force of meaning" of women's literary works and life experiences (Showalter 1981: 201, 205). With a nod also to Geertz's methods of thick description, both Rodriguez and Orsi use interviews to enrich their descriptions of festival events and plumb the inner meanings of religious symbols for women.

Carnivals and festivals fulfill Eliade's notion of religion as a kind of "nostalgia" for return to something more original and vital via myth and ritual. Eliade regarded religious notions of time, especially notions of time cultivated in rituals, as reversible and renewable. Religious persons thus reconstitute normal notions of time and space to create a sense of sacredness over and against the ordinary, "profane" times and places. In this sense, carnival can be cast as just such a ritual, albeit more playful than church liturgy. Burke's account notes that for the early modern European commoner, life was lived "in remembrance of one festival and in expectation of the next" (Burke 1978: 179).

But in what sense could the wild revels of carnival, seemingly brazenly profane, serve as an opportunity for rebirth and renewal, so crucial to Eliade's notion of religion? Especially given the role of asceticism and self-denial required to prepare for most standard forms of ritual, like the Roman Catholic sacraments? Perhaps another theorist can be introduced to help. Literary critic Mikhail Bakhtin saw in all this activity a kind of aesthetic impulse, the "carnivalesque" that revels in the "grotesque" body and all of its functions—sweating, eating, copulating, and defecating. In the whirl of carnival, these grotesqueries seem to lead to the tearing down of social propriety and personal degradation, the "anti-structure" of Turner's theories. This was not, however, just debasement for its own sake. Rather, Bakhtin felt there was a kind of affirmation of life, of the process of becoming, which took place through the processes of the body.

> The grotesque body . . . is a body in the act of becoming. It is never finished, never completed: it is continually built, created and build another body. Moreover the body swallows the world and is itself swallowed by the world. . . . This is why the essential role belongs to those parts [, the bowels, phallus, mouth and anus,] in which it outgrows its own self, transgressing its own body. . . . [T]he main events in the life of the grotesque body . . . [e]ating, drinking, defecation and other elimination (sweating, blowing of the nose, sneezing), as well as copulation, pregnancy, dismemberment, swallowing up by another body . . . are performed on the confines of the body and outer world, or on the confines of the old and new body. In all these events the beginning and end of life are closely linked and interwoven. (Bakhtin 1995)

Furthermore, carnival was, in spite of its lavish sinfulness, an essentially religious view of life, if by religious one looks for relief from drudgery of the everyday and the larger cosmic terror of death, again, a theme much discussed by Eliade as a primary function of religion. By seeking a return to what was essential and biological, even if done so in excessive ways, the carnival reveler entered into a visually potent, sensually vibrant, spontaneous and playful performances of life's elementals—joyfully communing with others, eating and drinking, erotic encounter, as well as destruction, suffering and pain. Done in the right spirit, festivals and carnivals *incarnate*, to use a pointed verb, a kind of elemental humanness.

Works Cited

Bakhtin, Mikhail. "The Grotesque Image of the Body and Its Sources," in *Bakhtinian Thought: An Introductory Reader*, ed. Simon Dentith, 225–53. New York: Routledge, 1995.

Burke, Peter. *Popular Culture in Early Modern Europe*. New York: Harper Torchbook, 1978.

Gilmore, Lee. *Theater in a Crowded Fire: Ritual and Spirituality at Burning Man*. Berkeley: University of California Press, 2010.

Mitchell, Joni. "Woodstock," *Ladies of the Canyon*, comp. Joni Mitchell. Audio recording, 1970.

Moss, Kenneth. "St. Patrick's Day Celebrations and the Formation of Irish-American Identity, 1845–1875," *Journal of Social History* 29 (1995): 125–48.

Orsi, Robert. *The Madonna of 115th Street: Faith and Community in Italian Harlem, 1880–1950*. New Haven, CT: Yale University Press, 1985.

Partridge, Christopher. *The Lyre of Opheus: Popular Music, the Sacred and the Profane*. London: Oxford University Press, 2014.

Pelikan, Jaroslav. *Mary Through the Centuries: Her Place in the History of Culture*. New Haven, CT: Yale University Press, 1998.

"Retail Holiday and Seasonal Trends: St. Patrick's Day," National Retail Federation (n.d.). Available online: https://nrf.com/insights/holiday-and-seasonal-trends/st-patricks-day (accessed November 30, 2019).

Rodriquez, Jeanette. *Our Lady of Guadalupe: Faith and Empowerment among Mexican-America Women*. Austin: University of Texas Press, 1994.

Schmidt, Leigh Eric. *Consumer Rites: The Buying and Selling of American Holidays*. Princeton, NJ: Princeton University Press, 1995.

Showalter, Elaine. "Feminist Criticism in the Wilderness," *Critical Inquiry* 8, no. 2 (Winter 1981): 179–205.

"The 10 Principles of Burning Man," Burning Man Project (n.d.). Available online: https://burning man.org/culture/philosophical-center/10-principles/ (accessed January 13, 2021).

"The Event." Burning Man (2021). Available online: https://burningman.org/event/ (accessed June 11, 2021).

Turner, Victor. "Carnival in Rio: Dionysian Drama in an Industrializing Society," in *The Celebration of Society: Perspectives on Contemporary Cultural Performance*, ed. Frank Manning, 103–24. Bowling Green, OH: Bowling Green University Popular Press, 1983.

Index

Page numbers in **bold** indicate references to the chapter associated with that author.